Making Sweatshops

Making Sweatshops

The Globalization of the U.S. Apparel Industry

ELLEN ISRAEL ROSEN

University of California Press

BERKELEY   LOS ANGELES   LONDON

University of California Press
Berkeley and Los Angeles, California

University of California Press, Ltd.
London, England

© 2002 by the Regents of the University of California

Library of Congress Cataloging-in-Publication Data

Rosen, Ellen Israel.
   Making sweatshops : the globalization of the U.S. apparel industry /
Ellen Israel Rosen.
       p.   cm.
   Includes bibliographical references and index.
   ISBN 0–520–23336–0 (Cloth : alk. paper)—ISBN 0–520–23337–9 (Paper
: alk. paper)
       1. Clothing trade—United States—History—20th century.   2. Cloth-
ing trade—History—20th century.   3. Women clothing workers—
United States.   4. Globalization.   I. Title.
   HD9940.U4 R666 2002
   338.4'7687'0973—dc21   2001005493

Manufactured in the United States of America
10   09   08   07   06   05   04   03   02   01
10   9   8   7   6   5   4   3   2   1

The paper used in this publication is both acid-free and totally chlorine-
free (TCF). It meets the minimum requirements of ANSI/NISO Z39.48–1992
(R 1997) (Permanence of Paper).

Contents

Figures and Tables

Figures

Tables

Preface

Before beginning the research for this book, I spent more than a decade investigating the problems of America's domestic apparel workers—the unionized women employed in New England's men's and women's apparel industry. By the early 1980s, like their male counterparts, the predominantly female workers in a variety of light industries, such as electrical assembly, jewelry making, and apparel production, had begun to lose their jobs. Technological change, deindustrialization, and the growth of competing imports from low-wage countries were beginning to erode manufacturing communities of the region.

Industry and union leaders, workers, and employers recognizing these global trends sought ways to maintain the viability of domestic production. In the apparel industry they looked to scholars, consultants, and other experts who were exploring the potential of new technologies, better human resource management, and new forms of work organization to improve competitiveness. Could industrial restructuring save at least a segment of the U.S. apparel industry and retain some of its jobs? Was it possible to improve, or at least maintain, the deteriorating wages and working conditions in the industry and to halt the trend of deunionization?

While costly efforts were being made to restructure apparel production, a major debate about trade protection for textiles and apparel was taking place in Congress and the White House. Ultimately, apparel producers who pressed for stronger tariffs and quotas to help solve their problems were disappointed, as America's presidents, with support from U.S. clothing retailers, began a major challenge to the Multifibre Arrangement, the managed trade regime that had regulated import levels since 1974. Since the 1980s, America's presidents have pressed for new accords to reduce tariffs, end quotas, and in other ways liberalize international trade in textiles and apparel.

By the early 1990s it was clear that new technologies and work reorganization were not likely to prevent the hemorrhage of apparel jobs. Nor were they likely to halt the deteriorating employment conditions in an industry that had, decades before, boasted that such problems had been solved. Indeed, it became apparent that sweated labor was emerging in apparel production in many countries of the developing world and was reemerging in the United States.

Such discoveries raised the questions that led me to write *Making Sweatshops*. In doing the research for this book, I saw that the process of remaking sweatshops in the United States began not in the early 1980s but more than thirty years before, in the period after World War II. The process of trade liberalization, not merely in textiles and apparel products, has played a major role in U.S. foreign policy since then. The policies that govern today's international trade were at the very heart of promoting American power and American hegemony in the postwar world. What follows, then, is not only about the globalization of the textile and apparel industries but also touches on important debates about the integration of the world economy.

Globalization is generating dramatic transformations that bring a multiplicity of new problems for the people directly affected by it. *Making Sweatshops* sheds light on a number of these issues. It will elucidate the process of globalization and argue that it ought to be promoted in a way that blends industrialization and economic development in both poor and rich countries, with concerns for social and economic justice.

I thank all the people who supported me as I spent more than half a decade researching and writing this book. Let me begin with the librarians of the Government Documents Division of the Boston Public Library. Before the flood of 1996 that severely damaged the room in which the government documents were stored, the room was housed in one of the most research-friendly environments I have ever worked in. Many of the documents I sought were nearly half a century old, and before the flood they were always there, to be found by some of the most resourceful, helpful, and courteous library professionals I have ever worked with.

I want to express my gratitude to the Women's Studies Scholars Program at Brandeis University. The program has provided me with a gloriously esthetic and comfortable place to work. But more important, being in the program has made it possible for me to meet and talk with many scholars steeped in the joy and despair of studying women's lives. I am also grateful to Nichols College for giving me a sabbatical year to spend in full-time research. I also thank Naomi Schneider, my editor at the University of California Press. It was her expertise and experience that made it possible to turn this sometimes awkward and lengthy manuscript into what I hope will prove to be a valuable book. I also thank Richard Appelbaum and Robert S. J. Ross for their comments on this manuscript, as well as Louise Lopman and Susan Tiano, whose own interest in this topic has been a source of pleasure and enlightenment. Thank you also to Judith Barrett, Corey Hope Leaffer, and Erika Büky.

This book is for Jeremy, whom I always reminded at dinner that I was not just proffering my own opinion on social issues but reporting "what the data said." He is now a published author in his own right. And it is for Richard, who, although he hasn't yet read this manuscript, knows what the book is about and, perhaps more important, what it means. And it is for Ruth Weinstein Israel, my mother, who was a garment worker and member of the International Ladies' Garment Workers' Union. Finally, it is for my father, Benjamin Israel, who still, on special occasions, wears his union pin.

1   Introduction

The red silk bargain dress in the shop window is a danger signal.
It is a warning of the return of the sweatshop, a challenge to us
all to reinforce the gains we have made in our long and difficult
progress towards a civilized industrial order.

Frances Perkins, U.S. Secretary of Labor, 1933

The Triangle Shirtwaist Factory fire in New York City in 1911 called attention to the sweatshop conditions under which women worked stitching clothes. One hundred forty-one workers, 125 of them women and girls, mostly immigrants, were burned to death or died after jumping from a window in the building, in which there was only one fire escape; the elevator was broken.[1] This tragedy was the first of many such fires to call public attention to dangers suffered by women employed in sweatshop conditions. This disaster, like similar ones that have happened since, called attention to employers who lack concern for the lives of their workers, who allow these conditions to continue despite the toll in suffering and human life. Tragedies like this one generate public support for the passage or enforcement of laws to ensure these incidents are not repeated. They are a metaphor for the conditions that women now face, less frequently in the United States, and more often in the developing world.

In New York City, the Triangle Shirtwaist Factory fire did lead to reforms. Yet it was not until after the successful organizing drives of the 1930s, the New Deal, and the prosperity of the early postwar years that the power of the International Ladies' Garment Workers' Union (ILGWU) was felt. Women sewing operatives, now often members of this union, received good wages, paid vacations, and medical benefits and, when work was slow, could collect unemployment insurance from the federal government.

In the 1950s New York City was the center of the women's fashion industry. The vast majority of U.S. apparel producers, mostly small businesses, and the ILGWU, which organized most of its workers, were geographically concentrated in New York, New Jersey, and Pennsylvania. The industry comprised thousands of small, private (often family-owned) firms

1

that in the 1958 season produced about 75 percent of the nation's Easter dresses.[2]

During these years of postwar affluence, when the apparel industry and its workers, like other U.S. industries, prospered, it may have seemed that sweatshop conditions were part of America's past, of a time before businesses were required to work within the New Deal social contract. Yet even as this prosperity unfolded, the seeds of new American sweatshops were being sown.

In 1983, Barry Bluestone and Bennett Harrison, in *The Deindustrialization of America,* analyzed the effects of a new form of economic restructuring that was leading to massive job displacement among America's industrial workers, particularly in Midwestern cities like Pittsburgh and Detroit. The authors saw this issue as one predominantly affecting male workers.[3] It was left to feminist scholars and journalists to demonstrate the role that gender played in the sweated labor of women in electronic assembly and apparel production in the emerging contracting shops of what was then called the Far East.[4]

By the 1980s, sweatshops were once more found in the United States, after a hiatus of almost forty years. A "sweatshop," as understood here, is not merely a firm that offers poorly paid jobs or an authoritarian system of industrial relations. The wages such companies pay are below the federally mandated minimum, or the conditions of employment they provide are substandard in terms of the criteria first set in 1938 by the U.S. Fair Labor Standards Act. Employers who provide such jobs violate federal law. The growing number of sweatshops in the United States demonstrates that the law is not being enforced. U.S. sweatshops began to gain national attention in 1995, soon after Kathie Lee Gifford identified herself as lending her name to clothing made for a U.S. retailer in a Central American sweatshop, and California state officials raided an undercover garment factory in El Monte, California, a middle-class suburb of Los Angeles. Asian traffickers held by force seventy Thai workers they had smuggled into the United States and were keeping in the basement of a house. When law enforcement officials approached the site, they found it ringed with barbed wire and spiked fences and doors locked from the outside. The building had no rear exit, and its small windows were reinforced with thick iron bars. The Thai workers, mostly impoverished women in their late teens or early twenties, were forced to sew clothing for about $1.60 an hour, from 7 A.M. to midnight each day.[5] The merchandise they were producing was destined for prominent retailers like Macy's, Hecht's, Filene's, and J.C. Penney.[6]

The exposure of such egregious conditions generated public shock and dismay. Yet, a year before the discovery in El Monte, the *New York Times* had published a broadside about apparel sweatshops written by two women administrators from the U.S. Department of Labor. They wrote, "The Labor Department estimates that in the San Francisco area more than half the 2,000 garment shops violate wage laws. And New York City has more than 3,000 apparel sweatshops with more than 50,000 workers, according to a General Accounting Office study. In El Paso, Los Angeles and Seattle, sweatshops are also common."[7] Further documentation of these abuses made it clear that El Monte was not an aberration but a problem that now exists on a national and international scale, despite a host of U.S. federal and statewide regulations on labor, health, safety, and immigration, and despite international trade accords that formally prohibit sweatshop conditions in all countries. These laws, however, fail to bring employers who run sweatshops to justice.

According to the International Labour Organization, during the late 1990s there were approximately 30 million jobs in the global textile, clothing, and footwear industries. The vast majority, over 80 percent, of the lowest-wage production workers are women. Men receive wages that are 20 to 30 percent higher than those of women.[8]

Apparel sweatshops in the United States tend to be concentrated in New York, California, and Texas, but they can also be found in most other large American cities, where they typically employ groups of new immigrant women.[9] Indeed, women in today's U.S. apparel industry often work more than eight hours a day in conditions that lack elementary safety and other legally required protections, earning less than the minimum wage.[10] Sweatshops in the apparel industry are not found only in the United States. In fact, they have expanded most dramatically outside America's borders, in the export-processing and free trade zones of low-wage, developing countries in Southeast Asia and Latin America. Most recently, new apparel sweatshops have emerged in eastern Europe, China, and sub-Saharan Africa. There is a growing body of information—data collected by organizations like the General Accounting Office, the U.S. Department of Labor, and the International Labour Organization,[11] and studies by social scientists too numerous to mention—that documents the excesses demanded of apparel workers in regions of the world where export processing is expanding. In these areas, child labor, indentured servitude, sexual harassment, environmental hazards, and employment-generated health problems have become the norm.

Concurrent with the growth of sweatshops has been the massive loss of jobs in apparel production in the United States and other industrialized countries. According to the U.S. International Trade Commission, over the past thirty years "roughly half the total productive capacity in the apparel industry has shifted from developed countries to [the less developed countries]."[12] Around the world, the vast majority of workers in apparel manufacturing are women. Indeed, a new study by trade economists shows that international trade between Organization for Economic Cooperation and Development (OECD) and non-OECD countries has produced gendered employment effects. It appears that the loss of manufacturing jobs in the developed countries in recent years is not associated with international trade per se but with international trade and trade deficits—specifically in textiles and apparel.[13]

Apparel production has always been a unique industry. It is labor-intensive, and its labor force has always been composed predominantly of women. Employed in traditionally female, sex-segregated jobs, these workers have typically been paid less than the men who perform comparable work in other types of manufacturing. Yet in the 1950s and 1960s, women employed in this industry in the United States, like many male industrial workers, earned relatively good wages and enjoyed reasonably good working conditions.

During that era, both the men's and the women's clothing industries were heavily unionized. In the early postwar years, the apparel industry was recognized for its aggressive union organizing and labor-management cooperation. Yet, over three decades or so, the industry lost almost half its jobs.[14] Its trade unions were severely weakened, and its wages and working conditions declined dramatically. *Making Sweatshops* is an effort to understand how and why these events occurred.

This volume does not contain any revelations about the abuses that apparel workers suffer today. Nor is it an exposé of the conditions that women workers face in contemporary clothing factories, either at home or abroad. More than a decade ago I wrote about American women factory workers who, over the years, had been displaced from their jobs.[15] A new chapter in this story is being written today by scholars, journalists, public agencies, and activist groups who continue to learn about and reveal the deteriorating working conditions in new apparel sweatshops.[16] These groups provide a stream of information about the ways in which current forms of international trade, patterns of economic development, and the policies of national governments are thwarting the efforts of women employed in apparel production to find work at wages that allow them to support their families and in conditions that support their dignity as human beings.

Confronted with this evidence, few are likely to publicly support, or even appear indifferent to, sweatshop conditions in the United States. Yet powerful interests in the textile, apparel, and retail industries; policy analysts; and neoliberal economists continue to legitimate sweatshop conditions. They argue that the global apparel trade will lead to economic development in poor countries. Not only will industrial production bring better employment conditions and higher wages in the future, but current forms of development and trade are already creating better jobs than developing countries previously have been able to offer. But will the expanding wealth produced by industrial development in poor countries inevitably trickle down the economic ladder? Or will we continue to see growing inequalities between the rich and poor, both across and within nations?

Critics of the neoliberal view point to the growing power of transnational corporations to transcend the dictates of national governments. They point to the institutions that support current neoliberal trade and economic policies—the World Bank, International Monetary Fund, and World Trade Organization (WTO)—which they argue have promoted efforts to expand global production at the expense of poor countries and poor people. As groups like these help direct flows of capital around the world, economists help legitimate and justify promoting these ventures as paving stones in the road to global economic prosperity.

Clearly, textile and apparel manufacturers and clothing retailers need to make a profit to continue producing and selling clothing. Making clothing more efficiently and cheaply so that it is more affordable is also a socially valuable enterprise. Fifty years ago many questioned whether it was necessary to transfer jobs to poor and developing countries to do this. Protectionists presented a challenge to those who tried to make it easier for American apparel producers to contract abroad. Since then, there has been a vast transformation in the apparel industry, in which half the jobs for women workers in apparel production have been transferred from industrialized countries to the developing world. We must understand, then, whether the efforts made to effect this global transformation will, in the long run, produce the economic development necessary to alleviate the existing social disorganization and expanding inequalities, or whether these efforts will only maximize profits and intensify inequality.

MAKING SWEATSHOPS

This book is also an attempt to explain the globalization of the U.S. apparel industry and to assess this project as it has occurred. My effort goes beyond the traditional explanation that the industry's need for lower wages suffices to explain the changes that have occurred. In this book I examine the complex political, social, and economic events that have transformed the apparel industry. I explore the forces that have made the textile, apparel, and retail complex into a network of large transnational and multinational corporate entities that rely on a vast network of low-wage, female-dominated production sites around the world.

In addition, I uncover the roots of these changes and question whether this transformation can be understood as the inevitable workings of pure market forces. I believe what is needed are historical and political perspectives that allow us a wider, more elaborate view of what markets are and how they work. Globalization of the apparel industry is a result of all these processes, and it began at the point at which the Untied States became the major world power.

TRADE POLICY

In this book I also analyze the formation of U.S. trade policy for textiles and apparel since World War II. The end of the war was a watershed in America's foreign economic policy, marked by the emergence of reciprocal trade. For over a century the United States had seen its economy grow behind the walls of trade protection. After the war, a continuous process of tariff reductions and market openings strengthened the country's postwar economy and its new international prominence. During the next half century, backed by U.S. military power, corporations at home and abroad would grow and flourish.

Trade liberalization is neither the primary motor of U.S. corporate growth nor the basis of today's global economy. Yet since the end of World War II, the international trade regime has been dominated by American power. Trade liberalization has been a major part of U.S. foreign policy and its domestic industrial policy. Both Democratic and Republican administrations have supported America's corporate players while setting the rules that govern the movement of goods and capital in the international arena. Continuing efforts by the United States to liberalize trade have been an important vehicle for corporate expansion and have helped to shape the world's industrial development during the past fifty years.

In *Making Sweatshops* I discuss the political and economic contexts in which trade policy for the textile, apparel, and retail industries were made and how they led to the globalization of these industries. Trade liberalization since World War II occurred in two phases. The first phase unfolded in Asia, in the quarter century or so after the war, as part of a larger strategy to contain communism and link the developing new economies of the region to the United States through export-led development—a concept that I will elaborate on in a later chapter. During this period a new trade regime was forged and imposed on the unwilling U.S. textile and apparel industries. Successive administrations committed to trade liberalization made it necessary for these trade-sensitive industries to restructure—to change the way they organized their production and sales, to respond to a new, more wage-competitive environment.[17] These organizational changes were designed to create a highly wage-competitive textile and apparel complex. The industries resisted, engaging heavily in efforts to introduce new forms of trade protection. These efforts generated vociferous debates between free traders and protectionists, and affected U.S. politics at the highest levels. Yet an effort was made to maintain the values of the New Deal social contract.

The failure of textile and apparel protectionists in the course of the first phase of trade liberalization allowed Congress during the Reagan administration to clear the way for the second phase. At the behest of a powerful group of emerging corporate beneficiaries, industry leaders pressed for a new and increasingly aggressive policy of trade liberalization. In the mid-1980s the Reagan administration forged a new trade regime for textiles and apparel in Latin America, a regime further expanded and strengthened by the Bush and Clinton administrations. The new regime sanctioned an unfettered, United States–dominated global competition in which U.S. transnationals could only be winners. It also signaled the end of America's postwar commitment to a social contract between labor and management. Sweatshops reappeared in American cities and were "discovered" in the developing world. The next two decades would see a massive hemorrhaging of American apparel jobs and the growth of new sweatshops both in the United States and abroad.

THE NEOLIBERAL ECONOMIC MODEL

As the 1980s wore on, segments of the apparel and textile industries aligned themselves with apparel retailers to press for a faster increase in imports of textiles and apparel made in low-wage countries. This effort was legitimated by professional economists who began to formulate a new approach to trade theory. The neoliberal paradigm that emerged allowed for the reshaping of trade policies. These policies were often supported by the World Bank and International Monetary Fund. The new agenda promoted the opening of new markets in developing countries, the expansion of low-wage apparel production in these countries, and the growth of low-wage textile and apparel exports to the United States. This agenda has made it possible for transnationals to move apparel production to ever lower-wage sites throughout the developing world. The neoliberal paradigm both explains the inevitability of existing trade policies and gives credence to the assumption that existing forms of trade liberalization are the most effective for generating economic benefits, for all groups simultaneously: for consumers, producers, and workers.

Clearly the discipline of economics is vital to an understanding of the new global economy. Yet neoliberal economists often make seriously flawed assumptions about the effects of trade on people and communities. Such assumptions tend to ignore the knowledge produced by historians and other social scientists about the role of institutions, power, culture, and gender in the workings of economies. As a result, neoliberal economists hold views about the behavior of individuals and markets that, since they are not grounded in empirical evidence, lead to erroneous conclusions and badly designed policies. *Making Sweatshops* is an effort to illuminate the flaws in the neoliberal model and explore how its implementation has affected women workers in the industry.

THE NEW DARWINIAN STRUGGLE

Today the textile, apparel, and retail complex is engaged in what the *Boston Globe* has recently called a new Darwinian struggle.[18] Dominated by a small number of retailers, textile producers, and apparel manufacturers, the industry is now primarily engaged in a competition that requires reducing the price and expanding the volume of clothing sold to consumers around the world. Competitive success for the individual corporation means not only capturing an ever larger share of the American market but also expanding sales to new consumer markets outside the United States.[19]

This competition, now linked to the financial constraints of the stock market, is driven by the need to generate higher profits to satisfy corporate stockholders and maintain a sufficient level of investment in the industry. As a result, transnationals are required not only to make an ongoing effort to reduce costs but also to locate ever lower-wage production-sites around the world.

The globalization of the apparel industry has indeed reduced the cost of clothing for consumers. The full-employment economy of the 1990s has been based on a strategy of low wages for American workers that makes lower cost apparel essential if the industry is to maintain and expand consumption. Yet the diminishing cost of clothing is providing little real economic help to American families, even those toward the bottom of the economic ladder. Moreover, the loss of jobs in the industry and the growth of sweatshops have not improved the lives of women who work in America's domestic apparel industry or the lives of apparel workers abroad.

GENDER AND THE GLOBAL APPAREL INDUSTRY

Employing women as the labor force of choice in such work has never allowed them to sustain themselves or their children particularly well. Nor has it allowed them to be economically independent of their families. Instead, it has sustained the profits of their employers and the prerogatives of male workers in other, more highly paid manufacturing work. There is no "pure market" reason requiring that women be employed in these poorly paid jobs.

Recent international trade agreements have created the potential for the growth of new economic structures: export-processing establishments that support the employment of women in apparel factories—in developing countries. These trade-oriented, export-processing regimes are built on traditional patriarchal expectations and customs that continue to define women as minor and secondary contributors to a larger family economy. Corporate profitability depends on the fact that women are paid only enough to supplement the earnings of a male provider, and considerably less than a living wage.

In chapter 2, I explain the tenets of free trade as they are now expressed by contemporary economists in what I call the *neoliberal economic paradigm*—as it applies to trade in general and to trade in textiles and apparel. I explain why the model that economists now offer in order to make trade policy and legitimate this trade is inconsistent with the empirical realities of contemporary global apparel production. I argue that labor markets are embedded in social, institutional, and gendered contexts. The practice of employing lower paid young women in apparel production is inconsistent with the assumptions about free markets, assumptions that are key to the neoliberal paradigm.

Chapter 3 is a historical analysis of the postwar changes in U.S. trade policy: the emergence of the early postwar reciprocal-trade regime in textiles and apparel, as it was first developed between the United States, Japan, and the Big Three—Hong Kong, Taiwan, and South Korea.[20] The U.S. military rebuilt Japan's textile industry during the American occupation, between 1945 and 1951, in response to the goal of American foreign policy to contain communism in East Asia after the war. In the decades that followed, the United States' continuing project to thwart left-wing insurgencies in the region contributed to the globalization of the apparel industry. Textiles and apparel played a major role in this process. As these industries helped bring about the "Asian Miracle" in Hong Kong, Taiwan, and South Korea, the continuing flow of exports from that region also transformed the U.S. textile and apparel industries.

Chapter 4 discusses the effect of the reciprocal trade agenda on the apparel industry. Here, I analyze congressional protectionism as it emerged in response to the political and economic relationship between the United States and the newly industrializing countries of Asia and the growing volumes of apparel imports that began to enter U.S. markets.

Chapters 5 and 6 examine how U.S. textile and apparel producers reacted to the impact of low-wage textile and apparel imports from Asia. These chapters explore the efforts each industry made to come to grips with the business environment promoted by the new trade regime as it was implemented by the Truman administration and later by Eisenhower and Kennedy. The textile and apparel industries, both labor-intensive, now faced a need to restructure, introduce new technologies, increase productivity, reorganize production, and reduce labor costs in order to compete with growing volumes of low-wage imports. Yet management also confronted its post–New Deal labor unions, who, in light of the new postwar prosperity, were demanding better wages and working conditions. In this context America's textile and apparel industries allied with their trade unions to support a protectionist agenda in Congress. Was protection, as analysts have argued, a "bad policy"? Or was it an inevitable response to the problems these industries faced?

Chapter 7 is an account of the demise of congressional protectionism in the context of the new neoliberal consensus. By the 1980s, the administration found ways to control implementation of the trade regime in order to circumvent the pressures of congressional protectionists and promote the free trade agenda in earnest.

In chapters 8 and 9, I examine the second phase of America's postwar trade liberalization: the neoliberal trade policies for textiles and apparel that were first put into practice in the 1980s for goods imported from Central America and the Caribbean. Chapter 8 is an analysis of the Caribbean Basin Initiative. In the early 1980s the region was seen as the last bastion of U.S. cold war containment policy. Reagan's new trade policy for the area soon made it a testing ground for a more aggressive form of trade expansion. The region became a growth area for low-wage offshore apparel production. Latin America's next set of low-wage assembly sites for apparel opened shop in Mexico. Chapter 9 is a discussion of the history and implementation of the North American Free Trade Agreement. By the end of the 1980s, Mexico and a small group of countries in the Caribbean and Central America were fast becoming a new American garment district.

Chapter 10 traces the history of the U.S. retail industry and the role it played in the new global trade agenda. Examining the early history of retailing, the chapter clarifies the links between the industry's corporate growth in the 1980s and its dependence on further liberalization of global trade. As retailers began to require an increasing stream of low-wage imports, they mustered political resources through the efforts of their new lobbying arm, the National Retail Federation.

Throughout the 1980s and 1990s, the industry persuaded successive administrations to remove barriers to global sourcing. However, new forms of competition generated trade-policy conflicts among textile and apparel producers and leaders of the new corporate retail industry. In chapter 11 I examine how these conflicts were resolved by further trade liberalization— the ending of the General Agreement on Tariffs and Trade and the Multifibre Arrangement, which was replaced by the World Trade Agreement (WTA) and the Agreement on Textiles and Clothing. These new international trade accords permitted continuous opportunities for opening markets in textiles and apparel throughout the world, challenging the older forms of protectionist trade liberalization desired by the textile industry. The WTA made it possible for newly industrializing countries in Asia, now producing low-wage textiles and apparel, to compete with the Western Hemisphere.

Today analysts are only beginning to understand the potential effects of the new free-trade agenda on the future of global trade competition in textiles and apparel. Yet neoliberal optimists often claim that freer trade will eliminate "unviable" forms of employment from the U.S. labor market and reduce the cost of clothing for American consumers. Opening the markets of developing countries to the apparel trade, they say, will provide new and better employment opportunities, thereby improving the living standards of people in the developing world. In chapter 12, I examine these propositions, looking at the effects of expanding low-wage imports on corporate producers, American consumers, and women production workers in both the United States and developing countries. Evidence suggests that the dramatic explosion of global apparel production may lead not to prosperity or the "greatest good for the greatest number" but to growing impoverishment and inequality. In the long run it may lead to a crisis of underconsumption and overproduction.

Trade liberalization has not freed the apparel trade from government regulation. It has merely replaced the old trade rules with new ones, which have been designed to boost the benefits of trade for transnational corporations. In both industrialized and developing countries, the women who are displaced from apparel production, like those who continue to work in apparel factories, are the least likely to benefit from this "race to the bottom." It is difficult to see these outcomes as the result of an invisible hand rather than as results of human and political agency. In this book I explain why it is essential to remedy the situation.

2   Free Trade, Neoclassical Economics, and Women Workers in the Global Apparel Industry

To understand the globalization of the American apparel industry, it is necessary to locate the process in its historical context. A policy of trade protection endured in the United States throughout the nineteenth and early twentieth centuries, supporting the dynamism of America's early industrial growth. The transition to a free trade agenda had its roots in the early 1930s but was not put in place until after World War II. After the war, the policy of trade liberalization, primarily the reduction of tariffs and opening of markets to trade and investment, began in earnest. Trade liberalization succeeded—but only after lengthy battles in Congress between trade liberalizers and protectionists.

The triumph of a global free-trade system must therefore be understood as more than the internationally driven imperatives of market forces: it is the long-term outcome of complex, major political efforts and complex negotiations among America's corporations, working people, the U.S. government, and the governments of developing nations. Finally, America's free trade agenda has played an important role in the maintenance of U.S. political power throughout the world.

Liberalizing trade has necessitated a new theoretical framework that I call the *neoliberal economic paradigm*. This framework, based in part on eighteenth-century neoclassical economic theories of free markets and free trade, has now been revised and modified to generate support for market-liberalizing initiatives on an international basis. The model dominates policy making; its ideas have a powerful hold on the way Americans think about trade policy issues. Yet today, scholars and activists concerned about the consequences of policies based on this approach are beginning to question not only its theoretical validity but also its usefulness in guiding the global exchange of goods and services.

POSTWAR TRANSFORMATIONS OF U.S. TRADE POLICY

America's shift to trade liberalization first began in the Great Depression of the 1930s, as Cordell Hull and others began to convince Franklin Roosevelt that the excesses of the Hawley-Smoot Tariff Act, with its high protective tariffs, had helped generate the "beggar thy neighbor" policies that contributed to international economic isolationism and laid the groundwork for the depression and World War II.[1]

The General Agreement on Tariffs and Trade (GATT), which regulated global commerce from 1947 to 1994, was designed to prevent the reoccurrence of the "war of all against all" that trade protection was seen to have created. What was then called reciprocal trade was designed to mobilize nation-states to regulate their international trade through negotiation and international cooperation. Multilateral negotiations were to be based on the most-favored-nation principle, which, despite the term, required that all nations be treated equally. Trade agreements were to be negotiated bilaterally, and the same trade regulations would apply to all countries,[2] guaranteeing a level playing field for the exchange of goods among nations. The new trade relations, involving the principles of reciprocity, mutual concessions, and nondiscrimination, held more promise for the creation of international prosperity than did economic autarky and protection. Countries linked economically by trade and investment would be linked politically. Global economic security would provide the motor to maintain world peace.[3] As one scholar puts it, "American officials have believed that trade barriers would have to be eliminated and a set of international rules enforced if the world was to avoid returning to a depression like the 1930s. The United States has wanted a 'Pax Americana' in which 'the establishment of a liberal trading system and the attainment of an expanding world economy' would be the central theme."[4]

America's postwar commitment to the GATT reflected British and American philosophical assumptions about economic rationality: free markets and free trade were the underpinnings of the optimal economic order. Reciprocal trade would solidify America's political influence on the postwar balance of power. It would also guarantee an ever-expanding and American-dominated world economy. Though domestic savings had led to a vast expansion of U.S. postwar demand, the growing size and productivity of American agriculture and industry made exports and investment abroad essential. America's major industries could now expand through both trade and investment outside the country's geographical borders in the interests of promoting the reconstruction of Europe.[5]

Although the GATT was primarily designed to regulate trade among the industrialized countries, especially Europe, by midcentury the exigencies of the cold war, as it played out in East Asia, transformed the objectives of the new liberal trade agenda. The U.S. administration saw the "loss" of China by 1948 and the growth of left-wing insurgencies in the region as jeopardizing American interests. One strategy of "containment" was to establish "reciprocal" trading relationships, first with a defeated Japan and, soon after, with many of Japan's former colonies in Southeast Asia, now formally liberated, independent developing countries.

Efforts to use the reciprocal trade paradigm to regulate exchanges between the economies of industrialized and less developed countries meant opening U.S. markets to a variety of low-wage, labor-intensive imports. In the past, high tariffs had protected U.S. producers from low-wage import competition. Now, for the first time in history, tariffs on textiles, apparel, and other products made in labor-intensive industries were significantly reduced. Despite the opposition of the textile and apparel industries to the tariff reductions, these reductions were nevertheless implemented as part of a larger U.S. political and military strategy to provide economic support to nations threatened by communism. By the early 1950s, reciprocal trade, initially designed to rebuild a war-torn Europe, had become a new policy option for use by the State Department to oppose the threat of "falling dominoes" in Asia.

In the United States, trade-sensitive industries like textiles and apparel were habituated to the exclusion of low-wage imports from their markets. Now they were encouraged to adjust to these imports, that is, to find new ways to remain competitive. Trade-sensitive industries were pressed by succeeding administrations to accept the new policy in the national interest. They soon began to protest in Congress.

In 1961 John F. Kennedy responded to the new congressional protectionism by implementing a quota regime on the growing volumes of textile and apparel imported from low-wage countries. In 1974 the Multifibre Arrangement extended this protection. Yet the United States also continued to promote a policy of export-led development, expanding apparel production in low-wage countries as a way to promote economic development. Increasingly, low-wage goods were imported into this country by the new U.S. corporate textile and apparel producers; they soon began to displace American-made goods.

FROM THE COLD WAR TO THE GLOBAL ECONOMY

It took until the debut of Ronald Reagan's administration to turn around
U.S. trade policy for textiles and apparel. In the 1970s, what Harrison and
Bluestone called the "Great U-Turn" led to a profound restructuring of
U.S. corporations, which was in part the result of the new microchip technology. The ability to coordinate global production systems as a result of
advances in the speed of transport and communication made possible the
switch from mass-production methods to more flexible and decentralized
forms of industrial production.[6] This approach is consistent with what others have called the "new international division of labor."[7] Internationally,
the completion of European and Japanese postwar reconstruction, along
with the entry of China into the world capitalist trading system, confronted the United States with a new tripartite world economy. As the cold
war waned and then ended, the new opportunities for U.S. corporate
growth and expansion required a new trade agenda to open the markets
of developing countries to flows of goods, capital, trade, and investment
that would link these economies with the United States and other parts of
the industrialized world.

The early postwar trade agenda had been legitimated by the need to
contain communism. A quarter of a century later, demands for expanded
trade led to a new role for American corporations as aggressive global
competitors. Trade liberalization was to make this competition possible. In
this context professional economists rediscovered and redefined an eighteenth-century trade paradigm and, with modifications, rejected the
Keynesian model. Resuscitating earlier notions about free markets and free
trade, they developed a neoliberal trade paradigm that was even more
keenly competitive and antiregulatory than the original classical economic
model on which the new approach was based.

Between 1980 and 2000—in less than two decades—the United States
initiated and entered into a multiplicity of new free-trade agreements, both
regional and global. By the 1980s a new group of economic and policy
analysts, neoliberal economists, began to dominate the national discourse
on global trade. They would shape and legitimate the direction of U.S.
trade and investment policy during the next twenty years.

Whereas Europe has hammered out an accord among its more or less
equally industrialized economies, many of the recent trade accords initiated
by the United States have been designed to link the U.S. economy with
the economies of much poorer, and less productive, developing countries.
This has been done to bolster the welfare of America's corporate players

as they compete in the tripartite economy. In the dozen years between 1983 and 1995, Reagan initiated and signed the Caribbean Basin Economic Recovery Act with twenty-two countries in Central America and the Caribbean, George H. W. Bush promulgated the Enterprise for the Americas Initiative, which has, in its turn, led to trade agreements with a number of countries in Latin America, and Bill Clinton pressed for, and won, congressional assent to the North American Free Trade Agreement (NAFTA) with Mexico. Then he presided over the completion of the Uruguay Round of the General Agreement on Tariffs and Trade, which led to the formation of the World Trade Organization (WTO). Clinton aggressively pursued, and won, most-favored-nation trade status for China, supporting that country's accession to the WTO. In 2000, Clinton signed new free-trade agreements for the Caribbean Basin and sub-Saharan Africa. Virtually all of these accords have and will continue to have important consequences for the U.S. textile, apparel, and retail complex.

In the past twenty years or so, the managers and executives of U.S. textile and apparel transnationals, taking their cue from mainstream economists, have overwhelmingly supported the neoliberal paradigm and its approach to doing business. The new trade agreements have made it possible for transnational corporations to increase their control over global capital flows, foreign investment, and international trade. Today, perhaps more than at any time since the end of World War II, the regulation of imports by quotas or tariffs, or by other, less visible means of controlling the flow of textiles and apparel from country to country, is considered bad policy.[8]

DISTORTIONS AND EXTERNALITIES

What, then, is this economic strategy that, according to one analyst in the *New York Times*, provides the "free trade lobbies [with] their imprimatur?"[9] According to one source,

> Neo-classical liberal economics builds models of how resources can be allocated and used efficiently to promote the maximization of utility (or satisfaction/security) of individuals, or of the greatest number of individuals. . . . The market promotes greater allocative and dynamic efficiency. . . . Generally, the most competitive markets are deemed by economic liberals to be the most efficient and most likely to contribute to the general welfare.[10]

In this context, free trade is a system that promotes self-regulating markets, allowing for the maximization of productivity growth and increased wealth. Trade protection thwarts such market efficiencies and inevitably leads down the slippery slope of Smoot-Hawleyism. It is said to put a fence around countries, limiting the economic transactions between them, creating economic isolation.

The neoclassical free trade paradigm is based on the well-respected assumptions of eighteenth-and nineteenth-century classical economic theory, developed in an age of aristocratic mercantilism by thinkers like Adam Smith and David Ricardo.[11] Neoclassical economists, who have become analysts of today's complex networks of international trade, finance, and global investment, have modified this argument. What is known as the Heckscher-Ohlin, or Heckscher-Ohlin-Samuelson, theory posits a set of assumptions that modify the original notions of Smith and Ricardo and define the economy as separate from politics.[12] In this context the only legitimate role for national governments in shaping markets is to remove political impediments—eliminating government-imposed regulations and market distortions that restrain trade.[13] The elimination of market distortions such as tariffs and quotas, it is argued, should increase the overall economic welfare of everyone concerned.

Since all government regulations are seen as serving political ends, such regulation is regarded as interference with market efficiencies and the production of wealth. The optimal economic setting, then, is "one of individual economic agents maximizing their marginal utility in a set of perfect market conditions."[14] According to Alfred Marshall, atomistic individuals detached from all social and political influences make rational economic decisions.[15] Presumably, in calculating economic efficiencies there is no society or social institutions; there are only individuals, individual choices, and individual preferences.

Inevitably, most critics of these assumptions point to the fact that a capitalist economy, indeed any economy, requires political structures to function with stability, regularity, and predictability. Political agency must always be understood as integrated with economics.[16] Geoffrey Underhill writes that a market "is not a natural phenomenon resulting from spontaneous interactions among individuals; it is instead a complex political institution for producing and distributing material and political resources. . . . Markets are open and contestable to manipulation by those who have the power to do so."[17] This is not to deny the existence of markets, which are real and important elements through which goods and services are exchanged. However, markets are not "resource allocation machines but social constructs that serve a social function."[18] They embody a set of rules through which goods and services can be exchanged for money, and these exchanges take place in a social and political context and in regularized and predictable ways. The rules that govern the exchanges, and the cultural and normative practices that are developed in making them, represent an infrastructure that underlies efficient market functioning. Without these parameters markets would be unable, over time, to support productive efficiencies. Indeed, industries often forgo investment opportunities when such forms of institutional regulation are absent. Corporate decision makers are frequently loath to risk trade or investment in regions of the world where the absence of an infrastructure impairs the predictability of business operations.

Political economists criticizing the neoliberal model have argued that the study of the economy presupposes that social and cultural factors define how wealth should be produced, how systems of production and markets should be organized, and how individuals and groups should share the wealth produced. Economic systems embody moral and cultural norms that shape the management of human resources and the patterns of labor relations. As Underhill writes, "The principal focus of political conflict, at the domestic or international level, concerns who gets what, when and how."[19]

Yet neoliberal economists often define institutional requirements of social life as externalities that have no place in the economists' calculations of economic efficiency, as issues that ultimately should be left to moral philosophers, sociologists, and politicians. They believe that the free market exchange of goods and services will simply maximize the size of the gross national product, increasing the overall economic welfare of the entire society. As a result, they avoid discussion of distributional effects.

Neoclassical economists support the recent efforts of the WTO to liberalize trade, arguing that the elimination of barriers will make the new international trading system freer of regulatory distortions than it has ever been. Yet political economists say that the WTO now embodies a new set of principles and rules that regulate capital markets and transnational corporations through politics and norms, just as previous regimes have done. Moreover, the new rules are constrained by the operations of supranational agencies such as the World Bank and the International Monetary Fund, which also structure markets. Thus, the neoliberal trade regime and the supranational agencies have merely changed the market structures and the rules that formerly governed trade. In so doing, they have created a new international political economy designed to support the global expansion of transnational corporations in the twenty-first century.

TRADE LIBERALIZATION IN TEXTILES AND APPAREL

Neoliberal trade policy analysts make two flawed assumptions here: first, that we continue to live in a world where capital is localized; and second, that the exchange of textile and apparel products between and among countries will yield a roughly comparable value to all trading partners. These assumptions do not effectively describe the empirical realities in which capital, goods, and labor are exchanged in contemporary forms of international trade. The assumptions have lead to erroneous conclusions and predictions about the economic consequences of trade liberalization.

In many cases the new forms of global exchange in textiles and apparel do not enrich all parties involved in this trade, and they may not lead to a generalized prosperity that benefits all participants, or at least not equally or equitably. The globalization of the apparel industry has accelerated job loss in the U.S. apparel industry and has led to wage reductions and sweatshop conditions for the workers who continue to be employed in this country. It has also generated sweatshops and job loss abroad while supporting higher levels of profitability, growth, and consolidation of the largest corporate enterprises that increasingly dominate these industries.

The concept of comparative advantage is used to explain capital flows and trade patterns. According to Paul Krugman, "A country has a *comparative advantage* in producing a good if the opportunity cost of producing that good in terms of other goods is lower in that country than it is in other countries."[20] For example, if it is less costly to produce apparel in Mexico, it is economically more efficient for the U.S. producers to cede the production of apparel to Mexico. The capital that producers would have used to manufacture apparel in the United States could be more efficiently utilized to make other products or services for which the United States has a comparative advantage, such as financial services.

Economists have argued that low-wage developing countries have a comparative advantage in their natural abundance of low-wage labor. Given the labor-intensity of the textile and apparel industries, with their low capital requirements, it is more efficient to locate production in low-wage regions of the world.[21] Industrialized countries, on the other hand, with their advanced technologies, produce capital-intensive manufactured goods and services more efficiently. Thus, textiles and apparel should be produced in low-wage countries and exchanged for higher-value-added manufactured goods from developed countries, making both countries better off economically.

Economists like Jeffrey Schott, Gary Hufbauer, Kimberly Ann Elliott, and William R. Cline have developed models that demonstrate, in precise dollar values, how tariffs and quotas on this type of international trade, mandated by the Multifibre Arrangement (MFA), have created market impediments that have reduced economic efficiencies and generated economic losses to the U.S. economy.[22] They show that tariffs and quotas under the MFA constituted a tax on clothing for American consumers while producing artificial subsidies in the form of employment and wages for domestic apparel workers. If consumers could purchase less-expensive clothing, they would be able to either spend more money on other goods and services and thus gain a higher standard of living, or save this money, which could then be used for other productive investments.

At the same time, these economists argue, trade in textiles and apparel would improve the standard of living in developing countries in which apparel is assembled. The earnings from the new jobs created there would start turning the wheels of capital accumulation and fuel industrialization. Schott and Hufbauer, Elliott, and Cline, writing in the late 1980s and early 1990s, urged tariff and quota reductions and favored eliminating the Multifibre Arrangement. Ending the MFA, they stated, would permit a freer, more efficient exchange of textile and apparel products across international borders.[23] Their arguments were influential. By 1995 the MFA was ended.

Yet the economic relationships that these economists loosely define as trade do not describe the way trade is carried on in the global apparel industry. Indeed, what is loosely called trade today is more descriptive of the economic relationship that resulted from the Taft-Hartley Act than of trade described in Adam Smith's *Wealth of Nations*. The Taft-Hartley Act, in particular section 14(b), commonly known as the "right to work" clause, gave individual states the power to ban the union shop.[24] This had the effect of allowing the flow of goods and capital investment across state boundaries; it allowed northern-based textile and apparel producers to invest in Southern factories and employ the labor of lower wage, nonunion workers. In the same way, U.S. postwar market-opening initiatives, which reduced tariffs for textiles and apparel imports, facilitated the transfer of capital to East Asian countries—first to Japan, later to Hong Kong, Taiwan, and South Korea, and after that to other East Asian countries. In 1983 the Caribbean Basin Economic Recovery Act, also known as the Caribbean Basin Initiative, expanded apparel trade between the United States and twenty-two countries in the Caribbean and in Central America. In the 1990s NAFTA made Mexico one of the largest producers and exporters of apparel to the United States.

In 1995 the World Trade Agreement superseded the General Agreement on Tariffs and Trade, and the Multifibre Arrangement was replaced by the Agreement on Textiles and Clothing (ATC). This act, which now regulates international trade in textiles, clothing, and footwear, will, by 2005, eliminate the quota regime that formerly ordered international trade in these products; new tariff reductions will continue to be negotiated. The ATC will open new markets throughout the developing world. In 2000, similar agreements with China and sub-Saharan Africa facilitated the development of new arrangements that will make it possible for American corporations to contract for the production of clothing at potentially lower wages than in either Latin America or Asia.

These changes in trade regulations, which will be thoroughly described in subsequent chapters, have created a political and economic context in which an almost unlimited amount of capital, textiles, and apparel can legitimately move across national borders. The rules embodied in these accords have made it possible for companies to invest in textiles and apparel and move across the globe, employing the abundant low-wage labor of women in a growing number of developing countries. This type of trade and the ideological paradigm that justifies it have been criticized by many of the same people who now challenge the role of the World Bank and the International Monetary Fund. These institutions, they argue, have encouraged—through their structural adjustment programs—unequal terms of trade, leading to the impoverishment, not the enrichment, of developing countries.

Clearly, unequal exchanges are less likely to occur when U.S. corporations trade with or invest in other industrialized countries where wages are roughly equal to those of the United States. Nonetheless, economists argue that despite this differential, Mexico, a poor country, will become better off economically by engaging in this exchange than not doing so at all. Yet without a systematic comparison of this form of development to others—a difficult comparison to make—such claims are empirically untestable; their predictions of growing wealth wait for the future for confirmation.[25]

Neoclassical economists describe the transfer of apparel manufacture to low-wage countries as in instance of the industry being "footloose," explaining outsourcing as the inevitable result of market imperatives that continually drive labor-intensive industries to areas of lower wage production. Yet, transnationals cannot contract for the low-wage labor of workers in other countries unless there are treaty arrangements that permit and encourage such transactions and, indeed, facilitate an infrastructure to promote such development. Today, new trade accords among nations impose rules that make it both legal and efficient for capital to cross boundaries. These rules create and structure the markets that make apparel production increasingly and globally footloose, allowing producers to continually search out lower wage labor.

WOMEN, APPAREL PRODUCTION, AND THE NEOCLASSICAL ECONOMIC PARADIGM

If the existing forms of apparel trade support an unequal exchange of value, the clear preference for the use of women's labor in this industry makes the exchange even more inequitable. To understand this inequality requires recognizing the effects of trade practices and unequal gender roles, both of which play a part in the new free trade. Disentangling the effects of these two factors—neoliberal trade policy and gender—requires reconceptualizing the way labor markets work. As Alice Kessler-Harris notes, economists believe the market treats men and women neutrally and compensates them on the basis of their talents and skill.[26] Kessler-Harris's careful historical analysis of women's wages in nineteenth-century America, however, makes it clear that women's wages are determined in ways that transcend the economists' models. They are fixed in the real world of "human relationships, political compromise and social struggle," conveying a message about the gendered norms and rules that define the kind of work socially assigned to women. Women's wages reflect the measure of value that men (and women) assign to their productive and reproductive work. To comprehend how employers calculate a woman's wage is to recognize how society views a fair and just recompense for workers whose primary activity in life is defined by their relationship to the family. Understanding these relationships as they play themselves out in the apparel industry requires a feminist perspective of women's traditional role in manufacturing employment or, as Kessler-Harris calls it, "the social construct hidden inside the wage."

Historical research suggests that, in primitive societies, where scarcity was the norm, women were responsible for spinning, weaving, and sewing—the making of cloth and clothing.[27] In the Middle Ages, as cloth production became a craft and a trade, women were assigned the less skilled tasks. Industrialization supported this sexual division of labor in ways that continued to maintain women's subordinate position in the production of cloth and clothing.[28] In both Europe and America, as women began to work for wages outside the home, one of the first industries to employ them was the textile industry.[29] The emergence of the ready-made, mass-produced clothing industry later in the nineteenth century made women the labor force of choice in apparel production too.

The segregation of women in low-wage industrial production has traditionally been legitimated by defining the work women do as rooted in their biological, anatomical, and psychological "nature"—for example, their small hands, their lesser intelligence, which presumably makes them unable to master more complex industrial work skills.[30] Not until the 1980s was it pointed out—by British feminist sociologists—that women's presumed lack of skill resulted from the normative beliefs about their abilities that men used to exclude them from skills training and better-paying industrial jobs.[31] Such beliefs, rooted in patriarchal traditions, were found in the demands of male workers and trade unionists that women be excluded from the better-paid industrial work in order for men to demand a family wage. As Veronica Beechey writes, "A number of studies have shown how definitions of skill can have more to do with men's attempts . . . to retain some control over the labour process and keep skill designations for their own work by excluding women from better paying jobs, than with actual technical competencies which are possessed by men and not by women."[32] Many of the low-wage industrial jobs relegated to women, sewing in particular, required elaborate skills but were nevertheless socially devalued and poorly paid because they were done by women.

Historically, industrial skills in the capitalist West have been understood as expertise in the technological aspects of the production process. Such skills frequently emanated from preindustrial craft traditions "owned" by men. Masculinity itself has often been defined as embodying an intrinsic facility for scientific and technical knowledge and activities. Men continue to be thought of as endowed with stereotypical characteristics of superior rationality, objectivity, and technical expertise, aptitudes and talents not seen as equally inherent in women.[33]

As older forms of craft production gave way to mass production, jobs were deskilled. Yet the need to maintain the legitimacy of the male family head (e.g., husband as breadwinner) continued to support men's demands for the exclusion of women from higher-paying industrial jobs and for a family wage, a norm that continued to be upheld by both labor and management. Thus manufacturing jobs allocated to men were typically in capital-intensive and more profitable industries like steel and auto assembly, while women were relegated to employment in labor-intensive industries with low levels of productivity like textiles and apparel production. Low productivity constrained employers to pay lower wages and employ women. This was considered acceptable since women were believed to have legitimate access to the economic support of husbands and fathers. Indeed, designation of the male breadwinner as the head of the family and the relegation of men and women to separate spheres has traditionally been supported by the male-dominated labor movement and has supported the demand for a family wage.

In the past decades, trade liberalization in textiles and apparel, promoted by U.S.-driven trade policies and accepted by the business and government leadership of many low-wage countries, has enhanced corporate access not merely to low-wage labor but to low-wage female labor. While the neoliberal paradigm continues to posit a free market in labor, free trade policies have intensified the use of gendered labor markets in the apparel industry on a global basis.

These new, more intensively gendered markets have been fostered by forms of industrialization that differ significantly from those of nineteenth- and twentieth-century Europe and America. They embody new forms of industrial relations and new human resource practices, which are embodied in the institutional structure of export processing.

Export processing—through which a significant part of the world's apparel is assembled for sale in industrialized countries—is typically carried out in special industrial zones, where the costs of infrastructure are borne by, and tax relief is provided by, the host governments. These zones are often isolated from the institutions of the larger society; the factories are sometimes surrounded by barbed-wire fences. In an environment where labor laws and other regulatory measures are suspended, employers have greater control over the workforce. In this framework, women, frequently young and unmarried women, are targeted as the labor force of choice. Apparel is assembled not at market wages but at women's wages, set at varying percentages of what is defined as a man's wage. In numerous situations, labor practices that many would consider worker abuse have become the norm.

APPAREL PRODUCTION IN EXPORT-PROCESSING ZONES

The promises of trade liberalization have not produced a win-win situation domestically. Nor is it likely that the continuing phase-out of quotas and tariff reductions, new market openings, and the expansion of apparel production in the export-processing zones (EPZs) of the world will promote the economic aspirations of people in developing countries. In 2000 the International Labour Organization (ILO) issued a report about these zones, where a large part of the apparel production in developing countries is done. The ILO findings do not offer hope that export processing of apparel, as it is now structured, is likely to generate stable forms of economic growth. Nor does the ILO expect this form of production to provide decent work for the women who work in these zones. According to the ILO, EPZs have been huge generators of employment, but

> their rise to ubiquity poses increasingly serious questions to the world's 27 million strong EPZ workforce (as much as 90 percent of whom are female) and for the legions of development strategists who see EPZ investment as a quick way for developing countries to acquire the industrial skills and resources necessary to compete in a global economy. . . . The evidence thus far points to pervasive absence of meaningful linkages between the EPZs and the domestic economies of most of the host countries.[34]

The world's growing apparel industry represents an expanding source of comparative advantage for textile and apparel transnationals. Yet the new forms of Darwinian competition, imposed by the retail end of the industry, create contemporary patterns of apparel employment that may ultimately threaten the continuity of family life in developing countries by impoverishing women and their families.[35] At their extremes, worker abuse and wages that generate impoverishment may threaten a person's health and longevity. John Galtung argues that violence against persons need not be limited to physical acts that do them direct bodily harm. Violence can also be understood as avoidable insults to basic human needs—and more generally to life—that lower the level of needs satisfaction to below what is required to maintain a stable and acceptable quality of life.[36] In that sense many contemporary forms of human resource practices can be considered forms of violence.

Today, conditions at what are presumably industrial settings are beginning to resemble those of slave labor camps. The economic pressures in the global apparel industry are creating incentives for increasing coercion of, and incipient violence toward, women workers. Such conditions may challenge our notions about where industrial discipline ends and violence begins.

3 Roots of the Postwar Textile and Apparel Trade

The Reconstruction of the Asian–Pacific Rim Textile Industry

THE AMERICAN OCCUPATION OF JAPAN

The story of the liberalization of American trade in textiles and apparel begins with the defeat of the Japanese at the end of World War II. In 1945, the country was occupied by the U.S. military under the direction of General Douglas MacArthur, the Supreme Commander of the Allied Powers (SCAP). The occupation was to last until 1952. Unlike the occupation of Europe, Japanese reconstruction took place under the direct authority of the American military, which acted on behalf of the U.S. Department of State and was directly answerable to the American president. The purpose of the occupation was to permit the United States to oversee the restructuring of Japan's political system, the democratization of its civil society, and its industrial reconstruction. None of the other allied powers participated in this endeavor.

A major part of SCAP's mission in Japan was to organize the population and materials in order to revitalize the country's industrial production and find markets for the new manufactured goods. MacArthur initially had a free hand in directing the process of Japanese reindustrialization—until 1947, when the State Department began to intervene more directly.

SCAP AND JAPANESE TEXTILES

SCAP's effort to rebuild Japanese industry entailed the reconstruction of Japan's prewar textile industry. The objective was to help Japan produce textiles for export that would generate foreign exchange to pay for what were then desperately needed imports. Textile exports had played a major role in Japan's industrialization in the late nineteenth and early twentieth centuries.

Japan is an island country about the size of California, with few natural resources. Before World War II, textiles had been among Japan's most important industrial products, earning the country a large part of its foreign exchange. In the early twentieth century, Japanese textile production and textile exports grew dramatically, peaking in the late 1930s. Between 1937 and 1939, Japanese textiles were among the most competitive in world trade, representing 35 percent of the country's total exports of industrial goods. In 1937, textiles accounted for 60 percent of the total value of Japanese exports.[1] By 1940, on the eve of World War II, raw cotton comprised 70 percent of Japan's raw materials imports, and textiles represented 40 percent of its industrial exports.[2]

Before the war, Japan produced cotton cloth, rayon, and silk. The Japanese never produced raw cotton but imported it from China, which before the war was one of Japan's major trading partners. In 1938, 42.2 percent of Japanese cotton-fiber imports came from China, Korea, and Formosa, and 61 percent of Japanese exports went to these three countries. Forty percent of all Japanese imports came from China, and 25 percent of Japan's exports went to China.[3] In the late 1940s, however, China was in the midst of its long civil war and was no longer selling raw cotton.

Japan had a long tradition of cultivating silkworms; before the war the country was renowned for its fine silk exports. In the 1930s the country exported silk to the United States and Europe, which did not have indigenous silk industries. Much of the silk was made into women's hosiery. After World War II SCAP developed a five-year plan to revitalize Japan's silk industry. The backbone of the country's prewar textile exports, silk earned most of the textile industry's foreign exchange.

Though silk represented only 22 percent of all textile exports in 1937, it earned a higher rate of exchange than cotton or rayon textiles.[4] Before the war Japan had also imported coal and wood pulp to make rayon. But the import costs of these raw materials represented a large proportion of the total cost of production for both rayon and cotton fabrics. This cost reduced the foreign exchange value of these goods. Therefore, although cotton textile exports represented 30 percent of textile production in 1937, cotton added relatively little to Japan's foreign exchange reserves.

The U.S. occupation targeted the textile industry as a key industry to rebuild, in part because of the "reluctance to encourage the rebuilding of industries which might aid future aggression."[5] Plans for Japan to produce textiles had been made even before the end of the war and were put into action almost immediately after the U.S. occupation began. As Stanley

Nehmer and Marguerite C. Crimmins wrote in 1948, "Action by the Supreme Commander of the Allied Powers (SCAP) toward rehabilitating the Japanese textile industry has been the result of the implementation of Allied occupation objectives as set forth in the Potsdam declaration and subsequent Far Eastern Commission policy decisions."[6] The reconstruction of the Japanese textile industry was entirely planned and coordinated by the U.S. War Department, the U.S. Commercial Company, the Commodity Credit Corporation, and the Department of State.[7]

As early as January 1946 the Allied powers sent a fact-finding mission to Japan to assess the potential for implementing this policy. The Textile Mission, as it was called, included representatives from China, India, the United Kingdom, and the United States.[8] The Mission made recommendations to rebuild an export-oriented textile industry that would earn war-torn Japan foreign exchange to pay for the import of needed food and other scarce resources.[9]

Although silk had ranked first among prewar Japanese textile exports, after the war nylon began to replace silk in the manufacture of women's hosiery. In 1947 the value of silk exports declined dramatically, defeating SCAP's plan to rely on silk exports.[10] Efforts to rebuild the rayon textile industry were equally unsuccessful because of the high cost of importing coal and wood pulp, as well as the costs of replacing the rayon textile machinery that had become obsolete during the war. Cotton textiles now seemed like the best option.

The war had ravaged about 80 percent of Japan's textile machinery, which had been uprooted from the factories and converted to war use. Some textile machinery had been destroyed by bombing, and a small proportion had been transferred to Japan's occupied territories overseas. By the end of the war, most of Japan's textile machinery was destroyed by war and left in rubble.[11] In 1947, SCAP began to authorize production targets for cotton textile reconstruction. The Japanese government "adopted a series of measures to promote textile production, the most important of which gave priority to the textile industry in the allocation of materials, working capital, power and coal. Extra rations of food and clothing were granted to textile workers."[12] SCAP rationed the consumption of textiles—30 percent of Japanese cotton fabrics were allotted for domestic use and the remainder allocated for export. SCAP was also responsible for production schedules and for setting the prices of inputs that went into textile production,[13] including the price of labor.

THE FIRST TEXTILE CONFLICT

Before any textiles were produced, it was necessary to find the raw materials. The difficulty of finding new supplies of raw cotton soon disrupted SCAP's schedule for producing and exporting textiles and was one of the causes of the first post–World War II congressional dispute over the United States–Japanese textile trade, a skirmish that was won by the State Department.

The United States made efforts to encourage Asian countries to sell low-cost raw materials like cotton to Japan. Yet many Southeast Asian countries had been Japanese colonies before the war and had suffered economic and political exploitation that had enriched Japan at their expense. These countries had been forced into trade relationships that made them exporters of raw materials and importers of higher-cost Japanese manufactured goods. As Burton I. Kaufman writes, "With memories of World War II still fresh in their minds, the countries of the region were reluctant to establish commercial ties with their former captors."[14] Although there was some trade between Japan and Southeast Asia, many of the former's trading partners were too poor to expand this trade with Japan after the war.[15]

Raw cotton was available from the United States, but Japan did not have the dollar liquidity to finance the imports necessary for the occupied country's textile reconstruction. Yet textile production was essential for maintaining a balance of payment between the United States and Japan.[16] Reestablishment of the textile trade was not left to market forces but was managed by SCAP and the U.S. War Department. It was decided that the United States would finance the sale of its own supplies of raw cotton to Japan. In June 1946, SCAP oversaw the first shipments of U.S. raw cotton to Japan, which were funded by U.S. government loans. John R. Stewart writes, "In August 1947 an Occupied Japan Export-Import Revolving Fund was created in Japan to utilize the $137 million in gold and silver of Japanese ownership in SCAP custody as a credit base for loans to finance imports of raw materials for processing into exports."[17] Stewart notes that "this was made possible by the conclusion of an agreement between the United States Commercial Company (USCC) the Commodity Credit Corporation (CCC) and the War Department for the shipment . . . of cotton to Japan."[18] In 1947 SCAP procured some raw cotton from India and Egypt, but 88 percent of the cotton exported to Japan for textile production came from the United States. SCAP also made provisions for the Japanese to pay for cotton in yen or in commodities and to sell Japanese cotton textiles for sterling.[19] While such interim solutions solved the immediate problem, these methods could not be used in the long term to finance enough raw cotton for Japan's new textile factories.

THE DEBUT OF COMMUNIST CONTAINMENT IN EAST ASIA

At the beginning of the occupation, and before the onset of the cold war in East Asia, SCAP made its plans to rebuild the Japanese textile industry. The cold war dramatically intensified the urgency to reindustrialize Japan and led to changes in relations between the State Department and the military occupation. The reconstruction of Japan's textile industry and its exports of textiles were a significant part of this larger goal.

By the late 1940s, the iron curtain began to fall—both in Europe and East Asia. In the immediate postwar years, most American planning for the reconstruction of war-torn countries focused on Europe.[20] The European Recovery Program (the Marshall Plan), along with new forms of international finance, had been designed to rebuild Europe and to fund European purchases of America's industrial products. Reconstruction of Europe's economies would increase worldwide demand and generate prosperity. In part this was a Keynesian vision that formed the rationale for economic aid to Europe in the postwar negotiations at Bretton Woods and Geneva.[21]

At the end of the war, the United States was the only industrialized nation whose infrastructure and manufacturing capacity had not been either destroyed or severely damaged; America produced 50 percent of the world's industrial output.[22] As noted in chapter 2, even though wartime savings fueled new consumer demand at home, American producers needed to export in order to avoid another round of overproduction and unemployment. Finding overseas markets for America's surfeit of agricultural and industrial output posed a major challenge to the continued stability and productivity of the U.S. economy. Trade liberalization embodied in the General Agreement on Tariffs and Trade (GATT) was an effort to encourage an alliance between the United States and Europe's capitalist countries. The United States began to export goods and capital to Europe and, reciprocally, to open its markets to the goods of a reindustrializing Europe.

However, as left-wing forces gained power in Europe and the West began to confront a powerful and expansionist Soviet Union occupying eastern Europe, the United States began to direct Marshall Plan aid at hastening the economic reconstruction of the war-damaged nations and at the remilitarization of NATO countries. The goal was to encircle and contain the Soviet Union and its eastern European satellites. As the cold war emerged in East Asia, the U.S. political agenda in that region changed too. Even before the defeat of the Chinese Nationalists and their retreat to Formosa (Taiwan) in 1947, the weakness and corruption of the Nationalists permitted the Communists to gain a secure foothold in China. As the Communists gained strength in China and left-wing insurgencies began to appear in the region, America saw a new threat to its control of the Asian-Pacific Rim. By 1947 America supported Chiang Kai-shek in opposition to Maoist communism,[23] but the increasing success of the Chinese communists led the State Department to question this approach. Even before Mao defeated the Nationalist government and the United States "lost" China, the State Department had already begun to take a more active interest in Japan's economic, political, and, particularly, military security. Japan's industrial reconstruction took on a new urgency. As Richard Barnet writes, "The workshop of Asia, as [U.S. Secretary of State Dean] Acheson had called the defeated island empire, was now designated in the emerging American grand design as the 'stabilizer' of Asia. Japanese economic policies had been tailored to meet U.S. security requirements. Nippon was once again encouraged to expand a 'coprosperity sphere' in Southeast Asia and to tie its economy to the dollar."[24] By 1949, when the Communists defeated the Chinese Nationalists, the State Department had clearly redefined its Japan policy.

In 1947, George Kennan was appointed the head of the newly created Policy Planning Staff (PPS) at the State Department. Kennan's thinking lay at the heart of the State Department's new political and economic agenda in the Far East—its determination to abandon China and make Japan the bulwark of democracy in Asia. Kennan's strategy was one that "prescribed the creation of positions of strength in Western Europe and Japan to curb Soviet and Communist influence." According to Kennan, "American occupation policies had succeeded in disarming and demilitarizing Japan, the PPS noted in November 1947, but 'they have not produced . . . the political and economic stability which Japanese society will require if it is to withstand communist pressures after we have gone.' "[25] As head of the PPS, Kennan had argued for a Marshall Plan in Europe that emphasized Soviet containment. As the communist threat in Asia grew, he began to see SCAP's earlier efforts as isolating Japan, and MacArthur's goal of breaking up the *zaibatsu* (industrial cartels) as threatening the country's rapid industrial recovery.[26]

The State Department became increasingly concerned to rapidly link the Japanese polity and economy with the West. At the beginning of the occupation, SCAP, under MacArthur's leadership, had been given a relatively free hand in directing Japan's recovery. However, by 1947, as the Communists began to take power in China, the State Department started to scrutinize MacArthur's leadership of the Japanese recovery, to question the direction of his efforts to promote democracy and break up the prewar industrial cartels.

MacArthur saw the defeat of Japan as the result of the country's failed militarism, a consequence of Japan's prewar, quasi-feudal sociopolitical system. MacArthur succeeded in getting the Japanese Diet to support agrarian reform and eliminate the power of the prewar Japanese landed aristocracy. He hoped to rebuild Japan's industrial structure and civil society along Western liberal, individualistic, and entrepreneurial lines. Consistent with the goals of the State Department, MacArthur also wanted to see Japan as a *democratic* bastion of Western capitalism in the Pacific. He envisioned a reconstructed Japan tied to the West through trade and investment, and sought a way to stabilize Japan and secure America's position in the Far East.

The *zaibatsu* had been pillars of the country's prewar colonialism and militarism, and MacArthur wanted to dismantle them. His views are expressed in one of his semiannual lectures to the Japanese. Allied policy should be, he argued, designed to transform

> that system which in the past has permitted the major part of the commerce and industry and natural resources of your country to be owned and controlled by a minority of feudal families and exploited for their exclusive benefit. The world has probably never seen a counterpart to so abnormal an economic system. It permitted exploitation of the many for the sole benefit of the few. The integration of those few with the government was complete and their influence upon government policies inordinate, and set the course which ultimately led to war and destruction.[27]

MacArthur's desire to create democracy in Japan was designed to promote more individualism and competition, and this motivated his plans to break up the *zaibatsu*. These plans were soon abandoned in the new efforts to speed Japan's industrial reconstruction and ensure Japan's economic security.[28] Japan was to become the hub of a new free world and a free-trade network in this region, and this required rapid economic growth and political stability.[29]

Despite Kennan's support for a new Marshall Plan for Asia, Congress was reluctant to approve additional foreign aid for Asia and now urged a

Japan policy based on "trade not aid."[30] This strengthened the hands of policy makers in the State Department who favored the rapid reindustrialization of Japan. Rebuilding Japan's textile industry and its textile trade now took on greater urgency. Kennan appointed William H. Draper to promote the new Japanese textile industry, and Draper tried to secure congressional approval to use foreign aid to finance the sale of raw cotton to Japan.

Draper had been a military officer during World War I, after which he enjoyed a prestigious career in banking, first at the National City Bank in New York, and subsequently at Dillon Read, where he became vice president ten years later. He rejoined the military during World War II, serving under MacArthur. In the early postwar years he was secretary of the army.[31]

Draper organized a new Textile Mission to Japan comprised primarily of American bankers and businessmen and financiers like himself, to "study" the feasibility of rebuilding Japan's textile industry. These men supported the state Department's program for Japanese reconstruction. The Textile Mission visited Japan in January of 1948, officially to assess the feasibility of this task, but its real goal was to legitimate the new United States–Japan textile policy. According to one firsthand report, the group stayed only two and a half weeks and got all its information in briefings from the U.S. Army's General Headquarters.[32] Upon their return they produced a report that supported this new State Department policy. Relying on former associates in the banking community, Draper also made efforts to arrange for private financing of American cotton exports to Japan, setting plans in motion "to form a North American Cotton Corporation with a capital of $60 million to be subscribed by cotton shippers or by a group of commercial banks, or alternatively by the Export-Import Bank."[33] This corporation never materialized. At this point, only government was willing to see its political capital invested in such a risky business.

Ultimately it was U.S. agricultural interests, particularly Southern cotton producers, who persuaded Congress to approve U.S. Army plans to finance the sale of America's raw cotton to Japan. At the end of World War II, the United States had a large surplus of raw cotton languishing in U.S. government silos—for which it was becoming increasingly difficult to find markets. U.S. cotton producers had suffered during the depression but had grown prosperous during World War II. With the war's end, agricultural surpluses, cotton among them, mounted once again and prices fell. Export of surplus cotton to Japan was close to the hearts of U.S. cotton producers and clearly consistent with SCAP's agenda for rebuilding Japan's cotton textile industry.[34]

As the Textile Mission left for Japan, Senator James Eastland, "a Mississippi Democrat and cotton producer," introduced what became known as the Eastland bill, written to authorize U.S. foreign aid appropriations that would finance the sale of cotton to Japan. The cotton lobby had been pressing for such an arrangement. Senator William H. Knowland, a California Republican "cotton senator," had already lobbied the Pentagon to develop the Japanese textile industry as an aid to both U.S. cotton producers and to Japan.[35] The plan's popularity was evidenced by the fact that forty-one senators sponsored the bill.[36] According to Howard B. Schonberger, there were many

> Washington policymakers encouraged by the rapid rehabilitation of the once mighty Japanese cotton textile industry. The failure of plans for restoring the Japanese silk industry, the relative technical and financial ease of raising cotton textile output, the pressure of raw cotton producers in the United States for foreign markets, and above all the expectation of a large foreign exchange surplus from Japanese textile exports, figure heavily in the decision of economic planners to make cotton textiles the key to launching a successful recovery program.[37]

After favorable testimony in Congress, the Eastland bill passed. As raw cotton arrived from the United States, textile production in Japan increased. By 1949, the combined efforts of Congress, the cotton lobby, and SCAP had financed the rebuilding of the Japanese textile industry to the point where the effort began to bear fruit; increasing quantities of textile product were readied for export.

FINDING MARKETS FOR JAPANESE TEXTILES

In 1948 the Draper Commission, working with the State Department, Congress, and American cotton producers, had temporarily solved the problem of financing American cotton exports to Japan. As Japanese textile production increased, however, a new problem emerged—how to find export markets for the growing volumes of Japanese textiles.[38] One aspect of the problem was the difficulty of linking these exports to the U.S. dollar. In 1949 the Truman administration described the problems Japan faced in finding Southeast Asian outlets for its cotton textiles. As Stewart puts it, "The principal markets for Japan's cotton textiles are in Southeast Asia and other colonial areas which are mainly in the sterling bloc. Here lies the primary problem of Japan's postwar textile industry—how to sell in sterling areas and still pay dollars for American cotton."[39]

Only countries with dollars—the United States and those strategically important to U.S. policy objectives—could buy Japanese textiles. The United States had financed the import of raw materials with dollar loans. With the largest supply of dollars in the postwar world, it made sense for the United States to buy Japanese textiles and urge other countries with dollars to open their markets to Japanese textiles. The United States was poised to purchase cotton textiles manufactured in Japan and became the world's principal advocate for reciprocal trade.

Before World War II, 40 percent of Japan's textile exports were sold to British India, the Netherlands Indies, Korea, Manchuria, Egypt, and other markets in Southeast Asia.[40] As noted earlier, after the war Japan's former colonies in Southeast Asia could not, or would not, purchase Japanese manufactures;[41] some were too poor to do so. According to one author, "*Per capita* annual income for all the countries of East Asia in 1955 was under $100 compared to about $220 for Japan."[42] Many of these countries also had access to U.S. foreign aid, allowing them to proceed with their own industrialization.

The loss of Japan's prewar export markets threw Japanese producers back on U.S. and European markets. Yet except for silk, the Western industrialized nations of the world had never been large buyers of Japanese textiles. In the 1930s the United States and European cotton-textile-manufacturing countries had raised their textile tariffs to ensure the health of their own textile and apparel producers against low-wage competitors. In the United States, even these high tariffs failed to keep Japanese imports down to levels that U.S. producers considered acceptable. American textile manufacturers had personally visited Japan to privately negotiate voluntary export restraints with leaders of Japan's textile industry.[43]

William Borden argues that the major concern of the U.S. State Department in rebuilding Japan's textile industry was not the problem of dollar liquidity but the new international conflict with Red China that had emerged.[44] By 1949 American foreign policy was primarily aimed at thwarting the industrial growth and political power of Red China. In order to contravene China's ability to influence left-wing insurgencies in Asia, it was necessary to build a Japanese "workshop" in Asia. To do this, the State Department tried to weaken Japan's trade with China and reorient Japan to trade with capitalist-leaning countries in Southeast Asia and the West.

Japan had traded extensively with China before the war but had lost a large proportion of its prewar textile investments in China. For the State Department, it was necessary to block the possibility that China might become an outlet once again for Japan's expanding textile production. In the 1951 peace treaty with Japan, the United States imposed an embargo on Japanese trade with mainland China.[45] Even though Japanese textile producers opposed their government's decision to accept this embargo, by 1951 Japanese trade with China had dropped off dramatically.

During the early cold war years, America's efforts to reconstruct the Japanese textile industry and to finance a renewed Japanese trade in textiles had little to do with efforts to unleash market forces. Neither Truman nor Eisenhower had any interest in providing American consumers with low-cost textile products from Japan. Until the late 1950s the reconstruction of the Japanese textile industry was important primarily to the effort to contain communism and promote the political and economic ties that would link Japan to the Western democracies. The State Department played a role in making these things happen.

THE EISENHOWER ADMINISTRATION AND THE TEXTILE TRADE WITH JAPAN

When Eisenhower entered the White House in 1953, as the cold war intensified, he continued the policies of the Truman administration. Like Truman and Kennan, Eisenhower and his secretary of state, John Foster Dulles, continued to believe "that Japan was 'the key to the future political complexion' of much of the Far East." Moreover, according to Kaufman, "the President and the Secretary of State supported the organization of something resembling the Greater East-Asian Co-Prosperity Sphere, which Japan had sought to establish between the two world wars."[46] The Eisenhower administration encouraged Congress to authorize aid and technical support to capitalist-leaning countries in East Asia and wholeheartedly supported the United Nations embargo against China. The State Department strengthened its efforts to both build and rebuild textile industries in a variety of East Asian countries and was soon to encourage their textile and apparel exports to U.S. markets.

The reconstruction of Japan's textile industry led to the opening of the U.S. market to imports of low-cost Japanese textiles and apparel. The growth of these imports in American markets was soon to create a rift in American trade politics. American textile and apparel manufacturers, along with trade union leaders in these industries, feared a deluge of cheap imports. They formed a coalition to oppose trade liberalization and support trade protection. This struggle over U.S. trade policy for textiles and apparel would continue through the 1980s.

In keeping with a policy of economic austerity, Congress rejected Eisenhower's initiatives to appropriate new funds for an economic recovery plan for Asia and instead urged a strategy of "trade not aid."[47] Yet in response to the State Department's cold war concerns, Congress was prevailed upon to appropriate funds for the purchase of new textile machinery to rebuild not only Japan's textile industry but also those in other selected countries throughout East Asia.

The International Cooperative Association (ICA), a U.S. agency engaged in disbursing foreign aid, played a large role in these developments. Throughout the 1950s it used some of the funds earmarked for technical assistance and financial credit for U.S. producers to assist in the construction and reconstruction of textile facilities in East Asia. As the decade wore on, the ICA spent less on projects to aid the U.S. textile industry and more of its funds for procurement and the promotion of textile production abroad.

According to the 1958 testimony of Frederick Payne, a Maine congressman and advocate for the U.S. textile industry, in 1951 the ICA spent $31 million for this purpose, followed by $12 million in 1952. Indeed, by 1958 the ICA had spent a total of $45 million.[48] This raised the ire of U.S. textile manufacturers who opposed government support for the construction and reconstruction of textile machinery firms competing directly with those in the United States.

Many of the American textile producers and their congressional supporters saw these expenditures as a way for the United States to compensate Japan for the voluntary export restraints (VERs) that the textile industry had demanded of the administration. Moreover, some of the funds were spent on rebuilding the textile industry in the Philippines, a country that, before the war, had been an important export market for U.S.-made textiles. Now a recipient of U.S. largesse, the Philippines was soon to become a new and competitive textile producer, as well as a significant part of the U.S. security perimeter in the Pacific.[49]

Yet despite these efforts, with the loss of Red China in 1949, Far Eastern dominoes would soon begin to fall. By February of 1950, the Chinese Communists concluded a military alliance with the Soviet Union. North Korea closed itself off behind the bamboo curtain, and South Korea found itself in economic and political distress. By June 1950 Communist forces in North Korea had invaded the south. Between 1950 and 1953, General Douglas MacArthur led UN troops in Korea in the unsuccessful attempt to defeat the Communists in the north. During the early part of the 1950s, left-wing insurgencies also posed a significant threat to Burma and Malaysia.[50] At the same time, the French were waging an anticommunist struggle in French Indochina.

The Korean War provided a new and important export stimulus not only for Japanese textiles but also for other types of Japanese industrial products, as Japan was awarded contracts to supply UN forces with military supplies.[51] However, in 1954 the Korean conflict came to an end. Korean War procurement had saved the foundering Japanese economy—but only until hostilities ended, whereupon contracts for Japanese industries dried up. With the China market closed to them and insufficient demand in Southeast Asia, Japanese textile producers once more faced a dearth of markets for their increased output.

After the Korean War, the Eisenhower administration generated new legislation for continued support of raw cotton exports and made a stronger case for Japanese textile imports, both of which succeeded in response to new invocations of the Far Eastern Communist threat. The administration also persuaded Congress to fund raw cotton exports to Japan by invoking the interests of the American farm community, particularly its cotton producers. At that point America's farmers still represented the American way of life.[52]

Subsidies for raw cotton had increased cotton acreage in the United States during World War II. Moreover, mechanization of cotton agriculture in the early 1940s made cotton acreage more productive.[53] A growing volume of unsold cotton was stored in government warehouses; the storage fees alone represented a significant cost to the American public. By the end of 1954 the United States was holding a surplus of 10 million bales of raw cotton that had cost the American government $1.39 billion to store.[54]

Subsidizing cotton exports for Japanese and other Far Eastern textile producers rewarded cotton growers, a group firmly in favor of open markets and reciprocal trade. There were about four million American farm families, many of them cotton planters. In 1955 cotton was, after wheat, the largest U.S. agricultural export. Forty million acres of U.S. land produced cotton valued at $14.3 billion dollars, accounting for 5 percent of all U.S. agricultural exports.[55] Japan was the largest importer of this cotton, taking 25.7 percent of America's total cotton exports in the 1953–54 season.

Congress also passed the Agricultural Trade Development and Assistance Act, or PL 480. Although PL 480 was known as the Food for Peace program, raw cotton was treated as part of America's agricultural surplus.

According to President Eisenhower's 1955 report to Congress on this act, Title II authorized the president "to furnish, out of Commodity Credit Corporation stocks, and on a grant basis, surplus agricultural commodities to friendly governments or peoples to assist in meeting famine or other urgent relief requirements."

Under Title I of this act, the U.S. government could sell cotton for dollars, providing Japan with $54.3 million worth of cotton between 1955 and 1956 for this purpose. Aid to Japan from this program represented 27 percent of all such funds provided during this period. Japan received an additional $29 million under Title II of PL480, or 15 percent of all such funds between 1955 and 1956. Under Title II, Japan could purchase cotton with its own currency, held in separate accounts to finance U.S. purchases of domestic goods and services from indebted countries.[56]

Between 1953 and 1957, the Export-Import Bank provided a total of $376 million to "assist cotton exports." A full 93 percent of this money, or $350 million, went to Japan.[57] Private banks also offered loans to countries that wanted to purchase cotton but lacked the dollars to pay for it. Finally, in 1957 Japan received $68.4 million under the CCC Export Credit Sales Program for Cotton, or 19 percent of all the funds.[58]

While the agricultural community supported the State Department on this issue, the country's textile producers did not. It is true that in 1946, in the aftermath of the war, American textile producers, unaware that they might have to compete with low-wage imports, were anxious to help the Japanese rebuild their textile industry. As Destler writes, "So confident were [America's textile industry] leaders that in 1946, they endorsed and cooperated in a mission to Japan—a fierce prewar trade competitor—to aid in reconstructing that country's textile industry during the American occupation."[59] However, in 1947 the War Department and SCAP began to urge Congress to open American markets to Japanese textile imports. By then the American Cotton Manufacturers' Institute (ACMI), the U.S. cotton textile manufacturers' trade organization, had changed its position, no longer supporting the rebuilding of Japan's textile industry. U.S. cotton textile producers sent their own mission to Japan in June of 1948 to discuss textile imports with Japanese producers—just as they had in the 1930s. The ACMI strongly opposed opening U.S. markets to imports, instead supporting the State Department's initial position, which had stressed the "recovery of Japan's 'normal' markets in Oriental and Colonial countries."[60]

With the end of hostilities in Korea, there was a rapid surge in low-cost Japanese textile and apparel imports, which led to a new round of "cotton politics." America's textile makers and the members of Congress who supported them came into conflict with the Eisenhower State Department over the extension of the Trade Agreements Act. After a long and acrimonious congressional debate, the leader of the textile coalition in Congress was suddenly called by a State Department official for a special briefing and informed about the defeat of the communists at Dien Bien Phu, in what was then French Indochina. The fear of communist expansion decisively turned the tide of congressional sentiment and led to the bill's renewal.

The 1954 extension of the Trade Agreements Act—which I discuss in detail in chapter 4—allowed Eisenhower to reduce textile tariffs by 5 percent each year for three years; the act was extended in 1954. The agreement also contained a number of protectionist features broadening the conditions under which American industry could seek relief from foreign imports, and it limited the extensive tariff reductions Eisenhower had hoped to enact.[61] Yet, between 1954 and 1956, following the tariff reductions made in each year, textile imports rose dramatically.[62]

Although the annual percentage increases rested on a very small base, the quantities of many types of cotton textiles imported from Japan began to increase with great rapidity. According to figures from the U.S. Department of Commerce and the Japanese Ministry of Finance, by 1956 U.S. imports of "cotton cloths" had increased by 695 percent over the figure for 1953; the increase for cotton velveteens was 1,977 percent; for cotton sheets and pillowcases, 1,391 percent; for cotton outerwear, 353 percent; for cotton wearing apparel, 3,250 percent; and for cotton handkerchiefs, 768 percent.[63]

Between 1951 and 1955 Japan's cotton textiles represented a full 39.5 percent of its exports of industrial products.[64] Indeed, by 1956, after three more years of successive import tariff reductions, the value of Japanese textile shipments to the United States "was seven times the 1952 level."[65] These imports continued to be a very small proportion of the U.S. market and can hardly be said to have created a market disruption. Yet such growth rates provided realistic fodder for the protectionists' argument that liberalizing trade in textiles by reducing tariffs would, if it continued, open the door to a flood of low-wage imports.[66]

Eisenhower, as president of the United States and leader of the free world, was trying to promote Japanese exports to the United States. He tried to persuade the European nations, particularly Great Britain, to do so as well. However, Great Britain now found itself trying to restructure its own textile industry, which had suffered from sharp declines in exports. As a member of the GATT, Great Britain was officially committed to reciprocal trade. However, in the immediate postwar period, the new British Labour government pursued policies to achieve full employment. Part of this approach involved a commitment to limit its imports from former trading partners in the British sterling bloc in preference to increased trade with Japan. According to David P. Calleo and Benjamin M. Rowland, "Such arrangements were anathema, however, to the votaries of multilateral free trade in the American State Department and Treasury. According to the prevalent State Department view, Europe's economic reconstruction depended essentially on a return to a liberal trading system as soon as possible."[67]

Eisenhower continued to urge Europe to accommodate Japan's economic needs throughout the 1950s. He sponsored and lobbied extensively for Japanese membership in the GATT.[68] Japan was admitted to the GATT in 1955, but this did not accomplish Eisenhower's real objective. Japan's membership encouraged some countries, many of them Commonwealth trading partners, to accept Japanese exports, but fourteen out of the thirty-three members of the GATT continued to bar imports of Japanese manufactured goods by using the Article XIX escape clause provision in the agreement.[69]

In 1957 the total value of Japan's textile and apparel exports to the United States represented 33 percent of all Japan's manufactured exports to this country. Eighteen percent of all Japan's exports to the United States were in textiles. Apparel exports represented almost half of this, or about 15 percent of all Japanese manufactured exports to the United States.[70]

The Japanese pressed the United States to accept these textile exports to compensate for the embargo that prevented their access to Chinese markets. At the same time, tariff reductions for Japanese textiles were testing protectionists' patience in Congress. By 1957 Eisenhower was forced to deal with these pressures. He negotiated voluntary export restraints with the Japanese, who at that point accepted the fact that they would have to limit their textile exports to the United States.

Tariff reductions between 1953 and 1956 had increased the volume of U.S. textile imports. The VERs went into effect in 1957, limiting the growth of these imports. Nevertheless, between 1950 and 1962 U.S. imports of Japanese cotton textiles went from being 2.1 percent of Japan's total exports to the United States to almost 9 percent—despite the fact that the majority of Japan's textile exports were now being shipped to Asia.

By the 1950s the textile industry's congressional battle against low-wage East Asian textile imports had begun, an issue I discuss in the following chapter. This battle would take another thirty-odd years to resolve and would encompass a region much larger than Japan.

Between 1947 and 1960, textiles played a major role in the trade between the United States and Japan. After that, however, Japanese textile imports began to wane as Japan began to export textiles to other developing countries in Asia—countries that the United States had also helped to industrialize in response to threats of communism.

The textile trade was to play a major role in Asia, first in the Big Three and the Association of Southeast Asian Nations (ASEAN), and was to become increasingly important in building economic and political links between the United States and developing countries in the region.[71] But textile exports to the United States were only a small part of the problem. The use of textiles in apparel manufacture was another part. Asian textiles were already being used to make apparel in Asia that was designed and financed by U.S. capital and sold in the United States. Clothing imports from Asia would soon threaten the U.S. apparel industry.

THE ASIAN MIRACLES: SOUTH KOREA AND TAIWAN

The United States never occupied South Korea and Taiwan as it did Japan. However, it did engage in direct military intervention to protect these countries from communist incursions. After World War II, America also provided massive financial and economic support for South Korea's and Taiwan's national military defense efforts and large-scale funding for their industrial revitalization—as it did for other former colonial and newly independent nations in the region, including Hong Kong, Malaysia, Thailand, the Philippines, Indonesia, and Singapore. This support was designed to link these nations to the Japanese "workshop" and thereby to Western-dominated, free-world networks of trade and investment. All these efforts were tied to the development and growth of export-led industrialization, which laid the groundwork for the globalization of the U.S. apparel industry.[72]

Taiwan is an island and Korea is a peninsula. Both lie close to China's borders. The two countries were intimately involved, historically and politically, through conquest and trade, with China and Japan. For the half century prior to 1945, Korea and Taiwan were Japanese colonies, during which time they were transformed into plantation economies and forced to grow rice, tea, sugar, and other raw materials for export to Japan.[73] In return, Korea and Taiwan were export markets for Japanese manufactured goods. By 1945 Korea had been divided—the Soviet Union occupied the north and the United States occupied the south. Liberated from Japan in 1945, Taiwan and South Korea by the 1950s were recovering from the impoverishing effects of colonization and a half decade of war.[74]

When the Korean War turned the cold war hot, Truman and then Eisenhower upheld the defense of the Far East by bearing the expenses of military leadership. Between 1945 and 1958, both before and after the Korean War, the United States provided economic and military aid to South Korea that, as estimated by the United Nations, amounted to $2.6 billion.[75] According to the calculations of Alice Amsden, "The average annual inflow of aid from 1953 through 1958 was $270 million excluding military assistance, or roughly $12 per capita per year. This was nearly 15 percent of the average annual gross national product (GNP) and over 80 percent of foreign exchange."[76] Amsden sees the huge influx of U.S. dollars into South Korea, which persisted even after the Korean War, as having allowed the Syngman Rhee government to engage in massive corruption. This corruption, she argues, was responsible in large part for the country's successful economic development. Rhee's government distributed foreign aid funds for investment to individuals on the basis of their political connections and willingness to make financial contributions to Rhee's private and political agenda. As Amsden sees it, this also gave rise to "an altogether new entrepreneurial element." She writes, "According to the *Government Audit Report on Illicit Wealth*, the industries to which these new enterprises thriving on venality belonged, included, textiles, paper, housing, mining, fertilizer, flour, alcohol, glass, pottery, livestock, construction, warehousing and trade."[77]

Parallel developments took place in Taiwan. In the early 1950s both Eisenhower and Chiang Kai-shek still harbored the hope of eventually returning the Chinese Nationalists in Taiwan to power on the mainland.[78] The futility of such hopes, however, led Taiwan's government to shift its priorities and make the country a showcase of free-market development, or as Neil Jacoby writes, "socially and politically stable, and an economically capable base for the recovery of all of China."[79]

Jacoby has carefully documented the range of policy discussions by, and programs developed by, the U.S. State Department—often in collaboration with the nation's armed forces—to support the military defense and economic growth of Taiwan in the fifteen years following World War II. In particular, he calculates that between 1953 and 1956 the United States funded Taiwan's economic development and military expenditures to the tune of almost $300 million a year. In addition, between 1950 and 1965 the United States appropriated $148 million in foreign aid alone to bolster Taiwan's economic and military defenses against communist incursion.[80]

In his detailed 1966 study of U.S. aid to Taiwan, Jacoby writes that Taiwan was "the beneficiary of a particularly rich aid program . . . aided by the full panoply of aid instruments, institutions and administrative techniques. Virtually every idea and formula invented in 15 years of U.S. aid administration was tried in Taiwan."[81]

As the primary donor for this massive military and economic project, "the US could have a significant influence upon Chinese [Taiwanese] policies."[82] Jacoby's assessment of the extraordinarily high levels of U.S. foreign and military aid to Taiwan is worth repeating here to demonstrate the intention of the United States to shape the economic policy of the region.

> The primary determinants of the size of the aid-investment multiplier—
> the total amount of investment induced by external assistance—are
> the economic policies of the government of the recipient country.
> If the recipient government pursues policies that provide a favorable
> climate for savings and for productive investment by its own citizens as
> well as by foreigners, aid can induce much additional investment and
> economic growth. If its economic policies discourage savings and
> investment, the aid multiplier will be low. In administering the country
> aid programs, AID [Agency for International Development] is expected
> actively to use the influence it possesses upon the government of
> the aided country to create optimal conditions for productive invest-
> ment.[83]

With its extensive support of the conservative, authoritarian governments of South Korea and Taiwan, the United States helped shape their political and economic systems. One student of "late industrialization" suggests that stable profits and continued economic development are the result of a stable infrastructure and the ability of the government to "sustain the policy over the long run." Authoritarian regimes may be more successful than democratic ones in generating rapid industrialization.[84] Indeed, as Donald B. Keesing puts it, "The roster of governments that have succeeded in instituting coherent, pro-trade policies is not exactly a list of repression-free, anti-authoritarian regimes. . . . Having labor leaders in jail as well as achieving enough political stability to take a long-run view seem to be very common accompaniments to the creation of pro-trade policies."[85]

Much of the economic aid to South Korea and Taiwan went toward building an infrastructure—toward paving roads, building modern harbors, and increasing electric capacity to facilitate private business investment.[86] These enterprises required large investments in foreign technology and capital goods that the indigenous economies of that region could not produce and could not afford to purchase. Economic development in this region may have had less to do with free trade and the elimination of distortions in the economy than neoclassical economists might believe.

With the U.S. military umbrella in place, along with large amounts of U.S. foreign aid, and an embargo against trade with China, a successful strategy against communist aggression was forged in South Korea, Taiwan, and Hong Kong. The rapid economic growth subsequently generated in this region was to make these three into "Asian Miracles."[87]

HONG KONG

Hong Kong is frequently cited as having one of the purest forms of free trade and as the paradigmatic example of the advantages of nonintervention in promoting economic development. Yet even here, government policy played an important role. Colonized by Great Britain, after World War II Hong Kong became a protectorate of that nation. Louis Turner notes that this government "took specific statutory actions that supported the growth of manufacturing industries by establishing the Federation of Hong Kong Industries in 1960, the Hong Kong Trade Development Council in 1966, the Hong Kong Productivity Council in 1967 and the Hong Kong Export Credit Insurance Corporation in 1968. Manufactured export growth was a deliberate national development strategy in Hong Kong adopted by both the government and the private sector."[88]

Hong Kong's economic development was deeply entwined with the major historical and political transformations that rocked the Asian-Pacific Rim in World War II and its aftermath—especially the Chinese revolution. The UN-imposed trade embargo on China in 1951 had a major effect on the region's economic future and contributed to the eventual growth of export-led development in Hong Kong. As one historian writes, "Like Singapore, Hong Kong launched its industrialization and manufactured exports drive in response to adverse circumstances in the early 1950s, in this case the reduction in trade with China resulting from the change in government and the trade restrictions associated with the Korean War."[89]

TEXTILE DEVELOPMENT

As the Communists took power in China, defeating the Nationalist forces, thousands of civilian refugees fled the mainland to Hong Kong and Taiwan. Many of these refugees, particularly those from Shanghai and Canton, brought with them the capital, production skill, and business expertise necessary to promote investment in new textile and apparel industries.[90]

By the mid-1950s both Taiwan and South Korea had developed textile and apparel industries that produced goods primarily for the domestic market. At that point, Japan "was virtually the only country with a modern textile industry in the East and Southeast Asian regions, and was competitive in exports."[91] Japan had made only a limited foray into the U.S. market, exporting about 9 percent of its textiles to the United States. In 1950, before Korean War procurement increased the demand for Japan's textiles, that country's textile producers exported most of its relatively small cotton textile output to Asia and Australia.

In the early 1950s Hong Kong's textile industry was tied to the British sterling bloc. A British Crown colony, Hong Kong benefited from free access to the textile markets of the United Kingdom. In 1959, however, the Lancashire Agreement, with which Great Britain began to restrict textile imports from its sterling-area trade partners, made Hong Kong's textile exporters turn to U.S. markets.[92]

In Taiwan the government began to subsidize production of textiles and, particularly, apparel for export by offering tax rebates to entrepreneurs. The government also built duty-free export-processing zones to encourage foreign investment in garment assembly.[93] The Korean government too made this type of apparel assembly a priority, offering exporters a variety of subsidies[94] and creating an infrastructure to facilitate the processing of apparel for export.

In the 1950s the United States directly subsidized the building and rebuilding of modern textile and apparel industries in other Far Eastern countries too, such as Singapore, the Philippines, Pakistan, and India. While some of these countries had produced textiles and apparel, none had ever produced Western clothing for export before World War II.

By 1960, only fifteen years after the conclusion of World War II, a productive and efficient textile and apparel complex emerged in Taiwan, Hong Kong, India, Pakistan, and the Philippines. These countries were on their way to becoming large-scale producers and exporters to the United States and other world markets. The United States played a big role in facilitating this development by reducing import tariffs on these imports—products that increasingly were in direct competition with higher cost and higher priced U.S. products.

In 1960, American politicians and textile industrialists toured a number of new state-of-the-art textile and apparel facilities in Hong Kong, Japan, and Singapore. What they saw and reported to Congress served to warn domestic industry leaders and other Americans about the future facing U.S. textile and apparel producers. Senator Robert Hemphill of South Carolina, a major textile-producing state, described his visit to the Far East to see its modern textile facilities:

> On November 29, 1960, while in Hong Kong, I visited the South Sea Textile Manufacturing Co., Ltd., located about 9 miles north of Kowloon. . . . In the textile plants of the US, the average pay is better than the $1.25 minimum which is a subject of controversy on our legislative scene today. The pay in Hong Kong is about the same per day as we pay per hour. In addition there is no withholding tax, no social security, and no medical plans such as we think of. . . . The plant employed 1,300 males and 500 female workers and ran three shifts of 8 hours per shift.

He continued,

> Later on Friday, December 2, 1960, I visited Osaka to see firsthand the textile plants there. In the briefing on the textile industry I was informed that the textile industry had been one of the most important in Japan, but for several years had made very little advance and was losing ground to other light manufacturing and heavy industry; . . . that the Japanese textile industry took some 2.5 to 3 million bales of raw cotton (600,000 to 1,600,000[)] from the US; that it produced some 3.5 billion square meters of fabric[,] . . . exporting some 40% of production (something less than the 247 million yard quota being shipped to the US), and delivering the balance for consumption within Japan.[95]

In 1960 Walter T. Forbes, a South Carolina textile manufacturer, also made a trip to the Far East—to Japan, the Philippines, Hong Kong, and Taiwan—to see the textile and apparel complex that was developing in these countries. What Forbes saw in the Philippines was

> the largest knitting plant in the Far East. It consumes 28,000 pounds of yarn per day, with the very latest tubular textile finishing equipment; capable US trained management, employing 1,300 people, including construction crews; 20,000 job applications on file; consuming approximately 15,000 bales of ICA program cotton, enjoying an export subsidy of 8.5 cents per pound under the price our American mills are paying [sic]. There are only two plants in America which can compare with this splendid new mill.[96]

The use of foreign aid to fund competitive enterprises abroad suggests why small businessmen often became protectionists and were likely to oppose foreign aid—earning the sobriquet of "isolationists." As one textile executive argued at the Pastore Committee hearings in 1958, "A case can certainly be made for selective foreign aid, as our allies need to be buttressed against the economic programs of Russia and its satellites. But we cannot see what good purpose is served if this money is used in such a way that, in the long run, its expenditures will contribute to the undermining of a sector of American industry."[97]

As U.S. textile and apparel producers began to hear more about this highly productive, U.S.-subsidized, direct, low-cost foreign competition, it is hardly surprising that they challenged foreign aid policies. Reports like these must have amplified the fears of U.S. textile producers and strengthened their attempts to build a base of support for legislation to protect their businesses from low-wage imports.

Soon, new types of man-made fibers were developed and transformed into apparel. Low-wage apparel made from such fibers would find its way from the Far East to U.S. markets in larger and larger volumes.[98] With U.S. foreign aid policies making it possible for the new Asian mills to purchase new technology and employ low-wage labor, U.S. textile producers inevitably perceived a serious difficulty in remaining competitive, given that 65 percent of the textile machinery used by domestic producers had been made obsolete by new technology.[99] Between 1947 and 1957, despite productivity growth—albeit growth at rates somewhat lower than in other U.S. industries—textile wages dropped: they went from being 16 percent lower than the wages of other U.S. industrial workers in 1947 to 30 percent lower in 1957.[100]

Before 1947 all textile trade between the United States and Japan was done through intergovernmental transfers—between the Japanese government and the agencies of SCAP. However, in February 1948, restrictions on the entry of businessmen to Japan were lifted. That year Nehmer and Crimmins wrote, "It is assumed, for example, that many American and foreign firms specializing in the textile trade will consider establishing offices or agencies in Japan through which they can arrange to secure Japanese textiles to fill the needs of their customers. Eventually Japanese nationals will be permitted to travel abroad for commercial purposes, and the marketing of textiles will be a fruitful commercial activity for such travelers."[101] By 1955 U.S. trade missions were appearing in Japan. Retailers, manufacturers, and importers now had carte blanche to seek out low-cost imports from a Japanese textile industry that had been rebuilt largely by U.S. military and foreign aid funds.[102] They began to recognize the new opportunities being made available to them. Reduced import tariffs encouraged entrepreneurs to contract out production of low-wage and low-cost apparel in duty-free production sites abroad. Clothing could be made in Hong Kong or Taiwan at a fraction of the labor costs that heavily unionized shops were demanding at home.

In 1957, in response to pressure by congressional protectionists, Japan committed itself to voluntary export restraints on textile and apparel exports to the United States. No such agreements existed between the United States and either Taiwan or Hong Kong. In the 1950s Hong Kong's textile and apparel producers began what was soon to become a lively business with American apparel importers. American businessmen visited the region regularly to contract with apparel producers for low-cost products to be sold in the United States.[103]

During the 1960s Japan's newly restructured chemical cartels began to increase their production of man-made fibers. By 1970 Japan had become the second largest manufacturer of man-made fibers in the world.[104] As real wages in Japan rose, textile producers shifted out of cotton textile production and began to develop a more capital-intensive, man-made fibers and fabrics industry. Rather than trade in cotton textiles with the United States, the Japanese began to invest in and export polyesters and acrylics to other Asian countries and the United States. These new fabrics could be used effectively, and more cheaply than cotton, in clothing production.[105] Cotton textile production soon constituted a much smaller share of Japan's industrial repertoire. Japanese textile exports went from 39 percent of industrial goods between 1951 and 1955, to 21.3 percent between 1961 and 1965, and to only 7.4 percent between 1971 and 1975.[106]

Japan effectively ceded the much more labor-intensive apparel industry to other Far Eastern countries. At the end of the 1950s Japan's direct foreign investment in, and exports of, man-made-fiber textiles to Southeast Asia transformed the Japanese into major textile suppliers to the growing apparel industries in Hong Kong, Taiwan, and other Far Eastern countries, which had begun to assemble and export apparel to U.S. contractors, retailers, and importers.[107] At the end of the 1950s, as the British market became less accessible to Hong Kong producers, they too turned their textile and apparel industries to producing fashion-oriented apparel for export to the United States.[108] As might be expected, leaders of the U.S. textile and apparel industries resisted becoming the market of choice for expanding volumes of low-wage textile and apparel exports, and began to plan a new protectionist campaign in Congress.

WOMEN IN THE FAR EASTERN
TEXTILE AND APPAREL INDUSTRIES

Women's low-wage labor played an important role in the growth of apparel production in export-processing zones throughout the Asian-Pacific Rim.[109] In prewar Japan, women's subordinate status and low wages made it possible for Japan to produce textiles that were of such high quality and low price that they could undersell the low-end products of other countries—even those of Asia and Africa. According to one perspective, the success of Japan's prewar textile industry was based on the "combination of strong management and low wages. [With its high technical standards and good equipment,] Japan was in a good competitive position against both the old exporting countries and the infant industries of the new countries."[110]

Initially, textile wages were set not by the market but by fiat. As Japan industrialized, women workers were recruited from the rural areas through a system of indentured servitude. Chiang Hsieh writes, "The traditional system was for contractors to recruit young daughters of farmers and advance loans to the latter on behalf of the employers in exchange for the girls' services; the young workers were then kept in bondage until the loans were fully repaid."[111] According to one observer, "The industrialization of Japan, which began with light industry, especially the textile industry, could never have been accomplished without young unmarried girls, brought from peasant villages throughout Japan. Cloistered in dormitories inside the factory compounds, they were forced to work for twelve to sixteen hours a day in unhealthy and dangerous conditions, and were then sent back to their families immediately if they got sick."[112]

This system of industrial relations existed until after World War II. In 1947, the older forms of recruitment to the industry were abolished under the auspices of the U.S. occupation and SCAP. The Japanese government established a system of free public employment offices to recruit industrial workers. When food shortages in urban areas continued to keep the labor supply confined to the countryside, SCAP authorized extra rations for textile workers to encourage women to join this workforce. The Japanese government also enacted protective labor legislation for women—a code regulating wages and working conditions—and made it permissible for workers to organize unions.[113]

The occupation improved the status of Japan's women textile workers, and SCAP continued to set wages. Employers hired women in the less skilled jobs defined as women's work—women's wage rates were set lower

than those for men, who were typically employed in the supervisory positions. The industry adopted the almost universal practice of hiring unmarried girls and young women as the preferred and lowest-wage labor
force in textile production, while the male supervisors were eligible to
receive a bonus when they married.

Japanese textile wages for both women and men were roughly comparable to wages in other Japanese industries. Japanese textile producers
employed a larger proportion of women, however, than did U.S. textile
producers. In 1947, 62 percent of workers in the Japanese textile industry
were women, whereas women represented only 27 percent of all workers
in Japanese manufacturing as a whole. In the larger textile establishments,
86 percent of the women workers were under twenty-six years of age. In
1956 Japanese women earned less than half (48 percent) of what men
earned.[114] Some suggest that the real ratio of women's to men's wages may
have been even lower than that. Figures from 1961 indicate that Japan's
women textile workers earned only 37 percent of men's wages; women
apparel workers earned only 40 percent of male wages in the same industry. The U.S. textile industry was among the lowest-paid industries in the
United States at that time, but the wage differential among men and
women was substantially smaller than it was in the Far East.

A large, gendered wage difference existed even in the larger, more productive state-of-the-art facilities that dominated the postwar Japanese textile industry.[115] Observed Senator Robert Hemphill of South Carolina in
1960, after his visit to such a plant in Osaka, Japan, "It was noted that the
Japanese textile industry pays the girls [sic] Y4,00 to Y10,000 per month
($12 to $30) and the more technically skilled men Y25,000 to Y50,000 per
month ($70 to $140), with amenities running up to 40 percent in addition
to basic salaries. It was also noted that the medical and social benefits were,
in most cases, more extensive than those given to American workers."[116]

According to Amsden, this gender-wage differential was just as large in
South Korea in the postwar period, a consequence of the prewar years
when Korea was a Japanese colony.[117] Even today, Korea and Japan have
two of the largest manufacturing-wage dispersions between light and
heavy industry. The high rates of female labor-force participation in light
industry in both Japan and Korea, and the large wage gap between men
and women workers within industries, even in the more productive modern facilities, have played an important role in making textile and apparel
industries in these countries so competitive internationally.[118]

Japanese women employed in apparel production appear to have had employment conditions even less desirable than those found in textile manufacturing. There is little hard data on wages paid in the Far Eastern apparel industry in the 1950s and 1960s. A 1955 article in the *Christian Science Monitor* by Gordon Walker, however, offers a sense of women's situation. Walker describes the life of the young Japanese worker Fumiko Tamashita, age seventeen and "just out of high school. . . . Like hundreds of other young girls in the smoky outskirts of Osaka[,] . . . she works in . . . a poorly heated and poorly lighted shed in which 28 girls gather each day to sew, cut and pattern cotton blouses."[119] Walker goes on to say that "unlike employees of the big textile mills with their labor standards laws, their company mess halls and dormitories, the garment workers of Japan are in a different class. There are no such things as labor standards, no unions, no wage levels except very low ones, and no such thing as fringe benefits." He cites a wage level of $9.25 a month for these young women working six days a week and ten hours a day; textile workers earned $34 a month for an eight-hour day, as well as free room and board above and beyond these payments.[120] Despite the official postwar labor regulations, some Japanese apparel firms had sweatshop conditions that may have been even worse than this. While there are few firsthand reports about the conditions of these women's employment, a 1950 report indicates that in some smaller firms the exploitation of young women workers was found "in its most deplorable forms."[121]

Asia's generally lower wages, the even lower wages paid to women, and the higher percentage of women workers all helped make production in these countries attractive to importers and retailers, particularly when productivity levels could, with up-to-date technology, be made comparable to those in the United States. The female labor force was seen as highly flexible: women worked only a few years before they left to get married, and they were easy to displace when the industry downsized or moved to a lower wage country. Women workers helped Asian textile manufacturers minimize the cost of textile and apparel production, a pattern that later continued as textile and apparel production spread to other countries in the Far East. It is not surprising, then, that American producers and trade unionists saw East Asian competition as a major threat to postwar gains—especially after decades of labor struggle and five years of war.

American observers of the Asian-Pacific industry in the postwar period saw these young girls and older women as enjoying reasonably good working conditions. According to these observers, most were not being abused or exploited but were merely being treated in accordance with the economic standards, culture, and traditions of their time and place. As we will see, the same arguments continue to be used by economists today to justify the treatment of women in export-processing zones.

Half a century ago in Asian countries, what we now call sex segregation in the labor force was seen as necessary for the protection of women workers—a way to keep them safe from the sexual and physical violence of predatory men. Today, economists claim that employment in export processing has the potential to free women from the patriarchal constraints of family life and provide them with opportunities for economic independence. I examine such arguments later in the text.

The marginal nature of women's participation in the labor force in East Asian countries—and women's treatment as family members and economic dependents—made it easy for textile and apparel manufacturers to move production to other countries or regions in response to market demands. Indeed, by the late 1950s Japan had already begun to move its textile production to the Newly Industrializing Countries.

In Taiwan, by the mid-1990s, women had become more permanent workers in textile production. When factories closed and production moved to the People's Republic of China, women employed in these plants, with many years of tenure, had vested pensions. Nevertheless, when they were summarily dismissed from their jobs, many found their employers had not funded these pensions. Older women, a large number of whom were widows, found themselves virtually unemployable and with no resources as they aged.[122]

In the United States, women also worked in sex-segregated jobs and were paid less than men. But U.S. apparel workers in the 1950s had unions to represent them, and textile producers had strong political representation in Congress to help keep them in business. As a result it took several decades of struggle between trade protectionists and trade liberalizers to dismiss protectionists' claims and dismantle these domestic industries.

The process of making low-wage textiles and apparel in export-processing zones was forged early in the context of America's postwar efforts to contain communism in East Asia. Yet the low-wage strategy and the use of women's labor persists in developing countries throughout the world. In the 1950s, America's textile producers and the workers they employed were just beginning to see the potential problems of trading with developing, low-wage countries in this way. As we will see, both labor and management responded to this issue in the political arena.

4 The Emergence of Trade Protection for the Textile and Apparel Industries

While Japan, Hong Kong, and Taiwan were rebuilding their textile industries and looking for export markets, on the other side of the world U.S. textile and apparel producers were gearing up for a political battle to protect their markets from East Asian imports. The battle emerged in Congress just as the cold war in East Asia was beginning—in the late 1940s during Truman's administration. The emergence of a protectionist movement for textiles and apparel might be dated to the debut of Eisenhower's presidency, when intense debate in Congress brought textile protectionism to the attention of the public and the media.

The already extensive historiography of the U.S. textile and apparel trade in the first quarter century after World War II is firmly grounded in the liberal assumption that protection is bad policy,[1] and that efforts by textile and apparel lobbies to legislate protection have been misguided. Free trade was seen as the best route to the achievement of a more enlightened, liberal, and internationalist foreign-economic policy. Protectionist concerns were defined as reactionary, provincial, and xenophobic responses to a more enlightened foreign economic policy—as the responses of self-interested small-town businessmen focused on local, rather than the more important international, concerns.

There is, of course, some truth to these characterizations. Yet it is necessary to go beyond the standard arguments to understand how and why trade protection became such an important political issue. The textile and apparel industries were not alone in demanding trade protection: a large number of other labor-intensive industries also protested the emergence of a new economic environment that threatened their prosperity and their survival.[2] Congressional protectionism in postwar America was a response to a transition in America's foreign economic policy after World War II which ended 150 years of trade protection that had, by the end of World

War II, contributed to unprecedented success for American business. The transition from protectionism to reciprocal trade occurred as the United States took on new international responsibilities as both the leader of world capitalism and the primary opponent of world communism. U.S. objectives in both roles were to expand America's political and economic interests around the world; reciprocal trade was a major part of this larger effort.

POLITICS AND THE GATT

The General Agreement on Tariffs and Trade represented an alliance among capitalist countries. Its purpose was to rebuild the countries of the Atlantic Alliance in the postwar world, which was America's first international priority after the war. The GATT provided the framework within which the United States opened its markets to imported goods from Europe. The European Recovery Program—the Marshall Plan—would provide the financing for European reconstruction.

The new trade regime was designed to link nations in strategic alliances through reciprocally reduced tariffs. It expanded trade among the member nations of the GATT—in Europe, America, and East Asia. As new countries industrialized and became competitive, they joined the GATT, through which tariff reductions were negotiated under the new most-favored-nation rule among member states.

The commitment to a process of continuous trade liberalization embodied in the GATT was also consistent with America's most immediate economic concerns. As noted earlier, at the end of World War II the United States was the only industrialized nation whose infrastructure and manufacturing capacity had not been destroyed or severely damaged. While U.S. manufacturers benefited from the demand born of wartime savings, the size and potential productivity of America's industrial capacity made it necessary for businesses to export in order to avoid another round of overproduction and unemployment. At the end of fifteen years of depression and war, the need to find overseas markets for America's surfeit of agricultural and industrial products had become a challenge to the stability of the U.S. economy.

The postwar period also gave credence to a Keynesian approach to economic policy, designed to promote demand, which was briefly embraced during the immediate postwar negotiations at Bretton Woods and Geneva.[3] This formula underpinned the rationale for economic aid to Europe. Foreign aid helped U.S. corporations regain and expand their prewar markets in Europe by providing the liquidity Europeans needed to purchase America's expanding output.

What was not foreseen at Bretton Woods were the changes wrought by the Pacific war, particularly the loss of China and the emergence of new communist insurgencies in East Asia. As the reconstruction of Japan took on new urgency, the Eisenhower administration invoked the reciprocal-trade principles of the GATT to reduce tariffs and promote the import of low-wage products like textiles and apparel into U.S. markets. Eisenhower tried to persuade the European countries to do the same.

However, encouraging the import of low-wage products from nonindustrialized, underdeveloped, poor, and low-wage countries represented a different type of economic relationship than did trading with an industrialized Europe. Trade between countries at the same level of development typically involves a relatively equal exchange of labor. Trade between advanced industrial and underdeveloped countries, however, is likely to reproduce previous colonial economic relationships—replacing the exports of commodities from underdeveloped to industrialized nations by manufactures made with low-wage labor.

As we have seen, the reduction of tariffs to encourage low-wage textile and apparel imports represented a sea change in U.S. trade policy and posed a fundamental challenge to the welfare of the nation's small, competitive, and labor-intensive industries. As Truman and then Eisenhower increased their determination to negotiate tariff reductions, many of these industries, particularly the textile industry, made their opposition known in Congress. Textile producers did not accept the new trade regime until the early 1960s, when the Kennedy administration found a way to motivate them to do so.

THE BIRTH OF TRADE LIBERALIZATION:
THE RECIPROCAL TRADE AGREEMENTS ACT OF 1934

To understand the postwar transformation in U.S. trade policy, one must begin with the prewar trade regime and the power of Congress to ensure that low-wage competitors were kept from American markets. The Constitution had initially granted to Congress the right to set tariffs. Before 1934, local businessmen could appeal directly to their congressional representatives to support their trade interests. Congressional representatives could introduce bills to increase tariffs for imports that were seen as competing with those produced domestically. Representatives could more easily mobilize support for such bills when the competing products were imports from low-wage countries.

By the mid-1930s, however, there was increased opposition in Congress to the logrolling employed to pass the Hawley-Smoot Tariff Act in 1930. "Smoot-Hawley" became a symbol of political corruption; many opponents began to see such politics as inimical to America's welfare. Other countries retaliated, raising their own tariffs for U.S. exports. The dramatic reduction in world trade that followed clearly contributed to the economic isolationism that bred the depression and World War II.

In 1934 Congress passed the Reciprocal Trade Agreements Act (referred to as the RTA), giving President Franklin Delano Roosevelt the right to negotiate bilateral tariff reductions with individual trading partners.[4] Tariff reductions, it was expected, would stimulate international trade. By 1945, the United States had entered into thirty-two bilateral trade agreements with twenty-seven countries, granting tariff concessions on 64 percent of all dutiable imports and reducing rates by an average of 44 percent.[5]

The genius of Secretary of State Cordell Hull was evident in his advising FDR to forge bilateral trade agreements, as opposed to a unilateral tariff-setting procedure. The purpose was to create harmonious trade regimes among nations. International trade agreements would make it possible to defuse potential conflicts that had made trade protection a cause of war.

Congress gave up the authority to set tariffs, a change that was to revolutionize the formation of U.S. trade policy in the postwar period: tariff setting was made into an act of foreign policy controlled by the executive office. As America began to play a new international role after the war, many congressional representatives found they could no longer vote in the interests of their local constituents: the president would negotiate with other countries to set tariffs. Indeed, after World War II all U.S. presidents, regardless of political party affiliation, have supported trade liberalization, while protectionist concerns have come from Congress.

When Congress ceded the right to negotiate reciprocal tariffs to the administration in 1934, it gave up a major prerogative. Therefore, Congress limited the time frame of this act to only three years. After that, the president's power to undertake such negotiations would be subject to congressional review and renewal. Although Congress could have voted against renewal of the 1934 Reciprocal Trade Act at any point during the remainder of the depression or during the war, it was not willing to do so. Only in 1949 did the act become a contentious issue in Congress; but ultimately it was made permanent and irreversible.

By the time the RTA came up for renewal in 1949, it was clear that the new trade regime would benefit some industries at the expense of others. Labor unions and representatives of domestic industries affected by a new influx of low-wage imports were already beginning to protest the competition and demonstrate the harm it was causing their businesses.[6]

On March 1, 1949, President Truman sent a message to Congress encouraging it to extend the RTA and allow the administration to negotiate further tariff reductions. Truman did not speak to the industry's need to restructure. Nor did he urge business leaders to find new ways to become competitive with the low-wage imports that would be inevitable. Instead he tried to reassure domestic producers that they would not suffer from import competition.[7] He said,

> The interests of domestic producers are carefully protected in the negotiation of each trade agreement. I assured the Congress when the Reciprocal Trade Agreements Act was last extended in 1945 that domestic producers would be safeguarded in the process of expanding trade. The commitment has been kept. It will continue to be kept. The practice will be continued of holding extensive public hearings to obtain the view of all interested persons before negotiations are even begun.

Yet tariff reductions negotiated through the GATT had already begun to increase the flow of imports that threatened domestic manufacturers in a variety of small, labor-intensive industries. By 1949, makers of hats, bicycles, woolen gloves, and other products; coal producers; and proprietors of fisheries found themselves in competition with lower cost imported products. As already noted, many of the affected industries, seeing a challenge to their livelihoods, brought their complaints to Congress. Initially, some of the imports they complained of came from the reconstructed war economies of Europe: postwar recovery meant that imports even from these countries were produced at wages lower than those earned by newly affluent American workers in the 1950s.[8]

The American Federation of Labor endorsed the renewal of the Reciprocal Trade Act—albeit with a number of qualifications, since so many of the industries represented by this trade union alliance would benefit from exports.[9] Yet labor representatives of trade-sensitive industries began to testify in Congress about the harm imports had caused them. A group called American Wage Earners Protective Conference appeared on the scene. Its executive secretary, O. R. Strackbein, testified in opposition to the Reciprocal Trade Agreements Act. He described the American Wage Earners Protective Conference as "a nonprofit organization composed exclusively of national and international unions affiliated with the American

Federation of Labor. We represent upward of 500,000 workers in a dozen organizations. In addition I represent the Allied Printing Trades Association[,] with a membership of almost 200,000."[10] Strackbein then read into the record a statement by the American Federation of Labor supporting the Trade Agreements Act. The letter, with its disclaimer on further tariff cuts, reads, in part, "In supporting the trade agreements program, we recognize the need of safeguarding American labor in some industries, especially where wages are a relatively heavy factor in the cost of production[,] against competition that threatens to undermine our labor standards."[11]

Despite Truman's belief that the imports he advocated would not hurt domestic producers, many labor-intensive and trade-sensitive industries were nevertheless asked to adjust to these low-wage imports rather than seek protection. The new postwar trade policy challenged the traditional expectations of both manufacturers and trade unions. Based on their prewar trade experience, low-wage competition called for raising tariffs on imports, not reducing them. These imports, made at low cost and sold at low prices, threatened the labor standards that had so recently been won and the profit levels domestic producers had gained since the 1930s.

If there were U.S. producers who opposed low-wage imports, there were also corporate producers who desired to expand their sales of American products and to invest abroad, and who favored reciprocal trade. In an era when American industry produced 50 percent of the world's industrial output, tariff reductions by other nations would increase the access of U.S. corporations to markets abroad.[12] Postwar reconstruction, in response to Marshall Plan aid, was about to generate new demand for goods. Expanding U.S. industries feared that protected European markets would, in the longer term, lead to another crisis of overproduction and depression in the United States and abroad, and this prompted many of America's large corporate leaders to support reciprocal tariff reductions.

Textile manufacturers were concerned with how the new GATT trade regime, as incorporated in the Reciprocal Trade Act, would affect their businesses. For example, at the 1951 Senate Finance Committee hearings a representative of the Forstmann Woolen Company in Passaic, New Jersey, which made woolen yarn and marketed woolen sweaters, testified about his business problems and how they were affected by imports. His claimed that the industry's low productivity and the continuous demand for higher wages, which in the United States were already higher than anywhere else, would not allow the U.S. textile industry to compete even with European products, let alone lower wage imports from East Asia. As he put it,

> The labor rates of our industry are approximately 4 times higher than those of England, 6 times those of Italy, 7 times those of France and 16 times those of Japan. In addition, to these differentials, the Textile Workers Union of America (CIO), which is currently on strike in approximately 160 mills in our industry, has presented demands that in total, exceed a further increase of 50 cents per hour. . . . According to studies by the United States Tariff Commission, the efficiency of the American textile worker as compared with the British is only 1.3 to 1 in our favor. . . . Our foreign competitors can build mill structures and install machinery at less than one half the cost which we must face in this country.[13]

The administration's insistence on reciprocal trade and the demands of labor for higher wages in this low-wage industry would be a continuing problem for the U.S. textile industry throughout the 1960s and 1970s.

As Truman's administration gave way to Eisenhower's, the new president faced a continuing confrontation with textile protectionism. Eisenhower, who entered office in 1953, appointed Clarence Randall to chair a committee that would set guidelines for American trade policy. Randall was a member of a lobbying group called the Committee for National Trade Policy, composed of U.S. corporate leaders whose business concerns were centered on exporting; they were staunch supporters of both free trade and communist containment. They included Harry Bullis, chairman of the board of General Mills; Joseph Spang Jr. of Gillette; General John McCloy of Chase National Bank; John Coleman of Burroughs Manufacturing Company; and George Ball, who had spearheaded the successful campaign against the protectionist Simpson bill.[14] In the spirit of bipartisanship, Eisenhower also appointed members of Congress who had supported the Simpson bill in Congress. These men were Dan Reed (R-New York), Richard Simpson (R-Pennsylvania), and Eugene Millikin (R-Colorado). Yet the political tilt of the committee was clear. The Randall Commission was to hammer out a report that would eventually provide the basis for renewal and expansion of the 1954 Trade Agreements Act.

TRADE AND COMMUNIST CONTAINMENT

By Eisenhower's time, American trade politics had become increasingly colored by the cold war. Domestically, McCarthyites warned Americans of the communist peril. With Eisenhower's first inauguration, in 1953, the expansion of trade and the further reduction of tariffs became more salient as a political issue. With John Foster Dulles as secretary of state, Eisenhower's trade agenda became wedded to trade expansion as a way to contain communism. The end of hostilities in Korea in 1953, and the slackening of U.S. military procurement in Japan, made the State Department see trade expansion as an even more important bulwark against the communist threat. In 1947 Truman's State Department, recognizing that the Nationalists could not win the civil war in China, had changed the direction of Japanese reconstruction. The Eisenhower State Department not only continued to promote "America's workshop in Asia," but began to speak of reindustrializing Japan as a way to prevent a falling-dominoes effect. Dulles expressed this concern in a talk on June 11, 1954, to the Los Angeles World Affairs Committee:

> Japan's population, now grown to 87 million, depends for its livelihood upon foreign trade. Trade is offered by the Communists—at a price. That price is that Japan—the only industrial power in Asia—should cease to cooperate with the United Nations and with the United States as it is now doing and should become a workshop where the abundant raw materials of Asia can be converted into implements for Communist use against the Free World. Japan must trade to live, and if the free nations fail to make it possible for Japan to earn its way, then inevitably, though reluctantly, her people would turn elsewhere. This would be stupid from an economic standpoint and folly from a political standpoint. Japan is an excellent customer for our cotton, wheat and rice. From a political standpoint it requires little imagination to visualize what would happen if Russia, China and Japan became a united hostile group in the Pacific.[15]

In 1954, the State Department bulletin was replete with official statements by speakers who linked the prevention of a communist offensive in East Asia with Japanese trade. The image of the communist threat was expressed differently in speeches addressed to different constituencies, but all of these speeches were similarly fraught with messages about the peril of the communist threat. For example, in a talk to the American Legion of San Francisco, Deputy Undersecretary Murphy offered the same warning—but in a slightly different vein: "The ambitions of Soviet imperialism are universal. Its goal has always been world domination. In the Pacific the Communists have three current objectives. They are (1) the manpower of China; (2) the industrial capacity of Japan; and (3) the resources of Southeast Asia."[16] A third message, a speech by the deputy assistant secretary for East Asian affairs, is infused with the McCarthyist rhetoric of the time:

> In Japan, the Communists will attempt to take advantage of the frictions always resulting from the presence of foreign troops to create and intensify anti-American feelings. They will exploit Japanese fears of being caught in the atomic crossfire of another world war in order to neutralize Japan. They will seek to dominate Japanese labor, utilizing techniques found effective in other industrial countries. They will wait for Japan's economic position to worsen, as it surely will unless wider markets are found for Japanese exports, and if their hopes for Japan's economic collapse prove justified, the Communists will use the situation to discredit the moderate democratic elements and to promote Japanese trade with mainland China as a means of obtaining Japan's economic tie-in with the Moscow-Peiping bloc.[17]

During these years the battle over free trade was not, as it would become in the 1980s and 1990s, a discourse about the need to unleash market forces or to provide American consumers with affordable products, but an effort to invoke the fear of left-wing insurgency. Hard-liners in the State Department under Dulles declared it almost essential to subordinate the needs of a segment of American industry to the principles and policies of anti-communist multilateralism. This stance was accompanied by messages designed to reassure those opposed that reciprocal trade policy advanced the general welfare.

THE TEXTILE PROTECTIONISTS AND 1954

The U.S. textile industry, with its protectionist trade agenda, had wielded a great deal of power in Congress since the late nineteenth century. By the mid-1950s it was among the largest and most significant industries threatened by the administration's power to reduce tariffs. Although much of the industry relocated from the Northeast to the South in the 1950s, New England textile manufacturers still had a significant presence in Congress.

As left-wing insurgencies erupted in East Asia in the early 1950s, U.S. textile manufacturers north and south once again began to face new trade problems.[18] The year 1954 was a watershed in the history of textile-trade-policy battles and the struggle to obtain import quotas.[19] The rapid surge of imports sparked a mobilization by the organized textile industry, led by the American Cotton Manufacturers' Institute (ACMI).

As fears about the spread of communism in East Asia grew, the conflict between textile protectionists and trade liberalizers in Congress came to a head. In 1953 Claudius T. Murchison, economic advisor to the ACMI, said that the textile manufacturers trade association represented

> about 85% of the country's total spindlage, and . . . has about two-thirds of the total American cotton consumption, which is by far the greatest textile industry, cotton textile industry, in the world. We are twice as great as India, which is second in importance, twice as great as the combined output of the United Kingdom and Japan. In fact, we consume 40% of all the cotton consumed in the free world and, naturally, we do not wish to be sacrificed as a tariff policy gesture.[20]

As the end of the Korean War prompted the dramatic surge in textile imports, the administration claimed the right to negotiate even further tariff reductions. In the next two years, as tariffs were reduced, textile and apparel imports increased. Though labor and management in the textile industry were fighting over unionization and wage increases, the Textile Workers Union and management cooperated in the congressional campaign for trade protection. Textile producers faced an administration whose trade policy concerns were much less worried about the fate of their industry than with the need for increased imports to promote American security interests in Asia.

As Raymond A. Bauer, Ithiel de Sola Pool, and Lewis Anthony Dexter put it, "The partisans on each side [of the trade issue] girded for battle."[21] The protectionist coalition, led by the American Cotton Manufacturers' Institute, clashed head on with the State Department over imports of Japanese textiles. Speaking in support of extending the Trade Agreements Act was Director for Mutual Security Harold Stassen, who defended the bill in terms of both these goals. He stated, "Under President Eisenhower's inspiring leadership, the United States today is bringing new hope to the people of the free world—hope for lasting peace and for rising standards of living. . . . No single country can stand alone against Communist aggression. . . . [Eisenhower has] said—'mutual security means effective mutual cooperation.'" Continuing in the same vein, Stassen said, "We are today at a crossroads in our foreign economic policy. No aspect of American policy is more important than the course this Congress chooses to adopt in our economic relations with other nations. The economic stability, and therefore the political stability of the free world, will be influenced by the wisdom of your decision."[22]

The need to contain communism ultimately won the battle to extend the Reciprocal Trade Act. As debate on the extension of the Trade Agreements Act in 1954 heated up, communist forces defeated the French at Dien Bien Phu.

In the face of another "falling domino," even Dan Reed, the powerful protectionist chair of the House Ways and Means Committee, was persuaded by the administration to back down. Reed had opposed Eisenhower's plans to negotiate further tariff concessions for Japanese textiles and had led the opposition to the president's Trade Agreements Act. Yet after he had vigorously opposed the bill, the fear of communism influenced him to reverse his position. He then asked the House to support, rather than oppose, the extension of presidential negotiating authority for another year. Reed explained his about-face as follows:

> We know the conditions in the world today. Let us lay the cards on the table. We know the situation in Japan. We know that . . . *there is a great reservoir of people out there out of work and the Communists are working to the best of their ability among these people. We need Japan on our side in this troubled world,* and we are not going to gain their support by starving them to death. We have to do at least this much for them, at least give them a chance to be heard through trade negotiations. I am not willing . . . to take the responsibility[,] under present conditions of the world[,] of killing this bill and shutting the door to such negotiations.[23]

Trade expert and free-trade advocate I. M. Destler argues that Congress was happy to cede its power over trade policy to the president. He claims that, by the postwar period, congressmen viewed it as a fait accompli. He argues that Congress's unwillingness to pass legislation that would challenge America's foreign economic policy demonstrates that Congress was largely in favor of free trade and opposed to protection. Destler writes,

> Beginning in the mid-1930's Congress did decide otherwise, changing the way it handled trade issues. No longer did it give priority to protecting American industry. Instead, its members would give priority to protecting themselves: from the direct, one-sided pressure from producer interests that had led them to make bad trade law. They would channel that pressure elsewhere, pushing product-specific trade decisions out of the committees of Congress and off the House and Senate floors to other governmental institutions.[24]

It is hardly surprising that, amid the anticommunist sentiment of 1954, congressional representatives became convinced that the administration's desire to support the Japanese and East Asian economies was justified— that subordinating trade protection to national security was necessary. Two days after Dan Reed made his speech about the defeat of the French at Dien Bien Phu, Congress passed the president's bill; not long afterward, so did the Senate.

Destler argues that members of Congress resisted the demands of their constituents for protection because they became convinced that it was "bad policy." This is an implausible explanation. During the 1950s and 1960s, representatives of textile interests in Congress continued to vote for protection. Yet the power of the Eisenhower administration, and especially the State Department, made it difficult for protectionist congressmen to deliver the higher tariffs their constituents wanted.[25] In 1954, for the first time, not only did textile protectionists fail to raise tariffs in the face of low-wage imports, they also failed to prevent further tariff reductions. By 1956 the value of Japanese textiles exported to the United States was seven times the 1952 level.[26] No doubt the large rate of increase was calculated from a very low baseline. But even this small level of import penetration was seen as portending worse in the future.

Some members of Congress understood the role of trade liberalization in containing communism in East Asia. John A. Pastore, a Democrat from the textile-producing state of Rhode Island and a staunch textile-industry supporter, was empowered to form a committee, subsequently known as the Pastore Committee, to hold hearings to analyze the "textile problem" and develop remedies. At one hearing he questioned W. T. M. Beale, a State Department representative who was asked to testify before that committee. Pastore, responding to Beale's efforts to evade a question, commented, "I can imagine what happens there at your meetings the minute you begin to feel one little measure is going to accelerate the possibility of communistic infiltration. . . . Then it becomes a political question. Then I think I suppose 2.5 or 3 or 3.5 percent of your entire importations, by comparison to your national production, doesn't become very important if it means peace or war in the world."[27]

CONGRESSIONAL PROTECTIONISM AND THE
MACHINERY OF TRADE POLICY FORMATION

From the administration's perspective, however, the textile coalition had the power to thwart future negotiations over tariff reductions. In the 1950s, the president negotiated multilateral trade agreements with the help of the Trade Agreements Commission. This body included the president's appointed cabinet members from the Departments of State, Commerce, Treasury, Defense, and Agriculture, as well as the Tariff Commission, which was officially a congressional agency. Both the GATT and the RTA gave the president the power to negotiate reduced tariffs. These laws also allowed for the inclusion of language and practices designed to protect industries like textiles from "unfair competition."[28]

The Tariff Commission had been established in 1916 as an agency of Congress, and had been invested with the power to determine the "peril point" of tariffs—that is, the point at which lowering tariffs created "unfair competition." Yet it soon became clear that this safeguard was more likely to legitimate the reciprocal trade agenda than to provide trade-sensitive industries with real recourse against the impact of competitive, low-wage imports.

Officially there were two regulations embodied in the Trade Agreements Act that sheltered an industry from unfair competition: the escape clause and the peril point, to be implemented by the Committee on Reciprocity Information (CRI). This body was designed to provide industry with the opportunity to consult with U.S. trade negotiators before entering the international arena to bargain for tariff reductions and concessions. Before such sessions, hearings were called by the CRI, whose mandate was to transmit the concerns of affected industries to the State Department and the president. The CRI, however, was not mandated to make recommendations to the negotiators on the basis of industry testimony, and the administration was in no way bound to use any industry recommendations in its international negotiations. Thus, industry concerns expressed to the CRI could simply be ignored.

The escape clause was the first, and perhaps the major, remedy for industries "injured by unfair trade." Leaders of industries that believed they were threatened by imports could make their case to the Tariff Commission, which then met and decided whether the case should receive a hearing. If it decided to hear the case, the commission was required to send a report with a recommendation to the president, who, in deliberation with the Trade Agreements Commission, could either accept or reject the Tariff Commission's recommendation. If the president approved it, he could raise tariffs on the injured product or he could renegotiate the agreement with interested U.S. trading partners. If not, tariffs continued at previous levels.

In the prewar period, imported products made with low-wage labor were often seen as representing unfair competition. Businessmen who believed their industry was suffering from unfair competition could and did appeal to their congressmen, who typically responded favorably to constituent demands by introducing bills or amendments to bills that raised tariffs on such products. In the early 1950s, the peril points for tariffs were described by an advocate in the following way: "Tariff making was regarded as lending itself to a scientific process, based upon an impartial system of fact and cost finding. Our tariff was to be determined, within limits set by Congress, by the difference in costs of production here and abroad. Cost studies were to arrive at mathematical conclusions. Bipartisanship of the Commission was intended as a guaranty that the procedures followed were fair and the results factual and unbiased."[29]

Textile manufacturers were particularly well represented among protectionists in Congress in the prewar period. In 1935, when Japanese textile imports reached a penetration rate of about 1.5 percent of the domestic market (about the same level they would reach in 1954), the textile industry found a way to protect itself. Initially the Japanese had agreed to voluntary export restraints. When, in 1937, these had failed to reduce import levels, American and Japanese textile manufacturers visited Japan and concluded a private, voluntary agreement with Japanese textile manufacturers to accomplish this goal.[30]

In 1943 Congress passed an extension of the Reciprocal Trade Agreements Act. In voting to renew the authority of the president to negotiate the reduction of tariffs, Congress also mandated that the official peril points be used to set tariffs. Yet as early as 1949, industries facing low-wage imports charged that the Truman administration had blatantly ignored the peril points and left import-sensitive industries in the dark about the content of the GATT negotiations.

In 1951, Secretary of State Dean Acheson addressed the Senate Finance Committee, which was once again considering renewal of the RTA.[31] In his opening statement Acheson objected to the efforts of congressional protectionists to amend the legislation as they had done in the past. Through these amendments, congressional protectionists had tried to limit the power of the Trade Agreements Commission. Protectionists had enjoined the commission to set rules that the latter believed would handicap the executive branch in opening U.S. markets and would bind U.S. trade negotiators to protectionist concerns. These amendments required (a) that the Tariff Commission mathematically calculate and fix a peril point, (b) that it investigate every complaint, and (c) that it participate in all the decisions of the Trade Agreements Commission. As Acheson put it, "The amendment would make any decline in sale, or increase in inventory, or any downward trend in production, employment and wages, regardless of cause, evidence of serious injury if import competition contributed to it in any way." The State Department charged that the protectionist amendments thwarted its Keynesian internationalism—its efforts to promote the expansion of world trade—a policy seen as essential to building a reconstructed Europe able to fend off Soviet advances.[32] At the same time, the administration continued to accept the right of Congress to control tariffs.[33]

As early as 1949, industries wanting trade protection were already disputing the usefulness of the escape clause procedure under the Truman administration. In the late 1950s, trade-policy making, with the help of the Trade Agreements Commission, became increasingly centralized in the hands of the executive. The Reciprocal Trade Act came up for renewal every three years, periodically reviving the conflict over tariffs. Each time, the textile coalition threatened to challenge this arrangement and revoke the administration's power to reduce tariffs. At issue was the right of the executive to pursue trade policies that seemed to sacrifice domestic industries for the anticommunist cause. Many textile producers could remember the years when high tariff walls had been taken for granted as an effective and legitimate policy to support America's labor-intensive industries. Not surprisingly, as low-wage imports moved beyond prewar levels, the congressional protectionists grew angrier at a president whose trade policies were seen as generating unfair competition. In 1956 a proposal for textile quotas failed by just two votes to pass the Senate. According to one source, "Veteran House members later said that opponents of reciprocal trade mounted the biggest pressure campaign that they could recall."[34]

By 1958 it had become clear that the administration could veto trade protection and may have done so frequently. Of thirty-one petitions to the Tariff Commission to maintain tariff barriers against import "injury," twenty were overturned by the president.

Although the majority of the textile trade with Japan consisted of cotton textiles, reciprocal trade also affected America's wool textile industry. Edwin Wilkinson, vice president of the National Association of Wool Manufacturers, claimed that reciprocal trade in textiles had been intended to allow British wool producers access to the U.S. market after World War II. However, new woolen textiles made in Japan were underselling British woolen textiles in the U.S. markets. Wilkinson also feared that Indian wool and woolen textiles might soon become more competitive than those from Japan. As a result, both the U.S. and British wool industries would suffer. Wilkinson became one of the staunchest textile protectionists, testifying in Congress, "In our view, as we have said many times, a trade and tariff policy will not be achieved until Congress regains ultimate control of policy from the executive branch."[35]

In other hearings that year, Senator Malone, questioning John Foster Dulles, outlined his understanding of the new trade policy, claiming the administration had appropriated "life and death powers over the economy of the United States which the Congress has illegally delegated to the President since 1934, and which three successive Presidents have now utilized."[36] He claimed it had been done without the consent of those who had the most to lose. According to Malone, "Congressmen who have been in Geneva during sessions of GATT have not been permitted to sit in on any of the actual tariff negotiations. No American industry, organization, or private citizen may appear there."[37] Dulles could not refute this charge. He implicitly acknowledged that the State Department's political aims took priority over those of America's textile producers. Dulles said, "I have pointed out, Senator, in my opening statement that almost everything that Government does, whether it is our defense program or anything else, has a competitive impact on the American economy."

Malone replied, "But isn't this the first time that we have ever given the Executive the right to trade an industry to further the foreign policy? Under this act, isn't it the first time it has ever been done?" Dulles responded to this challenge by simply saying, "Yes!"

There is evidence that the State Department did overrule decisions to provide tariff relief for industries and firms who claimed they were subject to import injury. Strom Thurmond, archconservative and strong textile protectionist, was quoted as asking W. T. M. Beale, a representative of the State Department, whether the State Department ever overruled the Tariff Commission in decisions to deny tariff relief to industries injured by imports: "Now what are the textile people going to do even after the fact-finding body, the Tariff Commission, says they are entitled to relief and the President declines to grant the relief? Isn't the President acting chiefly on the recommendation of the State Department in the action he takes?"[38] Beale made it clear that the textile industry might indeed have to forgo protectionism in the war against communism. Responding to Pastore, he said, "There are some people in the State Department who feel that[,] maybe in the interest of achieving the broad objectives of the foreign policy, part of the domestic textile industry might have to be sacrificed."[39]

Beale acknowledged that the administration might pursue a trade policy that would "sacrifice" the textile industry to the general good, implicitly justifying trade liberalization as being good for the "country as a whole"— anticipating the arguments America's neoclassical economists would make some twenty-five years later, though for different reasons. In 1958, the president of the American Cotton Manufacturers' Institute could say, "With each passing year our industry, as well as many other industries, was forced to raise its voice in ever louder protest against the procedures of the trade agreement authority, which progressively subordinated the interests and the recommendations of American industry."[40]

Congress still had the legal right to set quotas and tariffs on imports but such efforts required veto-proof legislation. It was not until the mid-1980s, with passage of the Jenkins-Hollings bill, that Congress risked this last and ultimately fruitless effort. In the early cold war period, the choice was between communist containment and the U.S. textile industry. To challenge tariff reductions, to reverse the growing volumes of low-wage imports in the 1950s, would have required a vote defying the expansionist and anticommunist objectives of the administration's foreign policy agenda.

Although the administration had the power to reduce tariffs, the U.S. textile industry in the 1950s was still able to challenge, if not to override, the president's multilateral trade initiatives. As Japanese textile imports increased during the years 1954 to 1956, Eisenhower found it necessary to respond to the political demands of the textile protectionists, and, in 1957, protectionists won a small but important victory when the president negotiated voluntary export restraints with the Japanese.

Elation over this victory was short-lived. As textile imports from Japan tapered off in the 1960s, imports from Hong Kong and Taiwan began to increase. By 1962, not only textile imports but, more important, clothing imports began to raise the ire of U.S. apparel manufacturers who now, like U.S. textile producers, experienced the consequences of low-wage competition.

These apparel imports were typically made of cotton or man-made fibers spun or woven in Japan, Taiwan, or Hong Kong and assembled in Taiwan or Hong Kong. They were made primarily by low-wage women workers at factories under contract for U.S. importers, clothing manufacturers, and retailers. They were sold in U.S. retail stores at substantially lower prices than comparable domestically made products. These trade relationships, in the early stages in the growth of export processing, bore little resemblance to the trade relations described by David Ricardo in his eighteenth-century treatise on the value of free trade, or to the exchange of goods between industrialized countries, where products made in one country were exchanged for those in another.

America's apparel makers and their workers, like textile producers, began to flex their muscles and demand import quotas.[41] Women who worked in America's apparel industry were union members: they belonged to the International Ladies' Garment Workers' Union in the women's fashion industry or to the Amalgamated Clothing Workers of America in the men's clothing industry. They began to enjoy the benefits of union membership only in the postwar prosperity of the 1950s.

THE KENNEDY COMPROMISE
AND THE TEXTILE-APPAREL COMPLEX

When John F. Kennedy became president in 1960, he inherited the "textile problem." Kennedy's concerns for trade liberalization and communist containment were the same as those of Truman and Eisenhower and were motivated by the same foreign-policy objectives. However, by 1958 the formation of the European Economic Community (EEC), a free-trade bloc of western European countries, threatened to create trade barriers for U.S. exports to Europe. As Kennedy saw it, European protectionism would leave both continents vulnerable to the Soviet threat.

Kennedy's objective was to reduce tariff walls between the United States and the six EEC nations, along with the latter's former colonies. Not only would exporting America's abundant industrial goods sustain a high-wage, full-employment economy in the United States, but it would also preserve the economic strength of the free world. Yet congressional protectionism threatened the Kennedy administration's ability to negotiate further tariff reductions with Europe. To overcome this barrier, Kennedy needed to assure the Europeans that his efforts would not be sabotaged by protectionists in Congress.

Kennedy was a Democrat and a liberal. In the 1950s he had been a senator from Massachusetts, a state that was fast losing its textile jobs to the South. He had seen firsthand how close the textile protectionists had come to overriding the new internationalist trade agenda. Their continued power in Congress challenged Kennedy's ability, as president, to negotiate tariff reductions designed to expand multilateral trade—both with Europe's Common Market and the former colonies of East Asia.

The textile lobby had pressed a reluctant Eisenhower to negotiate with the Japanese for voluntary export restraints. Eisenhower had not been able to persuade the European Economic Community to ease its opposition to Japanese imports of cotton textiles. Kennedy hoped to arrest the growing congressional protectionism that could, he feared, generate veto-proof legislation to impair his ability to negotiate reciprocal tariff reductions with Europe.

Kennedy, like Eisenhower before him, saw the developing countries as targets for communist takeovers and, like his predecessor, believed they must be offered access to the markets of industrialized nations to support their economic development and military security. However, as the international trade in low-wage textiles and apparel accelerated, American policy-makers eventually saw that the United States could not be the sole market of choice. Instead, a multilateral regime for regulating textile and apparel imports would strengthen the link between U.S. cotton exports and Japan's textile exports and divert a portion of East Asian textile and apparel exports to the European Economic Community.[42] Since, at the end of the 1950s, Congress was increasingly reluctant to continue its extensive foreign aid, the opening of Europe's markets to East Asian countries would also support America's trade-not-aid policy, which had significant support in Congress.[43]

Kennedy's response to these problems was a three-part program, a compromise that was offered in deference to the power of textile protectionists in Congress.[44] Ultimately, however, it served to legitimate and institutionalize the internationalist trade agenda that the United States had pursued since the 1934 Reciprocal Trade Act, later embodied in the GATT. Kennedy's willingness to negotiate import quotas in the early 1960s allowed him to succeed where Eisenhower and Dulles had failed. He was able to consolidate the administration's control over trade policy formation, which has since allowed subsequent administrations to further the objectives of trade liberalization. Kennedy's approach was more conciliatory than adversarial. Yet his compromise legitimized the administration's power in making trade policy while leaving him free to pursue the Kennedy Round of multilateral trade negotiations.[45]

THE TRIPARTITE COMPROMISE

The first element of this compromise was legislation creating quotas for East Asian imports. These quotas were to be negotiated with countries exporting textiles and apparel to the United States. Kennedy negotiated the one-year Short-Term Arrangement in 1961 and, a year later, the Long-Term Arrangement (LTA). The LTA created a special trade regime for textiles and apparel that lasted until 1971, when negotiations began for the Multifibre Arrangement. Anxious not to set a precedent, Kennedy treated the textile and apparel industries as special cases under the aegis of the GATT. Developed countries could negotiate bilateral trade agreements with low-wage exporting countries, setting import quotas only for products made of cotton.

The import-growth rate for cotton textiles and apparel was set at a maximum of 6 percent each year, which would accommodate developing nations' expected need for export growth while limiting the flow of textile and apparel imports to the United States. This approach was intended to allow America's textile and apparel industry to "adjust" to the new low-wage competition.

The second element of Kennedy's textile compromise—in conjunction with the special trade regime—was the Trade Expansion Act (TEA) of 1962, which replaced the expiring RTA, last extended in 1958. The TEA embodied a commitment by the federal government to balance the need for protection with the imperatives of free trade. The act gave the executive branch authority to reduce tariffs up to 50 percent. The Seven-Point Program, the heart of the act, was designed to provide income assistance, relocation assistance, and job training to displaced workers. Passed easily by Congress, the bill promoted federal support for "industrial adjustment" as well. Kennedy also accelerated the schedule of tax depreciation allowances for textiles and apparel producers investing in new technology. In the coming years the schedule for tax depreciation would be accelerated further. Furthermore, in 1964 the two-price cotton policy—in which the federal government subsidized the cost of raw cotton grown by foreign, but not U.S., producers—was equalized. This allowed for a 26 percent reduction in the cost of raw materials for textile producers, which freed capital for new investment in the textile industry. As the textile industry's move to the South was completed, expenditures on new plants and investment grew between 1962 and 1968, and production grew rapidly between 1960 and 1979.[46]

Through these measures, the federal government would help the industry to restructure and workers to deal with unemployment and job searches. Import growth would be regulated at a rate that could accommodate the needs of the textile and apparel complex to become more competitive with their Far East, low-wage competitors.

THE LIMITS OF THE KENNEDY COMPROMISE

Kennedy's compromise persuaded Congress to accept trade liberalization as the new paradigm. In exchange, Congress finally recognized the right of the administration to set tariffs as part of its foreign economic policy. This allowed the Kennedy administration to uphold its policy of trade not aid and fostered the opening of U.S. markets to the low-wage products of developing countries.[47] The Kennedy compromise represented a transformation in U.S. trade policy-making. Congress would no longer be required to renew the Reciprocal Trade Act every three years. Subsequent administrations could pursue further trade liberalization as part of foreign policy–making in the national interest. Kennedy's compromise created a new institutional framework to regulate trade and resolve trade disputes over textile and apparel imports. Trade-sensitive industries and their workers would have to adjust to the new regime of slowly expanding imports and potential job loss.

THE VIEW FROM DEVELOPING COUNTRIES

While textile and apparel protectionists in the United States fought the administration over trade liberalization, countries of the developing world took a different view. By the mid-1960s many of the contemporary conflicts about trade in textiles and apparel between industrial and developing countries were already being debated. In 1964 the United Nations Conference on Trade and Development held its first conference in Geneva. Seventy-seven of the developing countries participating in the conference demanded that the United States further open its markets to their exports as a way of promoting economic development and industrialization. They saw this as a necessary aid to overcoming the consequences of their colonial pasts.[48]

By the late 1960s demands for greater trade liberalization were being made within the United States, incipiently expressed in the context of the neoliberal paradigm. Lyndon Johnson's economic advisor Carl Kaysen wrote, "The whole country would be the gainer, if, over time, we could shift resources away from textiles, shoes and other unsophisticated manufactures to more advanced items where we have a real comparative advantage. These are mainly items which use resources that are higher paid and relatively more abundant here than abroad—capital, scientific and technological research, skilled and educated labor."[49] This perspective was not to be fully legitimized until the late 1980s. Indeed, the textile and apparel trade regime continued to be a political burden for U.S. administrations. In negotiating the Multifibre Arrangement, President Richard Nixon, like his predecessor, continued to deal with the need to balance divergent positions on the issue—to satisfy the protectionists led by the Southern cotton textile interests in Congress, to press the Europeans to absorb a larger share of East Asian exports, and to limit the growing pressure of East Asian imports on U.S. markets.[50] The administrations of Kennedy, Nixon, Ford, Carter, and, to some extent, even Reagan at least publicly acknowledged the needs of the protectionists in their textile and apparel trade policy. It was not until the late 1980s, during the Bush administration, that congressional protectionism would be defeated.

Kennedy's tripartite compromise signaled a turning point in postwar policy formation for the U.S. textile and apparel trades, legitimating and institutionalizing an internationalist free-trade agenda. Congress was forced to acknowledge the administration's right to control and administer the country's trade policy, leaving Kennedy free to pursue a new round of multilateral trade negotiations. The Kennedy compromise did not resolve the battle over trade protection. What it did was to finally end congressional power to set trade policy and further liberalize trade.

How did America's textile and apparel producers respond to the new trade policies, which forced them to adjust to the growth of low-wage imports? This issue will be addressed in the next two chapters, which describe what happened to the U.S. textile and apparel industries in the two decades between 1960 and 1980.

5   The U.S. Textile Industry
Responses to Free Trade

The progressive opening of world markets to textile and apparel exports began soon after the end of World War II and is still going on. Whereas the reciprocal trade approach defined the earlier decades of struggle between trade liberalizers and protectionists, by the middle of the 1980s the neoliberal trade paradigm began to dominate trade policy for the textile, apparel, and other industries. In 1995 the World Trade Agreement, and its Agreement on Textiles and Clothing, superseded the General Agreement on Tariffs and Trade. Embodying the neoliberal perspective, the WTA began eliminating all protective quotas on imports of textiles and apparel.

Much of the historiography of trade protection in general, and trade protection for textiles and apparel in particular, suggests protectionism is a bad policy and unsuited to the economic requirements of the world today. Why, then, did textile producers engage so vehemently and for so long in what was to become a fruitless battle? By illuminating the dynamics of textile production, I will show how and why the textile and apparel industries took a protectionist stance—and how protectionism was defeated.

HISTORICAL ANTECEDENTS

The U.S. textile industry originated in the early part of the nineteenth century, when the Boston Associates established their textile mill complex in Lowell, Massachusetts. By the 1880s the industry was already changing. Through a process of mergers and acquisitions, textile companies consolidated, over a period of time, as they moved from New England to the South. By the end of World War II, the U.S. textile industry was fast becoming a southern enterprise. The move to the South was completed by 1960.

In 1950, New England had 1,500 cotton-textile manufacturing plants with about 450,000 workers. By 1958, the New England textile industry employed only 124,000 workers, while the South had 477,600.[1]

The average size of an American plant in 1950 was about 300 workers. By 1954, mergers had increased the size and productivity of textile establishments.[2] Between July 1953 and September 1954 alone, the pace of mergers and acquisitions in textiles was more rapid than in any other U.S. industry. By March 1955, 43 U.S. companies in the cotton textile industry, engaged either in spinning, weaving, or finishing operations, owned 507 plants employing about 345,550 persons, or about 60 percent of all employees in domestic cotton-textile production. Seventy percent of the acquisitions were made by firms with $10 million or more in capital assets.[3] When cotton textile mills consolidated and moved to the South, 541 were closed and only 5 new ones were opened. Some 147,000 textile workers lost their jobs.[4]

The traditional explanation for the southward move of the U.S. textile industry, and for its lost jobs and shuttered plants, is the South's lower labor costs, its lower energy requirements, and the efforts of southern communities to lure textile mills to the region with state tax breaks.[5] Certainly these were important motivating forces, but they are only some of the reasons for the move. Barry E. Truchil and others have argued that the most salient incentive for moving south was the federal tax laws that made it possible for textile companies to deduct the losses of an acquired company against the purchasing firm's profits for at least two years. Northern banks had been financing the acquisition of Massachusetts and Rhode Island firms by larger corporations, a phenomenon many northern communities opposed. A New England firm would be closed and its workers displaced as a new facility was opened in the lower cost South.[6]

During the Kennedy administration, the Textile Workers Union of America commissioned a study of the textile industry by Seymour Harris, a professor of economics at Harvard University. The study, titled *New England's Textiles and the New England Economy: Report by the New England Governors' Textile Committee to the Conference of New England Governors*, was given the imprimatur of the prestigious Pastore Committee, which Congress had appointed to study the industry's problems. Harris addressed a variety of internal problems facing the textile industry. He saw the mergers and subsequent move to the South as responsible for the job loss and unemployment of Northern textile workers. He wrote, "While the industry was consolidating in the South with high levels of productivity and profitability, and new increased investment in man-made fiber production, the process of restructuring was accompanied by intense suffering among textile workers in the North."[7]

During the 1950s, as the U.S. textile industry was in the throes of moving south and restructuring, the first imports of low-wage textiles from Japan hit American markets. America's textile manufacturers opposed the reduction of tariffs amid the fear of growing, low-wage foreign competition. Japanese textile imports became anathema. Citizens of American textile communities in South Carolina picketed stores selling Japanese textiles, and one community passed a law requiring retailers to indicate by signs in their windows that they were selling Japanese textile products.[8] According to the Japanese press, "A California Republican Congressman was reported to have urged Americans to boycott Japanese goods temporarily." A South Carolina Democratic senator was also reported to have proposed "cutting off U.S. MSA and other economic aids to a nation which could not keep Communist agitations in check."[9]

If textile producers supported trade protection, the textile unions did not. As the labor movement in the textile industry saw it, America's textile producers—not Japanese imports—were responsible for the job losses experienced by the country's northern textile workers. Union leaders saw textile executives, who invoked the problem of job loss to justify protectionist demands, as disingenuous. They refused to support trade protection, seeing industry leaders as being concerned with East Asian competition, not the fates of their workers.

In the 1950s the U.S. textile industry was still a labor-intensive industry with relatively low requirements for capital investment. Moreover, because the technology was widely known, in the early part of this century investors enjoyed relative ease of entry. In part, as Emanuel Cellar points out in his 1955 report on the textile industry, "this comparative ease of entrance into the industry led to a condition of chronic overcapacity which resulted in a condition of low profit and instability." Textile producers feared that foreign competition would reduce their potential export market. Cellar also states, "The prospect is that the future will bring further expansion of textile manufacturing in foreign, low-wage areas. At the least this will result in a diminishing export market for the American textile industry."[10] Despite consolidation in the 1950s and 1960s, textile firms continued to be relatively unproductive and marginally profitable. Individual textile firms could succeed or fail in response to small differences in the cost of domestic labor. A close examination of the record shows that U.S. textile producers in the 1950s had real reasons to fear the growth of low-wage competition.

Low profits in the 1950s meant textile producers often did not have the resources to purchase new technologies. By the 1960s and 1970s, however, the Kennedy program's accelerated tax depreciations made it possible for U.S. textile factories, almost all of which were now located in the American South, to increase their productivity—just what trade liberalizers urged them to do. Federal support made it possible for the industry to buy up-to-date machinery and shed some of its labor force, making the industry more competitive with its counterparts in the Asian-Pacific Rim. At the same time, the industry continued to claim that imports were responsible for the "unfair competition" that led to plant closings and job losses.

TEXTILES: LOW WAGES AND CLASS CONFLICT

In part, textile protectionism must be understood in the context of the industry's labor-intensity and the class relationships that have traditionally characterized relations between textile workers and their employers in the United States. In the 1930s and again in the 1950s, workers made efforts to unionize the southern textile industry, but their efforts were thwarted by conservative employers aided by local governments. In the 1950s, organized textile workers in the North and unorganized workers in the South demanded higher wages. But their efforts were solidly defeated by southern employers, who could impose their authority on workers through cultural and political coercion and sometimes violence. Needing to compete with these low wages made it more difficult for northern textile employers to grant wage increases.

Textile producers moved to the South partly to escape an organized labor force and to benefit from the low-wage environment that the South could provide. Southern textile manufacturers had continued to resist unionization even after the passage of the Wagner Act in 1935. Moreover, in 1947 the Taft-Hartley Act strengthened the ability of southern textile producers to thwart assertive workers and union organizing efforts. Section 14(b) of the act permitted individual states to pass laws that bypassed federal legislation prohibiting unions from demanding a closed shop. Subsequently, all the southern textile states, and some western ones as well, passed "right to work" laws making union organizing even more difficult.

On April 6, 1955, as Congress was discussing the administration's trade bill to reduce tariffs on textile imports from Japan, the TWUA threatened a strike of forty thousand workers in the northern textile mills in response to a demand for a 10¢ an hour wage cut. The estimated average wage in the northern industry was $1.35 an hour, and the cotton textile workers had had a pay cut of 8.5¢ an hour in 1952; they had not had a wage increase since 1951. The proposed cut would make wages comparable to those in the South.[11]

On April 10, 1955, Seabury Stanton, chair of the Fall River–New Bedford Textile Manufacturers' Association (who also testified in Congress opposing imports) addressed the delegates of the TWUA in response to the union's refusal to accept a wage cut. He told them that southern manufacturers would continue to take away New England's textile industry unless they cooperated with management by following a policy of wage restraint.[12] The following March the TWUA demanded a 10¢ an hour raise from northern manufacturers.[13] In July of 1956, an election year, the now-united American Federation of Labor and Congress of Industrial Organizations (AFL-CIO) announced its support for a union-organizing drive in the southern textile industry. The major targets were thirty-five plants operated by Burlington Industries, Cannon Mills, and the Pepperell Manufacturing Company.[14] The TWUA's intense struggle to organize the southern textile industry in the summer of 1956 ultimately failed.[15] However, in September 1956 the union issued a widely distributed report that brought public attention to the poverty of textile workers and the legitimacy of their demands for better wages. According to the *New York Times*, the report "contended that one million textile workers and their families were 'condemned to an ever declining standard of living.'" The report also asserted that textile wages were "25 percent below the national factory average, with the gap growing wider each year. . . . The union urged employers and the government to join in a program to raise wages, spread unionization, curb imports, improve sales methods and ward off mill closings."[16]

It is important to keep in mind how poorly paid textile workers were, and how relatively little the difference was between northern and southern wages. In 1954, out of a listing of thirty-three manufacturing industries, textile workers ranked thirty-second, with an average hourly wage of $1.19, compared to $2.65 for the top-ranking building-construction industry. Southern workers earned $1.17 per hour, and northern, often unionized, textile workers earned about $1.32, a difference of only 11.4 percent.[17] However, textile manufacturers had moved south in large part to benefit from a nonunion, lower wage environment. Northern textile producers were adamant about the need to lower wages, because this 10 percent differential inhibited their ability to compete with the larger, more productive southern mills built in the 1950s.

While northern textile manufacturers asked their workers to accept a wage cut, southern textile workers mounted a union drive to raise their wages to northern levels. No doubt textile manufacturers were hostile to unionization on ideological grounds, but the textile industry was also sensitive to small differences in the cost of labor. As a result, what might appear to the observer to be a small difference could ultimately generate intense conflict between labor and management in this industry.

During this period, debates about further tariff reductions took place in the nation's capital. Japanese textile workers were earning the U.S. equivalent of $.15 an hour.[18] By 1960, Hong Kong had begun to take Japan's place as the new low-wage textile and apparel exporter to the United States. Textile workers there too earned $.15 an hour, or less than 10 percent of the average U.S. textile wage of $1.65 an hour.[19] Imports from Hong Kong and Japan were more competitive in U.S. markets, even with the added costs of tariffs and transport. Within this framework, it is not surprising that, three weeks after New England's textile workers were told they must agree to a wage cut, the outgoing president of the American Cotton Manufacturers' Institute made a heartfelt demand for import quotas, saying, "We are face to face with a life or death question of whether our own government will stand idly by and permit low-wage competition from Japan to seriously cripple our industry. Must there be closed mills and breadlines before the Administration in Washington concedes the possibility of irreparable damage to our industry?"[20]

THE TEXTILE INDUSTRY AT HOME AND ABROAD: WOMEN'S WAGES

Hong Kong's low-cost textile exports were a major threat to the U.S. industry, in large part because of the lower wages the Hong Kong manufacturers paid. They could pay such low wages because they employed so many young women. Walter T. Forbes, after his visit to Hong Kong in 1960, wrote about the South Sea Textile Company in Hong Kong and its workers. The working conditions and personnel policies he described were reminiscent of those prevalent in the U.S. textile industry in the cities of Lowell and Lawrence at the end of the nineteenth century. It was the availability of young, unmarried women, or "mill girls," in the early nineteenth century that made the New England textile industry so profitable,[21] and the same pattern of gendered employment aided East Asian producers in the mid–twentieth century. As Forbes tells us,

> The new dormitories house 500 men and 1,000 girls, whose ages
> average approximately 21. He [the owner] explained his best workers

are from 18 to 23 years old, and after 25 they are let go to other jobs, as their efficiency goes down. One girl was running two sides of a spinning frame and one weaver operates approximately 10 looms, which by U.S. standards is very low, but their wages are low too. . . .

At least 85% of the employees in the Far East textile industries are women[,] and approximately 85% of all employees are housed in mill dormitories. The average age in one plant was given as 19.5 years. Girls are paid 10,000 yen per month ($28), plus their board and lodging, which is estimated at about 20% of their wages. In off time, they are given excellent training in sewing, cooking, English, etc.— a very good educational program. At the end of 4 to 5 years, these girls have accumulated a dowry of about $600; they return home to their local communities with this money, a sewing machine, a hand knitting machine, and with their good vocational training have no difficulty finding a husband.[22]

This data is consistent with the findings of Ester Boserup, who as early as 1970 showed that women and men experience industrial development differently.[23] Later, Alice Amsden described comparable wage differentials between men and women in the early development of South Korea. She writes that "Korea has the dubious distinction of having one of the highest gender wage gaps, an honor shared by Japan. On average, Korean women earn less than half of what men earn. Korea, like Japan, also has one of the largest manufacturing wage dispersions between light and heavy industry."[24] The low wage paid to young women was particularly important, not only in South Korea but also for the postwar development of the textile and apparel industries in other East Asian countries, such as Hong Kong and Taiwan.

America's women textile workers too were employed in sex-segregated industrial jobs, and women's wages have always been lower than those of their male counterparts. But in America in the 1950s, not only were textile wages higher than those in Hong Kong and Japan, the wage differentials between men and women were not nearly so extreme. In 1960, the year Walter Forbes visited the Hong Kong textile factory, women employed in the U.S. textile industry earned an average wage of $1.40 an hour, or 94 percent of men's wages, which averaged $1.49 per hour. In both northern and southern textile firms, gender-wage differentials were relatively small. In the United States, women represented 46 percent of the textile industry's labor force, compared to 62 percent in Japan.[25]

America's women textile and apparel workers were a mature, skilled, and stable workforce. Apparel workers and northern textile workers were unionized. In 1964, apparel workers earned 77 percent of the men's manufacturing wage. They were considerably better off than women textile workers in the low-wage South during America's postwar prosperity. Indeed, it was in part the very welfare these workers enjoyed that made U.S. textile and apparel manufacturers begin to seek the comparative advantage of offshore production.

THE WAGES VERSUS PROFIT BIND IN TEXTILES

In the United States in the 1950s, despite all the mergers and consolidation in the textile industry, wage demands provoked by a reactivated labor movement in the textile industry were creating a dilemma for textile manufacturers. By 1956, southern cotton-mill profit margins had declined to between 55 and 75 percent of the 1947–49 levels and were lower than those in manufacturing as a whole: profit per dollar of sales, or profit on net worth, averaged little more than half the level found in manufacturing generally.[26] Manufacturers proceeded on the assumption that they had to keep all costs, including wages, to a bare minimum.

At the same time, a state-of-the-art textile industry was emerging in East Asia as a result of U.S. subsidies and foreign aid. The domestic industry was facing not only a slowed growth in demand in the U.S. market but also the threat of losing traditional export markets in East Asia. Along with the high price of cotton and increasing overcapacity, growing levels of Japanese imports loomed as one of the most significant potential threats. Given the wage scale for textile workers, however, it was virtually impossible to reduce wages further.

Low-wage competition from East Asia was not new. In the 1930s, conflicts between U.S. textile makers and their Japanese rivals had been resolved by the private efforts of U.S. textile manufacturers who, in 1937, went to Japan to negotiate a trade agreement with their competitors. But the new U.S. trade laws made attempts at another such solution illegal. With Congress having lost its ability to set tariffs, textile manufacturers could no longer control imports through the efforts of their congressional representatives. Many textile executives had been to Japan and Hong Kong; they had witnessed the dynamism of their foreign competition. Now, confronted by an administration that was at best indifferent to their concerns, textile manufacturers were at a loss to control the new business environment.

Between 1953 and 1956, textile and apparel imports had expanded.[27] If the expansion represented a low level of overall growth, it nevertheless had an impact on small segments of the industry, such as hats, gloves, and women's handkerchiefs. If only a few segments of the industry had thus far been affected by Japanese import penetration, there was every reason to believe that Asian competitors would increase and diversify their exports to the United States as much they could, expanding the spectrum, volume, and value of highly competitive products in the not too distant future.

Clearly, textile producers behaved cynically in demanding protection from imports, given the job losses they themselves were causing by moving from North to South. But it was only good business sense to realize that, even if imports constituted only 2 percent of domestic consumption, in the future they could increase dramatically. Thus, spokesmen for the U.S. textile industry were not being entirely disingenuous in arguing that they needed continued protection from low-wage imports even if they could not really claim that imports were causing immediate business failures or job displacement.

Such concerns are dramatized by the 1958 testimony of Halbert M. Jones, president of the American Cotton Manufacturers' Institute (ACMI), whose comments before the Pastore Committee explain why a 2 percent market share for imported textiles was seen as a problem. Jones said that low-wage imports

> affect our price structure far beyond any amount that you would
> normally believe to be possible. . . . There is a constant pressure. You
> may have a reduction in price of half a cent, and the domestic industry[,]
> because of competitive pressure[,] meets it. Then there is another
> half cent and it meets that, and a small reduction, which is repeated in
> a highly competitive industry such as we have, finally results in
> price deterioration, which is extremely serious for the industry.[28]

What appeared baffling to observers and threatening to America's textile producers was the way the Japanese did business. According to American textile manufacturers, Japanese textile promoters were charging less than the cost of production, or what trade analysts now call "dumping." Japanese business practices confirmed American manufacturers' worst fears about a foreign conspiracy to undermine the U.S. textile industry. The intense price competition fostered by Japanese vendors was a consequence of the way textile production and marketing were organized by the Japanese. Writing in 1964, Warren S. Hunsberger sheds light on this issue: "The handful of Japanese trading companies competing with each other in the sale of cotton textiles in New York sometimes resort to price competition in circumstances from which no one seems to gain but the American consumer. While an American may be pleased to see Japanese business houses accepting what appear to be less than maximum obtainable prices, the business motives of these Japanese are at times baffling to their American customers."[29]

Japanese trading companies acted as brokers for their manufacturers; sale prices were less important to them than volume. Their goal, encouraged by the cartelized Japanese economy, was to maintain an aggressive pricing system—and not to make the highest attainable profits. Their objective was to maximize sales volumes and foreign exchange while maintaining growth and amicable relations with important customers.

In the 1957 study he did for the northern textile industry and the Textile Workers Union, Seymour Harris, recognizing that job displacement in textiles was a consequence of domestic competition, made recommendations for industrial adjustment. Neither Harris nor the TWUA were protectionists. Nevertheless, Harris supported the demand for trade protection. His report states, "We believe the United States should not increase foreign competition in textiles by making trade concessions" and goes on to say that

> textile employment has greatly declined[:] . . . about 20 percent for the nation and more than 40 percent for New England in 7 or 8 years. The industry is affected with unsatisfactory prices, inadequate output, low profits, and frequent periods of liquidation. It is not wise policy to handicap a declining industry further through governmental policies.
>
> The problem that tariff reduction seeks to solve—the dollar shortage abroad—is one about which the whole nation should be concerned; it should not be solved by excessive sacrifice by one segment of the economy, and a declining segment at that. A larger part of the burden of reducing the dollar shortage should be borne by the taxpayer, the investor and the strong industries, notably those in export businesses.
>
> In view of the unsatisfactory condition of the industry, as evidenced by prices, output, exports and profits, and the even more unsatisfactory condition of the New England segment, the leaders of the industry feel they are being asked to bear an excessive part of the burden of saving Japan for democracy.[30]

Bauer, Pool, and Dexter, in arguing against the politics of protection, quite rightly point out that textile protectionism has often been represented by reactionary elements intensely hostile to labor.[31] We can hear an echo of this response even in the more recent popularity of Pat Buchanan during his short-lived 1996 candidacy for the Republican primary nomination for president.

Postwar protectionism appealed to the desire of local business elites to retain political power, at a time when it was waning in favor of larger national and international corporate entities whose interests lay in a more outward-looking international economic agenda. Bauer, Pool, and Dexter see the protectionist impulse as a case of provincial opposition to policies of an increasingly powerful federal government with global and cosmopolitan objectives and responsibilities. In the 1950s and 1960s the opposition of locally based southern textile manufacturers to internationalist objectives, including trade liberalization, characterized the political culture of southern mill towns. In 1947 this opposition was bolstered by the Taft-Hartley Act. These rural communities were dominated by mill owners who not only controlled the work lives of many of the townspeople but, before World War II, might even have owned the church, school, and company store.[32]

The history of American populism is replete with instances of extreme conservatism and xenophobia emerging from communities like these that were threatened with change.[33] Such populist conservatism is often the response of middling status groups experiencing the loss of privileges, stability, and security embodied in an older way of life. Such a view, however, is not inconsistent with the fact that domestic textile producers were responding to real economic threats from Asian producers. U.S. subsidies of foreign aid, modern technology, cheap cotton, and, by the mid-1950s, annual tariff reductions all meant that imported Japanese goods could be sold in the United States at bargain-basement prices. When Congress's loss of tariff-setting powers changed the norms and patterns of their previous market relationships, textile manufacturers lost their ability to prevent low-wage competition and believed, with justification, that this loss endangered the industry's future prosperity.

Political leaders, legislators, businesspeople, and the public are generally more responsive to human-scale threats of layoffs and poverty than to demands by an industry for industrial restructuring. Thus, when a 1950s union drive failed, adverse publicity about poverty among America's textile workers created the image of a rapacious textile industry. In the context of a presidential election only a month away, reports of impoverished workers and greedy mill owners contributed to Eisenhower's decision to negotiate voluntary export restraints with the Japanese. At the same time, Burlington Industries, after thwarting the union's organizing drive, agreed to give its workers a 10¢ an hour raise.[34]

COMPETITIVE STRATEGIES:
LABOR REPRESSIVE INDUSTRIAL RELATIONS

Southern textile manufacturers—having lost control of trade policy and facing competition from larger, more productive mills with advanced technologies at home and abroad—searched for new ways to maintain the industry's competitive position. As noted, one of the strategies they used to maintain a low-wage workforce was to sustain the traditional, paternalistic authority of rural southern communities that supported the labor-repressive system of industrial relations. The textile industry was centralized in three southeastern states. In the late 1960s and the 1970s, the corporate headquarters of the largest and most concentrated textile conglomerates in the industry were in North and South Carolina and Georgia; a full 70 percent of all U.S. textile workers lived and worked in the rural textile communities of these three states.[35]

This impoverished labor force worked longer hours than workers doing similar jobs in other industries, but earned less per hour for their labor.[36] Families improved their living standards only by sending a larger number of family members to work in the lower wage industries. Many supplemented paid industrial work with participation in an informal, noncash-oriented agriculture.

By the 1970s the traditional elites who had controlled the local and state governments in this region since the end of the Civil War were challenged by new, higher-wage or unionized industries that began to relocate their manufacturing facilities in rural southern textile communities in search of cheaper labor. When such companies offered wage or union pay scales higher than the textile, apparel, and furniture industries, textile management saw these attempts as disruptive of labor-market stability, and illegally obstructed their entry into the region. According to one analyst, in the 1970s "Raleigh North Carolina actually had a written policy that discouraged unionized industries from locating in the local vicinity. Xerox and Miller Brewing are two firms that located elsewhere after having their initial interest in the Raleigh area rebuffed by the local business community in 1975. The locals argued that unionized firms would 'disrupt the local economy.' "[37] Communities like Raleigh were able to maintain the industry's labor-repressive employment system until the 1980s.[38] Until that point, new industrial investment in the South was limited to three low-wage manufacturing industries—textiles, apparel, and furniture. At the same time, new organizing efforts intensified the industry's opposition to unionization. In 1963 the Textile Workers Union began a new struggle to organize the industry. One issue in this struggle was their demand that the government mandate installation of modern technology to remove cotton dust, which had been causing workers to contract byssinosis, or "brown lung disease." The J. P. Stevens campaign became a test case for the entire southern textile industry. It lasted almost two decades, during which time Stevens was found guilty of thousands of violations of labor law. Stevens earned the company and the southern textile industry notoriety for union busting and opposition to demands by the Occupational Safety and Health Administration (OSHA) for clean air. By the mid-1970s, OSHA and the Environmental Protection Agency (EPA) finally succeeded in getting cotton textile mills to install devices to prevent diseases caused by airborne cotton dust.[39] Although the union won its battle in the struggle to end brown lung disease, America's southern textile manufacturers continued to pay some of the lowest wages in U.S. manufacturing. Moreover, the required installation of devices for removing cotton dust was too expensive for many of the smaller textile mills. Many went bankrupt and were bought by the larger companies, which further concentrated the industry.

THE KENNEDY COMPROMISE AND THE RESTRUCTURING OF AMERICAN TEXTILE PRODUCTION

Advocates of industrial policy have questioned the value of the textile industry's protectionist stance, arguing that the industry was not competitive in the 1950s and 1960s, that it suffered from overcapacity and stagnating demand. They believe textile manufacturers ought to have looked inward instead of outward. Instead of focusing on trade protection, manufacturers should have retooled to increase textile industry productivity in light of the new investments in modern plants and equipment in East Asia.[40] Others contend that American exceptionalism was responsible for the focus on individual entrepreneurship and business opposition to state interventions in the economy. As Vinod K. Aggarwal and Stephan Haggard put it, "The American bureaucracy, in contrast to the bureaucracies of France and Japan, lacked an independent vision of industrial policy, independent sources of information, and policy tools to implement disaggregated, industry specific policies."[41] Or as Thomas W. Zeiler has written of protectionism, "The view sidestepped the real culprit of the problems—inefficiency—that was responsible for difficulties in many declining industries like textiles. But management preferred to capitalize on the highly emotional (and more visible) import issue rather than blame themselves for not reinvesting their profits into plant modernization."[42]

These are reasonable conclusions, ones that the industry shared. As we have seen, textile producers visited East Asia in the early 1960s to gauge their new competition. They did recognize that protection was not sufficient to maintain the international competitiveness of their industry without a large infusion of capital to restructure their production facilities.[43] In the 1950s the industry did not have sufficient capital to make such investments. Low profits had historically made it difficult for the industry to find resources for investment in new technology, and for the most part, textile makers were forced to rely on the internal generation of funds for this purpose.[44] This constraint limited their investment in plants and equipment to replacing worn-out machinery; it also contributed to producers' need for a labor-repressive system of industrial relations.

However, as noted earlier, during the 1950s the industry had engaged in highly profitable mergers and acquisitions, which, while displacing workers in the northern industry, provided textile producers with additional capital and allowed for some economies of scale. During Eisenhower's presidency, textile industry requests for financial support from the government were ignored or refused. The administration focused its efforts on expanding trade on behalf of more valued industries.[45]

It was not until the early 1960s that the federal government responded to the industry's needs, offering support that may ultimately have been more useful than the minimalist protection provided by the quotas of the Long-Term Arrangement. Kennedy's textile initiatives offered federal financing for industrial restructuring.

Despite the new law, for the first seven years after its passage no funds at all were appropriated either to aid firms or to support displaced workers. By 1970, the Department of Labor set up a small office to administer the program. By May 1973 thirty-one firms had been certified as eligible to apply for adjustment assistance. They applied for funding that presumably would allow them to restructure their operations. Six of the thirty-one firms were funded; of these, five produced textiles and one manufactured apparel.[46] Kennedy's program ordered a speedup of tax depreciation allowance schedules. In the early 1960s, Kennedy had explained the need for this program: "The industry is experiencing a major technological breakthrough in which advancing techniques engender further advances and make even recently developed equipment economically outdated before it is physically worn out. Their pressure for the adoption of technological innovations is accentuated by competition of foreign firms who, in most cases, enjoy the advantages of very liberal depreciation allowances as well as low wage costs."[47] Tax write-offs for technological innovation made more capital available for modernization and represented a new mandate for the textile industry to increase domestic productivity in a more competitive international marketplace.

In the 1970s, in order to offset the spiraling cost of crude oil, the U.S. textile industry shifted the emphasis of its technology development away from the development and production of new man-made fibers and focused on reducing production costs.[48] Textile industry executives focused on technologies that increased machine speeds, allowed operations to be combined, deskilled the labor process, and reduced the need for floor space. This mass-production strategy reduced the number of unskilled workers required and generated productivity gains. The new technology either eliminated labor or allowed the deployment of workers in ways that maintained the industry's traditionally low-wage workforce.[49]

In 1964, the two-price cotton policy—which had set the cost of raw cotton higher for U.S. textile producers than for foreign manufacturers—was equalized. This change made the cost of raw cotton 26 percent lower than it had been for domestic producers and freed capital for new investment. As a result of these measures, U.S. textile manufacturers made new expenditures on plants and equipment. Between 1960 and 1970, production expanded rapidly.[50] By the beginning of the 1980s, the move to the South was complete.

In the 1970s the government's mandate that the industry finance technology for environmental protection was seen as thwarting industry's efforts to promote domestic capital formation. Only the larger firms eventually agreed to comply with OSHA and EPA regulations. The mandate put the smaller, less profitable textile competitors at a severe competitive disadvantage, which led to further centralization and consolidation of U.S. textile production by means of new mergers and acquisitions. Many smaller firms, unable to afford the costs of environmental protection, closed their doors.[51]

One can argue, then, that the U.S. government in the 1960s and 1970s did have at least a minimalist industrial policy for the textile industry, one that included government subsidies for investments in new technology and environmental safety. Textile executives' demands on Congress for trade protection were often accompanied by less-public requests for government aid for industrial restructuring, an issue that many advocates of industrial policy have failed to note.[52] U.S. textile productivity increased, and the industry shed more of its labor.

There is an important relationship between the textile industry's restructuring and its demands for trade protection. The Long-Term Arrangement, in effect between 1963 and 1974, imposed import quota limits only on cotton textiles. Not surprisingly, during the 1960s and early 1970s there was dramatic growth in imports of man-made fibers and fabrics, imports from both Europe and Asia, which were becoming a source of greater competition for U.S. producers.

In response, American producers were forced to turn their attention to producing the new man-made (noncellulosic) fibers. Many textile producers built or rebuilt their facilities to process man-made fibers. These efforts contributed to the burst of capital spending in the industry and increased production, from 677 million to 3.2 billion pounds, between 1960 and 1968.[53]

Despite the tax depreciation allowances, only the largest companies managed to get financing for new capital investment and capitalize on new technologies in order to process man-made fibers. According to a 1976 study by the U.S. Office of Industrial Economics, this was due to the industry's low level of returns on sales and on stockholders' equity.[54] By 1983 W. Denney Freeston Jr. and Jeffrey S. Arpan would write, "A side effect of technological developments was increased industrial concentration of several segments of the textile complex. Man-made fiber producers increased their share of output, largely at the expense of the less concentrated natural fiber producers. New production technologies in the textile industry encouraged integration of spinning and weaving."[55] These larger textile mills began to integrate vertically and horizontally, which enabled them to finance a more diversified industry.

In 1974, tax depreciation schedules for new investments in textiles and apparel technology were accelerated once again.[56] Continuing technological innovation in textiles was also facilitated by the continued buyouts and mergers, which led the industry to consolidate further. From the 1960s to the 1980s, domestic and foreign competition, coupled with downturns in recurrent business cycles, led to the closing of many smaller, less efficient mills. This growing concentration in the industry increased productivity further, as the number of smaller and less efficient firms declined.[57]

By the mid-1970s a new, more concentrated textile industry was firmly relocated in an industrializing South. Four major corporations controlled 39 percent of cotton weaving mills, 42 percent of production in synthetics weaving, 67 percent in carpet weaving, 60 percent in synthetics finishing, 57 percent in thread mills, and 80 percent in tire cord and fabrics.[58] As the authors of a government study write, "After acquiring control of smaller mills, large companies like Burlington and J. P. Stevens applied mass-production techniques and consolidated diverse textile activities into larger integrated plants. Other companies, such as Texfi, sought greater control over its source of fibers and as a consequence began to manufacture man-made fibers for their own knitting mills. Together, these events trans-formed the textile industry into a smaller group of expanding firms en-gaged in integrated activities."[59]

In 1974 only eighteen textile companies were reporting gross sales over $200 million. According to *Fortune* magazine, their combined total sales of $10.5 billion accounted for about one-third of the industry's $31.2 bil-lion in total sales as estimated by the Federal Trade Commission.[60] The top three firms in 1974 were Burlington Industries, with $2.3 billion; J. P. Stevens, with $1.3 billion; and United Merchants and Manufacturers, with $962.6 million.

By 1981 the industry had grown even more concentrated. Among ap-proximately five thousand textile firms, the fifty largest firms accounted for 50 percent of the industry's total output. The largest of these were Burlington Industries, J. P. Stevens, Milliken, West Point–Pepperell, and Springs Industries.[61] These firms continued to increase their concentration and make new investments, particularly in computer-driven technologies imported from Italy, Japan, and West Germany.[62]

Aid to trade-sensitive industries for restructuring was a response to the international competition that resulted from America's new hegemonic agenda and new foreign economic policy in the postwar period. In that sense the Marshall Plan, the Mutual Security Act, the Food for Peace program (Agricultural Trade Development and Assistance Act, or PL480), and the Export-Import Bank, all operating under the U.S. military um-brella, lay at the heart of America's postwar industrial policy. Exporting industries were favored. The economic dislocation and losses caused by imports were discounted in the pursuit of larger goals; but these effects influenced which industries would become winners and losers. In the 1980s, trade expansion continued to dominate America's foreign-economic-policy agenda.

The reluctance of U.S. textile producers to invest in research and de-velopment—their inability to fund the development of their own tech-nology—made the industry dependent on foreign textile-machinery man-ufacturers.[63] During this period, the new technology was made primarily by Japanese and European companies. Brian Toyne and Jeffrey S. Arpan write, "A key competitive strategy is to slow the diffusion of new technology in order to maintain a competitive edge. However, this can be accomplished only if technology is developed in house, rather than by textile manufacturing and equipment companies, or by firms in other segments of the textile complex (e.g., man-made fibers). Otherwise textile firms will not be able to control the diffusion process."[64] Even if the U.S. textile industry was "the most productive and cost efficient in the world," this alone could not guarantee its ability to compete.[65] By the 1980s the international dispersion of advanced textile technologies had leveled out competitive advantages among the textile industries of the United States, Europe, and East Asia. It now became increasingly clear to textile manufacturers that the competitive advantage continued to lie in having greater size and lower labor costs. Even today, the low price of imports made by low-wage labor continues to threaten the U.S. textile industry. The higher costs of U.S. labor and capital mean that textiles imported from Asia continue to sell at prices below what it costs U.S. manufacturers to produce them.

In the 1980s, even after two decades of congressional struggles over trade policy, the protectionist concerns of U.S. textile and apparel firms began to merge. Increasingly, the expanding volumes of apparel produced on the Asian-Pacific Rim were made with Asian, rather than U.S., textiles. Segments of the U.S. textile industry that supplied apparel makers began to lose customers. Some U.S. textile producers turned to manufacturing textiles for home products rather than clothing as a way to avoid foreign competition. Yet the makers of fabric for clothing continued to press for import quotas, lest their already low profits turn into losses, bankruptcies, and shuttered mills. By the 1980s the textile industry would begin to profit from apparel made in low-wage countries of Latin America.

THE DECLINE OF TRADE PROTECTION

Throughout the 1960s and 1970s the U.S. textile industry invested in up-to-date technology, made a massive effort to prevent unionization, and resisted demands by OSHA to clean up the environment. Indeed, although Kennedy's Long-Term Arrangement and the Multifibre Arrangement did very little to stem the tide of import growth, the textile industry continued to lobby for trade protection.[66] By the end of 1967, members had introduced 729 bills in the House of Representatives to impose quotas on imports.[67] Initially, the textile industry's trade unions did not participate in the protectionist trade coalition. But by 1967, as textile workers saw expanding low-wage competition reinforce the industry's traditional labor-repressive strategies, the president of the United Textile Workers Union officially endorsed import quotas.[68]

Congressional protectionism may not have prevented trade liberalization, but it may have slowed it down. The power of congressional protectionists also helped the textile industry win the economic support it needed to restructure itself.[69] As Destler points out, even Richard Nixon, with no real political agenda for the industry, felt he could not antagonize the textile interests. Running for president in 1972, he sought support from textile industry leaders in the hope that Strom Thurmond and his political allies would aid him in his campaign for a second term in the White House.[70] Nixon negotiated the Multifibre Arrangement, which, after his resignation, was signed by President Ford. Indeed, as we will see, the power of the textile industry in Congress made it possible to press Reagan, in the mid-1980s, for a new form of protectionist "free trade" initiative in Latin America.

The protectionist agenda was not the outcome of a lack of wisdom among textile producers. Nor was it generated solely by the industry's conservatism. The need to deal with the new trade agenda in the postwar period also motivated apparel producers to support trade protection. While reciprocal trade strengthened American economic and political power abroad, it was not designed with the interests of the textile and the apparel industries in mind. As small, labor-intensive industries with low profits, textile producers, and soon after, apparel producers, resisted a policy that promised to put many of the small firms that then made up these industries in the 1960s and 1970s out of business.

6 The U.S. Apparel Industry
Responses to Capital Flight

The textile and apparel industries in the United States developed separately. Until quite recently, each had a distinct history, different types of production, and unique traditions. While America's textile industry had its roots in early-nineteenth-century New England, and later in the South, the U.S. apparel industry developed during the end of the nineteenth century and the early twentieth century in New York City.

Apparel manufacturers were largely from southern Italy and eastern Europe. The Jewish and Italian immigrants who became the owners of small manufacturing and contracting firms first came to the United States during the period from 1880 to 1920. The culture of these manufacturers, rooted in a craft tradition of tailoring and sewing skills, was urban and cosmopolitan. It was philosophically grounded in a sense of class consciousness, internationalism, and social democracy, as was the culture of their workers and the men who led the trade union movement in the industry—the International Ladies' Garment Workers' Union (ILGWU) in women's clothing, and the Amalgamated Clothing Workers of America (the Amalgamated, or ACWA) in the men's clothing industry.[1]

In the past, journalists and muckrakers had written about the poverty of textile workers in the South; now the brutality of working conditions in the lofts and garment factories of New York's Lower East Side became the subject of similar documentation. While the labor struggles of the 1930s had failed to organize the southern textile industry, similar struggles in the clothing industry succeeded, leading to a progressive set of labor-management relationships and trade unionism in the New York City apparel industry. By midcentury the policies of the New Deal, aided by postwar prosperity, had laid the groundwork for a thriving and unionized garment industry. By the 1950s, labor's alliance with the New Deal and the Democratic Party had allowed the apparel unions in New York, New Jersey, and Pennsylvania to organize the East Coast.[2]

Historically, the industry had been composed, in the United States as elsewhere, of small, family-owned firms. There were "inside shops"—producers who designed, manufactured, and sold garments—and "outside shops," run by contractors who might do either the cutting and assembly, or only the assembly work, required to produce a variety of garments planned and designed by different manufacturers. Like the textile industry, the apparel industry was highly competitive and marginally profitable. Productivity and profits here too depended on a labor-repressive employment structure. However, whereas the textile industry was unambiguously hostile to the labor movement, unionization of the apparel industry led to a unique form of labor-management cooperation.

The apparel industry, centered as it was in New York City, benefited from having a critical mass of manufacturers and contractors engaged in relationships that served each party well. Manufacturers agreed to provide work only to union contractors—to be done only in shops with contractually required wages and labor standards.

The small, competitive manufacturers and contractors were willing to cooperate with workers to promote wage and employment stability because the labor-management bargain offered management an alternative to the cutthroat competition that was endemic to this volatile industry. The fact that the union required manufacturers to work only with union contractors provided an incentive for contractors to unionize, because, as part of the union network, they were assured a relatively stable and steady supply of work from unionized manufacturers, who had to compensate them at a price that enabled them to pay union wages.[3] Concomitantly, the accord created a level playing field for manufacturers who might otherwise have had to struggle with competitors using lower wage labor. The contract also assured manufacturers ready access to a skilled workforce.

The ILGWU has been criticized for its top-down strategy of organizing manufacturers, thereby failing to involve the grassroots workers. The male leadership has also been criticized for unwillingness to reward women organizers. Despite these flaws, for a time the union accord offered a win-win situation for workers, contractors, and manufacturers. The union contract eliminated the intense competition that often drove employers out of business and workers out of jobs. Unionized workers had better working conditions, more employment stability, and higher wages. While some saw the industry's unique labor contract as "anticompetitive," in 1957 the courts upheld the ILGWU's right to organize in this way.[4] The unionization of the apparel industry created a semblance of labor peace and stability in the industry by developing a relationship that served the needs of contractors and manufacturers alike while providing decent wages and working conditions and some forms of employment stability for its workers.

In 1955 the ILGWU recorded 446,000 workers nationwide, up from 320,800 ten years earlier. When the large manufacturers became organized, they brought their contractors along.[5] In 1960 the Amalgamated claimed 385,000 members.[6] By 1960 New York City employed over 339,000 apparel workers, out of a national total of 1.15 million. In 1949, production workers in the industry earned an average weekly wage of $61.28, while the national average for all manufacturing workers was $54.92—good wages for the apparel industry's largely female labor force.[7] In 1956, apparel workers in New York and seven northeastern states were responsible for making three-fourths of the Easter dresses bought in the United States.[8]

As men's fashion dictated at that time, a large part of the output in men's clothing production consisted of tailored suits and jackets. Sidney Hillman was the original leader of the Amalgamated Clothing Workers of America in the men's industry; by the 1950s Jacob Potofsky had succeeded him, while David Dubinsky had become the president of the ILGWU.

RUNAWAY SHOPS

The bargain achieved by labor and management in the U.S. apparel industry has been viewed as a model of cooperation. At the height of this cooperation, during the years 1949 to 1960, a stable relationship between the two seemed to have ended cutthroat competition, sweatshops, and labor violence. The ILGWU and the Amalgamated were becoming regional power brokers in New York. But just as the hard-won labor-management contract in the U.S. apparel industry seemed most successful, the accord began to disintegrate. Clothing manufacturers found new opportunities and incentives to seek out low-wage labor, incentives that were stronger than the value of wage stability. Manufacturers began to move to lower wage, nonunion areas out of town. Indeed, it was the move to the South that helped end unionization in both textiles and apparel.

"Out of town" meant anywhere outside New York City—rural communities in upstate New York and southeastern Massachusetts, and in western Pennsylvania, where the decline of anthracite coal mining led wives and daughters of jobless miners to take jobs at any wage they could.[9] It meant Puerto Rico and Los Angeles, areas in which apparel manufacturing was beginning to expand. It also meant the South, where, as noted earlier, many small towns were looking for new investment and offered apparel manufacturers and textile producers tax breaks, cheap financing, and a low-wage, union-free environment.[10] Thus, New York's apparel workers, like the textile industry workers, began to see job losses and wage reductions even before the industry started to move to the Asian-Pacific Rim.

Whereas in 1949 there were over 339,000 apparel workers employed in the New York metropolitan area alone, by 1960 the number of workers in the state had declined to about 271,200, and the overall number of apparel workers in the nation had increased to 1.2 million from 1.15 million.[11] The years between 1949 and 1960 saw a major decline in the earnings of apparel workers compared to those of workers in other manufacturing industries. Apparel wages in New York City declined even more.

By the end of the 1950s the period of peace and prosperity for apparel workers had come to an end. In November 1958 a strike was called in seven northeastern states where the ILGWU had a large concentration of organized workers. The strikers demanded a 15 percent wage hike. But the employers of many western Pennsylvania locals, where wages were low and dresses were made for the low end of the market, claimed they could not sustain a wage increase in the face of the slow growth of demand and the wage competition from the lower wage South.[12] The strike was finally settled by arbitration, with the union winning an increase of 8 percent— basically an increase to match the cost of living.

The settlement of the strike appeared to restore the power of the ILGWU,[13] but after that the union's hold over the labor force began to slip away as the labor contract was challenged by "runaway" shops. The New York region was already beginning to lose its prominence as the center of U.S. apparel production. Perhaps most important at that time, companies were moving outside the union's jurisdiction, to the South. Sixteen southern states had passed right-to-work laws after the enactment of the 1947 Taft-Hartley Act, which severely weakened the power of organized labor to maintain and increase wages and improve working conditions; many industries moved south to take advantage of the open-shop provisions.

Clearly the ILGWU strategy to organize the industry from the top down made it difficult to build a more democratic union. The ILGWU, led largely by men, had a history of employing women to organize but then excluding them from the union's power structure. The more grassroots forms of organizing, where workers in individual firms mobilize others to sign union cards, has never had as much success as an organizing strategy in the small-scale and fragmented apparel industry as it has had in some other industries.

Efforts to organize apparel manufacturers or contractors on an individual basis in the South and other places was very difficult. First, the small southern towns to which apparel firms moved lacked a critical mass of producers. It was therefore not possible to organize from the top down. Second, even when apparel workers won union elections under such conditions, manufacturers or contractors often were unable to afford a union contract. In response to wage demands that could not be sustained, a marginally profitable firm had only undesirable choices with respect to its workers: the employer could "cheat" by paying workers less than union scale, go out of business, or move to another, lower wage area. Finally, as we have seen, the political environment of the South in particular was overtly hostile to unionization.

To sustain the type of unionization that was so successful in the apparel industry would have required the creation of disincentives for apparel firms to move to low-wage areas. Policy initiatives like the Taft-Hartley Act did just the opposite. Stephen Sylvia argues that the breakup of the labor-management accord in the apparel industry was due to the failure of the ILGWU's leadership to organize the South.[14] He states, quite rightly, that the union followed a policy of wage restraint in negotiations with New York employers as a way to discourage owners from moving out of town to lower wage areas where the organization was unable to enforce the union contract.

The movement of apparel firms to the South was virtually designed to weaken the labor-management accord that the ILGWU and the industry had made so successful in the Northeast. What had given the accord stability was the interdependent network of manufacturers and contractors that characterized the industry in the New York area. Incentives for manufacturers to move out of town to nonunion environments challenged the union's role as a conduit of labor, which had now become cheaper and more abundant elsewhere. When the Taft-Hartley Act created the opportunity to reduce the cost of labor, employers made use of it. In that sense, section 14(b) of the Taft-Harley Act encouraged the industry to become "footloose, as it helped to promote 'runaway shops.' "[15]

By the 1950s, apparel producers were being invited by the governments of small southern towns, desperately in need of jobs, to set up shop. In many of these towns, however, antiunion, local elites who supported a low-wage environment, dominated the political scene and found ways to pressure union organizers to leave town. As an increasing number of apparel producers moved out of town, especially to the South, the labor-management accord in the Northeast began to fall apart.

Efforts to organize textile unions in the South have never been successful. It is hardly surprising, then, that the ILGWU failed to organize apparel firms that began to open there in the 1950s. One could certainly fault the union for failing to put more resources into organizing at that time. Yet when we examine the evidence of the ILGWU's attempts to organize in the South, it appears that the leadership may have been unwilling to devote its resources to an effort that seemed a fruitless task.

The ILGWU did make some serious efforts in the 1950s to enforce the union contract in shops that had "run away." In one of these cases, that of a New York manufacturer who removed to a small rural southern community, the firm was prepared to honor its contractual obligations but was prevented from doing so. The owner of the firm made an initial effort to fulfill his contract with the union by honoring the wage commitment to the new workers. According to the *New York Times*, however, the community (local elites, townspeople, and even workers) initiated a campaign of violence against the ILGWU. Organizers later appeared on the scene in an unsuccessful attempt to rally the workers. The employer returned to New York to confer with David Dubinsky about reaching a compromise with the union in this seemingly impossible situation. Eventually the employer and Dubinsky agreed that the former would pay a significant fine to the union in lieu of honoring the labor contract.[16]

In 1954 the ILGWU also financed the purchase of an apparel plant in Appomattox, Virginia, at the cost of $40,000. A unionized New York apparel manufacturer had agreed to run it as a union shop.[17] According to the *New York Times*, the ILGWU was "doing this to combat what they think is 'unfair competition' by some southern cities in enticing new enterprises through 'bargain basement tactics' on the tax and labor front." In another example of creative labor strategies, the union gave a southern manufacturer three years of immunity from union organization when he consented to pay wages at least $.15 above the minimum wage.[18]

While the data on this issue is limited, the ILGWU strategy was to enforce the union contract in runaway shops, requiring that union manufacturers who moved out of town continue to pay union wages and employ union contractors. But trying to maintain this contractual arrangement in right-to-work states or in small southern towns like Birmingham, Alabama; Savannah, Baxley, and Appomattox, Georgia; Lynchburg, Virginia, and other small towns in the Carolinas where these firms moved was not generally successful in the face of extreme hostility to unions and the often violent efforts to destroy them. These efforts to organize in the 1950s and 1960s are not unlike the ones we are now seeing in apparel *maquiladoras* in Mexico and similar operations throughout the developing world.

In many of its efforts to sustain unionized shops, the ILGWU appealed to the National Labor Relations Board (NLRB) or to the courts to enforce their contractual relationship with the offending manufacturer or contractor. Yet while some of these efforts ended in court decisions upholding the union's position, runaway manufacturers and contractors found ways to continue avoiding the union.

In the 1950s and 1960s there was a large migration of African Americans and Puerto Ricans to New York City. Whites started leaving the central city for the suburbs. The mayor of New York, fearing the growth of an indigent population, appealed to employers and the Central Labor Council to increase wages in the city's manufacturing industries. However, the movement of industries, including the apparel industry, to the low-wage, right-to-work South made it hard to answer this appeal. Without incentives to keep manufacturing in New York, it became easier for labor-intensive apparel firms to move or open new plants out of town.

Federal requirements prohibiting union avoidance might have made it more difficult for the industry to leave New York. Indeed, as Sylvia himself argues, such a situation existed in the postwar Federal Republic of Germany. There, the national consensus supported unions, refusing to allow policies like open shops and right-to-work states. The Taft-Hartley Act and America's strong entrepreneurial values meant that in the United States neither business nor government was ever prepared to enjoin such a policy. With the industry's labor-intensity, its reliance on contracting out production, and the use of low-wage women's labor, the potential to move to low-wage areas offered manufacturers license to "run away." In 1954 a *New York Times* reporter commented on the federal role in this industrial change: "For both economic and political reasons it is unlikely that Uncle Sam will do much to put the brakes on the shift of industry or to outlaw any of the 'lures' that are being used in the Civil War on plants."[19] As a result of these trends, labor markets in the industry were reconstructed with incentives for moving apparel production to lower wage areas.

As firms pulled up stakes and left, the ILGWU saw the erosion of its membership base. Its new strategy of wage restraint—which had been intended to keep apparel firms in the New York area and save jobs at lower wages—was a bad bargain, one made in the context of major industrial changes that challenged the union's power. The bargain kept members subject to the union's jurisdiction and maintained the organizational unity of the ILGWU and the power of its leadership. But at best it was a flawed strategy, unable to prevent runaway shops or maintain wage equity among regions.

RUNNING AWAY TO EAST ASIA

Unlike America's textile producers, U.S. apparel producers had never suffered from low-wage import competition before World War II, not even from Europe. In fact, before it became policy, U.S. apparel manufacturers and both apparel unions had supported free trade. Theirs was a position based largely on principle—on the internationalist ideals embedded in social-democratic traditions. Low tariffs for consumer products also meant lower cost goods for American workers.[20]

In the early prewar period, apparel producers benefited from the low-cost imports of cotton textiles from Japan. However, just as they began to face runaway shops and the breakdown of the labor-management accord, Eisenhower's administration implemented the new East Asian foreign policy that would reduce textile tariffs in order to encourage Japanese textile imports. These imports included a small volume of low-wage apparel items assembled by Japanese workers in shops that contracted with American producers.

In the early 1950s, armed with samples of cotton blouses, U.S. producers went to Japan and contracted with Japanese manufacturers to produce them for export to the United States. They were sold in U.S. retail stores for one dollar each, while comparable blouses made in the United States cost consumers three to four dollars. These blouses were imported to the United States as early as 1947, when they began to enter U.S. markets. By 1954, with the end of hostilities in Korea, 171,000 cotton blouses were exported to the United States from Japan. A year later, the number had skyrocketed to 4 million dozen, accompanied by a variety of new apparel products in growing numbers. In 1956 shipments dropped to 2 million dozen as a result of voluntary export restraints, but were still about twelve times the 1954 level. Domestic production rose from 6.6 million to 10.8 million dozen. The growth rate of Japanese imports was higher than the domestic production rate.[21]

In 1957 another small decline in import growth provided a short respite from expanding increments of textile and apparel imports. This occurred because of the voluntary export restraints that Eisenhower negotiated with Japan. However, by 1959, apparel imports began to increase again—this time by 45 percent. Between 1947 and 1960 the volume of imports increased twelvefold.[22]

By the 1960s, producers in Hong Kong and Taiwan had also begun to mass-produce low-cost women's and children's clothing for export to U.S. markets. These products typically sold to bargain-basement retailers in cities of the American South. Much of the imported apparel was the result of the new practices by U.S. importers, retailers, and domestic apparel manufacturers who had begun to contract work to East Asian producers.[23] Such enterprising American importers, retailers, and apparel manufacturers became the first direct foreign competitors of U.S. apparel producers, most of whom were still making clothing for the American market at union wages in the New York City area. Thus, unionized producers suddenly found themselves competing with nonunion, low-wage producers not only in the South but also offshore at a fraction of the cost of U.S. producers.

As the Asian economies recovered from the war, Japan began to export its textiles to other countries in the region, particularly to Hong Kong. The Japanese also began to expand their investments in a vertically integrated textile and apparel industry. These textiles were used to make clothing for export to the United States.[24] Walter Forbes, during his 1960 visit to Hong Kong to see the textile competition that his industry faced abroad, was a witness to the expansion of this new Asian textile and apparel complex. In testimony before Congress he described Castle Peak Industries, a Japanese-owned apparel facility located in Hong Kong. Forbes said there had been a

> tremendous increase in the Hong Kong garment industry, to an estimated 100,000 sewing machines today (50,000 in plants and an estimated 50,000 in homes). Practically all of the garment industry's rapid growth has occurred since Japan adopted their voluntary quotas to the United States in 1956. . . . Seventy percent of the cotton cloth consumed in this Hong Kong garment industry in 1960 came from Japan, and Japanese firms are now buying garment factories and constructing new spinning and weaving plants in Hong Kong.

In describing Castle Peak, he said, "An inspection of this big garment plant revealed the entire plant had just been purchased by Japanese interests and was a well-run, even by U.S. standards, bundle-system operation, making sport shirts and pajamas consuming 35 million yards of cloth per year (primarily from Japan). Every case in the shipping room was consigned to Smithville, Tennessee, for distribution to the big American chainstores."[25] Forbes testified that textiles accounted for 68 percent of Hong Kong's total exports, which were primarily garments. Thus, Japan had avoided being locked into its voluntary export restraints by transferring its textile exports from the United States to Hong Kong and Taiwan. These fabrics were then made into clothing and exported to U.S. retailers.

Such arrangements—in which U.S. entrepreneurs contracted with East Asian textile and apparel makers, who assembled low-wage apparel for purchase by U.S. retailers—do not fit the model of exchange that writers like Adam Smith and David Ricardo describe. Although the Japanese had a history of exporting cheap textiles, some of which were sold in the United States, they had not exported clothing, and especially not Western clothing, before World War II. In a letter to the *New York Times* in 1959, Leo Ullman, the president of the Clothing Manufacturers' Association of America, the trade organization composed of manufacturers of men's tailored suits, wrote, "The Japanese consumer does not ordinarily purchase ready made tailored clothing. The new industry has been organized by so-called American entrepreneurs who have been setting up factories in foreign countries where sweatshop conditions prevail[,] for the sole purpose of exporting such garments to the United States."[26] Sylvia points out that this new import competition in the late 1950s was a mere 2 percent of the U.S. retail market—both in textiles and apparel.[27] He argues that its impact was not analogous to competition from the runaway shops that moved south. Industry and trade union leaders may have seen low-wage southern competitors at that point as more of a direct threat to the industry's health and to the strength of the labor-management contract. Yet this did not blind them to the new challenge posed by Asian contracting.

The process of trade liberalization, then, functioned in much the same way in East Asia as the Taft-Hartley Act in the American South, extending the range of U.S. capital mobility, by political fiat, to low-wage regions of the world. New York apparel manufacturers in the 1950s could open new factories in the South, benefit from lower labor costs, and avoid unions. Free trade allowed them to do the same in Hong Kong and Taiwan, to access even lower wage labor across national boundaries. If low-wage southern labor was an immediate threat to apparel producers and trade unionists, imports from lower wage countries overseas were even more of a threat in the long run.

The clarity with which American apparel producers saw the problem is demonstrated in a letter sent in 1961 by Jerome Asher, president of the Trouser Institute of America, to Lawrence Phillips, vice president of Phillips–Van Heusen, then a successful American shirtmaker. Asher wrote, "It would be quite possible for us to develop a line of slacks in Japan, Hong Kong, Formosa, Yugoslavia, and many other parts of the world, which in every respect would duplicate the product manufactured here. Even allow-ing for the various current import duties and the cost of transportation, we could undersell the domestic market by anywhere from 20 to 30 per-cent." His letter continues, "You can imagine what would happen if we were to open a warehouse in New York City or other key cities, offering this type of merchandise. In short order, little would be left of the Amer-ican pants industry."[28]

Phillips himself was among the staunchest apparel industry protection-ists of that time, and he testified prophetically in a 1961 hearing before the Pastore Committee, "The basic fear that hangs like a guillotine over the heads of domestic apparel producers is the potential further expansion of imports."[29] Lawrence's testimony continues, "We have great fears that what has happened in Hong Kong can easily be duplicated in many other areas; for example: South Korea, Taiwan, India, Pakistan, and maybe some-day even communist China, where there is no price on labor. There are numerous reports and rumors that preparations are being made in some or all of these countries to dip into the gravy bowl of the American mar-ket."

In 1963, imports of men's long-sleeve dress shirts constituted 8 percent of the total number of imported shirts sold; by 1972 they represented 30 percent of sales. In 1963, 14 percent of women's blouses were imported; by 1972 imported blouses represented 20 percent of all retail sales in vol-ume. By 1972 South Korea could produce and export to the United States men's long-sleeve dress shirts for sale at half the price of the same item produced in the United States.[30] Phillips–Van Heusen was soon to begin producing offshore. Today, it is a large, transnational apparel corporation. As a result of its contractors' alleged violations of labor standards in its Central American plants, the company has recently been a target of pro-tests against offshore sweatshops.

As early as the 1960s then, despite the low level of import penetration, American apparel producers were able to foresee the effect of offshore production on their industry. About twenty years later, Americans would see the reemergence of domestic sweatshops and new ones in the export-processing zones of East Asia and Central America.

THE EMERGENCE OF CONGRESSIONAL PROTECTIONISM

In the 1950s, as the textile makers began to demand protection, so did segments of the apparel industry, particularly manufacturers of products that competed directly with imports. The latter began to oppose tariff reductions as early as 1954.[31] By 1956, with the dramatic increase in the importation of cotton blouses, the National Association of Blouse Manufacturers voted to file a formal application for protection under the escape clause of the Trade Agreements Act.[32]

In the textile industry, the postwar surge of imports sparked a mobilization for trade protection in Congress, led by the American Cotton Manufacturers' Institute and joined by the textile workers' unions. The textile industry took the lead in the early years of the protectionist struggle for trade protection, since its power in Congress allowed it to threaten the administration's efforts to liberalize trade. The apparel industry, however, had virtually no political influence in Congress. The political power of the U.S. apparel industry in the years between 1950 and 1970 was centered in the Northeast, particularly in New York City and New York State.

Reciprocal trade and tariff reductions represented a paradigm shift in which the administration had changed the definition of fairness embedded in the previous understandings of the markets in these industries. The growth of state-of-the-art facilities in East Asia, like Castle Peak, was a dramatic example of this problem. In a government that favored policies making the industry increasingly footloose, apparel makers and their workers both saw a long-term threat. They rejected the sacrifice they were being asked to make in the interests of American security.

As apparel imports from East Asia began to arrive in the United States in noticeable numbers, both apparel producers and trade unionists in the apparel industry started to ally themselves with conservative textile manufacturers to promote a trade regime of higher tariffs and quotas on the new low-wage imports. By 1960, five apparel trade associations had formed the Apparel Industry Committee against Imports and had joined with apparel unions and the textile industry in asking Congress to urge trade protection. Indeed, while the ILGWU was vociferous in its denunciation of imports and its demands for protection, the Amalgamated Clothing Workers of America (ACWA)—the union that organized the men's clothing industry—initially took much bolder action in its attack on imports. In July 1959, at its yearly convention, the union adopted a resolution to oppose imports, and it demanded federal legislation to implement import controls. The ACWA proclaimed it would "join employers in the apparel field and other needle trades unions to seek legislative controls over goods produced in 'sweatshop' conditions in the Orient."[33]

The Amalgamated's protectionist position represented a drastic change from its original internationalism, a position it had shared with the ILGWU, and that had motivated the union to support the Eisenhower administration's liberal trade program. Now Jacob Potofsky, the Amalgamated's president, justified his apparent turnaround by saying that the Amalgamated was not opposed to the reciprocal trade program, but that the program had never been intended for "destroying an important American industry by unfair competition from sweated labor abroad."[34] Potofsky also claimed that imports were the result of American business efforts, of "large mail order houses, merchandising chains and department stores" who were seeking "a quick profit on cheap labor."[35]

The men's clothing industry, where more of the workers were men and were skilled tailors, was also beginning to suffer from import competition, although it did not employ as many outside contractors as the women's garment industry. According to Potofsky's testimony, the Amalgamated represented 385,000 workers in forty-one states in an industry employing over a million workers. At that point, most of the industry was employed making tailored suits, overcoats, topcoats, and sport jackets. However, when the Japanese started exporting men's tailored suits composed of wool and man-made fibers to the United States, the Amalgamated began to experience some of the same concerns as the industry's manufacturers. In 1959, Potofsky echoed the response of Leo Ullman, the head of the Clothing Manufacturers' Association. Potofsky said in his testimony, "Japan ha[d] begun to ship readymade tailored clothing to this country, and Hong Kong [was] developing a mail order business with the United States in made to measure tailored clothing."

Potofsky, like textile protectionists, saw the inevitability of import growth, even with only a 2 percent rate of import penetration. He described the effects of imports on the behavior of retailers—who, thirty years later, would help generate the reemergence of apparel sweatshops. Potofsky said,

> A relatively small volume of imports is highly disruptive. Most men's and boys' wear is promoted and sold at retail in this country in terms of price apparel. When a retail outlet undersells his competitors on the basis of imports from low wage countries, the competing retailers immediately demand equivalent price concessions from their domestic suppliers, and shop for them from manufacturer to manufacturer. When domestic manufacturers find that they are losing accounts to competition from abroad which they cannot possibly meet, they are under pressure to dilute quality, to lower wages, and to develop their own import sources. When any firm is forced out of business by import competition, the market is demoralized by uncertainty and fear.

He argued that the clothing imports were creating the same problem for his industry that imports were creating for U.S. textile manufacturers.

Like textiles, the men's clothing industry was limited by a narrow price margin. Competition from East Asia was already causing domestic manufacturers to cut costs, modernize domestic plants and equipment, and develop more efficient strategies of production. Yet Potofsky was not optimistic about the potential for advanced technology to stanch the influx of low-wage imports. He could foresee the advent of technological parity between the United States and offshore producers eventually eliminating the productivity advantages new technology might offer American industry.[36] Advanced technology would not permit—in either the long run or the short run—the U.S. apparel industry to compete with low-wage imports.

In an era before the "jeaning of America," when more men wore suits to work, men's tailored clothing represented a significantly larger segment of the apparel industry than it does today. The industry faced a steep reduction of its already low profit margins, and more bankruptcies. While much of the immediate problem was due to domestic competition, as it was in the women's garment and textile industries, men's clothing imports further limited the industry's freedom to generate an acceptable ratio of wages and profits—a major problem for this labor-intensive industry.

When Hong Kong, unlike Japan, refused to agree to voluntary export restraints, Potofsky announced that the Amalgamated would seek trade restraints on clothing and apparel imports. David Dubinsky, president of the ILGWU, joined him in announcing the ILGWU's support for import restraints.

Only a year later, in 1960, the Japanese sent 120,000 ready-made suits to the United States, after making an unofficial commitment to send only 25,000 to 30,000. Potofsky, after consulting with his members, threatened direct action by the union.[37] When the Japanese industry refused to agree to a new export-restraint agreement on suits, the Amalgamated unanimously voted for a boycott. A call went out to members not to cut or sew any textiles made in Japan.

Despite the sympathies of the new Democrat in the White House, John F. Kennedy rebuked Potofsky.[38] However, even more telling was the fury of Nelson A. Stitt, president of the U.S.-Japan Trade Council, who cautioned that this act could lead the union to find itself in legal and political difficulties. Stitt urged the industry "to proceed with care lest it find itself in trouble with the Justice Department, the NLRB and the Federal Trade Commission."[39]

THE KENNEDY COMPROMISE

Protectionists found it difficult to negotiate with either the Truman or the Eisenhower administration. Both administrations in the effort to pursue a policy of communist containment legitimated reciprocal trade and pressed for the opening of U.S. markets to East Asian textile and apparel imports. Truman and Eisenhower, and the trade-liberalizing businessmen who supported them, told Americans that imports represented only a small fraction of domestic production; that imports competed with only a limited segment of America's textile and apparel industries; and that, because of their poor quality, imported products would not, in the long run, be competitive with higher quality American products and, therefore, would not injure U.S. producers.

Yet the growing power of the protectionists in Congress made Kennedy worry that protectionists would thwart his efforts to negotiate tariff reductions in Europe. Kennedy offered to compromise with the textile and apparel industries,[40] and he put forward a program to support industrial restructuring and a quota regime to regulate imports. Ultimately, neither of these programs prevented the migration of the industry to low-wage countries.

TRADE PROTECTION

The quota regimes for textiles and apparel—the Short-Term and Long-Term Arrangements in the early 1960s and the Multifibre Arrangement (MFA), in effect from 1974 to 1994—have often been seen as political compromises with special interest groups. The industries themselves have been described as overprotected and as beneficiaries of a unique system of import protection not available to other industries. These special trade regimes for textiles and apparel, however, were never designed to protect textile or apparel producers from the expansion of low-wage imports. They were implemented instead to slow down the rate of import growth and to moderate the flow of imports to U.S. retailers and consumers.[41] The real objective of the Short-Term, Long-Term, and Multifibre Arrangements, as Robert Kuttner argues, was to "manage trade."[42] Indeed, the officially stated goal of the MFA was "to achieve the expansion of trade, the reduction of barriers to such trade and the progressive liberalization of world trade in textile products." Its purpose was also "to further the economic and social development of developing countries and secure a substantial increase in their export earnings from textile products and to provide for a greater share for them in world trade in these products."[43]

William R. Cline, a neoclassical economist, advocate of freer trade, and opponent of the Multifibre Arrangement (MFA), sees the quota regime as having distorted market forces. In 1987 and 1990, in a revised edition of his well-known book *The Future of World Trade in Textiles and Apparel*, he argues that the MFA should be abolished. Yet despite his opposition to protection, even he recognizes that the MFA has never been able to protect the industry from increasing imports.[44] As he puts it, "Protection under the MFA acts as a semipermeable screen that impedes imports but nonetheless does not fully stop their more rapid entry when the underlying economic forces intensify import pressures." Had protection been the objective of Kennedy's 1960s trade initiatives, annual import levels might have been pegged at a certain percentage of U.S. market share and linked to rates of U.S. market growth, as both the textile industry and the trade union movement in the apparel industry had initially advocated.[45]

The main function of the MFA was to balance the needs of developing countries for export markets with the needs of the United States and other industrialized countries to regulate the rate at which imports of textiles and apparel expanded. Both the Long-Term Arrangement, in 1962, and the Multifibre Arrangement, in 1974, required bilateral negotiations between importing and exporting nations to set import quotas. Such negotiations would lead to agreements that specified which products made in exporting countries could be sold in U.S. markets and in what quantities. This allowed U.S. negotiators to influence the export volumes of developing countries through quota regulations. The importance of access to the U.S. market meant that bilateral negotiations also provided a means for the United States to influence the policies of developing countries through the allocation of quotas.

When Kennedy introduced the initial quota regime for textiles and apparel, both the Short-Term and Long-Term Arrangements were designed to regulate imports from Taiwan, Hong Kong, and South Korea. His Seven-Point Program was enacted primarily at the behest of the American Cotton Manufacturers' Institute; it created a quota regime that regulated only cotton textiles and apparel made with cotton textiles.[46] There were no quotas for textiles and apparel made with the newly developed and increasingly popular man-made fibers, which in the 1960s and early 1970s were being produced in Japan and used to manufacture clothing in Hong Kong, Taiwan, and South Korea. Therefore, as the U.S. government proceeded with its program of tariff reductions, the "polyester revolution" of the 1970s dramatically increased imports of apparel made with man-made fibers. It was only in 1974 that the Multifibre Arrangement was negotiated by President Nixon, imposing a quota regime that covered textiles and apparel composed of man-made fibers.[47]

Indeed, even as protective legislation was enacted, exporting countries developed a wide variety of strategies to avoid the quota restrictions.[48] As David B. Yoffie puts it, "The exporting nations had to upgrade, diversify, bargain for their short run needs, and/or cheat."[49] The first quotas set by the Short-Term Arrangement in 1961, as well as by the agreements that followed, were defined by the quantity of items to be exported rather than the price of each item. Since the quotas were initially set at existing export volumes, America's East Asian contractors tried to maximize their exports just before this quota regime went into effect. Until then, Asian contractors had made a practice of exporting both textiles and apparel. With a quota limit, they recognized that the higher value of apparel products, as compared to textiles, would make it more profitable to export apparel, and they began to focus on apparel exports.

The early East Asian exports of apparel were initially standardized, mass-produced, low-value-added merchandise sold in bargain-basement stores. Soon foreign producers began to realize they could increase the value of their exports by making higher quality, higher-value-added women's "fashion products."[50] As American women began to enter the labor force in large numbers in the 1970s, East Asian manufacturers began producing an increasing amount of "career wear" and sportswear for export.

Quota regimes for textiles and apparel have always included language allowing domestic producers to appeal for protection from "import injuries," "import surges," and "market disruptions." Yet, for the most part, U.S. agencies charged with enforcement of MFA regulations could only react to these surges by reducing quota increases for the coming year. Therefore, importing countries could not stabilize or reduce the overall volume of imports over the years by pushing them back to the status quo ante.

According to MFA regulations, a new exporting country was given no quota limits until textile and apparel imports from that country began to exceed certain established levels. At that point, an overall quota limit was negotiated, with a maximum allowable 6 percent overall annual increase. Originally, the countries belonging to the Association of Southeast Asian Nations (ASEAN) had no quotas and had cheaper labor costs than the

Newly Industrializing Countries (NICs) (Hong Kong, Taiwan, and South Korea). This encouraged producers in the latter nations to subcontract production to the ASEAN countries for export to the United States. While the NICs remained the largest suppliers until the mid-1980s, producers in the ASEAN countries soon began to expand their own exports.[51] As sites for apparel production grew, export levels grew faster than projected. Indeed, total U.S. imports expanded faster than the increase in domestic demand and accounted for a larger and larger proportion of domestic consumption.[52] As figure 1 shows, apparel imports have been increasing since the early 1960s and have grown even more dramatically since the early 1980s.

By the mid-1970s the energy crisis, two oil shocks, and increased federal spending precipitated by the Vietnam War led to rising prices, sluggish growth, and stagnating wages.[53] By 1973 the Kennedy Round of tariff cuts and an overvalued dollar that reduced the ability of America's industries to export had undercut the U.S. trade surplus; a sizeable deficit emerged. Since then, the apparel trade deficit has continued to increase steadily.

DISPLACED WORKERS

Trade liberalization and the growth of imports dramatically increased the number of workers displaced from their jobs. President Kennedy recognized the need to compensate these workers and, as part of his Trade Expansion Act, instituted the Trade Adjustment Assistance Program for displaced workers. This program incorporated several programs: a compensation program, retraining program, and relocation allowances program. Like earlier programs, the Trade Adjustment Assistance Program fell short of providing the necessary financial compensation and services required by, and promised to, those who lost their jobs. Indeed, since 1961, when the program was implemented, it has not served workers well. Just as the quota regimes of the Short-Term and Long-Term Arrangements failed to protect U.S. apparel makers and their employees from low-wage competition, the Trade Adjustment Assistance Program has aided only a small fraction of displaced workers. It never provided workers with adequate retraining for new jobs or effective relocation assistance. In fact, the promises of this legislation have been honored more in the breach than in practice.

Trade Adjustment Assistance has failed to compensate women apparel workers. The rules of the program required that workers be certified as eligible. Eligible workers could then receive between 65 and 75 percent of

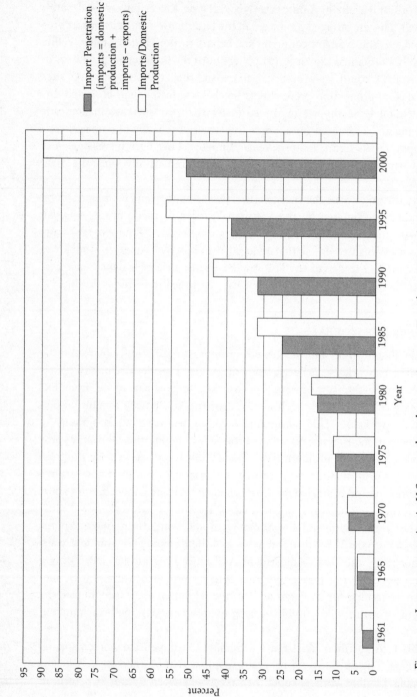

Figure 1. Import penetration in U.S. apparel products, 1961–2000. Data from *U.S. Industrial Outlook*, various years, 1961–2000 (SIC 23). Figure revised from Robert S. J. Ross, Ellen I. Rosen, and Karen Mc-Cormack, "The Global Context of the New Sweatshops," paper given at the Annual Meeting of the Society for the Study of Social Problems, New York, 1996.

their former wages for fifty-two weeks, considerably more than they could receive as recipients of unemployment insurance benefits, which lasted for only twenty-six weeks. Such payments could also be supplemented by additional support for training and by relocation assistance. However, funding for income assistance under the Trade Adjustment Assistance Program began only in 1970 and did not reach a significant level until 1975. After that, the numbers of displaced apparel workers receiving benefits under this program grew substantially until 1981. Between 1981 and 1985, apparel imports increased dramatically. Yet just as the cost of this program rose, the federal government opted out of its commitment to displaced workers.

As president, Ronald Reagan made it increasingly difficult for workers to receive benefits. In the Job Training Partnership Act of 1982, he tightened the eligibility criteria, allowing the administration to reduce funding for the compensation, retraining, and relocation allowances programs. The number of workers certified as eligible to receive support went from 88 percent to 14 percent. Between 1981 and 1987 smaller amounts of funding remained available; this funding was used largely for job retraining and relocation assistance rather than for income assistance.[54]

Most studies that have analyzed the sufficiency of these benefits and retraining programs show that displaced workers were seriously underserved. Short-term training produced few transferable skills, and workers were often reemployed at substantially lower wages. Moreover, even from 1975 to 1981, the years of highest benefits, displaced women apparel workers, despite their overrepresentation among women production workers, got only a tiny fraction of the support available. The bulk of the resources for all these programs throughout the years since 1970 went to workers in the auto, steel, and machinery industries, where the workforce was predominantly male.[55]

Earlier generations of women apparel workers had typically been young and unmarried. Most left their jobs to marry and have families. During the 1970s and 1980s, however, married women reentered the workforce. After being displaced from their jobs, most could not afford to leave the paid workforce to return to the role of homemaker, though many policy makers simply took for granted that they could do so. By the mid-to late 1970s, when layoffs in this industry began in earnest, U.S. wages and family incomes had begun to stagnate. America's mature female apparel workers at that time were typically middle-aged women who now needed paid jobs to help maintain their families or to support themselves. Many of these women were married to men likely to be displaced from jobs themselves. Such women and their families were likely to experience stagnating or reduced earnings.[56] They had very few options for reemployment at comparable wages.

Much of America's textile production and apparel assembly has been located in urban immigrant communities or rural areas, where the only employers are clothing or textile factories. Studies of displaced women apparel workers in the United States show that they have had the longest periods of unemployment and the most unfavorable reemployment options compared to other, typically male, manufacturing workers.[57]

STRUCTURAL ADJUSTMENT

In response to the growth of apparel imports, some producers embraced industrial restructuring in the hope that this would make their domestic-production capabilities more competitive with low-wage imports. As we have seen, in the 1960s U.S. textile producers were able to modernize their production facilities and benefit from the economies of scale so important to a mass-production industry. Apparel producers have not been able to do the same.

Both apparel and textile producers were entitled to funds for industrial restructuring as provided by the Trade Expansion Act of 1962. They were both eligible for tax-depreciation benefits. But textile producers were in a much better position to utilize these resources to restructure their plants. Moreover, their growing profitability in the 1970s was also a consequence of mergers and acquisitions that led to their increased consolidation and concentration. By 1974 the U.S. textile industry once more had a favorable balance of trade.

The apparel industry was not as successful in incorporating technology. Despite serious efforts to automate apparel manufacture, the inability to submit the sewing process to a "hard technology"—to make it more capital-intensive—forced the industry to rely on the traditionally labor-intensive sewing process.[58] As a result, the production of apparel continues to depend on contracting production and the use of women's low-wage labor. This has been a fundamental barrier to a more technologically sophisticated form of industrial restructuring that has transformed other manufacturing industries.

Kennedy's tax depreciation initiative had limited value for apparel producers; nevertheless, by the 1960s they had begun to spend more on new technology than they had in the past, particularly on automated sewing, cutting, and pattern-making technology. Such investments enhanced productivity. But the apparel industry spent only 40 percent of what the textile industry spent on new technology. By the 1980s the apparel industry was still investing less on technological change than textile producers were. According to Lauren A. Murray, textile companies were "spending $23 billion, or 4 percent of the industry's value of shipments, while the apparel industry spent only $8 billion, or 1.5 percent of that industry's value of shipments. In addition, the apparel industry directed only half of those expenditures to new equipment, while the textiles industry spent three-fourths of its outlays on new equipment."[59] Apparel producers using new technologies did enjoy significant productivity gains, but their increased productivity was not as high as in other industries.

Two explanations have been offered. The first is that the apparel industry was fragmented, and firms were typically small and had less access to financing than textile firms did. Second, although the new apparel technologies that became available were not as costly as new textile machinery, neither were they as laborsaving. Even today, it has not become possible to automate the industry.[60] There is as yet no known apparel-assembling technology more efficient than human hands or more cost-effective than limiting employment to a large, low-paid female workforce. Over the past forty years, neither publicly supported efforts nor private corporate efforts to develop cost-and labor-saving technology in apparel production have been able to reduce the labor-intensity of sewing technology.

In the 1980s, the introduction of quick-response, flexible manufacturing, and modular manufacturing techniques were initially seen as promising greater production efficiencies. Yet the productivity increases made possible by these changes have never been great enough to permit the industry to abandon the low-wage alternative. These technologies are still labor-intensive and can easily be transferred abroad. Other technological innovations, particularly those in transport and communication, further enhanced the footloose tendency of the apparel industry,[61] making it easier for producers to overcome the barriers of time and distance. The ability to relocate in lower wage regions of the country or world has, of course, been accelerated by growing industry support for a freer trade agenda.

Between 1960 and 1980, apparel production expanded to new countries throughout the world. By the early 1980s more than a hundred countries were exporting their apparel to the American market. Trade protection could not prevent an apparel-trade deficit.[62] Between 1974 and 1981, the U.S. trade deficit in apparel reached $7 billion.

Apparel produced offshore by American transnationals has also become a larger and larger proportion of domestic apparel consumption. Between

1973 and 1992 the textile and apparel industries lost 750,000 jobs, almost half the number that existed at the peak level of employment.[63] As workers lost jobs, organizing became more difficult, leaving the apparel trade unions unable to sustain their power to negotiate decent wages. This in turn led working conditions to deteriorate and the unions to lose their membership. It is hardly surprising, then, that as the viability of domestic production became increasingly problematic, many apparel industry leaders began to abandon domestic production and seek trade regulations that made it easier and less costly for them to move their production to lower wage areas.

In the early postwar decades, particularly during the Kennedy and Johnson years, it was more acceptable than it is now to argue that the federal government should bear responsibility for promoting a high-wage, full-employment economy and a social contract. But even in such a context, as early as 1961 the president of the American Cotton Manufacturers' Institute quoted Secretary of State George Ball as saying, "The problem is to find a way to shift American manpower as swiftly and painlessly as possible, out of the industries which cannot stand up to foreign competition into those which have stood the test."[64] As Johnson's Great Society programs were put into place, the president's economic advisors were advocating an approach to trade that would soon lead to deindustrialization and the flight of America's manufacturing industries to lower wage countries.

The transfer of large parts of industrial production to low-wage countries required the creation and acceptance of a new theoretical paradigm justifying greater liberalization of trade. A new set of political strategies was required to promote this objective and convince Americans that tariffs and quotas were distortions and barriers to trade. These views did not begin to gain acceptance until late in the presidency of Ronald Reagan, as the protectionist coalition finally lost its power in Congress.

Between 1980 and 1985, as apparel producers increased their offshore sourcing and imports grew dramatically, textile industrialists, domestic apparel manufacturers, and the apparel unions continued to fight for import controls and against Reagan's efforts to further reduce tariffs.[65] Apparel imports continued to climb. With the veto of the Jenkins-Hollings bill, to be discussed in the next chapter, all subsequent administrations, both Republican and Democratic, became poised for a new spurt of global trade-liberalizing initiatives. A new international textile, apparel, and retail complex was poised to expand. We now turn to an exploration of this change and what it accomplished during the Reagan years.

The 1980s
The Demise of Protection

THE REAGAN ERA

Ronald Reagan's tenure in the White House marked a turning point in the liberalization of trade and the development of free market initiatives. His administration challenged the legitimacy of trade protection and undermined the power of the trade protectionists. Indeed, during his administration the protectionist agenda was eliminated as a force in the formation of trade policy and replaced by the neoliberal agenda. As a result Reagan began to implement the new free trade agenda. He started with the Caribbean Basin Economic Recovery Act. Bush continued with the Enterprise for the Americas Initiative, and Clinton with the North American Free Trade Agreement. These paved the way for a new type of United States–dominated trade and investment regime with Latin America, and laid the foundations for a new round of trade liberalization that was to culminate in the termination of the GATT and the emergence of the World Trade Organization.

Increasingly, these policies were supported by the expanding transnational corporations involved in apparel merchandising and retailing. The new trade-liberalizing accords of the 1980s would expand the sites for the export processing of apparel in the Western Hemisphere. But perhaps most important, they would lay the groundwork for the completion of trade liberalization—the ending of the GATT and the Multifibre Arrangement—and the phaseout of quotas on textiles and apparel.

By the 1980s, the United States was no longer the world's primary manufacturer and exporter of goods. The country had begun to face new economic competition in a capitalist environment in which three major capitalist power blocs contended for new markets and investment opportunities. These blocs included the United States, as the leader of the Western Hemisphere; the European Economic Community and East Asian countries, now dominated by a resurgent Japan; and the NICs and the People's Republic of China.

By 1980 there had been two oil crises, a worldwide recession, a dramatic growth of foreign investment in the United States, and a crisis in U.S. manufacturing that was leading to a "new international division of labor" that was contributing to the "deindustrialization of America."[1] Or, as some would have it, an overvalued dollar was leading to growing imports of products like autos, steel, electronic equipment, and apparel from America's new industrial competitors. As U.S. exports declined, the United States experienced its first major trade deficit since 1917.[2] Economic analysts argued that the United States was facing a crisis of competitiveness. Sluggish economic growth and reduced profitability in the advanced capitalist countries were driving multinationals to promote the flow of capital beyond national boundaries—to seek new investment opportunities, particularly in developing countries. Foreign direct investment quadrupled between 1980 and 1990, as developing countries received an increasing proportion of the total share of that investment.[3]

Reagan's response to these conditions was to encourage corporate America's support for an antiregulatory and competitive market approach to doing business in the new global environment. In the earliest days of his administration, he made efforts to dismantle New Deal and Great Society programs. Such programs, which had given legitimacy to labor rights and had created a tradition of government responsibility for the socially and economically disenfranchised, had become considerably weakened since the 1960s. Now Reagan began an ideological campaign that emphasized the salience of individual rather than public responsibility for the welfare of the disenfranchised and impoverished.[4]

An heir of the post–World War II, hard-line, "cold warriors," Reagan began his first term in office by calling the Soviet Union an "evil empire" and making his Strategic Defense Initiative ("Star Wars") a political priority. Early in his administration, he summarily dismissed striking air-traffic-control workers, sending the message that the Reagan administration would applaud a new corporate challenge to existing labor laws and reduction of employment and wages. During this period there was a new wave of union busting, now implicitly licensed by a new National Labor Relations Board appointed by the administration.

Reagan retained a new group of economic advisors who began a campaign to resuscitate a nineteenth-century version of economic liberalism or, as it is often called, neoliberalism. Writers like George Gilder and professional economists like Milton Friedman urged a new policy of freeing

up markets, both national and international—a policy of industry dereg-
ulation and privatization, soon to be called "trickle-down economics."

TRADE LIBERALIZATION AND DOMESTIC POLITICS

To get reelected, Reagan, like his political predecessors, needed the votes
of Southern Democrats and Democratic congressmen, many of whom were
stalwart members of the protectionist coalition. As Nixon had done, Reagan made a formal commitment to aid the textile industry in order to get
their support. Yet Reagan's neoliberal views were at odds with the agenda
of the textile industry and congressional protectionists.

Despite the campaign promises he had made in response to the demands
of the textile interests, Reagan, a consummate politician, used a mixture
of coercion, reward, and incentives. But he also needed to deal with the
new transnational corporations in retailing and apparel importing. They
now favored freer access to low-wage, offshore production and the opening
of markets abroad. Although he responded to pressure by textile producers
to reduce textile and apparel quotas for Asian countries, he also found
ways to enforce the Multifibre Arrangement (MFA) in ways consistent
with the free trade agenda.

Reagan supported the enforcement of quota regulation and negotiated
reductions in the quota of East Asian apparel exporters. However, his administration also played politics with the MFA, encouraged imports from
the People's Republic of China, and vetoed major protectionist legislation.
The power of the protectionists, however, led Reagan to a new compromise
with the textile interests, but one that ultimately furthered the process of
trade liberalization for textiles and apparel.

Apparel imports had expanded rapidly between 1960 and 1980. During
the years of Reagan's presidency, 1981–88, they grew faster than ever
before (figure 1). In 1981 the value of apparel imported to the United States
was $7.75 billion, representing 17.6 percent of the U.S. consumer apparel
market. By 1988 the value of apparel imports had almost tripled, to $22.4
billion.[5] Clothing made at low-wage sites now comprised a larger share of
clothing sold in American retail stores. Apparel imports also represented
a large proportion of the growing U.S. trade deficit, a deficit that was
starting to provoke concern on Wall Street, on Capitol Hill, and particularly among U.S. textile and apparel producers.[6]

By 1983, textile and apparel imports from the Big Three—South Korea,
Taiwan, and Hong Kong—and other Asian countries in the region represented more than 80 percent of U.S. textile and apparel imports.[7] Textile

protectionists now claimed that these countries were no longer poor and undeveloped—it was no longer necessary for them to have special quota assurances to promote America's security in Asia.

However, the People's Republic of China was becoming a threat to the U.S. textile industry. Nixon had "reopened" China in the early 1970s. The PRC had not joined the Multifibre Arrangement, but China nevertheless had signed a trade agreement with the United States in 1980 and a second one in 1983, treaties that reversed a thirty-year period of cold war hostility and reopened U.S. markets to Chinese exports.[8] A significant portion of these exports was made up of textiles and apparel. Indeed, China now vied with the Big Three for access to U.S. markets. By the 1980s, China had been spending heavily for years on new textile technology, making its textile and apparel industries increasingly competitive with those of the United States.

A considerable part of the U.S. textile industry had focused on marketing to the "standard" apparel producers, using capital-intensive technologies to mass-produce fibers and fabrics for items like underwear, sleepwear, trousers, blue jeans, shirts, and other sewn products.[9] In the early 1980s this segment of the U.S. textile industry found itself competing heavily with the Big Three; it also saw that there would be even more intense competition with the PRC in the future. Although China was still twenty years behind the developed countries in textile technology, U.S. textile producers expected the PRC to fully modernize its textile and apparel industries.

Like other industrialized countries, the PRC found ways to manipulate the quota regime. However, unlike other countries, China's government during this period unofficially encouraged exporters to use fake visas to send illegal shipments of clothing to the United States, which led to the growth of low-cost Chinese textile and apparel products.

To make clear their opposition to the new Asian competition, in 1982 the American Textile Manufacturers' Institute (ATMI) filed a countervailing duty petition against thirteen nations. ATMI claimed that these countries "unfairly subsidized their exports of textiles and apparel to the United States," and it urged the U.S. government to impose retaliatory tariffs on this foreign merchandise.[10]

By the 1980s, a large and elaborate federal bureaucracy had developed to administer the Multifibre Arrangement. On December 16, 1983, to fulfill his promise to the southern textile interests, Reagan signaled the U.S. Trade Representative to take action to control the market disruption caused by recent surges in textile and apparel imports.[11] The Committee for the

Implementation of Textile Agreements (CITA) was now responsible for monitoring the textile and apparel trade and responded to the quota violations by issuing "calls," actions that placed sixty-to-ninety-day moratoriums on textile and apparel imports that had reached or exceeded the negotiated quotas.[12] Reagan also ordered new curbs on textile and apparel imports from the exporting countries in East Asia, including Taiwan, Hong Kong, South Korea, and the People's Republic of China.

As the Big Three began to reduce their exports to the United States, China's textiles and apparel exports increased. Consequently, the balance of U.S. imports shifted from Hong Kong, Taiwan, and South Korea to the PRC. Big Three manufacturers also began to subcontract in China, increasing the volume of apparel exports that were "made" in China. If the goal was to reduce imports from East Asia, these new quota regimes were only moderately successful. While apparel exports from the Big Three declined or even remained stable, exports from all these countries together continued to grow at substantial, if somewhat slower, rates.

By 1985 the PRC was strongly resisting new efforts to negotiate import reductions with the United States; talks between CITA and the Chinese government bogged down, dragging on until the end of 1987. During this period the Chinese government continued to encourage illegal transshipments. At first the U.S. Customs Service claimed, with some reason, a lack of resources to monitor these imports. Finally, the administration pressed the department to seize them through its right of embargo.[13] The PRC threatened retaliation. In response to protectionist demands and flagrant treaty violations, Washington officially cut Chinese quotas in key garment and textile products in retaliation of its own for continuing violations of the GATT.

ADMINISTERING THE MULTIFIBRE ARRANGEMENT

Reagan had publicly supported the textile industry's countervailing duty petition in his early years in the White House, taking a stand in favor of quota enforcement in line with the MFA. He had reduced textile and apparel quotas for Asian countries. Reagan was nevertheless able to use the institutional framework that had been designed to implement the MFA, in ways that were consistent with his trade-liberalizing objectives and consistent with the expansion of trade in textiles and apparel.

The United States did not interpret its MFA obligations as a mandate to protect its textile and apparel industries.[14] Just as in the past, the State and Commerce Departments continued to make trade policy in the interests of what was defined as the nation's "overall" interests.[15] Indeed, there is evidence that, under the Reagan administration, the State and Commerce Departments could use the apparatus of CITA to interpret the MFA regulations and America's MFA obligations in ways that helped promote policies consistent with their trade liberalizing agenda.[16] The rapid growth of apparel imports in the 1980s, then, was not simply the result of market forces, or even of officially agreed-upon quota accords, but was in large part made possible by the political and economic concerns of the administration.

CITA's role in this policy is clarified by the 1985 testimony of Walter C. Lenahan, Reagan's Deputy Assistant Secretary for Textiles and Apparel, and the chair of CITA. Lenahan testified before Congress that CITA's obligation was to determine when a country's imports were causing market disruption. Such a determination required that the "State Department advises [sic] that country that we would like to consult with a . . . view to reaching mutual agreement on quota."[17] It was then up to CITA to monitor the country's import levels and make such a determination. Lenahan's job was to conduct an investigation and submit recommendations for action to CITA, which was composed of representatives from the Departments of Commerce, State, Labor, and Treasury and the U.S. Trade Representative's office.[18] Lenahan told Congress that CITA had implemented an additional two hundred quota actions as a result of calls. He also said that twenty new quotas had been put in place through negotiations: "I believe we are beginning to see the fruits of those quota actions, because analysis of the most recent import data—that is, over the last four to six months—indicates a substantial decline in the level of trade from those countries and from a few other principal suppliers subject to quota action."[19]

Yet, despite the increased number of calls made by CITA in previous months, and despite the agency's negotiations of tighter quota limits with East Asian exporting countries, textile and apparel imports between 1986 and 1990 continued to rise dramatically. According to his own testimony, Lenahan himself did not have independent authority to make decisions about trade policy. His testimony indicates that his role was to transmit CITA's decisions to the Department of Commerce and the State Department, where decisions about CITA's recommendations would be made at the highest levels of the administration.

In 1985, Lenahan and the chief textile negotiator, Richard H. Imus, were called to testify at congressional hearings convened to investigate alleged MFA violations.[20] Although lengthy, the following testimony is useful here to show how the Reagan administration could limit CITA's regulatory power when it chose to do so, politically shaping what was ostensibly an administrative decision. Imus stated, "Policy is the primary responsibility of the U.S. Trade Representative, and is developed by him in concert with his Cabinet colleagues. In most cases that I have been aware of, the basic policy decisions have been made at that level in either the Trade Policy Committee or in a similar group, called the Textile Trade Policy Group." According to Imus, Lenahan, who was then chairman of CITA, had "the responsibility to monitor imports and to monitor the domestic industry, and to make a determination when those imports are disrupting or are threatening to disrupt domestic production." In this hearing Lenahan testified that "if, the chairman [Lenahan] believes, based on analysis presented by his staff, that disruption has occurred or that there is a risk of disruption, then he will submit a recommendation for action to the committee, the committee being comprised of Commerce, State, the U.S. Trade Representative, Labor and Treasury. And the Committee will then decide whether it is appropriate to take action to control those specific imports from a specific source." Typically, the United States follows up a call by CITA by requesting the importing country to resolve the matter through negotiations.

Lenahan was then questioned by the protectionist congressman Ed Jenkins about how CITA made decisions to issue calls. Lenahan replied that after a discussion of the issues, the five members of the committee made a decision based on majority vote. When Jenkins asked him whether the record of these votes was open for the committee's inspection, Lenahan replied, "I don't have it available with me. I would have to discuss with my Undersecretary the appropriateness of providing it."

Jenkins pressed the issue asking, "Has State ever refused, to your knowledge, to carry out a directive from the Chairman of CITA instructing it to make a call?" Lenahan responded, "Yes sir!" Jenkins then asked what happened when the State Department refused to allow a call made by the committee. Lenahan replied, "In some instances State has changed its position; in other instances, it has not."

> JENKINS: Does State have veto power, more or less?
>
> LENAHAN: I won't say whether or not they have a veto power. I will say that they have chosen not to take action.

After some additional parrying back and forth, Congressman Sam Gibbons entered the dialogue, pressing this issue by asking, "Did I understand you correctly to say that on no voted call had State refused? Is that correct?"

LENAHAN: Not to my knowledge, sir.

GIBBONS: But apparently the President gave you, as Chairman of CITA, certain authority to make a call, is that right?

LENAHAN: Under the terms of the White House directive of December 16, 1983, I am empowered under certain circumstances to authorize calls on our three biggest suppliers.

GIBBONS: And those are the kinds of calls that State has sometimes vetoed, is that right?

LENAHAN: Well, they have declined to transmit the message.

At that point Congressman Carroll Campbell entered the fray, saying, "[Are] you telling us that even though the President of the United States has empowered you in certain instances to make a call, that he has set forth new criteria to stop a disruption and a displacement in the market-place or displacement of workers, that because of a disagreement as to whether there is a threat or not, that we have instances where the State Department itself stops any action from being taken?"

LENAHAN: I'm certainly saying that, with respect to calls on the three major suppliers, I have . . . instructed the State Department to make calls, and they have declined to make those calls.

CAMPBELL: At that point, if they decline, . . . what steps do you then take? Where is your court of appeals?

LENAHAN: Well, it's normally been a discussion both within my department, between my department and the State Department, other agencies, of course, having an interest in this, from time to time have become involved.

CAMPBELL: . . . Would you give us a rough estimate, percentagewise, of the disagreements that you have not been able to reconcile with your department and with the State Department, or with this committee and with the State Department?

LENAHAN: About 15, sir.

According to Lenahan's testimony, it also appears that the enforcement of import regulations, particularly against Chinese products, was not a major administration priority. Under questioning about illegal imports of Chinese textiles and apparel, Lenahan testified that the administration failed to provide the appropriate government agencies with either the mandate or the resources to monitor these imports effectively. He described how responsible agencies had failed to enforce negotiated quotas, to report incidents of transshipment, or to check on clothing mislabeled to hide the real locus of its manufacture.[21] He said that Customs simply lacked the resources needed to enforce the rules of origin required by the MFA, and that it was unable to control imports of apparel when exporting countries shifted production from one low-wage country to another.

THE JENKINS-HOLLINGS BILL: WATERSHED
FOR THE EXPANSION OF TRADE LIBERALIZATION

The surge of apparel imports in the early 1980s galvanized congressional protectionists, bringing the battle over trade expansion to a head. Despite the different political orientations of southern textile manufacturers, eastern apparel manufacturers, and trade unionists, the members of these groups shared common goals: maintaining domestic production and domestic employment. Textile and apparel producers and the unions representing apparel workers—the ILGWU and the ACTWU—formed the Fiber, Fabric and Apparel Coalition for Trade (FFACT), which supported increased protection for domestic producers, a stronger MFA, and tighter global import controls.[22]

This group introduced the Trade Enforcement Act, also known as the Jenkins-Hollings bill, in 1985. The bill was modeled on the 1981 MFA agreement that the European Economic Community struck with its own East Asian suppliers, which curbed the annual growth rate of apparel imports at 1 percent. The bill required that the expansion of apparel imports be tied directly to the growth of apparel consumption in the United States.[23]

In 1985, large majorities in both the House and Senate passed Jenkins-Hollings, but Reagan vetoed it. Although Congress came close to overriding this veto, it could not quite muster sufficient votes. In 1987 Congress introduced a comparable bill. This legislation required a "global quota" that would limit the combined apparel imports to an overall growth rate of 1 percent annually.[24] This bill, too, passed both houses of Congress and was vetoed by Reagan, in 1988. Congress passed a similar bill in 1990—the Textile, Apparel, and Footwear Trade bill. This time President George H. W. Bush vetoed the bill.[25]

The battles over these trade bills were among the last major conflicts over import protection, and with their loss the protectionists suffered a major blow. The bills' failure finally cleared the way for the free trade initiatives that were soon to be implemented. The protectionists' defeat came at a time when the trade policy interests of the different segments

of the textile-apparel complex had begun to diverge, leading to new conflicts among textile producers, apparel manufacturers, and retailers. In
chapter 8, I analyze the compromise that the Reagan administration bro-
kered between these groups—a compromise that went far beyond new
trade regulations and made the industry more footloose than it had ever
been before.

The defeat of Jenkins-Hollings, and with it virtually all administrative
support for trade protection, cleared the way for free trade. By 1984, advocates of the neoliberal paradigm were demanding an end to the Multifibre Arrangement—a goal that was achieved in 1994. To accomplish this
objective, economists began to promote a new discourse about national
economic policy that called for a dramatic opening of global markets.

This paradigm for trade liberalization went far beyond demands to end
quotas and reduce tariffs. It embodied new norms about fairness in global
trade that helped create a framework for new regulations to legitimate a
dramatic increase in apparel production sites and an expansion of the role
of women in the global apparel industry. The new trade accords that were
to emerge between 1980 and 2000 also legitimated government financing
of technology and infrastructure to promote and benefit private export-
processing ventures. These trade agreements contributed to the integration
and concentration of U.S. apparel corporations and the growth of new
profit centers in apparel retailing.

Despite claims that the developing world could not compete with the
United States because of its technological deficits, it is now clear that the
new technologies that have penetrated the developing world have eliminated the productivity advantages of America's textile and apparel makers.
As a result of this distribution of technology, there have been massive
transfers of apparel production offshore. Low wages have become the bottom line.

In the past two decades, efforts like these helped promote the growth
of new lower-wage export-processing sites in the Caribbean, Central
America, and Mexico and an increase of textile and apparel exports from
this region to the United States.[26] Further, the WTO and the conclusion
of the Uruguay Round of the General Agreement on Tariffs and Trade
have made it possible for America's vertically integrated textile, apparel,
and retail complex to embark on a new global effort to expand production
sites and increase imports of low-wage apparel from developing countries
around the world.

8 The Reagan Revolution
The Caribbean Basin Initiative

THE U.S. ROLE IN LATIN AMERICA

THE U.S. ROLE IN LATIN AMERICA

The first act of America's trade liberalization was played out in the Far East; the second act took place in Latin America—in selected countries in the Caribbean, Central America, and, later, Mexico.[1] U.S. apparel manufacturers had begun to produce apparel in some of the Caribbean and Central American countries and in Mexico in the 1970s, but Reagan's Caribbean Basin Initiatives, the first in 1983 and particularly the second in 1986, dramatically accelerated the growth of assembly operations in the Caribbean and Central America. If the U.S. textile and apparel industries opposed America's efforts to rebuild the textile industries in Japan and the NICs in the postwar period, by the 1980s the changing U.S. textile and apparel industries actually pressed the Reagan administration for a new offshore option in Latin America.

Eisenhower's presidency had been marked by the growing communist menace in the Far East. In 1981, when Reagan entered the White House, he saw a new communist threat in the Caribbean and Central America— the stepchild of the Castro regime in Cuba. In addition to supporting military intervention against the left-wing insurgents there, the Caribbean Basin Initiative (CBI), or as it was officially called, the Caribbean Basin Economic Recovery Act, was a new trade and investment program designed to promote economic development and political stability in the region and to check the spread of Soviet-Cuban influence in the Americas. Textiles and apparel once more became part of an anticommunist strategy.

When the cold war came to an end, the U.S. textile and apparel industries were playing a major role in the new trade and investment regime that had been developed by the Caribbean Basin Initiative. This regime was not merely the result of market imperatives but was designed by the

Reagan administration to meet the needs of powerful segments of the U.S. textile and apparel industries.

REAGAN'S CARIBBEAN BASIN

For at least the past hundred years, the United States has been extensively involved in the military, political, and economic affairs of the Caribbean and Central America. Between 1953 and 1990, America's cold war policy for this region was to prop up, both militarily and economically, a continuing stream of authoritarian regimes in opposition to popular democratic and left-wing insurgencies. This approach played a role in the larger struggle between East and West, and was supported by U.S. corporate elites concerned with maintaining a secure environment for trade and investment in the region.[2]

A number of theoretical perspectives have been developed to explain the economic relationship between the United States and the Caribbean and Central America nations, and indeed, much of Latin America.[3] Although these are too complex to discuss here, what many of these theories have in common is an understanding that the economic relationships between the United States and Latin America have traditionally involved trade and investment patterns in which Latin America has suffered economically, while producing commodities for export to the United States—primarily raw materials such as coffee, sugar, tin, and minerals. The United States, in turn, has exported capital to the region and—in exchange for commodities—manufactured goods. This has helped make Latin American nations economically and politically dependent on the economy and government of the United States.

Until the mid-1970s, Latin America supplied about one-fifth of the crude oil used by the United States, about one-half of its petroleum products, about 90 percent of its bauxite, and 70 percent of its bananas. The United States purchased one-third of all the sugar produced in these countries and one-fifth of the coffee.[4] U.S. corporations handled much of this production and exported these products to the United States and other world markets. Then, in the late 1970s, the world prices for sugar dropped, and two oil shocks dramatically increased oil prices.

The United States dealt with this crisis by placing quotas on sugar, petroleum, coffee, and bauxite imports—products that had earned Latin American countries a major part of their foreign exchange. Between 1982 and 1987, exports of raw sugar from the Caribbean Basin countries to the United States went from 985,000 to 349,770 short tons. During the same years, exports of petroleum from these countries to the United States went from $5.062 billion to $1.393 billion. In the short run, this reduction dramatically worsened the region's balance of trade and triggered a new and massive spate of borrowing, which by the early 1980s had sparked a debt crisis in many countries. As the value of the region's cash exports declined, many countries were drained of income, and their people experienced more unemployment and poverty. As Reagan entered the White House in 1981, the growth of left-wing movements heightened his concern about Soviet-inspired insurgencies. He responded with a new round of economic aid to counter these insurgencies, developing new U.S. military initiatives in the region predicated on his belief that Soviet influence had to be rooted out and destroyed. As he told the *Wall Street Journal* in 1980, "The Soviet Union underlies all the unrest that is going on. If they weren't engaged in this game of dominoes, there wouldn't be any hot spots in the world."[5]

The Reagan administration stepped up U.S. support of pro-American regimes in Central America. Total aid to Central America grew from $194.2 million in 1980 to $1.2 billion in 1985.[6] Between 1980 and 1983, military aid to U.S. allies in Central America increased by 1,841 percent, from $20.7 to $401.7 million. By 1983, the U.S. military presence in the Caribbean Basin reached its highest level since World War II, as the United States dramatically increased its troops stationed there.[7]

In discussing the United States' offensive response to the possibility of dominoes falling so close to America's southern border, a 1982 report evoked once again the earlier forms of anticommunist vigilance and focused on the economic interests of corporate America in the region. According to this report,

> U.S. security and military interests in the Caribbean and Central
> America region are widely known. The region's shipping lanes are
> vital to U.S. defense and prosperity. Two-thirds of the oil imported by
> the United States, nearly half of U.S. trade, and many strategic
> minerals pass through the Panama Canal or the Gulf of Mexico. Other
> U.S. economic stakes in the region are also quite extensive. With
> more than $5,652 billion of U.S. direct investment (1980 figure) in the
> Caribbean and Central America, and with total U.S. exports to the
> area of $6,842 billion, the economic and political instability of these
> countries affects our own economy.[8]

A new policy emerged that replicated the dynamics that had characterized earlier periods of the cold war.[9] Strongly supported by the *National Bipartisan Report on Central America* (known as the Kissinger Commission Report), the Caribbean Basin Initiative was formulated within the framework of America's cold-war foreign-policy agenda, with a focus on Latin America.[10] Military support was accompanied by foreign aid, just as it had been in the 1950s and 1960s in Europe and in Japan and other underdeveloped countries in the East Asian countries, in order to prevent communist subversion and preserve America's political and economic interests. The U.S. government provided about $16.8 billion in bilateral aid between 1980 and 1992, given largely to selected countries of Central America and the Caribbean for military aid, balance of payments aid, and aid for economic development.[11] Many of the funding programs were established in the early postwar period—like the Food for Peace program (PL480), the Economic Support Fund, and the U.S. Agency for International Development (USAID). In 1981 USAID developed a program in Latin America called the Private Business Initiative.[12] One analyst estimates that about 58 percent of all funding for economic development was provided through this program.[13]

It was in this context, as a relatively minor effort in a larger set of policy initiatives, that on March 17, 1982, Reagan sent Congress a bill to implement the CBI. The act was described by a congressional report as legislation to support the restructuring of the region's export regime in ways that would promote employment and root out the poverty that generated support for left-wing alternatives. The trade initiatives embodied in CBI programs would bolster open markets and, according to a House report, support democracy:

> The Caribbean Basin countries have been seriously affected by the escalating cost of imported oil and declining prices for their major exports (e.g., sugar, coffee, bauxite). This has exacerbated their deep-rooted structural problems and caused serious inflation, enormous balance of payments deficits, and a pressing liquidity crisis. The economic crisis threatens political and social stability throughout the region and creates conditions which Cuba and others seek to exploit through terror and subversion.[14]

The CBI trade agenda was designed to promote restructuring of the region's quasicolonial trade and investment relationship with the United States. An infusion of new American capital would become the basis for export-led development, a strategy that had been developed earlier in Japan and the NICs and had fueled the Asian Miracles.[15]

Ultimately, however, the administration sought to prepare the region for a new kind of economic and political dependency on the United States based on free trade and new forms of market-oriented U.S. investment. But first it was essential to reestablish political and social stability. As one foreign business analyst later wrote, "Washington's commitment to roll back revolutionary processes close to its southern border is demonstrated by the action it has taken on Grenada and Central America, and is a major aspect of the New Caribbean. Without this commitment, any political risk analyst and almost any investor would have serious doubts about the region's future business climate."[16] The CBI did not help the countries in the region become economically autonomous. Instead it established a dependent integration through a new trade and investment regime between the United States and the region's countries, in which the United States continued to profit at the expense of these less developed countries.

The United States had a large trade deficit in the early 1980s, and the CBI nations were among the few with which it had a trade surplus. Enacted by Congress on August 5, 1983, the CBI was intended to maintain and expand that surplus by supporting the growth of new exports in lieu of the traditional raw materials. The centerpiece of the CBI was ostensibly a new round of tariff reductions for "nontraditional" exports. It was a market-opening gesture, described as consistent with the expansion of free trade. Acceptance of trade benefits would tie these countries to the United States.

The U.S. president alone had the right to offer or withhold from participating nations the advantageous tariffs and other benefits embodied in the program. Its benefits were to be allocated individually to each nation, through bilateral negotiations, and depended on the willingness of each to cooperate with U.S. policy. According to the bill, the president could not designate a country as a beneficiary of the CBI if it "(1) is a Communist country; (2) fails to meet criteria regarding expropriation of U.S. property; (3) fails to recognize arbitral awards to U.S. citizens; (4) affords 'reverse' tariff preferences to other developed countries; (5) engages in piracy of copyrighted broadcast material; or (6) has not entered into an extradition treaty with the United States."[17]

Both direct and indirect financial aid were made conditional on acceptance of U.S.-mandated exchange-rate adjustments, privatization of government services, wage controls, elimination of energy and food subsidies, and rescheduling of the debt.[18] Such "structural adjustment" policies allowed the United States to impose an export-oriented growth model on beneficiary countries.

The purpose of tariff reductions was to provide incentives for American corporations to make nontraditional export-oriented investments in CBI countries. The southern climate would encourage market-oriented U.S. agribusiness firms to invest in the production of winter fruits and vegetables for duty-free export to U.S. markets.[19] These exports, it was argued, would produce jobs and reduce poverty, thereby removing the incentive for supporting local, communist-dominated insurgencies. Exports would play the same role they had played in the Asian economic miracle, allowing the indebted CBI countries to earn the foreign exchange necessary to reduce their expanded indebtedness.

The poverty in much of Latin America was an outcome of the economic relationships established by the alliance of the landed oligopoly with U.S. corporations. Many Latin American countries had seen "the expansion of export agriculture at the expense of domestic food production, and the lack of linkages between the export sector and the rest of the economy." Yet with the reduced demand for commodity exports like oil and sugar, and growing indebtedness, many countries in the region found themselves casting about for a solution to their economic problems. The CBI was designed to restructure the traditional trade, investment, and financial links between selected countries in the Caribbean countries and Central America and the United States.

With the inception of the CBI, the Reagan administration mobilized U.S. agencies to develop programs to publicize and promote new business opportunities in the Caribbean. An Interagency Task Force was created, to be chaired by the U.S. Trade Representative.[20] The Department of Agriculture was enlisted in formation of the Agribusiness Promotion Council, composed of about three hundred private agribusiness leaders whose goal was "to promote U.S. investment in the Caribbean Basin and help beneficiary countries participate in international agricultural trade."[21]

The Department of Commerce created the Business Promotion Council (BPC), which offered a series of "VIP Business Missions." These missions involved "hundreds of seminars and workshops for U.S. businessmen." The BPC also distributed "CBI Starter Kits and Guidebooks" and began to publish the *CBI Business Bulletin*, which described the rules and potential benefits of the program.

Parallel to this, the U.S. government encouraged Caribbean businessmen to invest in the development of nontraditional exports through a Department of Commerce mission called "Caribbean Connections," in which "Caribbean businessmen with ready-to-export products travel to various cities in the United States to meet with potential buyers, agents and distributors."[22] The Department of Commerce also planned a series of technical seminars. The purpose of these seminars was to "assist Caribbean business in assessing the most efficient and effective way to penetrate the US market."[23]

Funding for the CBI was supplemented by monies borrowed individually by each nation from the world's multilateral lending institutions: the International Monetary Fund, the World Bank, the Inter-American Development Bank, and the Caribbean Development Bank.[24] In large part this aid was designed to stabilize the CBI nations' monetary situation and encourage market-oriented fiscal and industrial reform. The restoration of political stability was to complement "a hospitable macroeconomic and legal climate for domestic and foreign investment.[25]

Although the publicly stated objective of the Caribbean Basin Initiative was to promote foreign investment in the region, the final version of the CBI did not include any of the original proposals that could have created real incentives for investment (e.g., tax credits and accelerated depreciation allowances).[26] The only incentive that did remain in the final version was a small modification of section 936 of the U.S. tax code. Under existing law, U.S. corporations could receive a 100 percent tax credit on the profits earned in their Puerto Rican subsidiaries. Section 936 allowed the repatriation of U.S. profits in Puerto Rico on a tax-free basis. In 1986, section 936 was modified to require that $100 million per year of the $15 billion then on deposit in Puerto Rican banks be used for investment loans in CBI beneficiary countries.[27] CBI beneficiary countries were required to sign a Tax Information Exchange Agreement with the United States, which many countries were reluctant to do.[28] By late 1987, only Jamaica, Barbados, Grenada, and St. Lucia were program participants. The CBI could do little to make the region attractive to American investors without new efforts to revise the trade agenda.

U.S. protectionism was perhaps the biggest brake on U.S. investment in the region. Sugar had been a major export to the United States. Yet American producers of ethanol and rum, products made from raw sugar, had opposed tariff reductions on imports of these two products because they threatened to compete directly with their own sales in the United States.[29] Armco, Bethlehem Steel Corporation, North Star Steel, Northwestern Steel and Wire Company, and Raritan River Steel Company joined forces to oppose higher import quotas for steel pipes and tubes made by CBI countries.[30] The Florida citrus industry and U.S. flower growers mobilized to impose import restrictions on orange juice concentrate and cut flowers.

Protectionist pressures in Congress thwarted tariff reductions on trade-sensitive products that could be made in the CBI countries. Items like canned tuna, footwear, gloves, handbags, luggage, flat goods, textiles and apparel, leather apparel, and watch parts from particular countries were exempted from the duty-free status that the CBI initiative now offered. This made potential investors wary of the power of protectionist lobbies at home to impose restrictive tariffs on items produced in the CBI countries.[31]

The requirements of congressional oversight meant that hearings were held in 1986 to investigate the progress of the first eighteen months of the CBI. Records of the hearings show that the CBI was far from successful. Nontraditional investments by both U.S. and indigenous investors were unimpressive. A small number of new ventures were cited, but the investigation found that many of these projects did not result from the CBI tariff reductions or other federal efforts to promote the program.[32] U.S. protectionism, weak infrastructure, and the politically volatile environment discouraged investment. Furthermore, in 1981, two years before the CBI was implemented, 87 percent of all imports from the Caribbean and Central America that were to have duty-free status in 1983 were already duty free as beneficiaries of the preexisting Generalized System of Preferences and most-favored-nation regulations.[33] By 1989 one U.S. business specialist on Latin American investment concluded that "CBI has fallen far short of its goal of boosting Caribbean Basin exports to the United States and catalyzing private investments in the region."[34] What was notable, however, was the dramatic growth of apparel assembly in many of these countries, despite the fact that apparel imports were excluded from CBI tariff benefits by specific trade protections. This was noted by that same business specialist, who questioned the role of CBI tariff reductions in expanding nontraditional exports. He states, "What has increased tremendously in the time the CBI has been in existence—by some 400 percent in dollar terms—are U.S.-destined exports of apparel goods."[35]

PRODUCTION SHARING AND THE BIRTH OF "APPAREL REPUBLICS"

As we now know, many CBI countries ultimately became major sites for the assembly and export processing of apparel. By the mid-1970s, large corporate retailers, department store merchandisers, marketers of brand-name products, and trading companies had begun to play a pivotal role in setting up decentralized production networks in a variety of low-wage exporting countries. East Asia had become the hub of the U.S. apparel industry's growing network of textile-production and apparel-assembly facilities.

While the corporate offices of fashion-apparel producers located their financial, marketing, and design facilities in the Northeast—primarily in New York City, increasingly in Los Angeles—they also carried out much of their production abroad. Producers of women's fashion products—suits, coats, dresses, and sportswear—used East Asian production sites centered in Hong Kong, Taiwan, and South Korea. The Big Three had also developed contracting and subcontracting networks in lower wage countries in the Asian Pacific where apparel was produced. The sluggish growth in consumer sales of apparel in the United States had pressed the U.S. retailers, importers, and producers of women's fashion products to expand and diversify their production sites, using the MFA quota system to access lower wage sites in more remote developing countries.

As we have seen, America's textile industry had spent the 1960s and 1970s increasing its capital investment in labor-saving technology. By 1980, U.S. textile producers had become heavily concentrated and vertically integrated as a result of mergers and acquisitions.[36] Located primarily in the South—and in Texas, New Mexico, California, and Florida—many of these firms were close to the Mexican border and Central America. In the early 1970s, considerably before Reagan's CBI, America's textile producers had begun to outsource their apparel production to a small number of low-wage assembly sites in the Caribbean countries, Central America, and Mexico. These textile producers, who made fabrics for apparel, saw Mexico and the Caribbean Basin countries as fertile ground for expanding apparel assembly by means of U.S. Tariff Schedule (USTS) 807.00, a tariff regime that offered incentives to U.S. producers to assemble components of manufactured goods abroad.[37] Manufacturers used USTS 807 to develop and facilitate a new and unique kind of trade. According to the International Trade Commission's report, "Under Item 807.00 imported articles assembled in foreign countries with fabricated components that have been manufactured in the United States are subject to duty upon the full value of the imported product, less the value of the US-fabricated components contained therein."

Item 807 had been implemented in 1963. Initially, it was used not to ease the access of U.S. corporations to low-wage labor but to facilitate "production sharing" by reducing tariffs for U.S. goods most efficiently manufactured in more than one country. Throughout the 1970s, between 5 and 6 percent of all U.S. imports came into the United States under HTS 806.30 and 807. Most of these products (68.4 percent) were imported from developed countries—Canada, West Germany, Belgium, Luxembourg, Italy, and France—rather than underdeveloped or developing countries.[38] Indeed, between 1982 and 1985, manufacturers of metal products, primarily motor vehicles and motor vehicle parts, and office machines and parts, were the most prominent beneficiaries of this tariff regime. The 807 regime was valued for its tariff-reducing potential more than for its ability to facilitate access to low-wage labor: by 1985 the duty-free portion of imported goods eligible for the 807 tariff regime was twelve times higher than in 1970. U.S. apparel producers, wanting to have their products assembled offshore, soon found a way to make the 807 trade regime work to their advantage in Latin America.

Textile and apparel protectionists were opposed to the implementation of USTS 807. As early as 1973, concerned with its potential for displacing U.S. apparel workers, Lazare Teper, research director of the ILGWU, saw this program as a "direct enticement" for apparel firms to seek offshore sources. In his congressional testimony, he condemned these companies for producing offshore, saying,

> Aside from the lure of lower unit labor costs and lower US customs duties, domestic entrepreneurs are also enticed to move their contracting operations abroad by tax concessions, remission of customs duties on imports of machinery and other material, subsidized plant construction, special low interest loans and remissions of income and other taxes provided—and that is an important proviso, that the goods processed in the particular foreign country are not sold in that country, but the whole output is exported.[39]

The MFA bilateral agreements had accorded individual quota regimes to Mexico and Central American nations. However, when the CBI was introduced in 1983, congressional protectionists demanded stricter import quotas for textiles and apparel from the region.

In 1982, a year before the CBI was passed, textiles constituted the second most important use of exported components for apparel assembly.[40] Women in countries like Haiti, the Dominican Republic, El Salvador, Nicaragua, and Barbados, where wage rates were among the lowest in Latin America, assembled and exported apparel to the United States. These items represented 7.4 percent of all goods imported under the 807 tariff regime—and 3.4 percent of all U.S. apparel imports.

As early as the 1960s, American apparel producers, particularly those making bras and girdles, had begun to see the advantage of production sharing. The detailed construction of these garments required a considerable amount of sewing and, therefore, more labor than required by many other items. Many large and well-known American companies opened offshore subsidiaries and assembly plants during the 1960s and 1970s, in Mexico and in what were later to become CBI countries. Item 807 gave apparel producers access to abundant low-wage labor, and they opened small factories to test the waters.[41]

In 1965, Sears set up operations to assemble clothing in Honduras. Maidenform set up operations in Jamaica. In the early 1970s, Lovable built a plant in Costa Rica.[42] McGregor Sporting Goods, Phillips–Van Heusen, Farah Manufacturing, Haggar, Blue Bell–Wrangler, and Fruit of the Loom also started sourcing in these countries, because they saw them as ideal places for mass production of large volumes of low-end to middle-range trousers, slacks, shorts, shirts, and blouses,[43] products typically sold in discount stores like J. C. Penney and Sears.

Offshore assembly operations in the area were designed to promote cost sharing. Producers would calculate the cost of domestic production and then average this cost with their offshore production cost. The two production sites—the U.S. site and the lower wage offshore site—would "share" the mean cost of labor per unit of total production. Reduced tariffs for apparel assembly operations encouraged textile producers to integrate vertically into clothing production.[44]

Despite the deepening debt crisis in Latin America, when the CBI went into effect in 1983 congressional protectionists had succeeded in exempting apparel imports from the accord's special benefits. Textile producers chafed at the fact that preexisting quotas and tariffs thwarted their plans to further expand the export-processing platform that the industry had begun to develop in the 1960s and 1970s in countries that now participated in the CBI.[45]

In the early 1980s, U.S. firms producing apparel in the Caribbean Basin countries argued that much of their production in the United States was no longer "viable." By this, they meant that high wages in the United States inhibited their ability to compete with lower cost imports from Asian countries. Moreover, by this time U.S. textile producers were losing their U.S. apparel customers to East Asian countries whose flourishing textile industries produced a wide variety of fabrics cheaply and plentifully. These were purchased by U.S. apparel makers with factories in the region.

U.S. textile producers were reluctant to move the nonviable production to the Far East. The higher costs of transporting finished apparel products from East Asian countries was also an inhibiting factor, particularly in the face of emerging demands by retailers for "quick response" and "just-in-time" delivery. But even more important, producing in Asia meant competing with Asian textile producers.

The Caribbean Basin countries, however, had no textile capacity. Expanding apparel production in the Caribbean Basin meant U.S. textile producers could sell their merchandise to U.S. apparel producers. The expansion of apparel production south of the border would create a new market for textile producers without the need to compete directly with Asian producers. Though proximity to the United States kept the costs of transport relatively low, the CBI countries' quota limits stalled the development of these new Latin American production sites. Without higher quotas, the CBI countries could not remain competitive with Asian textile producers and would go out of business. An expanded USTS 807 regime would solve the problem.

Less than a decade after the passage of the Multifibre Arrangement, there were new pressures for the textile and apparel industries to open additional assembly sites in low-wage countries. When Jenkins-Hollings was defeated in 1985, the U.S. textile corporations challenged the restrictive quota limitations that the CBI initiative had imposed in 1983, limitations the textile industry had earlier pressed hard to maintain.[46] Now they saw that the export processing of apparel in the Caribbean Basin would allow them to compete with Asian producers.

As already noted, the initial thrust of the 1983 CBI mandate was to encourage investment in and export of winter fruits and vegetables. By 1986, however, the expected growth of these commodity exports had not materialized, challenging the prestige of Reagan's CBI program. The trade program, encumbered by domestic protectionist measures and lacking investment incentives, did little more than the existing HTS 807 regime had done to promote trade between the United States and CBI countries. Apparel was on a list of products specifically exempted from the special CBI tariff privileges between 1983 and 1986. Nevertheless, the value of exported apparel from eight of the Central American and Caribbean countries doubled during these years.[47]

By 1986 the value of apparel exports from the CBI beneficiary countries represented 40 percent of the value of all products, and 37.3 percent of all manufactured products, exported from the Caribbean Basin to the United States. Apparel exports from Mexico in that year represented slightly less than 2 percent of that country's exports to the United States and about 3 percent of all its manufactured exports.

By 1984, the year the CBI first went into effect, capital-intensive, vertically integrated textile corporations; southern-based apparel firms; and many importers and retailers began to lobby for the loosening of import quotas and tariff reductions in these countries. The powerful corporations in the yarn and fabric segment of the American textile industry were represented by the newly formed lobbying association the American Caribbean Trade Association (ACTA), which began to agitate on Capitol Hill for increased quotas for Caribbean and Central American countries. Indeed, ACTA developed the rationale and blueprint for the Special Access Program, adopted for the CBI countries in 1986.[48]

The Textile and Apparel Group of the American Association of Exporters and Importers (AAEI-TAG) worked with ACTA in mounting this campaign.[49] Led by Sears and J. C. Penney, eight retail associations formed the Retail Industry Trade Action Coalition (RITAC) in 1984 to represent the major U.S. corporations in the U.S. "soft goods" retail industry.[50] By the early 1980s this increasingly powerful retail industry had become a major political force for free trade. Large corporate retailers had opposed protectionists for years, trying to ensure their suppliers freer access to lower wage sources of production, on which their own competitive position increasingly depended.[51]

With total sales exceeding $1 trillion, this segment of the retail industry now employed 15 percent of the national workforce. Anxious to benefit from growing levels of low-wage imports, retailers began to organize a powerful lobby for the further liberalization of apparel trade, not only in the CBI countries but throughout the world.[52] William Andres, president of Dayton Hudson, and other RITAC members met directly with Reagan's aides Edwin Meese and Craig Fuller and planned a series of congressional breakfasts to discuss its trade agenda with key members of Congress, an agenda that included the ending of the Multifibre Arrangement.[53] Andres now claimed that "US consumers in the previous year had paid a hidden price tag of more than $23 billion because of textile apparel import restrictions."[54] With an initial budget of $750,000, in 1984 RITAC launched a major political campaign to oppose the renewal of the Multifibre Arrangement and make the case for freer trade.[55] Part of its effort was directed at opening U.S. markets to Caribbean textile and apparel exports by modifying the CBI. In 1985 RITAC spent another $1 million in pursuit of this goal.[56]

America's textile and apparel industries soon found themselves at the center of a strategy to promote export-led development that was to reshape the thrust of the Caribbean Basin Initiative. Textile and apparel industry executives argued that broadening the HTS 807 tariff regime would facilitate access to a new and growing pool of low-wage workers in Central American and Caribbean countries, thereby reducing the cost of clothing for American consumers. In 1986 the U.S. textile and apparel industries were to play a willing rather than a reluctant role in U.S. foreign policy, one supporting the administration's goal of restructuring America's trade and investment in the Caribbean Basin countries. Soon Mexico would be incorporated in this plan through the North American Free Trade Agreement. The Reagan administration and the textile and apparel industries began to define the production and export of apparel as the "engine of growth," or the "starter industry," for export-led development in the CBI countries. Apparel exports could finance a portion of the foreign exchange for the growing debt owed to multilateral institutions and U.S. banks. Export-processing zones for apparel assembly and other industrial assembly operations, it was argued, would create the industrial structure for a takeoff into export-led development. Producing in the region would also allow U.S. textile and apparel producers to export to the European market, as many of the CBI countries were members of the Lome Convention, which gave them preferential access to trade with the European Economic Community.[57]

Both industry and government benefited from the expertise and backing of prestigious free-trade economists who joined the effort to make free trade acceptable to Americans. According to a 1984 issue of *Fortune* magazine, "Additional free trade pressure is coming from 63 economists of varying political convictions, ranging from Michael Bluenthal and Barry Bosworth, former Carter advisers, and Nobel Prize winner James Tobin to conservatives like Milton Friedman, Norman Ture and Herbert Stein. The group is talking tough to both Democrats and Republicans."[58]

In the 1980s a new chapter in the history of postwar trade liberalization was initiated. Although the conflict between protectionists and trade liberalizers continued, protectionists now found themselves on the defensive. Large retailers represented by RITAC, importers represented by AAEI-TAG, and major segments of the textile industry, represented by ACTA, challenged the necessity of continued quotas and tariffs. These groups favored the expansion of apparel assembly in the CBI nations and other regions of Latin America. Professional, mainstream economists supported their interests, arguing for increased trade liberalization, offshore production, and foreign investment. These economists legitimated not only the interests of the textile and apparel producers and retailers but also the trade agenda of the Reagan administration; they favored the new market orientation that stressed the value of export-led development and the opening of global markets. Economic models showed that the new trade agenda was more efficient—good for corporations and good for American consumers.

On the other side of this issue, still in favor of protection, were the much less powerful domestic textile and apparel producers. The Fiber, Fabric and Apparel Coalition for Trade (FFACT) represented these groups in

Congress.[59] The trade unions in the apparel industry—the ILGWU and the ACTWU—were also part of this coalition. Protectionists saw the new market orientation, which stressed production in low-wage countries, as opposed to the interests of workers and domestic producers. The former would lose their businesses while the latter would inevitably be displaced from their jobs. For protectionists, the free trade agenda favored large corporate interests rather than small businessmen and working people.

With the veto of the Jenkins-Hollings bill, trade liberalizers engaged in efforts on all fronts to solidify relations with CBI countries and to pressure Congress and the administration for increased quotas. In 1984 Jamaican prime minister Edward Seaga invited U.S. textile executives of the American Textile Manufacturers' Institute (ATMI) to visit that country in order to explore the possibility of "expanding Items 807 operations into the Caribbean Basin region."[60] The ATMI planned similar trips to Barbados, Dominica, and the Dominican Republic. The president of the University of South Carolina helped organize a "Caribbean leaders conference" at the university to discuss ways the South Carolina textile industry could benefit from apparel sourcing in the CBI countries.[61]

THE SPECIAL ACCESS PROGRAM FOR THE CARIBBEAN

The American Caribbean Trade Association wrote the blueprint for the Special Access Program (SAP), which Reagan implemented unilaterally and which went into effect in 1987. The SAP was described as a new effort to expand "free trade and free markets" in Central America and the Caribbean. In the context of the political turmoil and economic crisis in the region, the SAP promised the participating nations that the expansion of trade under HTS 807 would, by encouraging apparel assembly for export, lead to economic growth. It would reproduce the "Asian Miracle" in the Caribbean Basin and keep the region politically democratic.[62]

The SAP, defined as a trade-liberalizing program for textile and apparel producers, was ultimately a quasi-protectionist measure designed primarily by and for the vertically integrated textile transnationals. It was a market-opening initiative structured to increase the amount of apparel exported by developing countries to the U.S. market, but whose manufacture was planned and financed by U.S. textile and apparel manufacturers.[63]

The Special Access Program created a new trade regime in which particular Caribbean and Central American nations could enter into bilateral agreements with the United States for Guaranteed Access Levels (GALs)—unlimited quotas for apparel exported to the United States. The program was based on the former Tariff Schedule 807 and was also called the Super 807 or Tariff Schedule 807A. Eligibility for unlimited quota and tariff reduction was defined by "rules of origin." These rules defined which exports qualified for these free trade benefits, giving preference to products made with U.S. textiles. In other words, GALs could be negotiated for apparel assembled in the CBI nations—but only apparel made of textiles "formed and cut in the U.S." Apparel imported from the region and assembled from foreign-made textiles could still enter U.S. markets at tariff rates consistent with Item 807, but it was not eligible for an unlimited quota.[64] As one analyst wrote,

> As a *quid pro quo* for this generous treatment for the new 807A products, the U.S. government made it plain, in the negotiations of [bilateral] agreements offered under the program, that it would also introduce a much more restrictive regime than before for equivalent goods in the same apparel categories which did not qualify for GAL treatment. . . . The main object here [was] to inhibit the further growth of operations by subsidiaries of Far Eastern groups using investment in Caribbean locations as a means of securing further quota allocations.[65]

Not only were wages dramatically lower in the region, but tariffs for apparel imports were generally higher than those for most other imports. The proposed tariff reductions were significant. The Super 807 reduced the tariffs on eligible items by 50 percent, because the tariffs were based only on the value added abroad, which was largely the cost of the labor. These tariffs were applied only to apparel that met the requirements of the rules of origin. The Caribbean Basin tariff regime offered a clear advantage over the higher duties on Asian imports, which were based on 100 percent of the product's value. In 1986, the year before the Super 807 program went into effect, the duty-free portion of textiles, apparel, and footwear imported into the United States from CBI nations averaged 51 percent of the products' value. By 1989, the duty-free portion of apparel made in CBI countries entering the United States through the Super 807 program had reached 64 percent.[66] Ultimately, then, the Super 807 did not give the CBI countries a "freer" market but instituted a new trade policy skewed in favor of America's corporate textile and apparel producers and retailers. The new trade regime also eliminated the competition with Asian manufacturers that U.S. textile producers had faced.

THE CARIBBEAN BASIN INITIATIVE AND THE FAR EAST

With liberalization of textile and apparel trade, the industry became divided over protection along a number of different lines. As noted in chapter

7, by the mid-1980s many Far Eastern apparel-producing countries, including China, were competing with U.S. producers in a rapidly expanding global apparel industry. The Special Access Program of the CBI and the reduction of import quotas for the NICs were policies designed to protect textile manufacturers and their customers—the makers of standard and basic apparel—from competing low-wage imports from China and other countries in the Asian-Pacific Rim. The program created incentives for apparel makers to shift their assembly from Asia to the Western Hemisphere, an issue that continues to concern U.S. textile producers today.

Many of the textile giants who had production facilities in the Caribbean countries, Central America, or both were also members of FFACT, the protectionist coalition in Congress. Others were members of ACTA, the textile trade group that had created the blueprint for the Special Access Program.[67] The American Textile Manufacturers' Institute and the American Apparel Manufacturers' Association (AAMA) historically had been organizations of domestic producers. Now each organization had a membership composed of companies that were often on opposite sides of the trade debate, depending on whether they focused on maintaining domestic production or producing abroad. Some firms did both. Though the AAMA officially supported protection, according to one 1985 account in *Bobbin Magazine*, the official trade journal of the AAMA, many of these companies favored the SAP: "Privately, many members of these organizations have been encouraging the Government to liberalize its treatment of 807 goods from the Caribbean, while tightening controls on the major Far East producers."[68]

The retail and fashion-apparel segment of the industry, however, was opposed to the Special Access Program and the rollbacks of NIC quotas. Hong Kong and Taiwan were major manufacturing centers for this segment of the industry. These producers sourced their textiles in the region. Many of them claimed that the fabrics they needed were available only from manufacturers there. The NICs also had a mature apparel industry with a skilled labor force. U.S. fashion producers, importers, and merchandisers had established strong ties with these firms.

Thus, apparel producers were split three ways over their Special Access Program. Producers of standard apparel favored the rules of origin, which they saw as the heart of the program. Fashion-apparel producers, however, had large sourcing networks in the Far East, and they opposed the strong rules of origin, according to which trade benefits depended on using textiles formed and cut in the United States. Domestic producers, of course, opposed the program entirely.

U.S. textile producers initially acknowledged their inability to provide American apparel manufacturers with many of the fabrics they required,[69] and they vowed to do better in the future. Apparel produced in Asian countries used textiles made in the region and had a U.S.-labor content of only 17 percent—the labor involved in the financial and managerial aspects of designing, ordering, and shipping the clothing to U.S. retail stores. Apparel assembled in the CBI nations and made from fabrics manufactured in the United States had a U.S.-labor content of 70 percent. Supporters of Super 807 argued that the SAP would not only expand employment in the CBI countries (a good thing for developing nations) but would also help maintain jobs in the United States. Even though employment would drop in the manufacturing sector, the new trade accord would help retain higher-wage jobs in finance, design, marketing, cutting, and services.

Low-wage imports had been expanding for the past quarter-century. The industry had been unable to develop a hard technology to replace the labor-intensive assembly process. In the January 1986 edition of *Bobbin Magazine*, an editorial by the journal's chairman and chief executive, Ronald Segal, reflected the insoluble dilemma this situation had produced. Segal writes, "It is clear now that technology, methods and productivity improvements in domestic manufacturing plants will not render the industry competitive during the decade. . . . The industry is left to fend for itself to maintain its viabilities. Yet a support vehicle is in our midst—807."[70]

In 1993, Andrew Postal, president of the U.S. blouse-making company Judy Bond, was a member of Caribbean/Latin American Action, a lobbying group for apparel producers sourcing in the CBI countries. Testifying in Congress, he described the value of the production-sharing regime. As he put it, "My company has faced over the last ten years substantial competition from Asia, and it was by linking our US plants with Caribbean plants that we were able to compete. Without these Caribbean plants we would have no US production. Our option would be to go to Asia and compete for US market share."[71]

As U.S. industries pressed for reductions in East Asian quotas, the CBI countries became increasingly desirable locations for Korean and Taiwanese apparel contractors and manufacturers, who could both benefit from lower wages in these countries and avoid the reduced import quotas through their access to USTS 807. By 1988, apparel assembly by Far Eastern companies in the CBI nations grew significantly. Three of the largest apparel-exporting countries—Jamaica, Costa Rica, and the Dominican Republic—identified 103 export-oriented apparel-assembly plants located in these countries. Thirty-six of these facilities (35 percent of all apparel-assembly plants exporting to the United States) were owned by East Asian interests. The remainder of the other comparable plants (67) were owned by American investors.[72] Indeed, of the foreign-owned plants, 23 (62 percent) had set up their operations between 1984 and 1986, the years just after apparel quotas from the Far East had been reduced and before the Special Access Program went into effect. Among the 67 U.S.-owned firms, only 19 (28 percent) had set up operations in the Caribbean Basin during this period.[73]

Between 1989 and 1991 at least 82 Korean and Taiwanese manufacturers moved to the region, investing about $85 million in plants and equipment, mainly electronics and apparel assembly plants. Koreans opened 55 apparel *maquiladoras* in Guatemala alone, compared to 20 started by U.S. companies.[74] In 1993 the U.S. General Accounting Office reported that there were a total of 95 Korean and Taiwanese assembly plants, and 63 assembly plants that were owned by other (non-U.S.) foreign countries, in the CBI region. These were located in Costa Rica, the Dominican Republic, El Salvador, and Honduras. In 1993 the Taiwanese and Korean assembly plants engaged in apparel and electronics assembly represented about 17 percent of all the assembly plants in the export-processing zones of these four countries.[75] Some Japanese firms have also made significant investments in Guatemala and Honduras.

If the apparel industry was no longer "viable" in the United States, it could nevertheless be "saved" by facilitating access to low-wage labor in the Caribbean and Central America. Yet, according to Adam Smith and David Ricardo, trade is about exchanging products made in one country for those made in another. The Special Access Program provided lower tariffs, higher quotas, and access to lower wages, all designed to expand production sharing. It had less to do with trade than with preserving apparel markets for U.S. textile corporations and gaining access to low-wage labor for apparel assembly. A representative of the American Caribbean Trade Association explained how the new Super 807 regime differed from the more traditional process of sourcing—as it was done in the Far East— arguing that production sharing yielded American-made products rather than imports. Production sharing, then, was not a process through which apparel was manufactured abroad and exported to the United States; it was not really "trade." As he says,

> Our industry is one of the few segments of the American apparel
> complex able to compete effectively against the rising flood of imports.
> Yet we have not grown in the last few years as imports have,
> because of the quota restrictions placed on us. We are hybrid importers.

Our fabrics and raw materials come overwhelmingly from the United States. We buy our fabrics, buttons, bows, plastics, zippers, cartons, bags, everything, here. We cut the fabric here. We ship the cutwork offshore for sewing assembly, bring the finished products back, pay duty on the foreign value added and distribute to our customers across the United States.[76]

Those who emphasize the salience of market forces in the footloose character of the apparel industry often fail to acknowledge that political rather than economic forces have promoted the geographical mobility of apparel production. There is no doubt that the lower cost of labor in the region was a large factor in the expansion of apparel assembly in the Caribbean, but it was not the only one. The region was only marginally valuable as a site for apparel assembly before the Special Access Program was passed. Moreover, the program was passed at a time when an economic transformation led to political concerns that jeopardized the region's relationship with the United States. The proximity of the region to the United States became valuable only at the point when retailers' demands for quick response had become an increasingly important component of production and Asian competition increased.

Apparel imports from the Caribbean Basin countries grew substantially between 1983 and 1986, even before the SAP went into effect.[77] However, it was not until 1987, with the dramatic change in tariffs and quotas, that imports from the region began to increase rapidly. While apparel imports from the CBI nations between 1983 and 1986 rose by 116 percent, between 1987, when the SAP was implemented, and 1997, total apparel imports to the United States from the region rose by 584 percent.[78] In less than a decade a significant proportion of apparel imports shifted from the Far East to the CBI nations, as textile and apparel producers had argued they would. By the end of the 1980s, despite the expansion of apparel imports from China and other developing countries in Asia, the Caribbean Basin region went from being a minor supplier to being a major one. In 1990 *Forbes* magazine would state, "The Caribbean is becoming America's garment district."[79]

SUPER 807 AND THE ROLE OF U.S. FOREIGN AID: THE GROWTH OF EXPORT-PROCESSING ZONES

The CBI countries' development of export-processing zones for apparel would not have been possible without the infrastructure constructed to support the Special Access Program for apparel. Building this infrastructure made the region increasingly safe and attractive as a place to do business. The World Bank, the International Monetary Fund, and USAID—the same agencies that funded earlier efforts to build the textile and apparel industries in the NICs—funded the infrastructure in the CBI nations.

Today's export-processing zones (EPZs) use in-bond plants for assembly operations, apparel assembly, and assembly of other labor-intensive products like shoes, toys, and other nondurable consumer items. EPZs provide a number of essential services that facilitate a secure and efficient transfer of goods and services across borders, often in areas of developing countries that are politically volatile or economically unstable or both, and that would not otherwise be able to sustain efficient manufacture or trade methods.[80] In 1982 Congressman Richard T. Schultz stated in his testimony on the Caribbean Basin Initiative, "One of the major deterrents to investment in the area is fear of the political risks. Many businessmen have told me that, were it not for fear of losing their investment through war, rebellion, expropriation or the inconvertibility of profits or earnings into U.S. dollars, they would consider investing in the Basin."[81]

According to a study on EPZs prepared by the Business International Corporation, titled *Improving International Competitiveness through Sourcing in Latin America*, a wide variety of factors are necessary to the success of offshore production in low-wage areas. These factors include infrastructure: water supply, transport, and telephone and other communication services. Other requirements are tax holidays, rental subsidies, training grants, special credits for employment creation, indirect subsidies for the purchase of domestic raw materials, a skilled and disciplined labor force, and freedom from foreign exchange controls. Since EPZs operate on a hard-currency basis, they shield investors and contractors from foreign exchange controls. Contractors are protected from the political risks of investment, which is particularly important in regions of the world where political turmoil can create major risks.[82] According to the Business International Corporation study, "Central American production sites have suffered from the region's image of political turmoil. Also in much of Latin America, business is often hamstrung by misguided state interference in economic and investment policies, although government interference is diminishing in many countries. Here again, EPZs hold a critical advantage: By their very enclave nature they often isolate producers from the local economy and government intervention."[83] The article goes on to say that, while "it is safe to assume that many Latin American nations will continue to maintain competitive wage rates in the future, labor costs may not be a pivotal factor. Even in labor-intensive sectors, deficiencies in other areas may dim the allure of cheap wages."[84] Thus, in the 1980s, the attractiveness of EPZs went beyond the potential profitability of offshore apparel assembly. In the context of a depreciating U.S. dollar, declining wages in the CBI nations, and a new and abundant source of low-wage labor, EPZs were an essential ingredient, a necessary condition for the CBI region's rise as a center for apparel assembly. They provided contracting services that producers could use with confidence and security; they were a sine qua non that assured the profitability and long-term growth of apparel contracting and textile investments.

PAYING TO LOSE OUR JOBS?

In 1992, a report by the National Labor Committee for Worker and Human Rights found that USAID funds earmarked for the Caribbean Basin were being used to encourage apparel manufacturers to relocate their assembly facilities offshore. According to estimates, total funding for development projects in eleven CBI countries had cost U.S. taxpayers $289.7 million.[85]

USAID, in existence since the early postwar period, funds programs to support the infrastructure and social programs of developing countries. Yet according to a GAO report, part of its mission changed with the Reagan administration. In 1981, the agency announced its Private Enterprise Initiative, which increased "its emphasis on encouraging the growth of competitive markets and private business, as a vehicle for economic development. The initiative has had its greatest influence on programming within the agency's Latin America/Caribbean Bureau, where it reinforces overall regional U.S. foreign policy."[86]

USAID funding was now channeled to apparel-producing CBI countries not through their governments but through these countries' business-promotion agencies—FIDE in Honduras, CINDE in Costa Rica, FUSADES in El Salvador, and the IPC in the Dominican Republic.[87] Essentially, these funds created export-processing zones and in-bond facilities. The agency "aggressively worked to increase exports to foreign markets, especially the United States, and to persuade foreign (including U.S. and Asian) companies to locate production facilities in their countries."[88]

By the late 1980s, with the waning of the cold war, the dual specter of deficits and deindustrialization brought politically motivated foreign aid under public scrutiny. The National Labor Committee challenged USAID for using taxpayer money to facilitate the shift of domestic employment to low-wage countries by funding export-processing zones.[89] Such funding, the committee also argued, facilitated violations of U.S.-supported labor-standards requirements embodied in treaty regulations that defined the terms of the Caribbean Basin Initiative.

A year later, in response to adverse publicity, the U.S. General Accounting Office (GAO) did its own investigation, confirming the revelations of the National Labor Committee.[90] The GAO data on the actual sums spent by U.S. taxpayers differed from data found in the committee's reports, but both organizations agreed that the funds spent on building export-processing zones were spent inappropriately.

The recommendations of the GAO review led to the introduction of section 599 to the 1993 Foreign Operations Appropriations Act. Section 599 makes it illegal to use foreign aid to induce a manufacturer to relocate production facilities offshore if doing so reduces domestic employment, provides funding for export-processing zones, or contributes to the violation of worker rights. The GAO report claimed, however, that USAID funding in itself was not responsible for U.S. investment and the expansion of USTS 807 trade with the CBI countries, and that market forces—the low-wage advantage and proximity to the United States of this region—were responsible for the growth of apparel assembly.[91] The GAO concluded that the use of USAID funds to promote export processing in the CBI countries "had a marginal impact on company decisions to locate a facility offshore." Yet, while export processing of apparel could have grown in the region without USAID funding, it might not have expanded so rapidly without EPZs.

The building of EPZs and in-bond plants in the CBI countries and Mexico accompanied the expansion of apparel sourcing in both areas in the 1970s and 1980s. *Maquiladoras* were financed and built, for the most part, by indigenous sources of capital. The CBI countries, more impoverished than Mexico, had few sources of domestic capital for private investment in such facilities. With the growth of the Special Access Program, part of the task was allocated to the United States government via USAID.

The USAID effort in the Caribbean was an adjunct to the Special Access Program that advanced the interests of corporate trade groups like ACTA and RITAC. The financing of export-processing facilities must be seen as a significant effort on Capitol Hill to promote apparel assembly in the CBI countries, and therefore as part of the Caribbean Basin Initiative, rather than as an isolated element in the context of a free trade regime.

In the early 1980s Reagan's anticommunist and free trade agendas generated an effort to restructure the economies of Central America and the Caribbean countries. Suffering from dramatic declines in the price of traditional commodity exports, many of the small nations in this region accepted the structural adjustment policies implemented by the Caribbean Basin Initiative. However, when investment in targeted industries began to falter, Reagan redirected his free trade objectives to allow America's textile and apparel industries to expand production in the Western Hemisphere in order to better compete with the Far East.

Such efforts can be seen as either structuring or distorting the free market, depending on one's point of view. Yet, as long as the CBI region lacked the needed legal and infrastructural foundations, U.S. textile and apparel producers did not relocate much of their production there, because of concerns about business risks. Trade Item 807 (which facilitated production sharing), as it was used in the SAP, and construction of export-processing zones were the primary ways the U.S. government facilitated apparel production in the region.

Only when the federal administration and the CBI countries themselves were willing and able to commit themselves to this type of economic restructuring was there a dramatic increase in the flow of capital for apparel-assembly operations in the region, and the growth of apparel exports from this region to the United States took off. U.S. trade and foreign policy gave apparel producers a comparative advantage, as they made it safe and profitable for them to do business in the region.

Ultimately, the Super 807 seemed an ideal policy: it included benefits for almost every interested party—U.S. textile and apparel producers, importers, the retail industry, and potentially, the American consumer. Soon, only the industry's trade unions would oppose such foreign sourcing ostensibly designed to make the industry more competitive and to save jobs for U.S. citizens. By 1990, the protectionist coalition had been fragmented and defeated. The increase in apparel shipped in from the Far East, the CBI countries, and Mexico would challenge domestic manufacturers, as women apparel workers lost more jobs, and sweatshops began to reappear.

9 Trade Liberalization for Textiles and Apparel
The Impact of NAFTA

In the fall of 1993 Congress ratified the North American Free Trade Agreement (NAFTA), which went into effect on January 1, 1994. Since that time, NAFTA has facilitated the growth of a vertically integrated textile and apparel complex in Mexico increasingly owned and controlled by U.S. textile and apparel transnationals. This new investment has ushered in a dramatic rise in low-wage apparel production in Latin America and has contributed to the demise of Mexico's indigenous apparel industry. Efforts are now being made to establish "full package" apparel capacity, which incorporates all the processes of clothing production—from fiber to fabric manufacture, through the final packaging of the product ready to send to the retailer. This enterprise targets U.S. markets almost exclusively. Mexican production, like that in the Caribbean Basin countries, offers the textile and apparel industries a way to compete with Asian suppliers.

If the Special Access Program implemented for the Caribbean Basin in 1986 was designed to satisfy U.S. textile corporations suffering the sting of failed protectionism, NAFTA was a much larger project. It was designed to liberalize trade and investment in the manufacture of a variety of more highly valued goods—like machinery, automobiles, and electronics. Yet by 1998, textiles and apparel had become Mexico's fifth-largest export, and the United States was the recipient of 97.4 percent of the country's apparel exports.[1]

MEXICAN *MAQUILADORAS* AND APPAREL

Export processing of apparel in Mexico did not, however, start with the implementation of NAFTA, but began to develop a full thirty years before. The opening of the first *maquiladoras*, or subsidiaries of U.S. transnationals, in 1965, as a result of the Border Industrialization Program, was not intended to promote export processing but to establish manufacturing plants in the northern border regions of Mexico to provide alternative forms of employment for Mexico's seasonal migrant workers. This program was designed to provide alternative employment in Mexico to deter the illegal migration of seasonal workers who crossed the border to work in California's agricultural economy.

An agreement between the United States and Mexico allowed foreign investors, largely American transnationals, partial or complete ownership of *maquiladoras* in order to assemble U.S.-made components into finished or semifinished goods for reexport to the United States.[2]

During the 1970s, Mexico's discovery of oil and its robust petroleum-export market allowed the country to borrow extensively. However, oil prices fell, and by 1982 Mexico was embroiled in yet another of its economic recessions and a new debt crisis. As the value of Mexico's oil exports dropped, the country found itself unable to support its high debt burden, and the crisis led to a peso devaluation in 1982. As a result, Mexico's *maquiladora* program became a much more significant element in the country's economy. Between 1975 and 1985 Mexico's debt went from $1.6 billion, or 58 percent of its gross national product, to $97 billion. Debt service threatened Mexico's economy, becoming $11 billion, or seven times higher than it had been—representing 37 percent of the country's exports of goods and services. Unable to continue financing its high level of U.S. imports, Mexico found it had a deficit in its trade balance with the United States. By the early 1980s *maquilas* had created 200,000 jobs and were contributing $2 billion to Mexico's balance of payments. In the late 1980s, these plants were the second largest source of foreign exchange—after oil exports—and more important than tourism.[3] As one analyst put it, the *maquiladora* program had become "one of the few shining stars on Mexico's economic scene."[4]

Joseph Grunwald and Kenneth Flamm state that there is little consensus about the earlier distribution of ownership of the *maquiladoras*. According to one study,

> In 1979, [regarding] the majority of the capital in 259 of the 540 firms
> operating as maquiladoras—48% was foreign; 95% of that came
> from the US. Another Mexican study says that 55% of the maquiladoras
> are wholly foreign owned. The US embassy in Mexico cites a report
> that 35% of the firms had Mexican capital and managers in 1979.
> A recent publication of the Third World Center in Mexico asserts that

US companies controlled 90% of all maquila operations in Mexico as of 1981.[5]

Other sources suggest that, by the mid-1980s, 90 percent or more of all the products assembled in *maquiladoras* were made in facilities owned by U.S. corporations and were produced for export to the U.S. market.[6]

Before the crisis, Mexican wages were higher than the average industrial wage in Hong Kong, Korea, and Taiwan; in the *maquiladoras* they had increased to $1.69 an hour, including fringe benefits. This was 15 percent of the $11.52 hourly American wage, but 26 percent more than the Korean and 17 percent more than the Taiwanese rates.[7] *Maquiladora* expansion, fueled by the 1982 peso devaluation in Mexico, brought the average earnings of Mexican workers in 1983 to about 57 percent of the 1981 level.[8] In 1982 wages plummeted below those found in the Big Three.

The quantity of apparel assembled in *maquiladoras* under the HTS 807 trade regime had grown substantially between 1970 and 1976.[9] However, as the 1982 peso devaluation reduced wages, the growth of apparel assembled in these plants accelerated even faster than it had during the previous decade. Between 1980 and 1987 the number of apparel plants went from 117 to 187, while the number of workers almost doubled, from 17,568 to 30,273. With the Special Access Program just implemented, investments in *maquiladoras* became increasingly desirable.[10]

The political and economic crises in Latin America created substantial uncertainty for foreign investors in the early 1980s, and foreign direct investment (FDI) declined significantly in the region. During this decade the lion's share of these funds went to East Asian countries, particularly the People's Republic of China.[11] However, after the left-wing insurgencies in Latin America were put down, the United States guided the restructuring of political and economic institutions in many countries in the region, and stability returned. Much of the funding that had been rechanneled to other parts of the developing world was restored to Mexico and the CBI nations, promoting renewed growth of trade and investment in the latter part of the 1980s.

Mexico was considered more desirable than the CBI countries as a location for the more profitable forms of investment, accounting for 36 percent of total annual FDI inflows between 1990 and 1991. Excepting the Caribbean Basin tax havens, the CBI nations had a 4 percent share of regional FDI inflows in the late 1980s; by 1990 this increased to only 7 percent.[12]

Despite the severe debt crisis of 1982, Mexico had a much larger and more diversified economy than most Caribbean and Central American nations. The leading Mexican export to the United States was petroleum. A third of Mexico's exports to U.S. markets were manufactured goods, including internal combustion piston engines and electrical distributing equipment. Mexico also exported agricultural products to the United States.[13] Between 1983 and 1990, apparel represented only 3.7 percent of all Mexican exports to the United States.

In 1985 Mexico hosted 734 plants on the border. By the end of 1991 there were 1,925 *maquiladoras* employing almost half a million workers, most in labor-intensive manufacturing. About 55 percent of the plants manufactured electrical goods or electronics; textiles or apparel; or furniture, wood, or metal products.[14]

From 1983 to 1990, the value of Mexican exports to the United States increased from $16.618 billion to $19.379 billion. Mexico's apparel exports—still a very small percentage of all the country's exports to the United States—doubled, going from 1.2 percent in 1983 to 2.4 percent of all Mexico's exports, and 3.7 percent of all Mexico's manufactured exports, to U.S. markets in 1990.[15]

During the 1980s, export-oriented apparel production played a much smaller role in Mexico than it did in the CBI countries. In 1983 the goods that Caribbean Basin countries exported to the United States were worth almost $8.9 billion; a small fraction of these (about 13 percent) were manufactured goods. Among these, apparel was valued at only $360 million, comprising 4.1 percent of the total goods, but 23 percent of the manufactured goods, exported to the United States.

While Mexican manufacturing for export increased during the 1980s, the opposite was true for the CBI countries. In 1990, seven years after passage of the 1983 CBI, and four years after implementation of the 1986 SAP, the value of all CBI exports to the United States actually declined. Only apparel exports grew, and grew quite rapidly. Between 1983 and 1990 the value of apparel exported from these countries to the United States under Item 807 went from $360 million to $1.973 billion. In 1990 this represented 23 percent of all exports, and 51.3 percent of all manufactured exports, to the United States.[16]

Whereas the CBI countries dominated Mexico in the export of apparel during the late 1980s, almost two-thirds of all apparel entering the United States under Item 807 came from both Mexico and the Caribbean Basin countries.[17] Apparel production would grow dramatically in both of these areas in the 1990s.

THE SPECIAL REGIME FOR MEXICO, 1988

In 1988, before leaving office, Reagan enacted a new program to expand Mexico's apparel exports to the United States by establishing an accord on textiles and apparel. Called the Special Regime, this new trade agreement made it possible for U.S. producers to expand their USTS 807 production-sharing regime in Mexico by $240 million a year.[18]

Unlike the CBI countries, Mexico had indigenous textile and apparel industries. These industries—with their aging technology, high employee turnover, and low productivity—were not internationally competitive. Products made in these firms were not destined for export but primarily for the Mexican market.[19] The Special Regime was not designed to restructure the Mexican textile and apparel industry. Had this been the intent of the agreement, Mexican producers could have invested in a higher-value-added export product, which could have generated the higher levels of foreign exchange needed to retire the country's debt. The Special Regime was, however, intended to support the growth of Mexico's export-processing sector and the country's expanding *maquiladoras*, at the expense of its domestic producers.

In many ways it was comparable to the CBI's Special Access Program, but it was tailored to fit the Mexican economy, allowing an automatic increase in quotas at the exporter's request. Unless there was a threat of market disruption, Mexico was permitted virtually unlimited quotas. At the discretion of the Committee for the Implementation of Textile Agreements, Mexico could export as much as the industry could produce.

As a result, Mexico's indigenous producers went bankrupt, ceding the country's domestic apparel industry to American investors. Before 1988, Mexico's textile and apparel export quotas could be filled under MFA-negotiated quotas. This could include exports to U.S. markets from domestic producers and from companies engaged in production sharing under Item 807 or 9802.[20] But the Special Regime's rules of origin—rules that governed quota allocations—favored *maquiladora* exports. Now, products assembled from fabric formed and cut in the United States were given a quota that was 200 to 500 percent higher than apparel made from textiles not meeting this criterion. As a result of this agreement, Mexico was now required to open its own markets to U.S. textile and apparel products. Between 1990 and 1993, even before NAFTA, U.S. sales of imported apparel from Mexico increased 202 percent.[21]

By the late 1980s the export processing of apparel in the CBI countries had generated new industrial growth in Florida. Twenty-five percent of what the state exported, it exported to the Caribbean nations.[22] Efforts to expand the CBI now had the vocal support of Florida businessmen, who claimed that firms in the port of Miami provided much of the cutting and supply services for the 807 apparel trade—trimming, customs expertise, and shipping.[23] Florida boasted that its thirteen deep-water seaports made foreign trade the predominant force in the state's economy, surpassing tourism and agriculture. Florida's business community, Caribbean politicians, and U.S. producers sourcing in the CBI countries began to demand a program for trade parity among all Latin American countries benefiting from the 807 apparel trade.[24] President George H. W. Bush sent a memo to his cabinet urging that, "CBI countries should continue to enjoy special and more liberal treatment under our textile import program. The CBI's effectiveness should be enhanced through appropriate assistance to investors, traders, and entrepreneurs in the region. . . . I call on Congress to act quickly to pass balanced legislation to extend and expand the CBI program in a way that is consistent with U.S. obligations under the GATT."[25] In fact, in 1990 Congress passed the Caribbean Basin Economic Recovery Expansion Act, making the Special Access Program, which had been scheduled to expire at the end of 1995, a permanent program and further reducing many 807 tariffs for a variety of CBI exports to the United States, particularly apparel.[26]

THE BUSH ADMINISTRATION
AND THE WESTERN HEMISPHERE

After Reagan's efforts defeated left-wing insurgents in Central America, Latin America became a new focus of American foreign-economic policy. Both George H. W. Bush and Bill Clinton would strengthen the ties of the United States and Canada with the Latin American nations. The Bush administration launched the Enterprise for the Americas Initiative, a first step toward a Western Hemisphere Free Trade Association. Congress gave Bush "fast track" authority to negotiate a U.S. treaty with Canada and Mexico, which laid the foundations for the North American Free Trade Agreement. NAFTA was the first building block and the centerpiece of the larger initiative.

Bush began to negotiate a series of trade accords between the United States and a number of Latin American nations. Ostensibly designed as market-opening initiatives, these new trade accords were instituted in cooperation with the World Bank and the International Monetary Fund, and, as noted earlier, they imposed obligations on these countries that went far beyond tariff and quota reductions. Their regulations were designed to restructure the economies of Latin American countries by promoting fiscal, trade, and investment reforms that would make them more hospitable to new types of U.S. trade and investment. At the end of the 1980s, with the cold war coming to a close, these trade accords were crafted in the interests of promoting competitiveness rather than containment. To link these countries more closely to the United States, both politically and economically, they were required to enact "major changes in legal and regulatory arrangements—especially the reduction of barriers to foreign participation in host economies, the introduction of debt equity swap programmes and the opening of a larger number of industries to private participation."[27]

Some of the required changes were similar to those demanded of CBI countries, and they included the privatization of state-owned resources and production facilities, the building of export-processing zones, the liberalization of banking, foreign majority participation in property ownership, tax-free imports of equipment used in the production of export goods, and the elimination of controls on remittances of profits. According to reports by the United Nations Conference on Trade and Development, the economic performance of these developing countries was "stimulated" by their continuing efforts not only to liberalize trade but to build an infrastructure that would create a stable and secure environment in which U.S. transnationals could invest and do business in Latin America.[28] Like comparable agreements that preceded them, the new trade accords would promote the flow of capital to these countries in exchange for access to their pools of low-wage labor and potential new markets for manufactured goods. As one optimistic expert put it,

> The newly market-oriented economies will have an insatiable appetite for capital goods, consumer goods and services from the old industrial countries. In fact, while the newly market-oriented economies account for only about a third of world output, they have 80% of the world's people and will account for more than 95% of the growth in world labor supply during the next half century. . . . There will be a surge in the potential supply of low-cost labor, agricultural output and raw materials.[29]

NAFTA AND THE PESO CRISIS

Bush may have initiated the Enterprise for the Americas Initiative and NAFTA, but Clinton, the first Democratic president in twelve years, was even more zealous in pursuing trade liberalization than his two Republican predecessors. After a vigorous national debate to build support for legislation enabling the treaty with Mexico, Congress ratified NAFTA in late 1993. As one analyst saw it, NAFTA represented "a significant point in the process of a longer series of efforts by transnational corporations to promote economic liberalization in Mexico."[30]

Less than a decade after it went into effect, the national debate about the success or failure of NAFTA continues. Not surprisingly, neoliberal economists and politicians who initially supported the accord now see it as a success. Those who favor free market theories point to data showing that the growth of U.S. exports to Mexico since NAFTA has led to an expansion of high-wage jobs in the United States. And while the peso crisis has been an incentive to transfer low-wage U.S. jobs to *maquiladoras* until recently, economists have noted the full-employment economy that emerged in America in the late 1990s,[31] which presumably obviates the distress of domestic job displacement.

Even if the loss of jobs is regrettable, say NAFTA supporters, the peso crisis, rather than NAFTA, was responsible for the Mexican wage declines. What is often ignored, however, is the fact that, even if the peso crisis was an independent development, once NAFTA was a reality it became more difficult, if not impossible, for the Mexican government to take steps to deal with the problems caused by the fiscal crisis, since it was obliged to uphold its treaty obligations with the United States and Canada. As one textile manufacturer in Fall River, Massachusetts, pointed out, "The outcome of the Mexico peso devaluation is a case in point. In response to this crisis the Mexican government raised tariffs on European and Asian exporters, and the resulting tariff hikes caused their exports to fall between 20 and 30 percent. A comparable tariff hike on US business probably would have had a similar effect. However, due to its NAFTA obligations, Mexico could not unilaterally increase tariffs on US goods."[32]

Yet those who question the free market approach see it as no coincidence that a new peso crisis occurred just as NAFTA was phased in. The causes of the 1994 fiscal debacle, they believe, had been building for some time in a Mexico whose corrupt politics had traditionally been deeply enmeshed in its economy. Corruption and indebtedness have plagued Mexico "virtually since the country's independence from Spain in 1821."[33] In 1986, however, as Miguel de la Madrid presided over Mexico's joining of the GATT, some believed the country would begin to reform its corrupt, state-dominated economy and make it more democratic and market-oriented. Indeed, by the late 1980s Mexico agreed to the Brady Plan, designed to resolve the nation's debt problems and privatize state-owned enterprises.

The plan stimulated increased levels of foreign direct investment in Mexico.

In the early 1990s, Mexico's new president, Carlos Salinas de Gortari, with the support of Mexican industrial and banking oligarchies, convinced the United States that Mexico was prepared to make a commitment to neoliberal economic reform, trade liberalization, and democratization. Salinas's commitment was met with great optimism by the American business community, which looked forward to Mexico's integration with the American economy.[34] Concluding NAFTA with Mexico would lead to a rapid expansion of new, highly profitable corporate investment south of the border.[35]

Yet many believed NAFTA itself was flawed, and that it contributed to the peso crisis. During the years of negotiation immediately preceding the accord, the promise of NAFTA led to a massive flow of U.S. capital into Mexico in the form of portfolio investment. According to one analyst, "This prospect helped to immediately reverse Mexico's decades of capital flight. Suddenly, $60 billion in global portfolio capital (hot money) catapulted into Mexico as NAFTA took shape[,] turning it, briefly, into the fast buck capital of the world, with speculative returns routinely in the range of 60 percent to 120 percent per year."[36] A full eighteen months before the December 1994 Mexican peso devaluation, Thea Lee, a trade economist at the Economic Policy Institute, warned Congress of what might happen. She testified that "there has been an increase in foreign direct investment in Mexico in the last few years, but there has also been a very big increase in speculative investment in Mexico, in the stock market and portfolio investment which is part of the financial bubble that people worry about bursting if NAFTA is rejected. . . . Investors have bought Mexican treasury bonds and stocks in anticipation of NAFTA going through, and some of them will be disappointed if NAFTA is rejected." Lee continued, "The Conference Board, a New York–based research organization, has estimated that in 1992 virtually all the new investment in North America went to Mexico."[37]

Jeffrey Schott, a neoliberal economist from the free-trade-oriented Institute for International Economics, spoke in support of NAFTA. At the same hearing that Lee addressed, Schott testified that U.S. investment was financing a trade surplus with Mexico. Congressional failure to approve NAFTA, he warned, would lead to the withdrawal of investment funds from that country and would turn the U.S. trade surplus with Mexico negative. As he put it, "Our concern is that rejection of the NAFTA would cause a shock in the capital markets."[38]

During the early 1990s, when this vast amount of capital was flowing to Mexico, there were constant revelations of the government's corruption. It became dubious whether the industrial and financial oligarchy that controlled the Mexican government could ensure that the massive new portfolio investment would support the country's takeoff into free market growth. Such fears were confirmed in January 1994, when new revelations of the political corruption in the Salinas administration accompanied the peso devaluation. As Lee predicted, portfolio investors saw their assets shrink dramatically. Mexico plunged into a new debt crisis, only to be bailed out by the United States once again.

Since that time, new studies have continually tried to assess the economic impacts of NAFTA on both Mexico and the United States. The Clinton administration and professional economists found evidence that the program was sound, arguing that there had been a significant trade surplus between the United States and its NAFTA partners between 1994 and 1999. According to testimony by Deputy U.S. Trade Representative Richard W. Fisher, "During NAFTA's first five years, U.S. goods exports to our NAFTA partners increased by $93 billion, or 66 percent, to a total of $235 billion. The $156 billion in goods we exported to Canada were as much as we exported to all the countries of East Asia put together. This year we will export more than five times to Mexico what we export to China. Our exports of $79 billion in Mexico make it our second largest export market, as I mentioned, after Canada."[39] In contrast to this optimistic view, critics of NAFTA argue that the U.S. trade surplus with Mexico is a myth, that the figures indicating a trade surplus result from calculations based on erroneous economic assumptions about the ways in which comparative advantage drives United States–Mexico trade.

Neoliberals argue that the lower labor costs of developing countries are offset by the higher productivity of industrialized nations. Thus, trade between developing countries, with their abundance of low-wage labor, and industrialized countries, with their advanced technologies, facilitates exchanges of equal value for both trade partners. However, free trade economists ignore the new potential to transfer the newest technology to low-wage countries. This transfer soon unbalances the presumed equity of such transactions, to the advantage of the industrial nations.

Critics of the neoliberal position point to the fact that U.S. exports to Mexico, as to other low-wage countries, are bound for subsidiaries of U.S. transnationals—there to be transformed by cheap labor into finished goods and reimported to the United States. This interindustry trade, they claim, does not lead to trade surpluses but to trade deficits for America. Indeed, the United States has had a trade deficit with Mexico of $10 to $12 billion each year since 1995.[40] Such trade deficits also mean higher profits for U.S.-dominated transnationals.

Supporters of NAFTA argue that Mexicans benefit from jobs created in the new *maquiladoras* and export-processing zones. Yet such workers now earn wages far below the cost of purchasing the goods they produce for export. Clearly, Mexico was a poor country before NAFTA. Yet NAFTA has intensified that poverty by helping to create continuing inflation and currency devaluations, which have impoverished most Mexicans. Since NAFTA went into effect, wages have declined dramatically. In 1993, compensation for manufacturing workers was 85 percent below U.S. costs; in 1999 this fell to 90 percent below U.S. costs. Mexican wages have dropped 20 percent since NAFTA.[41] Much of this is due to the repeated devaluation of the peso, which was valued at 3.1 to the dollar in 1994 but by early 1999 was 10 to the dollar.[42] A 1999 study by the InterAmerican Development Bank indicates that Mexican consumers had suffered a 39 percent drop in their purchasing power in the years since NAFTA. The report, written for the UN Development Program, shows that two-thirds of Mexico's population had slipped below the poverty line; before NAFTA, less than half that number were considered poor.[43]

THE TEXTILE-LED APPAREL INDUSTRY AND NAFTA

With NAFTA, Mexico saw the loss of billions of dollars of portfolio investment, followed by a new peso devaluation, both of which contributed to reductions in wages and the standard of living among Mexican workers. NAFTA has been a great benefit to the U.S. textile industry, however, in their competition with Asian producers. Indeed, the president of the ATMI was even willing to support trade parity for the Caribbean Basin in the pursuit of this goal. In support of a recent effort for parity legislation, he stated, "Our key objective in supporting an enhanced Caribbean trading agreement is to help the United States continue its trend of displacing apparel imports from the Far East and bringing apparel production back to the Western Hemisphere."[44] Despite the scandals revealed in Mexico's pre-NAFTA politics, when the treaty took effect leaders of the U.S. textile industry were clearly overly optimistic about its impact on Mexico's political future. But they were right about its potential to promote corporate investment. In 1993 *Textile World* reported,

> While allegations of fraud are routine in the Mexican election process, today's political environment seems to be improving under the

presidency of President Carlos Salinas de Gortari, who has dismantled many of the business practices and regulations blamed for stagnant growth during the last decade. Unproductive centralization and corrupt business practices are being eliminated, and foreign investment regulations and procedures have been significantly modified to make it easier for foreign countries to establish private enterprises in Mexico.[45]

Since its enactment, NAFTA and the peso crisis have both made Mexico a more attractive site for apparel production. Post-NAFTA Mexico allows America's textile corporations not only to benefit from the abundance of its low-wage labor for apparel assembly but also to develop new investment in a vertically integrated textile and apparel complex.[46] NAFTA has made Mexico a serious competitor to the Caribbean Basin countries as a site for production of apparel for export to U.S. markets.[47] These changes are the consequences of both the peso devaluation and the benefits embodied in the trade agreements.

FASHION PRODUCT, STANDARD PRODUCT, AND THE RULES OF ORIGIN

Just as the implementation of the Special Access Program for the Caribbean Basin in 1986 generated disputes within the U.S. textile, apparel, and retail complex, similar disputes emerged over the implementation of NAFTA. On one side of the dispute were the textile makers and their apparel customers who made standard and basic apparel, represented by the American Textile Manufacturers' Institute and the American Apparel Manufacturers' Association, respectively. On the other side of the dispute were the fashion apparel producers and their retail customers, represented by the Textile and Apparel Group of the American Association of Exporters and Importers (AAEI-TAG) and the National Retail Federation, respectively.[48]

As mentioned in chapter 8, the textile-led apparel group was competing with lower wage Asian producers and was anxious to promote the growth of apparel assembly in the Caribbean Basin countries; the SAP gave full trade benefits to importers of apparel produced in Caribbean Basin countries when the apparel was assembled from fabrics "cut and formed" in the United States. Retailers, importers, and makers of fashion apparel preferred to source globally rather than regionally, to purchase fabrics and choose assembly sites throughout the developing world. Domestic manufacturers and contractors, however—represented by the American Apparel Contractors' Association and the new Union of Needletrades and Industrial Textile Employees (UNITE)—opposed the CBI entirely, saying that it was inimical to domestic production and the employment of apparel workers.

In 1993, as Congress geared up to vote on NAFTA, U.S. textile manufacturers and their customers contracting apparel assembly in CBI nations pressed for more tariff reductions on U.S. apparel imports from the CBI countries. They sought tariffs set at the same levels that NAFTA had set for Mexican apparel imports. As they saw it, a trade regime for products from the CBI countries comparable to that for products from Mexico was essential to protect their existing investments in the CBI nations. The textile-led segment of apparel producers feared that, without "CBI parity," there would be a large-scale movement to Mexico.

Concerns about parity were reflected in the debate over the rules of origin instituted by the NAFTA-enabling legislation. One of the major areas of contention between the two groups was the NAFTA "yarn forward" rule. Item 807, as it was applied to apparel imported from the CBI countries, imposed import tariffs based solely on the value added by assembly operations, but only in the case of apparel assembled from textiles cut and formed in the United States. Importers of apparel made with other textiles owed full duty on the value of the entire product.

The NAFTA rule entitled producers to the full complement of duty-free and quota-free privileges—but this applied only to apparel assembled in Mexico from fabrics and fibers made in any of the three NAFTA countries: the United States, Canada, and Mexico. This rule of origin encouraged use of more U.S.-made content, and it favored textile producers. It posed an obstacle for fashion apparel producers who wanted the special NAFTA tariff benefits but who also valued the ability to source globally. While the fashion apparel group and their retail customers opposed this rule, the textile-led interests supported it.

Also in dispute were "trade preference levels," or TPLs. These were rules that determined which textiles and textile fibers were deemed unavailable from manufacturers in any of the three NAFTA countries and, thus, could be purchased only from suppliers in other countries. Apparel made from materials named on the list of approved materials received full quota and tariff benefits in NAFTA trade. While the U.S. textile industry and its standard and basic apparel customers wanted to limit TPLs as much as possible, fashion apparel producers who wanted to source globally fought to extend the list.

When NAFTA was passed, all quotas on apparel assembled in Mexico were abolished and exports to the United States became duty free. The textile-led apparel makers continued to press for CBI parity. Apparel tariffs were considerably higher than other tariffs. According to the International Trade Commission, "The average trade weighted duty on apparel is 16 percent ad valorem, compared with about 3 percent ad valorem for other products."[49] The SAP trade benefits reduced apparel import tariffs by about two-thirds compared to apparel imported from other countries, a reduction crucial in determining both the cost and selling price of apparel items.

In 1995, two years after the initial bid for CBI parity failed, a second bill was introduced.[50] That year, testifying in support of CBI parity before the House Ways and Means Committee, a representative of the Central American–Caribbean Textile and Apparel Council—a consortium of textile and apparel companies sourcing in the CBI countries—claimed that, after NAFTA, the cost advantage of sourcing in Mexico rather than CBI countries was between 8 and 25 percent.[51] By 1997, still arguing for parity, industry leaders argued that assembling apparel in Mexico, rather than the CBI region, could mean an 8 to 18 percent price advantage for American firms.[52] Moreover, the same witness estimated that textile and apparel operations in CBI countries could be closed, moved, and reopened in Mexico in a matter of six to seven weeks. According to the Caribbean Textile and Apparel Institute, between 1995 and 1996 more than 150 apparel plants closed in the Caribbean, and 123,000 jobs were lost.[53] In Jamaica, by the beginning of 1997 there were reported losses of over 17,000 apparel jobs and an unemployment rate of 16 percent.[54] But despite potential problems, the second parity bill also failed. In July 1997, a new one was introduced in Congress but was eliminated from consideration when it went into reconciliation between the House and the Senate.

Even without parity there is no evidence that massive numbers of CBI apparel producers in the 1990s pulled up stakes and moved to Mexico, as parity advocates predicted they would. Instead, the export processing of apparel in this region continued its steady growth. Even though the growth rates of the region's apparel exports to the United States slowed somewhat during these years, in 1997 CBI countries exported $7.5 billion worth of apparel to the United States, compared to Mexico's $6.3 billion.

When the Special Access Program was passed in 1986, Caribbean and Central American countries rapidly expanded their apparel exports to the United States. However, when NAFTA went into effect in 1994, Mexico expanded its apparel exports to the United States even more rapidly. As a result U.S. textile and apparel producers saw a slowdown in the expansion of apparel imports from the CBI countries—not a reduction of these imports from that region. By 2000 Mexico's apparel exports had caught up with and slightly surpassed those from the CBI countries, $8.8 compared to $8.7 billion.

Some of the CBI countries have been more successful than others in competing with Mexican apparel production. Table 1 shows that, between 1993 and 2000, apparel exports from the CBI countries to the United States were from the same regions that had been successful in export processing in the 1980s—the Dominican Republic, Honduras, Guatemala, El Salvador, Costa Rica, Nicaragua, and Haiti. Exports to the United States from other CBI countries, including Panama and Jamaica, declined.[55] This may account for the plant closings and job losses reported in Jamaica. Indeed, despite the dire warnings of the NAFTA-parity advocates, and despite the more advantageous NAFTA trade benefits and the low wages brought about by the Mexican peso devaluation, apparel exports from selected CBI nations have continued to grow rapidly.

Caribbean countries that experienced the steepest wage declines between 1989 and 1998 have been the highest-volume exporters of apparel to the United States. Furthermore, "countries where wages have fallen the most are also the countries that have the worst record of abusing workers' rights."[56] At the same time, productivity in the apparel industries of the most repressive countries has decreased, as measured by value added per employee. Manufacturers compete by "sweating labor," a human resource strategy not compatible with long-range growth and social equity.[57]

Whatever the rules that govern quotas and tariff rates, they are successful only to the extent that they are enforced. Textile and apparel makers are becoming more concerned about this, and have pressed for legislation to tighten the U.S. Customs Service's border control efforts. An inability to control the Mexican border could neutralize enforcement of the rules of origin. By 1995 not only drug traffic but also rampant cargo theft had become a pervasive problem in South Florida and along the Mexican border.[58] An acceleration in drug traffic has made the accompanying cargo theft a continuing problem.[59]

VERTICAL INTEGRATION IN THE TEXTILE, APPAREL, AND RETAIL CHAIN

NAFTA's rules of origin allowed tariff-and quota-free exports of U.S. textiles, and tariff-and quota-free imports of assembled apparel, but only when the components were made with fabrics and fibers produced in any of the three NAFTA countries. These new rules made it possible for textile

Table 1. Value of CBI Apparel Exports to the United States,
1993–2000
(US$ billions)

	1993	2000
Large exporters:	3.50	9.20
Dominican Republic, Honduras, Guatemala, El Salvador, Costa Rica, Nicaragua, Haiti		
Small exporters:	0.41	0.23
Jamaica, Belize, Guyana, St. Lucia, Panama, Barbados, Trinidad and Tobago, St. Kitts, St. Nevis, St. Vincent, British Virgin Islands, Netherlands Antilles, Bahamas, Dominica, Montserrat, Aruba, Grenada, Antigua/Barbuda		

SOURCE: United States International Trade Commission, "Apparel Imports" (SIC 23), Customs Value of Imports for All Countries, U.S. Imports for Consumption Annual Data (DATAWEB), http://www.dataweb.usitc.gov/scripts/REPORT.asp, February 13, 2001.

and apparel manufacturers to build a full-package operation in Mexico, a vertically integrated textile and apparel industry that started with the weaving of fibers and ended with the production of clothing that was packaged, tagged, and exported to U.S. retailers. As a result, apparel firms developed textile capacity, textile firms opened apparel divisions, and retailers began to manufacture merchandise for sale in their stores.[60]

The inability of the textile and apparel industries to get CBI-parity legislation passed limited the increase in vertical integration in the Caribbean Basin countries. This was, at least in part, the result of the CBI trade rules mandating that textiles used in clothing assembly in these countries be cut and formed only in the United States—and not in Mexico or Canada. NAFTA trade rules, however, allowed U.S. textile and apparel producers to seek out opportunities to develop joint ventures and strategic alliances with textile and apparel firms in Mexico. Some of these are partnerships between U.S. firms located in Mexico, while others are joint business ventures between U.S. firms and the more competitive Mexican textile- and apparel-producing firms. Many of Mexico's textile and apparel companies suffered from "high costs, outdated technology, poor quality, prolonged machine down time, and excess capacity"; other, more competitive firms have been "rescued" by forming joint ventures with American corporations in this new process of vertical integration.[61]

The ease with which the latest technology can be transferred has meant that new "technology, manufacturing experience, technical expertise, management training and capital . . . provide the cornerstone for the development of the critically important textile and apparel sectors of the Mexican economy."[62] The chief executive of one company making high-niche men's clothing reports, "There are many markets where it makes sense to own production resources . . . because you have to have the latest technology to be price competitive."[63]

A major new communications technology introduced at the 1995 Bobbin Contexpo, the apparel industry trade show, was the Sourcing Network, a computerized matchmaking service that links the buying offices of U.S. retailers, catalog houses, and importers with potential Latin American partners. In 1994 Mexico City hosted its first Sewn Products Expo to educate producers about the latest technological innovations and sourcing opportunities.[64] As one industry spokesman puts it, "While some of the manufacturers . . . produce or provide their own fabrics, such vertical operations are not the norm in Latin America. But they will have to be if the region is to keep the Far East and other competitors at bay."[65] Companies who engage in these new partnering arrangements can produce higher quality apparel, and are expected to move the U.S. textile, apparel, and retail complex up the value-added chain.[66]

Since 1994, textile investment in Mexico has grown. In January of that year, just as NAFTA went into effect, *Bobbin Magazine*, the AAMA trade journal, published an article titled "Mexico's Road to Transition." The article discussed the projects of U.S. textile firms like Cone Mills and Guilford Mills and the low-end retailers like Wal-Mart, Price Club, Dillard's, Burlington Coat, and Fleming Companies. These and other firms had recently implemented joint ventures with Mexican firms or planned to invest in Mexico.[67] Galey and Lord acquired Dimmit Industries, S.A. de CV of Mexico, which made finished trousers and shorts composed of U.S.-manufactured textiles.[68] The industry made denim fabrics and denim clothing, albeit not exclusively. In the mid-1990s Cone Mills of North Carolina and CIPSA of Mexico were "in the process of building the world's largest and most modern denim complex in northern Mexico, which will incorporate all segments of the fashion chain from textile manufacturing to the production of finished clothes."[69]

In 1997, Guilford Mills of North Carolina built, at a cost of $6 million, a "26,000-square-meter complex" to "facilitate the growth of the integration of the entire textile chain—textile fibers, fabrics, cutting and sewing," eighty miles south of Mexico City, in Morelos, Mexico. Called Nustart, it was a joint venture between Guilford Mills, Burlington Industries, Dupont

Corporation, and Grupo Alfa of Mexico and was financed in part with an $8 million subsidy from the Mexican government.[70]

According to the *Miami Herald*, the Nustart venture included eighteen factories and provided employment for "several thousand seamstresses."[71] The *Herald* stated that "[Nustart] is also intended to boost Guilford's textile sales . . . [in] an attempt to reverse the trend in the US apparel industry of subcontracting cut-and-sew operations to Asian companies that use Asian textiles to manufacture the clothing." This venture was designed to benefit from the capacity of Mexico, an oil-producing nation, to manufacture synthetic fibers, such as polyester and nylon, using advanced technologies. Burlington Industries, one partner in this effort, provided manufacturing services for companies producing denim.[72] The goal of Nustart, or "Textile City" as it is called, is to provide "one-stop shopping" for apparel manufacturers who want to do their apparel assembly in Mexico— and to make Nustart's customers "more successful so that they are likely to buy more fabric."[73] "Cone will build a denim operation and Guilford will construct a warp knit operation. . . . The objective then [was] to attract apparel customers producing denim and knit apparel to set up shop within the compound and share the infrastructure."

In 1997 the Tarrant Apparel Group, which had been consigning 80 percent of its production to China, began to build a full-package apparel operation in Mexico,[74] purchasing fabric and then subcontracting the cutting, sewing, and finishing of its products. A year later Tarrant purchased its own production facilities under its wholly owned Mexican subsidiary—a large denim mill, twill factory, and distribution center.[75]

By 1999, Cone Mills, the largest denim producer in the world, initiated a new joint venture with Deborah/Starlite to manage full-package production of apparel to be sold to private-label producers and retailers in the United States and Mexico.[76] In June of that year, Guilford Mills and Cone Mills announced a joint venture to open in the year 2000. This project was to be "an innovative textile and apparel industrial park in Mexico, the first large-scale industrial development in the country in which textile plants, garment manufacturers and laundering facilities are located in such close proximity. The park will be built on more than 500 acres in Altamira, near Tampico, a northeast coast port city in the state of Tamaulipas."[77] In November 1999, Burlington Industries opened a $2 billion enterprise to produce denim for jeans, and wool and wool-blend fabrics for use in men's and women's tailored clothing. It purchased a second facility to cut and sew denim and, in partnership with a Mexican firm, a laundry operation.[78] As NAFTA became law, Burlington, which had been making denim in

Mexico for years, decided to end its reliance on contract assembly work and to set up a full-package operation to make denim clothing, with direct sale to retailers and brand-name-fashion manufacturers.[79] In 1999 Cone Mills began a joint project with Guilford Mills in Mexico to make denim for high-fashion jeans. The purpose of this arrangement is to build an infrastructure to bring to the area the natural gas, electricity, and water essential for washing the jeans.[80]

Dan River, a textile producer that has focused primarily on home products rather than apparel, has signed a letter of intent with Grupo Industrial Zaga, a Mexican textile company, to build an integrated apparel fabric plant in Mexico to produce "high-count apparel and sheeting fabrics that are in demand in the Western hemisphere, but are currently supplied primarily from Asia."[81] The company's apparel fabrics will be sold to Dan River's customers, who make shirts and uniforms "at practically any location in the Western hemisphere."[82]

Once textile and apparel firms started moving to Mexico, the pressure for other American firms to do so increased. Perhaps no company felt the pressure more than Levi Strauss. Committed to making its jeans in the United States, the company saw most of its competitors go offshore—to Asia and, increasingly, Mexico. In 1990 Levi Strauss had a 48.2 percent market share in men's jeans. However, as apparel-manufacturing capacity grew in Mexico, competitors like the Gap, Tommy Hilfiger, and others began to produce jeans in alternative market niches. J. C. Penney and Sears began to target the lower niche markets, while Donna Karan, Ralph Lauren, and Versace started selling upmarket jeans.

In 1992, with a declining market share, instead of moving to Mexico, Levi Strauss committed itself to domestic production. Rather than move to Mexico, the company embarked on a massive reengineering of its U.S. plants to meet new demands for quick response from its department store customers.[83] In early 1991, the company looked for ways to cut the time it took to replenish retail customers' inventories from days to as little as twenty-four hours. Initially, the focus of the project, called Quick Response, was on implementing electronic data interchange systems that would speed communications between retail customers and Levi Strauss.[84]

Yet as the firm was doing this, retailers demanded that Levi Strauss "be able to do better forecasting and even deliver goods already packaged and tagged so they could go directly from the loading dock to the selling floor." Despite the effort to meet these requirements, by 1998 Levi Strauss's share of the men's jeans market had fallen from 48.2 percent to 25 percent.[85] Some saw the reengineering program designed by the company as having been unrealistic, expensive, and poorly conceived. By 1997 it was clear that the project had failed. Levi Strauss then made a decision to discontinue its domestic production and move offshore.[86] In November 1997, the company announced it would close eleven factories in four states, laying off 3,400 workers.[87] In March of 1999 it announced 5,900 more layoffs.[88] Even Bruce Raynor, secretary-treasurer of UNITE, which lost thousands of members as a result of these closings, nevertheless recognized the competitive pressures facing the company, noting that all of Levi Strauss's competitors had long been making their jeans in Asia and Mexico.[89] As one denim maker said, "It's difficult to understand how any of our competitors could think they can remain in business without pursuing Mexico as a strategic location."[90] Ventures like the ones described above—those manufacturing denim, jeans, and undergarments—are seen as contributing to the increased productivity of the Mexican textile-apparel complex.

NAFTA did not initiate the process of export-oriented apparel assembly in Mexico. This process had begun years earlier. However, since the inception of this accord, which has changed the trade rules, Mexico has become a major new export-processing platform for textile and apparel products sold mostly in the United States but also in other parts of Latin America and the world.[91]

Passed almost a decade after the Caribbean Basin Initiative, NAFTA allowed Mexico to rapidly catch up to the Caribbean Basin countries as an exporter of apparel. As we have seen, between 1983 and 1990, the years after the CBI was passed, the Special Access Program accelerated the growth of apparel exports from the Caribbean Basin to the United States, exports which increased much faster than those of Mexico. Between 1990 and 1993, apparel exports to the United States from CBI countries and Mexico expanded at about the same rate. However, from 1994 to 1999, the years just before and after NAFTA went into effect, Mexico was able to develop a full-package industry concentrating on the production of denim, jeans, and undergarments, and now equals the CBI nations in its exports of apparel to the United States.[92]

The significance of this transformation for the future of Mexico's industrial development is the subject of ongoing debates. Research is being done on the role that "lead foreign firms are playing in the cluster's growth, and the extent to which the networks they are establishing . . . promote industrial upgrading." Some argue that these vertically integrated ventures will promote positive benefits for the Mexican economy in the long run.[93] But many believe that this type of growth will only lead to the further "maquiladorization" of Mexico.

THE IMPACT OF TRADE LIBERALIZATION
ON LATIN AMERICA

In the 1990s, free trade agreements proliferated among countries in Latin America. In a strategy designed to equalize the benefits of the trade regimes that had been created for Mexico and the CBI countries, the United States signed new bilateral trade agreements with Bolivia, Argentina, and Uruguay.[94] Soon after this, a variety of Latin American countries formed three free trade alliances among themselves. Argentina, Paraguay, Brazil, and Uruguay formed Mercosur. Mexico, Colombia, and Venezuela signed a pact known as the G-3 Agreement. Venezuela, Ecuador, Colombia, Bolivia, and Peru signed the Andean Pact. Mexico participates in the G-3 Agreement and the Andean Pact, as well as a trade pact among Caribbean nations known as the Association of Caribbean States.[95] In 1996, the Andean Pact and Mercosur nations voted to merge, becoming a ten-member organization that encompasses almost all of South America.[96] These accords opened U.S. markets to imports of apparel from Bolivia, Colombia, Ecuador, and Venezuela (members of the Andean Pact) as well as from Peru and Chile.[97]

When it got the first Item 807A program in South America, Colombia began to increase its exports of underwear to the United States.[98] In the early 1990s Colombia and Peru were seen as poised to become major apparel exporters. Yet, after 1994, apparel exports from these countries to the United States suffered a major decline, while those from selected CBI countries and Mexico rose.[99] By 1996, two years after NAFTA was implemented, "textile and apparel exports to the U.S. by the Andean's two largest shippers hit the doldrums." In 1998, while apparel imports from the CBI nations and Mexico comprised close to 30 percent of all U.S. apparel imports, those from the rest of the Latin American countries made up only a tiny fraction of the total—slightly more than 1 percent.[100] These countries included Colombia, Peru, Brazil, Bolivia, Ecuador, Uruguay, Venezuela, Argentina, Paraguay, Bermuda, Anguilla, and the Cayman Islands.

What have been the consequences of the new free trade agenda? Despite the ability of many countries in the Western Hemisphere to export apparel to the United States, Mexico and the CBI countries are still the major competitors producing apparel for U.S. markets. Moreover, the growth of free trade in the Western Hemisphere has led to a shakeout in Mexico's indigenous textile and apparel industries. Most of Mexico's domestic producers have not gained access to U.S. import markets. Moreover, the new free trade accords in Latin America have opened Mexico's markets to low-wage goods from other Latin American countries and have challenged what remained of Mexico's lower-end apparel manufacturers who were producing for local rather than export markets. Mexico's domestic apparel producers are facing higher interest rates and lower levels of demand for their products.[101]

The 1997 financial crisis in Asia also affected Mexico. At the same time that America's denim and jeans producers moved to Mexico, Mexican producers faced an influx of low-wage denim products from Asian textile producers who were attempting to deal with their own crisis. Overproduction of denim and denim products made by U.S. producers has also taken its toll on the profits of many of these companies.[102]

In 1995, only a year after NAFTA was passed, Chuck Hayes, vice president of the ATMI, said, "U.S. textile manufacturers have certainly benefited from this production shift since the January 1, 1994, implementation of NAFTA."[103] Hayes is quoted as having said of NAFTA:

> The theory is simple. If garment makers can be lured to low cost manufacturing sites in Mexico they won't go to the Orient, where they end up buying fabric from Japan, South Korea and other Asian countries.
>
> To me[,] NAFTA was truly the beginning of a renaissance for the textile industry in the United States. . . .
>
> If we don't have NAFTA we'll be out of business. Ten years from today I'd have to close my doors.

To this statement, the Deputy U.S. Trade Representative added, "China is now the industry's greatest competitor."[104]

If economists see the enhancement of market forces as enhancing trade, industry specialists often see political clout as responsible for advantageous markets. Sharon Jacobs, an attorney specializing in international trade and a frequent contributor of articles to *Bobbin Magazine*, has been quoted as saying, "Some parts of the US industry already have mastered the art of getting our negotiators to draft provisions that make their business irresistible." She continues, "The casual apparel companies who now dominate the 807 and 807A operations in Mexico are the obvious prime examples. Those companies were very much in evidence during NAFTA negotiations, and it was a great investment of their time and resources, which is paying off handsomely."[105]

NAFTA AND THE LOSS OF U.S. APPAREL JOBS

In 1993, before Congress approved NAFTA, a study by Amy Glasmeier, James M. Campbell, and June M. Henton predicted that, should NAFTA

Table 2. Employment Changes in Manufacturing Industries, 1983–1998

	NUMBER OF JOBS					CHANGE (%)				
Region	1983	1986	1990	1993	1998	1983–1986	1986–1990	1990–1993	1993–1998	1983–98
					Apparel Employment					
South Central[a]	523,803	513,596	498,362	487,979	319,345	−2	−3	−3	−35	
NY/NE[b]	361,196	313,288	254,448	217,490	151,546	−13	−19	−15	−30	
West Coast[c]	115,165	125,118	146,734	143,609	139,741	9	17	−2	−3	
All Other	117,258	122,828	124,891	121,016	60,289	5	2	−3	−50	
TOTAL	1,117,422	1,076,816	1,026,425	972,087	672,919	−4	−5	−5	−31	−40
					All Manufacturing					
South Central	5,356,739	5,619,565	5,796,722	5,750,610	5,431,399	5	3	−1	−6	
NY/NE	4,622,222	4,534,677	4,057,147	3,587,545	2,933,534	−2	−11	−11	−18	
West Coast	2,383,730	2,576,695	2,752,704	2,417,889	2,374,453	8	7	−12	−2	
All Other	5,918,519	6,363,602	6,515,291	6,379,564	5,932,068	8	2	−3	−7	
TOTAL	18,281,210	19,094,539	19,121,864	18,135,608	17,031,454	4	—	−5	−6	−7
					All Manufacturing Except Apparel					
TOTAL	17,163,788	18,017,723	18,095,439	17,163,521	16,358,535	5	—	−5	−5	−5

[a] North Carolina, Georgia, Texas, Tennessee, Alabama, South Carolina, Virginia, Mississippi, Florida, Kentucky, Arkansas, West Virginia, Louisiana, Maryland
[b] New York, New Jersey, Pennsylvania, Massachusetts, Connecticut, Maine, Vermont, Rhode Island, New Hampshire
[c] California, Oregon, Washington
SOURCE: Calculated from U.S. Bureau of the Census, *County Business Patterns* (Washington, D.C.: U.S. Bureau of the Census, various years).

pass, the American South would experience a heavy loss of manufacturing jobs in the decade to follow.[106] In particular, since its passage NAFTA has dramatically affected the rate of job loss in apparel production compared to job losses in other manufacturing industries. Table 2 shows the pattern of job loss in apparel production, which has varied by region during the last two decades or so. By 1983, the New York–New England region, with New York City as the fashion center, had lost its predominance. At that time, the South had the highest concentration of apparel employment in the country. The New York–New England region continued to lose apparel jobs at a rapid rate during the 1980s, while the apparel industry on the West Coast, located mostly in California, saw a net gain in employment.[107] During this time, the South was affected only modestly by job loss. Between 1993 and 1998, the years immediately preceding NAFTA and the WTA, the employment situation in domestic apparel production changed rapidly. The New York–New England region lost 30 percent, and the South 35 percent, of remaining apparel production jobs.

When the new regime of global sourcing replaced the older quota system, the U.S. textile and apparel complex was confronted by a large and growing textile- and apparel-producing industry in selected Caribbean Basin countries and in Mexico. The Agreement on Textiles and Clothing (ATC) continues to pose a major challenge to the regional protection that NAFTA and the CBI had facilitated for a sector of the U.S. textile industry and its apparel customers. The ATC renewed the threat of low-wage competition by Asian firms, an issue that I treat in chapter 11. But before we can understand the potential outcomes, we must look at the role the U.S. retail industry played as it grew, became concentrated, and helped shape the U.S. textile and apparel trade agenda during the past twenty years.

10　Apparel Retailing
in the United States

*From Mom-and-Pop Shop
to Transnational Corporation*

Only twenty-five years ago, mom-and-pop clothing stores flourished alongside large department stores and discount chains. Today, however, the highly concentrated, vertically integrated U.S. retail transnationals— like Wal-Mart, Federated Department Stores, and the Gap—selling vast quantities of apparel, have put many of the smaller stores and even some of the larger department stores out of business. New forms of corporate retailing have played a crucial role in the globalization of the textile-apparel complex. Today, transnationals compete for retail market share and market power, both nationally and internationally.

For the past twenty years or so, retailing has been driving the thrust of U.S. trade liberalization in textiles and apparel. As a result, clothing stores have gained access to ever larger supplies of low-wage imports from developing countries. Trade liberalization has made it possible for retailers to enhance their power over the textile and apparel manufacturers who supply them, and to direct the restructuring of the textile, apparel, and retail complex.[1]

The elimination of quotas, the reduction of tariffs, and the opening of new markets around the world have not only accelerated the globalization of apparel production—leading to a new round of vertical integration and concentration in apparel retailing—but have also intensified the competition in textiles, apparel, and retailing. All the players are now engaged in efforts to sell more textiles or clothing and to increase their market share. Concomitantly, textile and apparel producers press the government for more and different kinds of trade liberalization, seeking even lower-wage production sites, as retailers open more stores to sell their ever expanding volumes of lower cost clothing.

This history of U.S. apparel retailing begins with the emergence of department stores, which first appeared during the early part of the twentieth century. Department stores initially occupied the main shopping district of the downtown area of cities, making it possible for the new urban middle- and upper-middle class consumers to enjoy the convenience of one-stop shopping; stable prices; and reliable, quality merchandise. Individual merchant families owned these department stores. In 1916, Lincoln Filene, president of Filene's in Boston, recognized the value of "collaboration between retailers in buying merchandise, recruiting executives, training employees, improving advertising, and other associated aspects of the retail business."[2] He started the Retail Research Association, which two years later was superseded by the Associated Merchandising Corporation.

Recognizing the industry's need for a centralized corporate structure that would diffuse risk, permit expansion, and earn higher profits, Filene began to advocate formation of a national retail holding company. In 1918 Filene's joined with Abraham and Strauss of Brooklyn and F and R Lazarus and Company of Columbus, Ohio, to form Federated Department Stores. Holding companies like this one increasingly became the dominant form of retail ownership in the industry. Department stores selling clothing and other household items put many smaller, local mom-and-pop specialty stores out of business.

Department stores enjoyed high and stable profits during the affluent years just after World War II. Increased car ownership and the expansion of highways led to massive suburbanization. Following their customers to the new bedroom communities, department store chains built new stores as "anchors" in suburban shopping centers. Shopping center construction accelerated between 1965 and 1975.[3] By 1977, four large holding companies controlled the majority of America's regionally based department store chains—Federated Department Stores, Allied Department Stores, May Department Stores Company, and Dayton Hudson Corporation. Together, they owned 807 retail outlets, with total sales in excess of $11.4 billion—five times the sales of the whole J. C. Penney chain with its 1,686 stores nationwide.[4] However, as department store chains reached the limits of suburban growth they began to expand their geographic coverage to a national market. By 1986 Neiman Marcus had "stores in Florida, and Massachusetts. Lord and Taylor, Saks Fifth Avenue and Bloomingdale's, have all followed with similar moves."[5]

THE CHALLENGE TO DEPARTMENT STORES

Department store expansion slowed during the 1970s, when an economic downturn and stagnation in family income reduced the growth of consumer demand for apparel. Traditionally, department stores had served the large middle class. With the downturn, the middle class began to shrink: some families moved up the economic scale, but almost twice as many moved down.[6] Moreover, by the end of the 1970s, new off-price and discount store chains, and niche-oriented specialty stores, began to outprice and outsell department stores, drawing off their clientele.[7]

Reduced buying power among a declining middle class meant traditional retailers could no longer sustain stable margins by catering to a large, growing, and relatively undifferentiated market. Retailers were forced to develop niche marketing and market segmentation, targeting their products to particular age groups, income levels, and ethnic groups among the buying public.[8] This new approach was designed to satisfy the full range of consumer demand in order to maintain and expand market share. Some retailers moved upscale, but these smaller, high-niche markets soon became saturated. Others, such as Wal-Mart and Kmart, who moved downscale, were more successful.

In a slow-growing economy, clothing retailers in every market segment found themselves competing for a greater share of a stagnant or slower growing market. By the 1980s, as the period of American prosperity drew to a close, America had become "overstored" and "overmalled." Shopping center and mall construction slowed sharply, as retailers faced a crisis of productivity and profitability. Not only were small retailers unable to compete, but the new and more competitive environment meant that only a few "power retailers," like the Limited and Macy's, succeeded, and a shake-out ensued. Stores became targets for mergers and acquisitions.[9] Ten years later, apparel retailers would face debt, bankruptcy, and new and higher levels of concentration.

According to Daniel W. J. Raff and W. J. Salmon, in the early 1980s the organizational structure of department stores made them unable to respond to changes in the selling environment. Market saturation increased, and competition for market share intensified. Department-store holding companies, unable to seek new profits by expanding retail markets and retail space, began to merge with, and acquire, competing retail formats: discount and specialty store chains. And discount and specialty stores acquired department stores. For example, Federated Department Stores merged its smaller divisions—Shillito's, Bullock's North, I. Magnin, Sanger-Harris, etc.—with some of its larger divisions. It has moved its high end department stores, Bloomingdale's and Burdines, to a broader geographical coverage. It has started its specialty discount chain, Gold Circle. It owns one of California's largest supermarket chains, Ralph's. It has turned its Filene's Basement Stores into a high end discounter. It has started its own specialty chains with The Children's Place, the Boston Store and Levy's. Over history, it has experimented with several discount formats: Fedway, Gold Triangle, and Goldsmith's.[10]

By 1987, apparel retailing had grown ever more concentrated. Kurt Salmon Associates, a leading consulting firm for the industry, claimed that the five largest apparel retailers accounted for 35 percent of all retail sales, a figure that has continued to increase.[11]

In the early 1980s, trade organizations and consultants implied that retailers had become profligate during the heyday of expansion and needed to increase their efficiency.[12] Corporate restructuring required a more efficient use of labor, new technologies, and perhaps most important, a new and more demanding relationship with apparel suppliers.

RESTRUCTURING FOR COMPETITION

Needing to reduce operating costs in order to increase sales and margins, retailers began to impose new kinds of economic pressures on their apparel suppliers, making significant changes: they implemented a quick-response program in order to reduce their traditionally large and costly inventories, and they expanded their lines of private-label merchandise. Retailers also altered their labor practices by cutting their full-time, trained sales staffs made up of career employees.[13] Much of this was made possible by new technologies that greatly increased worker productivity in both production and sales. The new retail competition required fewer managers and minimal sales help; the practice of customer service became economically unsustainable.[14] Employment in apparel retailing grew by 31 percent between 1973 and 1985, as stores reduced their full-time workers and increased their part-time help. By 1985 the earnings of workers in retail sales had declined dramatically—and were only slightly higher than those of the lowest paid workers employed in eating and drinking places.[15]

QUICK RESPONSE AND JUST-IN-TIME PRODUCTION

Perhaps the most important element of the changes was the effort by retailers to restructure their relationships with apparel suppliers. As one analyst points out, "Manufacturers have traditionally been responsible for making the product and delivering it to the retailer in a timely fashion. . . . They were responsible for delivering salable merchandise that would generate profitable margins, handling reorders of the best selling items, giv[ing] markdown allowances when goods weren't selling, provid[ing] cooperative advertising money, allow[ing] for easy returns and [giving] retailers the right to cancel orders."[16] Now apparel suppliers were forced to restructure their production to respond to additional retailer demands. Quick response and just-in-time deliveries meant retailers now changed their mix of merchandise every six to eight weeks, or even more frequently. This change reduced retail inventory costs and transferred expenses to producers, who were required to deliver more frequently and closer to the point of sale. Quick response also let retailers avoid too frequent markdowns of excess inventory. In an era of intensifying competition, markdowns threatened retail profit margins and retail profits.[17]

Traditionally, department stores had an average of 3.3 "turns," or seasonal deliveries of merchandise, leaving them with costly inventories. With just-in-time deliveries, domestic suppliers and importers had to produce and deliver small batches of multiple styles and models of fashion merchandise six to eight times a year.[18] As merchandise sold, retailers required rapid replenishment to avoid depleting stock. Today, retailers have new merchandise delivered as often as once a month.

Quick response also amounted to a new marketing strategy for retailers. The frequently changing merchandise heightened buyers' fashion consciousness, helping to increase consumer demand for rapidly changing styles and led to more clothing purchases. According to a major trade magazine, "A Quick Response System can reduce by half the revenue losses due to markdowns and stock-outs of apparel while benefiting customers by offering more of the right product at the right time and lower regular prices. . . . An average of about 8% of net retail sales is in forced markdowns. The closer to the retail season, the smaller the forecast error on new products."[19]

Many of the changes were made with new technologies that increased worker productivity. As desktop computers began to replace mainframes in the early 1980s, electronic technology restructured supplier-retailer relationships. The technology permitted retailers not only to reduce their inventories and operating expenses but also to collect demographic information from consumers that enabled them to plan marketing strategies. New software allowed retailers to tag individual items of merchandise, or, as they are called, "stock-keeping units," with bar codes. Retailers could monitor both inventories and sales instantaneously and save on inventory costs. The technology generated new sales strategies and marketing efforts. Electronic mail, and then the Internet, made it possible to gather information by means of electronic-data inventory control and transmit it over long distances between suppliers and retailers. By sharing information with their suppliers, retailers could order, reorder, and rapidly replenish their stocks; suppliers began delivering new merchandise to stores almost constantly.

Quick response allowed retailers to transfer the risks of unsold goods to suppliers and made possible new types of advertising. Large, centralized manufacturers were most successful in acquiring new technologies and restructuring their operations. Smaller merchandisers and importers, less able to afford these technologies, found it more difficult to establish and maintain the long-term "partnerships" with retailers that became necessary.[20]

THE ECONOMICS OF FASHION

The transformations in apparel retailing in the past two decades began in the 1970s in the context of a declining couture industry. Well-known couture fashion designers had produced individualized clothing for wealthy patrons. As this clientele began to shrink, many designers discovered the advantages of higher volume sales in high-niche, ready-to-wear women's apparel. These designers began to license their names to clothing producers, who hired their own designers to turn out fashions bearing the labels of designers like Oleg Cassini and Gloria Vanderbilt.

This new approach lent itself to the production of clothing for the high end of the clothing market to the low end. As the number of women in professional and managerial occupations increased, they needed wardrobes that would permit them to "dress for success." American designers like Liz Claiborne began to produce a new kind of clothing. By 1974, her firm and those of other designers were producing high-quality "career wear" in Asian countries like South Korea, Hong Kong, Taiwan, and Singapore.[21] More modestly priced clothing was sourced in low-wage nations in Latin America, like Brazil and Mexico, and more often in Asian countries like Thailand, Malaysia, the Philippines, and Indonesia.[22] Mass merchandisers and discount stores like Wal-Mart and Sears made even lower priced store-brand clothing in Caribbean Basin countries such as Guatemala, Jamaica, and the Dominican Republic.[23]

Gary Gereffi and Mei-Lin Pan describe a process known as "specification contracting": "Local firms carry out production according to complete in-structions issued by the buyers and branded companies that design the goods; the output is then distributed and marketed abroad by trading com-panies, brand name merchandisers, large retailers and their agents." This is often called a "buyer driven commodity chain." Such networks, usually controlled by foreign capital, are common in the apparel industry.[24]

Private-label merchandise became important as a way to create greater levels of backward integration. As Sergio Pais writes, "The ultimate in bargaining power is the ownership of the supply sources through backward integration. There are two forms of backward integration: partial integra-tion, where the retailer owns the brands that he sells but does not man-ufacture, or a full backward integration, where the retailer owns the brands and the manufacturing facilities for the goods he sells."[25]

Retailers from J. C. Penney to Saks soon discovered the value of private-label merchandise, which differs from brand-name merchandise in that it is commissioned by retailers rather than those who traditionally have been manufacturers. Clothing that carries a retailer's label (e.g., Saks Fifth Av-enue) has been designed by personnel employed by the retailer, who com-missioned it directly from producers instead of purchasing it from a brand-name manufacturer (e.g., Liz Claiborne). Retailers employ hundreds of people all over the world to make and sell their private-label clothing—in places like Florence, Hong Kong, Singapore, Taiwan, South Korea, Buda-pest, Indonesia, India, and the Philippines. In 1995, Macy's of New York had an in-house staff to do product design and development; the goal was to expand the repertoire of the company's private-label offerings.[26] Lucie Cheng and Gary Gereffi note that "some importers are like industry 'scouts' who operate on the outer fringes of the production frontier and help develop potential new sources of supply for global commodity chains (e.g., VietNam [sic], Burma, Saipan)."[27]

The growth of private-label clothing blurred the lines between different segments of the apparel industry—between large corporate retailers, mer-chandisers, importers, and manufacturers. Retailers began to compete with importers and manufacturers. Retailers today do their own manufacturing, and brand-name manufacturers (e.g., Liz Claiborne) also sell them cloth-ing. The Gap is among the best models of a highly integrated enterprise, selling the merchandise it designs and contracting abroad for its manufac-ture. Efforts are constantly being made in the textile, apparel, and retail complex to repeat the Gap's success, as firms try to increase their forward and backward integration. For example, full-price retailers like Brooks Brothers, Ann Taylor, Nordstrom, and Saks Fifth Avenue have opened their own off-price retail divisions rather than sell their unpurchased inventories to discount stores. Manufacturers of brand-name clothing, such as Liz Claiborne, Levi Strauss, Reebok, Nike, Calvin Klein, Nine West, Danskin, Speedo, Dana Buchman, and French Connection have also opened retail stores.[28] By eliminating the profits of merchandisers and other middlemen, retailers can sell at lower prices, potentially increasing their sales volumes and profit margins.

Although department stores must continue to maintain a high proportion of brand-name items, shoppers are also attracted to private-label merchandise when it bears the name of a high-niche retailer or offers the cachet associated with an exclusive store. Through advertising, today's apparel products are identifiable as "designer brands." These products are easily recognized by consumers, who often are unable to distinguish between them and private-label merchandise,[29] and who make purchases based on their evaluation of the price and of the quality of these names.

As apparel producers began to open their own retail shops, stores multiplied and retail space grew. Companies centralized their buying operations. Retail buyers were eliminated as retail corporations began to purchase a large part of their designer clothing and other merchandise through corporate merchandisers like the American Merchandising Corporation, Frederick Atkins, and the Batus Retail Group. Merchandisers such as these worked with retailers to plan their orders, contracting with both domestic and overseas producers for the manufacture and delivery of large volumes of brand-name apparel and private-label merchandise.

The years between 1975 and 1985 saw increased apparel exports to the United States, especially nationally branded clothing and private-label designer fashions produced largely in East Asian countries.[30] Discounters like Kmart and J. C. Penney opened Hong Kong buying offices in 1970, soon to be followed by new branches in Taiwan, Korea, and Singapore.[31] May Department Stores and the Associated Merchandising Company also opened buying offices during the 1970s. According to Cheng and Gereffi,

> Asian governments set up semiofficial associations and commissions to promote garment export and actively encouraged the formation of trading companies. In response, US retailers began to organize their global sourcing efforts in some new ways. One example is the Associated Merchandising Corporation (AMC)[,] . . . the world's largest retail and merchandising organization, and a major importer with 31 offices on five continents. The AMC serves as a link between the US consumer and the Asian factories.[32]

DISCOUNTING

The growth and expansion of discounting among apparel retailers in the early 1980s played a large role in the restructuring of the textile, apparel, and retail complex. Discounting was deeply implicated in efforts by retailers to further liberalize trade in textiles and apparel. Discount stores have existed in the United States since the 1950s. Initially they sold lower price goods rather than the well-advertised, brand-name goods found in department stores. Discounters were not a competitive threat to department stores until the mid-1970s, when state and local fair-trade laws across the nation were finally abolished.

Fair trade laws required retailers to sell national brand-name products at prices determined by manufacturers. According to one analyst, "Fair Trade Laws were legal mechanisms that permitted manufacturing firms to set a minimum on the price that retailers (and wholesalers) could charge for products they produced. These laws gave manufacturers the power to require retailers to sell a manufacturer's brand name of trade marked products at a fixed price."[33] Fair trade regulation had existed in retailing since the 1930s—a depression-era measure intended to maintain price stability and protect small retail enterprises from bankruptcy. The regulations existed through the postwar period, when dramatic growth mitigated intense competition.

The fair trade laws were repealed at the behest of the growing number of discount retail merchants. Repeal allowed them to compete with traditional retail outlets by selling brand-name products at discounted prices. The main spokesperson for repeal at the House hearings in March and April 1975 was Kurt Barnard, president of the Mass Retailing Institute (MRI), a trade organization of "companies representing 6,500 discount department stores in the United States."[34] Other trade organizations representing a variety of small-business groups opposed the MRI in both Senate and House hearings. The representatives of America's department stores, however, were absent—from both Senate and House hearings. They did not make themselves heard on Capitol Hill until several years later—when they opposed trade protection. The absence of department stores from the fair trade hearings suggests that the retail industry was not well-organized politically, or was not aware of the potential consequences of this change, which was destined to transform domestic retailing. Raff and Salmon write, "Department stores, carried by the tide of buoyant consumer demand, paid only minor attention to the growth of non-department store competition. . . . As a result, first discount department stores, then regional and national specialty store chains, and, more recently, power retailers began to erode their market share."[35] Others believe that "the repeal of fair Trade [sic] laws . . . had a profound effect on the department store industry as a whole. Repeal precipitated a virtually total restructuring of the retail sector."[36]

The passage of the Consumer Goods Pricing Act of 1975 allowed the expansion of off-price retailing. According to one analyst,

> When their inter-state fair trade regulations were repealed, discounters were no longer bound by manufacturers' pricing policies. . . . As the discounters started to discount more freely and grow faster, new types of discount formats were created. The newer ones are the warehouse stores, the offprice stores, limited assortment stores and discount specialty stores. The appearance of these new retailing formats has had serious impacts on the previously well established National Chains and the traditional department stores.[37]

Now off-price retailers could acquire and discount the same national brand-name or designer clothing that full-price retailers obtained abroad and sold at higher prices. They could sell at lower cost by purchasing at more favorable terms—buying manufacturers' overstocks, irregulars, closeouts, and discontinued items. Operating with lower markups and margins than department stores, discounters could sell a higher volume at lower prices—between 20 and 70 percent off department stores' prices. By the early 1980s off-price outlets began to erode department stores' market share, retail leadership, and financial viability.[38]

The success of discounting intensified the profit crisis facing the perhaps too rapidly expanding U.S. apparel retailing industry. At first, department store executives sometimes refused to purchase from suppliers who sold the same merchandise to discounters. Kids 'R' Us brought suit against Federated Department Stores for refusing to sell their branded merchandise. Federated subsequently countersued Kids 'R' Us, arguing that the department stores were making efforts not to violate the Sherman Act.[39] Yet conflicts like these ultimately failed to halt the growth of discounting. By 1983, "off price retailers rang up 6.5 percent of the $100 billion retail apparel business[, and it was estimated that] . . . the 30 percent annual growth of off price could give it 15% to 20% by 1990."

In 1983 merchandiser Frederick Atkins started an off-price division and began supplying discount stores. The divisional manager of this new off-shoot claimed that reduced consumer spending was not the only reason off-price retailers flourished. Even more important was the expanding volume of fashion apparel that had become available to discounters. He pointed out that "manufacturers' productive capacity exceeds the ability of traditional department and specialty stores to dispose of all that merchandise at regular prices. Otherwise there would be little room for off-price."[40] Much of that "productive capacity" was now offshore and growing.[41]

In 1984, another merchandising executive told a group of offshore apparel producers that the new competitive pressures in retailing made imports more important than ever. He said, "A function of importing is to obtain product at less cost to sell it at a higher mark-up and to offer the consumer value over and above that obtainable domestically."[42]

Now, specialty store chains developed their own overseas production organizations. For example, Mast Industries, the overseas sourcing arm for the Limited and reputedly the largest retailer of women's apparel in the world, communicates electronically with its home office in Andover, Massachusetts, on a daily basis. New fashion ideas may be developed in Andover in conjunction with production information available from East Asia. The garments, including the textiles, are then sourced abroad, delivered by air freight to Mast Industries' U.S. warehouse in Ohio, and distributed to retail outlets thirty to forty days after the day of order.[43] Jack Wexler, president of Mast Industries Far East, claimed, "Mast doesn't do anything different than anyone else, except that we keep the pressure on the factories to meet their deadlines and we ship by air."

The off-price stores forced department stores to adjust their strategies.[44] When purchasing slowed and competition accelerated, full-price retailers were forced to behave more like discounters, to hold more sales and clearances. The result was higher and higher markdowns. In 1985 *Women's Wear Daily* noted that even at Macy's, "while fashion and excitement are emphasized, the store keeps about 25 percent of its departments on sale to compete with the off-pricers."[45] In the same year, a Kurt Salmon executive told the National Retail Management Association that markdowns had taken a serious toll on retail profits in 1984. He said, "The overall picture presents what some view as a far more disturbing look at the impact of 'markdown madness.' "[46] Department stores were caught in a struggle to reduce their operating costs while sales slumps caused margins to fall. By 1983 a study by Kurt Salmon Associates found that, "while the retail industry handled $97 billion worth of merchandise in 1983, as much as $15 billion–$17 billion in additional revenues were lost to markdowns. That figure is approximately six times the total net after tax income that retail companies generate from apparel sales."

By the mid-1980s, large corporate retailers again sought new ways to reduce their operating expenses by reducing labor costs, introducing technological and organizational innovations, and increasing their private-label merchandise; the objective was to lower the cost of their merchandise to consumers in order to improve sales and margins. Retailers pressed their suppliers to seek lower and lower cost imports.[47]

THE PROFITABILITY PARADOX

By the mid-1980s, department stores had begun to experience a serious profitability crunch. As already noted, this resulted in part from the postwar expansion of retail space and the accompanying oversupply of merchandise. A biennial survey found that between 1974 and 1984 the number of shopping centers went up by 70 percent, and square footage increased by 80 percent. Over the decade, as the population rose by 12 percent, shopping center space per capita went from 7.7 to 14 square feet. If discount stores were doing well, department stores were not. In 1985, department store sales per square foot, adjusted for inflation, were below the levels of 1975.[48]

The overexpansion was making it more difficult for department stores to maintain profitability levels high enough and stable enough to meet the new expectations of public corporate shareholders. While sales had increased, levels of gross margin had fallen. Lasker Meyer, Irwin Cohen, and Laurence N. Garter offer one explanation for the failure of retail profitability.[49] They argue that the excess number of stores and the slow-growing consumer demand made it difficult for sales growth to keep up with operating expenses because efficiencies of scale had decreased as competition continued to increase. Intensified competition led retailers to confront a productivity paradox: High operating costs challenged profitability, yet as competition forced retailers to reduce prices, reduced margins required them to increase sales. Retailers were involved in a struggle to reduce operating expenses while searching for greater market share. They used a variety of new strategies to do this: for example, reduced labor costs, new technologies, strategic partnerships, private-label merchandise, and new niche-marketing techniques.

But the productivity loop confronted most retailers with a new risk-laden paradox and led to problems that were difficult to remedy. Unlike automakers, retailers found it was not always feasible, even with creative marketing strategies, to cut operating expenses or expand their sales enough to compensate for reduced margins, because they could not raise prices. Operating costs could not be reduced indefinitely. At some point in the productivity cycle, "operating costs as a percentage of sales reach a point of diminishing returns."[50] Therefore, the intense new competition made retailing a dangerous game for all but the most powerful retailers. A report by Management Horizons, a retail consulting firm, states, "The more productive the industry, the less profitable the individual players. This paradox is the heart of what now plagues retailing." The report also notes that "the application of the productivity loop has helped retailers become more efficient in their chosen market positions. This path, however, has led to deflation, bankruptcy and industry consolidation."[51]

By the mid-1980s, apparel retailers could remain profitable only by capturing a larger share of a considerably slower growing market. Retail corporations began using the "portfolio approach" to increase their corporate power. The chief executive of one leading department store chain told textile distributors, "Department stores are trying private brands (traditionally national chain turf), the National Chains are getting into fashion, some of the original discounters are going upscale, and specialists are niching into every one of those markets with every one of those strategies. Everyone is trying to get the other's market."[52]

THE THREAT FROM WALL STREET

As early as 1985, a year before Robert Campeau bought out Allied Department Stores, retailers were already concerned about leveraged buyouts. Between 1980 and 1990, 80 percent of the department store industry changed hands and nearly one-third of discount department stores were involved in some type of merger or acquisition activity.[53] Between 1990 and 1992, as the recession hit and family incomes fell, sales dropped dramatically below expectations. In these two years, more than one hundred thousand retail firms filed for bankruptcy protection, a 60 percent increase over the years 1984 to 1989.[54] In 1990 retailers struggled to find ways to cut their operating expenses and maintain their profit margins. As sales slipped, the highly leveraged retailers were unable to cover their expenses. In 1991, the annual meeting of the National Retail Federation offered its members seminars on how to deal with bankruptcy.[55]

When Wall Street began gearing up to finance the new wave of corporate consolidation, the retail industry was among those targeted. Financial and retail analysts predicted that the next few years would see a "flurry of mergers and acquisitions." America's banks and investment houses in the early to mid-1980s had been looking for new investments,[56] and many, like Manufacturers' Hanover Trust, Citibank, Bankers' Trust, General Electric Credit Company, and Drexel Burnham Lambert, became heavily involved in these leveraged buyouts. Retailers were seen as good loan candidates in part because of their large and valuable nonretail assets—their stores and real estate. The leveraged buyouts of Allied Department Stores and Federated Department Stores, orchestrated by Campeau between 1986 and 1988, took place because Campeau had credibility on Wall Street as a result of his own real estate fortune, "which served as collateral for his retail binge." Seeking to protect the independence of Macy's, its chief executive, Edward Finkelstein, borrowed $3.6 billion to finance a leveraged buyout that would take the world's largest department store private.[57]

Unlike the Wall Street financial establishment and real estate speculators like Campeau, retail executives were in the business of selling clothing. They understood that the best way to avoid becoming a leveraged-buyout target was to keep their stock prices high.[58] Stock prices responded not to a retailer's real estate holdings but to its retail profitability, measured by its return on investment and market share.[59] Because financial capital prompted the frantic level of mergers and acquisitions, retailers saw that it was necessary to rein in operating expenses and increase sales.[60]

The retail industry emerged from this debacle considerably leaner, and continued to face a slow-growing market demand for apparel. Now larger and more concentrated than ever before, large retailers faced even higher levels of debt. New efforts to reduce costs led to the introduction of new computer technologies to increase retail productivity. In 1992 a major retail consultant claimed that these changes had dramatically increased productivity in a period of sluggish consumer demand. Yet he also pointed out that the intensified competition and the need to reduce prices led to pressures for even greater efficiency. Those who could not keep pace, he said, were being "mowed down": "A record 19,000 retail companies slipped into bankruptcy . . . and retailers' profit margins have shrunk to just 1.2%—the lowest in 38 years. [He claimed that] . . . half of all retailers will be bankrupt or acquired by 2000."[61]

In large part, bankruptcies and declining profit margins were at the heart of the growing retail concentration in the 1980s, a concentration fueled by the large volumes of low-cost merchandise being imported. It is hardly surprising, then, that the retail industry was eager to further liberalize trade in order to develop new low-wage production sites around the world.

THE RETAIL INDUSTRY AND GLOBAL TRADE

Retailers began extensive lobbying for regional and global sourcing in the early 1980s. During the next two decades the industry played a significant role in supporting NAFTA and the CBI, expanding trade with China, ending the Multifibre Arrangement, and securing replacement of the latter with the Agreement on Textiles and Clothing.

In 1984, William Andres, retiring chief executive officer of Dayton Hudson, along with chief executives from Sears, J. C. Penney, seventeen other retailers, and the heads of eight retail associations, formed the Retail Industry Trade Action Coalition (RITAC). The new retail lobby hired a Washington management consultant to manage RITAC and "began holding breakfast meetings with congressional trade experts." By the mid-1980s, retailers and their fashion-merchandise suppliers had begun to see their future in the expansion of offshore assembly. In 1983, when the U.S. textile industry joined forces with the apparel industry and its trade unions to promote trade protection, the retail industry went head-to-head with the protectionist Fiber, Fabric and Apparel Coalition for Trade (FFACT). The following year, in a *Fortune* magazine article, the retail industry acknowledged its agenda: "One goal is to do away with quotas on footwear and apparel, which Andres says amounts to 'a triumph of politics over economic common sense.'"[62]

The reintegration of China into world trade sparked new conflict between the textile and retail interests. This conflict would continue to reassert itself over the next two decades. In 1983 the U.S. textile industry pressed the administration to "call," or halt, illegal Chinese transshipments of merchandise. These shipments, labeled as made in Hong Kong but actually made in the PRC, violated U.S. customs regulations. The ATMI asked for stricter rules of origin to halt customs fraud in order to constrain importers who "ship almost finished goods to countries with available quotas, sew the last button on in that country and use the second country's quota to get the goods into the US."[63]

One call by the U.S. Customs Service threatened the delivery of merchandise for the Christmas holiday season. The call was directly challenged by both RITAC and the Textile and Apparel Group of the American Association of Exporters and Importers when the latter group "filed for a permanent and preliminary injunction against the rules in the Court of International Trade in New York."[64] RITAC challenged the sixty-to-ninety-day moratorium that the Immigration and Naturalization Service had placed on the entry of their merchandise to the United States.

Trade protectionists, represented by FFACT, consistently claimed that China had violated MFA quota provisions with its illegal transshipments.[65] China had also been "illegally" subsidizing its textile industry with free raw materials and electricity while closing its doors to independent investment and joint ventures in textile production.[66] RITAC claimed that the moratorium on the shipment of goods made the situation chaotic for business, especially since goods designed for the Christmas season were delayed.[67] Despite protests from the Chinese government, the Reagan administration was reluctant to change its course. The call was not lifted, and litigation against the court's decision ultimately languished.

The conflict between the textile and retail interests intensified. In 1984–85 RITAC geared up to oppose the Jenkins-Hollings bill, which, if passed, would have reduced import growth to an overall increase of 1 percent annually. Large retailers launched a $1 million corporate campaign against the bill[68] and defeated the protectionists.

Participants in the retail coalition included the Retail Merchants' Association, American Retail Federation, and Volume Footwear Retailers of America. According to *Women's Wear Daily*, "The main thrust of the lobby is reportedly being provided by individual retail organizations and their chief executive officers. . . . Companies that have joined the coalition are said to include Sears, Roebuck & Co., R. H. Macy, Federated Department Stores and Associated Merchandising Corp., as well as about 15 other retail firms."[69] Other members of this new lobbying group were some of the largest and most powerful retail corporations in America: Kmart, Zayre, May Department Stores, J. C. Penney, Associated Dry Goods, Federated Department Stores, and Tandy. Retail trade groups like the National Mass Retailing Institute, Association of General Merchandise Chains, National Retail Merchants Association, and the American Retail Federation also joined this effort. The total annual sales of the companies represented by these organization exceeded $1 trillion. Among them, they employed 15 percent of the national workforce.[70]

According to William Andres, president of RITAC, the new free-trade lobby allied with the agricultural and financial services industries "in order to battle the strong protectionist lobbies in Washington." Andres, joined by Lee Abraham of the Associated Merchandising Corporation, had testified in Congress against Jenkins-Hollings, quite rightly claiming it would override the much looser import restraints of the Multifibre Arrangement.[71]

In 1986, when trade negotiations of the Uruguay Round of the General Agreement on Tariffs and Trade began, corporate retailers pressed for ending the Multifibre Arrangement. In 1986 RITAC published a position paper opposing rollbacks of textile and apparel imports from the Big Three, and calling for "a definite termination date for the MFA," described as a "bureaucratic dream and a retailer's nightmare."[72]

In April of that year, before the MFA negotiations began, after Reagan had vetoed Jenkins-Hollings but before it was known whether Congress would override his veto, a U.S. government delegation flew to East Asia to negotiate a freeze on imports from Taiwan and South Korea, which then had the largest apparel quota and the lion's share of apparel imports to the United States. Fearful that the new negotiations would jeopardize the flow of merchandise from Big Three suppliers, Abraham also made a special trip to Asia, presumably to consult with his business associates there. According to the *Daily News Record*, Abraham made "a swing through Far Eastern nations. . . . Abraham will touch base with trade groups, government officials, and textile/apparel manufacturers in Singapore, Taiwan, Hong Kong, Japan and South Korea."[73]

RITAC also took a strong position opposing a new tax bill being considered that year by the Senate Finance Committee, which threatened to eliminate tax deductions for payment of import duties. Abraham claimed that eliminating this deduction would "increase import duties by an average 54 percent, and would hit particularly hard at apparel and textile imports, which already are subject to substantial tariffs." The retail trade group claimed that an end to this tax deduction would cause a price jump for consumers of about 5 to 10 percent.[74]

Retailers also tried to influence tariff and quota regulations by influencing the bilateral agreements through which quotas and tariffs are set. In 1991, RITAC sent its lobbyists to influence the GATT talks at Geneva. RITAC opposed the tentatively agreed-upon growth rates, which, they complained, were entirely too low and would "not be sufficient to meet consumer demand in the coming years." They warned that the low rates would "cause harm to US merchants."[75]

In 1992, Congress passed a bill that would punish China for piracy of intellectual property and tie the country's most-favored-nation status and tariff rates to improvements in human rights. The retail industry opposed this policy.[76] Before George H. W. Bush could veto the bill, Leslie Wexner, chief executive officer of the Limited and then-chair of RITAC, headed a delegation of six leading retail executives to Congress to urge that the veto be sustained and to press upon members the importance of the China trade for providing inexpensive goods.[77] The group also included Donald G. Fisher, chair of the Gap; Joseph Antonini, chair of Kmart Corporation; John

J. Shea, president of Spiegel; Thomas A. Hays, president of May Department Stores; and one manufacturer—Linda Wachner, president, chief executive officer, and chair of the Warnaco Group. Leslie Wexner made a statement outlining RITAC's two trade priorities at that point: "First, to underscore our support of the administration and our mutual commitment to a successful conclusion of the Uruguay Round of GATT that would finally phase out the MFA. . . . Second, to make it clear that there should be one rule of origin covering all products, including textiles and apparel, in the North American Free Trade Agreement."[78] The well-funded and highly organized U.S. retail industry has continued to support these positions.[79] The retail lobby mobilized to support each and every new free-market, free-trade initiative pressed by the administrations of George H. W. Bush and Clinton, including measures to further liberalize trade accords with the CBI countries and Mexico through NAFTA.[80]

By the early 1990s the American Merchandising Corporation began investigating the potential to establish manufacturing sites in countries like Cambodia, Vietnam, and Africa, the last of which was described as the "greatest new import frontier."[81] In October of 1990, only months after the reunification of Germany, executives from the retail merchandiser Frederick Atkins held a conference in Munich to develop new overseas sourcing opportunities in eastern Europe.[82] By 1992 a spokesperson for the American Merchandising Corporation was advising prospective producers about the best assembly sites around the world, claiming that Turkey and Egypt were the best places to make cotton knits and fleece, Israel was best for swimwear, and eastern Europe was the best place for tailored clothing.[83] In 1998 a representative of the Gap said the company was sourcing not only in the United States but also in fifty other countries around the world.[84]

The retail and apparel industries began lobbying to end the MFA in 1984. A decade later, in 1994, it was eliminated. The Agreement on Textiles and Clothing had made it easier for fashion producers to access new sites for the export processing of apparel. As we will see, after 2005 the process is likely to accelerate.

CONTEMPORARY CORPORATE RETAILING

If trade liberalization has helped to foster global competition, it has also helped to further concentrate America's apparel retail industry by wiping out many small- and medium-sized players. In 1987 the twenty largest retailers of apparel and accessories accounted for 33.3 percent of all U.S.

sales; the fifty largest firms accounted for 41 percent of sales. By 1992 these figures had risen to 41.3 percent and 52 percent, respectively.[85] In 1997, among department stores, the top ten chains—J. C. Penney, Federated Department Stores, May Department Stores, Dillard's, Nordstrom, Dayton Hudson, Mercantile, Neiman-Marcus, Saks, and Proffitts—accounted for one-third of all department store sales.[86] Today, Wal-Mart is the world's largest retailer. Its sales are greater than the gross domestic products of 192 countries in the world.[87]

The mergers and acquisitions that contributed to this increased concentration have also increased debt among America's retailers. In 1996, with profit margins falling in all but the largest retail corporations—and with profits rising in industries like pharmaceuticals, high tech, and aerospace— retailers found it increasingly difficult to find low-cost capital for operating expenses or expansion.[88] Given retailers' continuing efforts to reduce operating expenses, higher interest rates made it difficult to borrow money and tended to squeeze profits. These problems made it more difficult to cope with the profitability paradox. The solution was clearly global expansion. Moreover, as more of the smaller, and some very large, retailers went bankrupt, those that remained would get the market share of the failed retail companies. Experts anticipated that retail bankruptcies would continue until the square footage declined enough to roughly meet consumer demand.[89]

Although retailers complained about the excess of shopping space in the 1980s, a decade later the problem had only intensified. In 1984, shopping space amounted to 14 square feet per capita. In 1995, in the 39,000 shopping centers in the United States, there were 18 square feet for every U.S. consumer. The productivity of selling space was half what it had been in 1987.[90] Under such conditions, it is hardly surprising that there continue to be so many retail bankruptcies.

Such expansion threatened to outstrip demand. In 1997 the disposable income of American consumers increased 5.7 percent over the previous year. A large proportion of this income, however, was spent on servicing consumer debt and not on new purchases of apparel. In the 1980s Americans were spending more on fashion apparel than they do today; by the 1990s an aging population of consumers spent less on nondurables, including fashion apparel, and more on consumer services.[91] In February of 1998, following a weak Christmas season, retailers were forced to slash prices, especially at apparel and specialty stores.[92]

Retailers try to capture consumer dollars by focusing on changing demographic patterns, by carefully scrutinizing consumer wants, and by reducing prices. Pricing distinctions between department stores, specialty stores, and discount stores are now blurred. Today, virtually all clothing retailers discount their apparel in response to the competition of off-price and discount outlets.[93] Not surprisingly, a 1993 study of New York consumers found that 95 percent believed that retailers set prices artificially high in order to discount them. One might say that consumers have been "educated" by full-price retailers who now offer "preseason, midseason and post-season discounts." Consumers do not buy at full price but wait for sales before buying. According to one industry magazine, "Surveys . . . indicate that about three-quarters of female shoppers in the USA regard the sale price of merchandise to be the real price."[94] Markdown percentages have increased significantly in recent years. Retailers now expect that only about 25 percent of their apparel will be purchased at the "full retail value." As a result, executives have developed a new pricing strategy: they calculate average margins for particular lines based on the variation in price at which clothing is sold, before and after successive markdowns.

Between 1979 and 1984, the overall markdown percentages in all categories of apparel merchandise, for both department and specialty stores, increased. The increased volume of low-cost clothing made abroad led to deeper markdowns. By 1997 markdown percentages had grown even deeper. As retail space expanded and the flow of low-cost apparel imports to the United States increased, the cost of clothing for consumers fell below the average increases in the cost of living.

Ten years later, after recovering from this crisis, the retail industry has experienced another cycle of growth, shakeouts, and consolidation. Indeed, at this writing, three months after the events of September 11, 2001, and the emergence of an economic recession that was already in the making, the retail industry is seeing another weak holiday season. More bankruptcies are expected, along with increasing retail concentration resulting from ensuing mergers and acquisitions.

At the heart of the profitability paradox is the inability of retailers to raise prices. There has been a decline in the real wholesale price of domestically produced apparel. Domestic production has declined. Such a constellation of events did not occur in the preceding quarter century.[95] A writer for *Bobbin Magazine* noted in February 1997: "It's no secret that the U.S. apparel contracting industry has been fighting an uphill battle against factors that run the gamut from international trade law and a flood of imports to sweatshops, the welfare system and the higher minimum wage. Or that compounding the negative impacts of these forces has been the drive of the retail market for lower priced goods."[96]

Wages remain low at home as well as abroad. A recent study of the New York City garment industry indicates that retailers pay their contractors "less every year for the same product."[97] As a result the city's contractors are staying in business only by reducing their labor standards below legal levels. New York City contractors are convinced that employment will decline further in the coming decade.[98]

LEAN RETAILING AND SOURCING ABROAD

Offshore sourcing has not only pared labor costs but also made it necessary to find more efficient ways to transport the large quantities of apparel from the points of production to the points of sale. According to Frederick H. Abernathy, John T. Dunlop, Janice H. Hammond, and David Weil in their book *A Stitch in Time*, the process of "lean retailing" has become essential to managing the logistics of supplying stores with merchandise, and thus an essential element in the new forms of competition.[99] They note that lean retailing is not a response to the demands of sourcing abroad but a new state-of-the-art strategy for solving the problems of inventory control in today's competitive retail environment. In 1997 Federated Department Stores moved more than 700 million individual items of clothing—many of them made at offshore production sites—from suppliers to their domestic stores.[100] Retailers focus on "continuously adjusting the supply of products offered to consumers at each retail outlet to match actual levels of market demand, thereby reducing their exposure to the risks of selling perishable goods."[101] With such vast inventories, they need more efficient ways to manage the supply chain.

The process of lean retailing, say Abernathy and his colleagues, captures the benefits of backward integration. During the decade between 1985 and 1995, retailers began to form strategic partnerships with their suppliers. Using elements of just-in-time production, today's clothing retailers and manufacturers now share information—and can do so more easily than ever before—through the use of bar coding and electronic data inventory control systems. Retailers must also have electronically sophisticated distribution centers, built to ensure that the right merchandise is received from producers and shipped to the right store at the right time.[102]

Abernathy and his colleagues focus on production in the CBI nations and Mexico. They describe how suppliers provide transportation from the factory, move the goods through customs, and ensure timely delivery to the distribution center and, from there, to stores. By 1998 a whole new software industry had been created to provide a variety of strategies to deal with these logistics. Consultants even offered advice about how to prevent drug dealers from secreting their own merchandise into the large containers that hold the clothing as it crosses national borders.

Lean retailing is heavily linked to retail success in today's competitive markets. According to the authors of *A Stitch in Time*, companies who employ the full panoply of lean retailing methods are three times more profitable than those who do not. However, it is just as likely that corporate profitability is a cause, as well as a result, of lean retailing: the most successful corporate retailers have the necessary capital to invest in the new technologies that the restructuring now requires.

The authors also state that lean retailing is not a response to the growth of freer trade and offshore production. Instead, they argue, "channel integration"—the new "partnerships between retailers and suppliers"—accounts for the emergence of lean retailing:

> These dramatic shifts cannot be ascribed simply to the passage of favorable trade legislation affecting Mexico and the Caribbean Basin countries. The preferential treatment under the Caribbean Basin Initiative and the tariffs it established for those countries dates back to the Caribbean Basin Economic Recovery Act of 1983 (amended in 1990), *well before the onset of the increase in trade flows from the CBI region.* Similarly NAFTA only began to be implemented in 1994, and tariff elimination under its provisions is still being phased into effect. Instead, these trade agreements have further heightened the benefits of proximity that channel integration has made increasingly important.[103]

The authors identify 1989 to 1997 as the period when imports from the CBI nations and Mexico expanded. Yet if, as they argue, Dillard's, Wal-Mart, the Gap, J. C. Penney, and the Limited all began to practice lean retailing between 1985 and 1995, these were also the years that U.S. textile and apparel producers were pressing the administration to open U.S. markets to imports from Latin America.[104]

Apparel imports from Latin America began to enter U.S. markets as early as the late 1960s, but Mexico's exports surged after the 1982 peso crisis, again after the Special Regime for Mexico was enacted in 1988, and once again after NAFTA and Mexico's 1994 peso crisis. Apparel exports from the CBI nations began to grow in 1983 and accelerated after the 1986 Special Access Program was enacted. It was trade liberalization that accelerated the growth of exports to the United States from these countries.

Channel integration—so desirable for retail profits—has increased the pressure on apparel suppliers, many of whom find the demands of retailers increasingly onerous. In 1999, *Apparel Industry Magazine* ran a series of articles dealing with the issue of supply-chain management. One analyst notes that "retailers continue to automate and add technology in order to squeeze supply chains and get goods moving faster. They [retailers] are demanding more value-added services from vendors." As Edna Bonacich and Richard Appelbaum see it, the large retailers are "price makers." They "know how many minutes it takes to sew a particular garment, and calculate, on the basis of the minimum wage, how much they need to pay per garment to cover it."[105] Those who contract for apparel—and retailers are increasingly among them—ultimately determine the price paid to production workers in export-processing zones all over the world.

Trade liberalization and technological developments in transport and communication have allowed apparel retailers access to low-wage sourcing on a global basis. Yet in today's competitive environment, retailers must continue to reduce the costs associated with time and distance. Abernathy and his colleagues argue that many retail executives today prefer to produce in Mexico and the CBI nations rather than Asian sites. Lean retailing enhances the value of proximity and gives this region a competitive advantage over lower wage regions in Asia.

No doubt lean production offers greater efficiencies in overcoming the problems of time and distance that result from the offshore, lower wage option. However, the authors do not explain why lean retailing could not be used by those who source in Asia. Is Latin American proximity to U.S. markets a real advantage to U.S. retailers? If proximity is the advantage, lean retailing might be most efficient with domestic production, except for the fact that the latter requires higher wages. Ultimately, then, the most sophisticated supply logistics must always be weighed against the significance of proximity to markets and the cost advantages of lower wage options.

As we will see in chapter 11, China is a major competitor to the CBI countries and Mexico for access to the U.S. apparel market. America's clothing retailers and other groups who source their production in developing countries now envision the expansion of export processing around the world. Retailers have been among the strongest supporters of global trade options. Since the 1980s they have been major advocates for trade initiatives that reduce quotas and tariffs and open up markets—not only in Latin America but around the world. Only the future will tell if lean retailing will support the competitive advantage that sourcing in the Caribbean Basin countries and Mexico is presumed to offer, or whether regions that lie at greater distances and produce goods for even lower wages will challenge this enterprise.

GLOBAL RETAILING

In the past decade America's retailers have expanded the numbers of retail outlets abroad. The growth of European and Japanese retail outlets in the United States sparked this effort. Between 1989 and 1991, European retail companies garnered 20 percent of the real growth in the U.S. retail market. By 1992 Europe was leading America in global retailing, and the U.S. market was its "prime target."[106]

Today, French hypermarkets like Carrefour—which sell a vast array of consumer goods—the Swedish furniture empire Ikea, the Dutch company Ahold, the British firm Marks & Spencer, and specialty retailers like Benetton and Laura Ashley have entered the retail markets of a number of developing countries, particularly in Asia. Thus far, only Wal-Mart, Toys 'R' Us, and the Gap can compete internationally on this level.[107]

As Europe's retailers look to eastern Europe and Africa, U.S. retail executives are exploring Mexico, Central America, Brazil, Chile, and Argentina. Before the 1997 fiscal crisis, European and American retailers looked to Asia—to Indonesia, Malaysia, Thailand, and most particularly, China— as a new place to open stores. By the mid-1990s, China, with the fastest growing domestic market for manufactured consumer goods, had opened its doors to British, French, and American retailers.[108]

Today the majority of U.S. retailers, even the largest, continue to do most of their business domestically. Two-thirds of the world's top one hundred global retailers still operate in only one country. Only five American retailers earn more than 50 percent of their consolidated revenues outside the United States.[109] American retailers are making an effort to expand abroad. In 1994 Price Waterhouse and Management Horizons, two retail consulting firms, were advising executives about the "narrow window of opportunity to expand their operations internationally,"[110] before the ATC quota phaseout is completed in 2004. Another consultant, Coopers and Lybrand, emphasized the urgency of this deadline: "Being first in a market doesn't ensure success, of course, but being there before the serious competition does increase one's chances. Because of the dearth of expandable markets locally, the international field is getting crowded and those on the inside track have a distinct advantage."[111]

Apparel manufacturers like Levi Strauss, Russell Corporation, and Sara

Lee, and sports and entertainment corporations like Disney, now sell recognized American designer and brand-name apparel abroad from their own retail outlets.[112] Mass market companies like Wal-Mart and its affiliate, Sam's Club, use their efficient supply networks to provide basic commodities to purchasers in foreign countries at a lower cost than existing small-scale domestic suppliers can.

According to Coopers and Lybrand's 1995 annual study of global retail corporations, thirty-six of the top one hundred global retailers, in terms of sales, were American companies. Nine of these corporations sold apparel products. Wal-Mart was the world's top global retailer, with 2,561 stores in operation worldwide, followed by Kmart, Sears, Dayton Hudson, J. C. Penney, May Department Stores, Federated Department Stores, Montgomery Ward, and Dillard's.[113] By the end of 1997, forty of the top one hundred global retailers were U.S. chains; twelve of them sold apparel. The new companies listed among the top one hundred global retailers were the Limited, the Gap, Nordstrom, and TJX, which owns the two clothing discounters Marshalls and T. J. Maxx.[114] The global success of these retailers suggests that apparel, because of its relatively low cost as a consumer product, is among the easiest products to sell abroad. Between 1994 and 1998, retail sales increased a full 20 percent.[115]

The growing market penetration of American consumer products and retail outlets abroad has been translated into effective demand among a relatively small proportion of foreign elite and middle-class consumers with enough purchasing power to fuel U.S. retail investment.[116] The limits of global retail expansion, however, are ultimately a function of the demand for consumer goods produced by U.S. textile, apparel, and retail transnationals. But demand ultimately may founder if American consumers find they have a surfeit of clothing, if a recession brings lower demand, and if American clothing is not affordable to people in developing countries.

11 Finally Free Trade
The Future of the Global Apparel Industry

One year after the enactment of the North American Free Trade Agreement, the Uruguay Round of trade talks led to the ending of the General Agreement on Tariffs and Trade and its replacement by the World Trade Agreement. The GATT, which had endured for more than fifty years, was terminated in 1994. The following year, the Multifibre Arrangement, which had regulated textile and apparel imports to the United States since 1974 under the GATT, ended and was replaced with the Agreement on Textiles and Clothing (ATC).

The year 1994 ended a forty-year period of regulated trade for the U.S. textile and apparel industries, an era that started with the Short-Term and Long-Term Arrangements in 1961 and 1962, respectively. On January 1, 1995, the world's textile and apparel trade entered a ten-year-transition period in which quotas are being phased out and lower tariffs for textiles and apparel are being negotiated. According to the U.S. International Trade Commission, "The main purpose of the ATC is to provide a systematic and gradual means of integrating world textile and apparel trade back into the trade norms set by the GATT. The ATC requires WTO members to phase out all MFA quotas in three stages over a 10-year period ending January 1, 2005."[1] The ATC "requires importing countries to increase the quota growth rates for major supplying countries by 16 percent on January 1, 1995; by an additional 25 percent on January 1, 1998; and by another 27 percent on January 1, 2002."[2] By 2005 all quotas will have been eliminated. During this period, importing countries are expected to open their markets to products exported by other countries.

In the next decade it will be increasingly possible for transnational corporations to have textiles and clothing manufactured anywhere in the world, wherever they find that technological requirements, labor costs, infrastructure, and proximity to markets are optimal. The new global accord is designed to culminate in more heavily concentrated and vertically integrated world textile and apparel industries, and is already creating new forms of competition among emerging corporate giants.

The changing trade regime is having new consequences for ongoing trade-policy conflicts between the textile-led apparel industry and the retail-led fashion industry. A rapid acceleration of textile and apparel production for export in Asian countries—indeed, in a large number of countries in the developing world—has intensified competition in the U.S. textile, apparel, and retail complex. The ending of quotas is likely to create a new political agenda among the industrialized and developed nations.

THE LINES OF CONFLICT

The textile industry and the textile-led apparel industry, as we have seen, have benefited from the regional and preferential trade accords with the Caribbean Basin countries and Mexico. Often described as trade-liberalizing measures, the detailed rules of origin embodied in these trade regimes have offered apparel producers, who may actually source in all these regions, what I call a "nonprotectionist form of protection"—special tariff advantages that give them access to low-wage labor and allow them to avoid competition with Asian exporters.

With the threat of NAFTA and the MFA phaseout, textile executives and their apparel customers pressed throughout the 1990s for CBI parity. Yet as we have seen, few moved their assembly operations to Mexico for better tariff treatment. CBI parity was designed to equalize trade benefits between the CBI nations and Mexico, but its goal was also to improve the U.S. textile industry's competitive advantage with Asian producers.

In 1993 Andrew Postal, chief executive officer of blouse-maker Judy Bond, a company sourcing primarily in the Caribbean Basin region, testified in Congress in favor of CBI parity. His concerns were centered on the fact that his competitors made women's blouses in low-wage countries around the world—particularly in countries like India, Pakistan, and China. He said, "On the one hand we are faced with the Uruguay Round textile negotiations. . . . And if that were to become law, the Pacific Rim would no longer be constrained by the MFA, and over 10 or 15 years, . . . we would be facing an unrestrained PRC, India, and Pakistan. . . . I submit that in the face of that, NAFTA becomes meaningless, as does the parity question."[3]

However, clothing retailers, fashion merchandisers, and importers in the retail-led fashion industry saw the preferential trade accords for the CBI nations—with their strict rules of origin—as embodying unjustified regulatory elements. They opposed NAFTA's strict yarn-forward rules of origin while favoring the trade preference levels that gave them greater freedom to choose fabrics from around the world than was otherwise possible when sourcing in Mexico or the CBI countries.[4] As early as 1990 the U.S. Apparel Industry Coalition began to lobby to end the customs fee for apparel transactions with CBI nations, and to simplify paperwork requiring importers to document their compliance with the rules of origin.[5] The retail-led fashion segment of the industry won regulations allowing retailers and their suppliers to source globally. Likewise, apparel producers in places like the Dominican Republic—the largest CBI exporter of apparel to the United States—were concerned that the trade-liberalizing effects of NAFTA and the WTA, by eliminating their preferential access to U.S. markets, would erode their ability to compete with producers in Mexico, Africa, China, and other parts of Asia.[6]

AFRICA AND EAST ASIA

In 1996, only a year after the Multifibre Arrangement was ended, the U.S. textile, apparel, and retail complex began to fix its sights on Africa. Before that, Africa had been seen as too distant and underdeveloped to be incorporated into international trade networks. Now, many of the war-torn and impoverished countries of sub-Saharan Africa have been included in the global trade regime. Few of the countries in this region are actually members of the WTO, and many are too poor to afford even the expense of membership. However, by 1996, well over a dozen African countries had begun to embrace trade liberalization and open export-processing zones.

In 1996, and again in the spring of 1997, in a bipartisan effort by Democrats and Republicans, Congress introduced the African Growth and Opportunity Act. While the act mandates private-sector investment in a variety of industries, "Section 8 of the Act consists entirely of a discussion of ways of facilitating textile and apparel exports from Africa to the United States, under detailed conditions which it specifies."[7] In support of this new trade move, Clinton announced the Comprehensive Trade and Development Policy for Countries of Africa in 1997. With this initiative he increased the number of personnel attached to the U.S. Commercial Service and the number of trade missions to Africa. The program established an advisory panel at the Export-Import Bank to encourage more investment in Africa and created equity and investment funds under the guidance of Overseas Private Investment Corporation. It authorized new funding for debt relief and reduced duties on African imports.[8]

At the same time, the countries of sub-Saharan Africa began to offer investors a variety of regulatory waivers and exemptions from taxes, waivers of industry regulations, exemptions from import and export duties, suspension of rules requiring that foreign investors partner with local entrepreneurs, strict guarantees against expropriation, assurances of physical security, and access to efficient communication and transportation networks.[9]

By 1997 U.S. retailers and importers, represented by the International Mass Retail Association, started to support these measures, seeing them as a way to "develop sub-Saharan Africa's competitive position vis-à-vis Asia."[10] Their objective was to make African countries into new low-wage start-up sites for apparel assembly.[11] The textile producers of the American Textile Manufacturers' Institute (ATMI) and their apparel customers opposed the bill, claiming that China was using African countries as bases for illegal transshipments of apparel destined for the U.S. market.[12]

America's African American community, led by Congressman Jesse Jackson Jr. and his Project HOPE, also opposed the bill. In February 1999, Jackson introduced the Hope for Africa Act, which would require labor rights provisions and debt relief and would request the Development Fund for Africa to help fund AIDS treatment. This counterbill was also supported by the Union of Needletrades and Industrial Textile Employees and the Southern African Clothing and Textile Workers Union. Inevitably, the bill, seen as protectionist, failed.

In 2000, the Clinton administration succeeded in getting the textile and apparel industries to compromise on a plan for African trade liberalization that was coupled with trade parity for the CBI nations. Congress introduced a bill that would both permit fashion producers to open new markets in Africa for low-wage production and give the textile industry CBI parity. This bill to implement the Trade Development Act (TDA) finally passed after the textile industry, represented by the ATMI, agreed with the House and the Senate on the rules of origin. The TDA, which took effect on October 1, 2000, opened trade in textiles and apparel between African countries and the United States.

Until recently, Africa participated in the global clothing trade primarily as an export market for used clothing.[13] Only Mauritius and South Africa have had globally competitive textile manufacturing facilities and have exported significant amounts of apparel to Europe. These two countries are now leveraging their ability to export to the United States. Liabilities inherent in trade with African nations include the many unstable and corrupt governments and the lack of infrastructure, such as roads, rail service, and port facilities.[14] The large proportion of the African population afflicted with AIDS is also seen as a barrier to development. Given all these conditions, it is unclear whether the TDA will ultimately promote the development of apparel production in sub-Saharan Africa.

Ostensibly, the pact is designed to encourage an indigenous textile industry in the region. According to *Women's Wear Daily,* "For two years, apparel produced in the least developed countries [of Africa]—excluding South Africa, Madagascar and Mauritius—could be made of fabric from other countries in order to encourage the creation of a textile industry." Yet because African-made textile exports to the United States will not qualify for trade benefits,[15] Africa is poised to become a perfect location for production sharing dominated by the U.S. textile-apparel complex. Moreover, the forty-two sub-Saharan African countries that have already participated in the Generalized System of Preferences are eligible for the benefits of this pact—but only for one year at a time, dependent on certification that they are "actively encouraging the liberalization of their external trade relations." Indeed, the act imposes criteria similar to those of the original Caribbean Basin Initiative.[16] Countries like Kenya, Zimbabwe, and Tanzania pay wages comparable to those paid by Chinese and other Asian producers.[17]

The Agreement on Textiles and Clothing allows retailers and fashion producers to develop global sourcing strategies. The TDA represents the efforts of the Clinton administration to respond to the political demands of the textile-led apparel industry, but only after clearing the way for China's accession to the WTO.

At present, the implications of the Trade Development Act are much more salient for the CBI countries than they are for Africa. Sub-Saharan countries have virtually no textile industry. The act is designed to let U.S. textile producers fill that gap, by making it possible for them to sell their products to African apparel producers, as they now do to apparel producers in the Caribbean Basin countries. At this point, however, sub-Saharan Africa has a very small apparel capacity.

More important, U.S. textile producers will get the equivalent of CBI parity—the tariff and quota advantages they have been demanding since before the passage of NAFTA. Apparel assembled in CBI countries from U.S. textiles—like Mexican apparel assembled from textiles made in the United States, Canada, or Mexico—will get the same quota-free and tariff-free treatment when it is exported to the United States. Such terms are much more favorable than those in other production sites in developing countries. The objective is to give CBI producers a window of opportunity to ready themselves to compete globally. In September 2000, a former chief textile negotiator for the U.S. Trade Representative told apparel producers in Greensboro, North Carolina, "You've got five years to get your act in gear to deal with the onslaught that will come from China and other countries when quotas are gone."[18]

According to the ATMI's trade director, the Trade Development Act is expected to reduce the U.S. textile industry's tariff costs by $700 million a year. ATMI analysts estimate that the act will increase the nation's textile sales by $8 billion a year.[19] Moreover, the TDA has made it possible for U.S. mills to form alliances and joint ventures with partners in CBI nations in order to build textile mills in those countries, and producers in the region are now able to plan for the development of full-package production.

Industry experts agree that during this period it will be important for countries to develop a well-rounded sourcing matrix that includes high-quality products, full-package production, rapid turnaround capabilities, and excellent customer service. Over the long term, these capabilities will be necessary if Latin America is to compete with East Asia as a supplier of apparel to the United States.[20]

THE CHINA TRADE

America's textile producers, and the apparel producers who purchase their fabrics, today focus most on the growing competition by the People's Republic of China (PRC) and other developing countries in Asia. This concern began in the 1980s, not long after President Nixon reopened U.S. relations with the People's Republic in the early 1970s.

Spending heavily on labor-saving, state-of-the-art technology, China began to bring its textile industry up to globally competitive standards. Its textile and apparel capacity became heavily concentrated and vertically integrated. U.S. textile producers making fabric for clothing increasingly found themselves in direct competition with not only the Big Three but also Chinese and other Asian textile makers. Textile producers had some protection, since China was not a member of the MFA. During the past two decades, however, China's growing trade with the United States was regulated like that of other member nations. In 1980 the United States signed a bilateral treaty with the PRC; it signed a second one in 1983.[21] At that time, textiles and apparel already comprised a large proportion of Chinese exports to the United States.

Like the nations who exported to the United States under the MFA, China was accorded a quota regime based on regulatory mechanisms defined by the Arrangement. The PRC first entered this trade regime with a small number of new product categories put under quota, in conformity with the regulatory system designed to encourage the expansion of trade. The first bilateral agreement between the two countries put eight product categories of textile and apparel products under the quota regime. By 1983, the Chinese government recognized the potential of textile and apparel exports for earning foreign exchange, and it expanded the mix of its exported products. The second bilateral agreement (in effect from 1983 to 1987) put twenty-five new items under quota.

Because it encompassed a wider range of goods, the second agreement was defined as a more comprehensive, or restrictive, agreement than the first. However, such definitions had little to do with the annual percentage increase of the PRC's exports to the United States, because a greater level of Chinese exports entered U.S. markets. When in 1982 U.S. textile producers filed a countervailing duty petition against thirteen Asian nations to oppose their governments' "unfair" subsidies of textile and apparel exports to the United States, Reagan responded by ordering curbs on textile and apparel imports from these countries.[22] However, Big Three countries began to subcontract apparel production to the PRC. By the mid-1980s, textiles and apparel became the PRC's largest foreign exchange earner, accounting for 28 percent of that nation's total exports and 43 percent of all its exports to the United States.[23]

Recognizing the potential of their textile and apparel exports for earning foreign exchange, the PRC took full advantage of all the MFA rules and practices that allowed exporting nations to expand their trade.[24] For example, they produced new items of apparel not yet covered by import quotas—shifting their production, and their exports to the United States, from controlled to uncontrolled categories. China never subscribed to the neoliberal approach to free trade that is embodied in the GATT, and in various ways has manipulated the quota regime to its advantage.[25] Like Japan in the early postwar period, China throughout the 1980s continued to govern the growth of its textile and apparel industries and expand its exports of their products. These exports had become the country's largest source of foreign exchange earnings.[26] The government offered tax rebates and bonuses to producers who reached or surpassed their export quotas.[27]

The PRC unofficially encouraged illegal transshipments of apparel, which set off "allegations by the U.S. Customs Service that Chinese exporters are evading quota limits by shipping products with fraudulent country of origin certification. In other cases, unmarked goods are being routed through places as widely flung as Hong Kong, Macau, Taiwan, Mozambique and Panama."[28]

In 1987 China agreed to cap its export growth at 3 percent annually until 1991. While the United States had previously limited individual categories of imports, that year was the first time it imposed aggregate limits on China's textile and apparel imports. In 1990, however, bilateral agreements between the United States and China further increased Chinese textile and apparel exports to American markets.

U.S. administrations have always played "textile politics" with the PRC, with a view to managing China's role in the global balance of power.[29] Clinton, responsible for foreign policy from 1993 to 2000, was a staunch free-trade advocate and had the support of America's corporate exporters in a wide variety of industries. He pressed for China's accession to the WTO regardless of that country's purported violations of trade rules and despite its political agenda, which was often at odds with the goals of the United States. He believed that trade expansion and membership in the WTO would improve China's human rights record. He encouraged the Chinese government to comply with WTO trade rules and to open Chinese markets to further U.S. trade and investment. These policies, he argued, would bring China, which was among the largest of the big emerging markets, in line with America's interests.

U.S. administrations have used tariffs and quotas to regulate access to American markets and, thus, to further their political objectives. Before November 2000, Congress was required to renew China's status as a most favored nation every year. America's goal was to enhance the opportunities for selling American products and services in Chinese markets. Although U.S. textile corporations continually ask for quota reductions and oppose tariff reductions, import levels of products from other Chinese industries believed to be more critical to the economy have often been allowed to grow in order to promote new trade and investment links between the United States and the PRC. In 1993, however, Washington cut China's textile and apparel quotas in key products in retaliation for continued violations of GATT regulations. Clinton threatened to revoke the annual approval of China's status as a most favored nation.[30] The U.S. textile industry has also pressured the government to block China's access to the WTO. Between 1994 and 1996, a three-year bilateral accord froze quotas at an overall 1 percent rate of annual increase.

In 1996 the United States condemned the Chinese government's implicit support for the thriving traffic in counterfeit videos, compact discs, and comparable forms of intellectual property. When the Chinese government refused to stop such ventures, the United States published a $3 billion "hit list" of Chinese imports, threatening to charge 100 percent tariff on these products. About two-thirds were textile and apparel products. That same year, the ATMI once again claimed that the Chinese government was illegally subsidizing its textile industry with free raw materials and electricity and closing its doors to independent investment and joint ventures in textile production. But on February 2, 1997, the two nations signed a new trade agreement on textiles and apparel that extended the existing quotas for Chinese exports of these items to the United States and reduced quotas "in areas of repeated transshipment violations."[31] China also agreed to further open its markets to U.S. textile and apparel products, including yarns, fabrics, and apparel items like T-shirts, sweatshirts, and underwear, items that U.S. companies are anxious to export.

In 1998, the ATMI again accused the Chinese of dumping.[32] The following year it continued to oppose China's accession to the WTO. Moreover, it insisted that, if China did become a member of the organization, quotas for Chinese goods should be fully phased out in 2008 rather than 2005, when all the other members' quotas are scheduled to be phased out. ATMI representatives testified in Congress,[33] basing their comments on a new study predicting that China's entry into the WTO in 2005 would triple the existing level of U.S. imports of Chinese textiles and apparel, which then totaled $27.5 billion, and that China would capture 31 percent of the U.S. market for apparel imports.[34]

In November 2001 China formally became a permanent member of the World Trade Organization. The nation is now among the top three exporters of textiles and apparel to the United States, running neck and neck with the Caribbean Basin countries and Mexico. Now that China has become a member of the WTO, all import quotas are to be removed in 2005 in conformity with the Agreement on Textiles and Clothing. The U.S. textile industry and their apparel customers fear the PRC will become a truly formidable competitor with America's textile-led apparel industry.

China is among the world's largest and most efficient textile producers today; it is the world's largest cotton-producing country and has the largest man-made fiber- and fabric-producing industry. It is also the largest producer of silk, accounting for 50 percent of global production.[35] By 1998 textile and apparel products accounted for one-fourth of China's exports worldwide. These two related industries employ about one-seventh of China's industrial workforce, accounting for 6 percent of China's industrial output.[36]

China's state-owned textile and apparel industries are now being closed, as the government promotes the construction of a more modern and efficient privatized textile industry in anticipation of increasing its exports. By devaluing its currency, the Chinese government has been able to amass large foreign exchange reserves and, at the same time, to promote its exports and discourage imports.[37]

With the return of Hong Kong to Chinese control in 1997, China also began to expand and upgrade the quality of its apparel exports, which at that point represented 70 percent of all its combined textile and apparel exports. The Big Three have seen their exports reduced. However, with their lengthy traditions of apparel production and fashion expertise, they have become new design and planning centers for the Asian apparel industry. Production, cutting, and assembly now take place in low-wage China. The Big Three offer full-package production to Europe and Japan, as well as to retailers and importers in the United States. Together this textile-apparel complex has the potential to become both a formidable competitor to similar complexes in other developing countries and an even larger supplier to U.S. retailers and importers.

The U.S. International Trade Commission has recently done a study to forecast "the potential impact of China's participation in the ATC's quota phaseout." One model was based on a scenario in which China gained access to the WTO. The study predicted that with access to the WTO China was likely to have about a 30 percent share of the American apparel import market by 2010, a figure close to that reported by the ATMI after a similar study. Perhaps even more important, the model predicts that the doubling of apparel imports from China between 1998 and 2010 would be at the expense of imports from the Big Three, South Asia, and significantly, from Canada and Mexico.[38] While the model does not disaggregate the CBI countries, it predicts that Canada and Mexico will have only a 3 percent share of the U.S. apparel market—a significant loss.

Such econometric forecasts can, of course, be wrong, and it is too early to predict the long-term outcomes of these events. Yet the vehemence with which the U.S. textile industry has opposed expanding imports from China since the early 1980s, and fought for CBI parity since NAFTA was passed, evidences its continued concern about Asian competition. Whatever happens, China will continue to be a player in this global industry. The U.S. textile transnationals are also hedging their bets—investing globally as well as locally—and apparel producers are increasing their sourcing operations in China. According to the Commerce Department's PIERS import-export database—a record of all cargo entering U.S. ports—some of the largest and most powerful retailers, as well as clothing and footwear transnationals, are now sourcing in the new export-processing zones of China. They include retailers like Federated Department Stores (Macy's and Bloomingdale's), the Gap, the Limited, Spiegel, Wal-Mart, New Balance, Nike, Timberland, Fila, and Agron.[39]

EMERGING ASIAN COUNTRIES

No doubt a wide variety of political and economic forces as yet unknown will influence the way transnationals pursue global trade in textiles and apparel in the twenty-first century. Developing countries throughout Asia are now, more than ever, playing a large role in this trade and are more likely to do so in the future. Many of these poor countries previously hesitated to participate in the international trade in textiles and apparel because the MFA quota regime limited the power of developing countries to influence the allocation of import quotas. Yet many Asian countries willingly participated in the Uruguay Round of discussions because they hoped for greater access to the textile and apparel markets of developed countries.[40] With the emergence of the WTO, new trade relations were swiftly negotiated between the United States and India, Pakistan, and Bangladesh. According to the U.S. International Trade Commission, market-access agreements with India and Pakistan permitted these countries to expand their imports to the United States for the first time in forty years. At the same time, these countries agreed to open their markets to U.S. textiles and apparel imports.[41]

The International Textiles and Clothing Bureau (ITCB) represents many developing and less developed countries, including India, Pakistan, Brazil, Bangladesh, Egypt, Indonesia, Hong Kong, Colombia, China, Costa Rica, Mexico, Sri Lanka, Thailand, and others. Just before the WTO meetings in Seattle in November 1999, ITCB members said that the Agreement on Textiles and Clothing had not fulfilled their expectations, had not significantly increased their access to the markets of developed countries. Since the WTA's implementation, they claimed, quotas had increased by only 5 to 6 percent, and that the United States had eliminated only 13 of 750 quotas[42]—a point with which the president of the World Bank, James Wolfensohn, could only agree.

As the fiscal crisis gripped Asia in 1997, stock markets and real estate values fell, devastating family assets and destroying family budgets. Economic growth faltered and unemployment soared.[43] Because currency devaluations reduced wages in East Asian nations like Indonesia, Thailand,

South Korea, and Malaysia, the value of these countries' apparel exports to the United States dropped. These nations saw that expanding their now lower cost textile and apparel exports to developed countries was a way to regain some of their lost capital. The Asian fiscal crisis ratcheted up their demands to increase their quotas faster than initially planned by the ATC, a push that U.S. textile producers once more resisted. The ATMI cited the crisis as the cause of an 8 percent drop in the average price of Asian fabrics, a 35 percent increase in cotton fabric imports, and a 51 percent increase in fabrics composed of man-made fibers, all occurring between 1996 and 1998.[44] These textile manufacturers described the United States as a " 'life support system' for these countries . . . [who] are . . . trying to export their way out of their difficulties and to our detriment."[45] The ATMI believes the Asian fiscal crisis caused not only an increase in U.S. imports but also a decrease in U.S. exports to its traditional markets in Asia (Japan, Hong Kong, Taiwan) and Europe.

U.S. textile producers also faulted the WTO for failing to fulfill its promise of opening new markets for U.S. textile exports to Asia. They pointed to the fact that more than half of the twenty-seven major textile-exporting countries were still relatively closed to U.S. textile exports, even more than when the WTA went into effect in 1996.[46]

It is difficult to imagine how these claims and counterclaims can be resolved, particularly in the shadow of the fiscal crisis that beset developing countries in Asia after 1997. Moreover, just at the time of this crisis, China began to further privatize its inefficient state textile sector and to expand its exports of textiles and apparel destined for American markets. Competition with lower wage Asian exports has reduced prices for China's exports.[47]

Even as American textile producers oppose the new market-opening trade initiatives in China, America's apparel retailers, overseas merchandisers, and importers of fashion apparel have seen their market-opening objectives realized by these events. Since the early 1980s, the retail industry has continually pressed for full expansion of trade with China, urging administrations to grant China access to most-favored nation status and, later, access to the WTO. In 1996 the *Wall Street Journal* wrote that "retailers were enraged at the steady deterioration in the United States–China relationship. The two countries have been locked in a war of words all year: The United States has objected to China's aggression toward Taiwan, its sale of nuclear material to Pakistan and its desire to join the World Trade Organization in Geneva. Added to that is the annual battle over whether to renew China's 'most favored nation' trade status."[48] According

to the retail industry's perspective, the United States' "decision to hit textiles was calibrated for maximum political benefit," domestically and
abroad, presumably to win the support of labor unions and workers in the
southern textile states, whereas U.S. clothing retailers wanted to make and
sell clothing throughout the developing world.[49] When the Asian fiscal
crisis hit in 1997, a Macy's executive told the *New York Times*, "We expect
to receive price concessions from our existing overseas manufacturers, allowing us to pass on savings to our customers." The same executive made
the point that "the economic weakness there [in East Asia] translates into
desperate manufacturers willing to cut prices in order to unload goods that
otherwise would go unsold."[50]

THE NEW GLOBAL COMPETITION

In the past two decades, successive U.S.-led trade-liberalizing agreements
have continued to open and expand low-wage production sites for apparel
in Mexico and the Caribbean Basin countries. These trade agreements have
been particularly valuable for the U.S. textile sector that makes fabrics for
clothing.

However, the fashion-apparel-led retailers were in favor of global sourcing. On December 1, 1993, in response to the passage of NAFTA-enabling
legislation and the potential for a tariff-free Mexico, the USA Importers
of Textiles and Apparel sponsored a one-day conference in Hong Kong
attended by over 250 major Hong Kong apparel exporters. The leaders of
this conference "stressed the vital interdependence of U.S. importers and
Hong Kong manufacturers," many of whom subcontracted to China.[51] The
fashion apparel industry—represented by retailers like Carter Hawley
Hale, Federated Department Stores, and Dayton Hudson—and fashion-
apparel producers like Anne Klein and Liz Claiborne, were sourcing or
purchasing full-package merchandise directly from Asian producers. So
were mass-market discounters like Wal-Mart, and other merchandisers
represented by the Associated Merchandising Corporation. U.S. fashion
importers, however, were also doing a substantial Item 807 business with
Caribbean exporters.

At the same time, U.S. textile producers are also working to open new
production facilities around the world.[52] In the two years between 1994
and 1996, the U.S. textile industry added new global subsidiaries. Rather
than put all their eggs in one basket, textile corporations have been building integrated-manufacturing capacity in Asia to produce fashion-
oriented apparel products, instead of the jeans and T-shirts they make in

Central America and Mexico.[53] By 1995 Burlington Industries, Alamac, Threads USA, and VF Corporation had announced joint ventures with Indian companies.[54] The Department of Commerce, in cooperation with U.S. textile and apparel manufacturers, has helped the industry maintain a major export drive for the last fifteen years.[55] In recent years U.S. textile transnationals have been making new investments globally. About half of these have been in Europe; the other half were in India and Latin America.[56]

China is a particularly important competitor, having 15 million of its workers employed in the textile and apparel industries. With the labor pool needed to expand low-wage production, China's exports of textiles and apparel can increase almost infinitely. In 1997 Hong Kong was reintegrated with the PRC; China's combined textile and apparel capacity now makes it an especially formidable apparel producer. Its State Council Development Research Center predicted a doubling of textile and apparel exports between 1998 and 2005.

What are the patterns in global apparel exports to U.S. markets? In 2000 the United States imported $67.5 billion worth of apparel from 188 countries. Mexico and China are now officially considered the two most important exporters of apparel to the United States. In 2000 China exported $9.6 billion to the United States, compared to Mexico's almost $9.8 billion.

But these figures alone do not reveal the reality of global production. Twenty-three Caribbean and Central American countries now export clothing to the United States, and most of them benefit from the Caribbean Basin Initiative. If we aggregate the exports of the 23 countries that exported apparel to U.S. markets in 2000, they amount to almost $9.5 billion—almost as much as Mexico's $9.8 billion.

After getting a slow start in the 1980s, Mexico increased its apparel exports to the United States by 987 percent between 1989 and 2000, compared to the CBI nations' increase of 499 percent. In these years, the production and export of apparel products from the Caribbean Basin countries and Mexico together have grown from $2.9 billion to $19.2 billion, or more than 660 percent. This level of expansion is certainly a tribute to the trade accords that have made the region America's new garment district. The CBI countries and Mexico's $19.2 billion of apparel exports to the United States represented 28 percent of all apparel imports to the United States.

Apparel imports from Asian countries to the United States rose dramatically as well. Between 1989 and 2000, apparel imports from Indonesia grew 281 percent; from Thailand, 397 percent; from Malaysia, 81 percent;

from Bangladesh, 575 percent; from Pakistan, 405 percent; from India, 300 percent; and from Sri Lanka, 326 percent. While imports from the Big Three—Hong Kong, South Korea, and Taiwan—declined by 13 percent between 1989 and 2000 (from $10.5 billion to $9.3 billion), they still represented almost 14 percent of the world's apparel exports to the United States. This was about the same proportion of apparel exported to the United States from China (14 percent), Mexico (14 percent), and the CBI countries (14 percent).[57]

In little more than a decade, the center of production for U.S. apparel imports has shifted away from the Big Three. Apparel exports to the United States from every major exporting region in the world, except for the Big Three, have grown.

Many researchers argue that the industry's need for proximity to the point of sale will encourage American apparel manufacturers and retailers to source in the Western Hemisphere—and even relocate their sourcing operations from Asia.[58] Judi Kessler, in a new study of the California-Mexico apparel commodity chain, also cites a number of fashion apparel corporations that have begun to produce in Mexico since the implementation of NAFTA.[59] She argues that the growing apparel commodity chains developing between California's fashion apparel companies and Mexican producers are making the industry less footloose, because delivery time and reliability have become more important than cost in sourcing abroad.

In early 1997 the Limited announced that it was shifting its lingerie sourcing operation from East Asia to Mexico. As a Limited executive put it, "Although wages in Mexico are still three times the $60 a month apparel workers make in countries like Sri Lanka[,] . . . it is cheaper and faster to move goods from Mexico City to the US than from Colombo. . . . The clincher is that under NAFTA there will be no tariffs on Mexican goods, while Sri Lankan goods will pay a 19 percent duty."[60] According to *Women's Wear Daily*, the U.S. textile industry is now gearing up to increase the sale of textiles to U.S. apparel producers as the new parity regulations take effect. Textile executives acknowledge that the industry will have difficulty producing all the fabrics that apparel producers want. A U.S. textile maker reported, "The domestic textile industry is so eroded, so small, relative to what it was five years ago, that the variety of product that the consumers and manufacturers want to have in the stores doesn't exist in America. . . . We're not selling imports because they're cheaper, but because we can't get them domestically anymore. There's not enough production."[61]

The dearth of specialized U.S. fabrics for apparel production is, in part, a result of the way the U.S. textile industry has responded to low-wage competition. For the past twenty years, textile producers have concentrated their efforts on making long runs of standard fabrics—textiles for underwear, T-shirts, and particularly, denim. This type of production is reflected in the new integrated manufacturing centers of Mexico. The large U.S. producers of fabric for apparel have relied on mass-production methods and the trade benefits embodied in NAFTA and the CBI. They do not make all the fabrics required by fashion producers that are available in other regions of the world. Whether U.S. textile producers will be able to diversify their production and still meet the requirements of their own rules of origin remains to be seen.

In the long term, will the trade advantages of NAFTA and the CBI parity programs continue to promote the comparative advantage of Latin America as the major source of U.S. apparel production? Will the CBI countries and Mexico, because of their proximity to the United States, replace East Asia as the major source of low-wage apparel production for America's apparel transnationals and their retail customers? Or will increasing competition from developing nations of the world particularly undercut the value of Latin American production?

GLOBAL SOURCING

Trade liberalization has facilitated new levels of global concentration in the textile and apparel industries. In February 1996 VF Corporation, for example, was selling Lee, Wrangler, and Rustler jeans and other local brands of blue jeans and intimate apparel through its 133 licensees and 50 distributors in 150 countries throughout the world. Between 1991 and 1996, that business alone grew threefold, from $250 million to $750 million. Kellwood Company, another major U.S. transnational, owns state-of-the-art textile and apparel facilities in the United States, the Caribbean countries, Central America, and Asia.[62] Since the mid-1980s this company, the fifth largest in the United States, has pursued an "aggressive external acquisition strategy. . . . The company operates 34 company-owned plants and distribution centres in nine U.S. states . . . plus facilities in Hong Kong, Taiwan, Costa Rica, Saipan, Sri Lanka, China, Dominican Republic . . . , Honduras and Canada."[63] Almost half, or 46 percent, of its goods are sourced offshore among contractors in thirty countries. Eastern European countries—particularly Hungary, Poland, and Russia—with their new free-market economies and low wages, increasingly are vying to produce textiles and apparel for sale in the United States, as American transnational textile, apparel, and retail conglomerates are developing new strategies to export to the European Economic Community.[64]

While the fashion segments of the apparel industry are likely to benefit from the global sourcing made possible by the new trade agreements, the U.S. textile industry may be in deep trouble. For the past half century, American textile producers have been claiming that trade-liberalizing and market-opening trade initiatives will be their death knell. In the 1950s and 1960s they fought hard to maintain trade barriers against Asian imports. In the 1970s they were helped to make large investments in new technology in order to increase productivity and reduce labor costs in an effort to compete with Asian imports. In the 1980s, when protection failed, the Reagan administration offered them a special production-sharing arrangement with the Caribbean Basin region to insulate textile producers from competition by the Big Three, with their growing low-wage exports, and then, perhaps more important, from competition with other Asian producers—including the People's Republic of China, with that country's even lower wage exports.

By the late 1990s, NAFTA, the World Trade Agreement, and the Trade Development Act had all intervened to promote global sourcing. The phasing out of all quotas by 2005, China's accession to the WTO, and the new Trade Development Act all threaten to challenge the competitiveness of the U.S. textile industry by reducing the regional protectionism America's textile producers have enjoyed since implementation of the CBI initiatives in 1983 and 1986. Even though the industry has fought hard to create a full-package production capability to rival that of Asian producers before the quotas are fully phased out in 2005, China and other low-wage Asian countries are serious rivals.

In part the U.S. textile industry is now suffering from the ramifications of the fiscal crisis that hit Asia in 1997 and the spillover effects of this crisis on the apparel industry. As I write in December 2001, the American Textile Manufacturers' Institute now claims that "the U.S. textile industry is suffering from the worst economic crisis since the Great Depression." According to their report written in August of 2001, in the four years since the Asian fiscal crisis hit, there has been a 40 percent decline in Asian currencies against the U.S. dollar, and textile imports from Asia have increased by 80 percent. As a result, U.S. textile profits have evaporated and more than a hundred mills have closed.[65]

Only the future will tell whether the U.S. textile industry is crying wolf, or whether the new global trade agenda, which has opened the door to the low-cost imports of Asian and African nations, will really lead to its demise. Both Latin America and Asia are now poised to compete in the U.S. market, and there soon may be new competition from African export-processing zones. How this market will be shared after 2005 is anyone's guess.

12 The New Global Apparel Trade
Who Wins, Who Loses?

By now, Americans are aware of the globalization of the U.S. apparel industry. They know about the loss of apparel jobs in the United States, the reemergence of sweatshops at home, and the growth of new ones abroad. They understand that "free trade" means low-wage imports, and that it has led to the development of substandard working conditions in apparel factories, whether these factories are in Latin America, Asia, or the United States. At the same time, they hear from neoliberal advocates of free trade, experts who claim that sweatshops, though inevitable in the short run, will lead to economic progress for the poor countries of the world and to new economic opportunities for women who come from these countries.

Embedded in this view is an optimism that the current trade and investment agenda will lead to a win-win situation for all the players involved—for workers and transnational corporations, both at home and abroad. If women lose jobs in American clothing factories, they find new and better ones in the high-tech and service industries, better jobs that require more education and skill. If new groups of immigrant women are working in America's apparel factories in substandard conditions and below the minimum wage, they are filling jobs Americans will not take, jobs that, despite their limitations, offer better opportunities than would otherwise be available to them.

The growth of low-wage production in the export-processing zones of developing countries has been defined as part of a larger plan for industrialization. Economic development is expected to generate new wealth for poor countries, creating greater economic opportunities for the current generation of impoverished workers and certainly for their children. Moreover, Americans benefit from the lower cost of clothing, and this is especially important for America's low-income families. Ultimately, then, hard work and faith in the workings of the market will improve economic conditions. The alternative is economic stagnation, which is guaranteed to produce only more poverty in the future.

Yet many Americans are beginning to question the view that existing forms of development represent the best of all possible worlds, and to doubt the premises of the neoliberal paradigm because of its potential to create a "race to the bottom," to extend the downward harmonization of standards. In the United States we are seeing greater job insecurity, declining wages, and growing inequalities throughout the economy. Internationally, we are seeing growing inequality both between and within nations.

Who are the winners and who are the losers of the globalization of the apparel industry? Executives and managers of the large retail and apparel transnationals have clearly been winners, while those who have been displaced from their jobs, mostly the women who now work in the industry's sweatshops—in the United States and in the export-processing facilities of developing countries—are some of the losers. While it is argued that consumers' economic welfare increases as a result of the free trade regime's ability to offer clothing at lower cost, evidence suggests that the benefit consumers derive from this is minimal.

THE WINNERS

Despite intense competition in the U.S. retail industry, its financial debacle in the late 1980s, its benefits from trade expansion, and its constant struggle with fluctuating levels of consumer spending, apparel manufacturers' profits rose dramatically in the last two decades of the twentieth century.[1] The U.S. apparel industry, as measured by all indices of profitability—including return on equity—became more profitable than the average of all other U.S. manufacturing industries.[2] Not surprisingly, the industry's chief executive officers have benefited from this (see table 3). In this five-year period, new trade liberalizing agreements allowed imports to reach new levels.[3] In June 1997, *Women's Wear Daily* ran the following headline: "Most Apparel CEO's Saw Their Incomes Swell during 1996."[4] The author of this article wrote, "Overall, 27 of the 38 apparel executives surveyed received raises. Apparel industry executives' salaries were on average 5.5 percent higher than in 1995, as apparel companies' earnings gained 38 percent to $2.6 billion. The average salary of the CEO's in the group came to 1.64 million against $1.55 in 1995."

In 1997 bankers were courting apparel executives to offer them loans.[5]

Table 3. Profitability Ratios, Apparel and All Manufacturing,
1993–1997
(calculated on operating income)

	1993	1994	1995	1996	1997
Return on sales					
Apparel	5.0	6.0	4.8	4.8	6.6
All manufacturing	6.0	7.4	7.6	7.4	7.6
Return on assets					
Apparel	9.7	9.4	8.0	8.7	12.4
All manufacturing	6.3	8.0	8.3	7.9	8.0
Return on equity					
Apparel	25.5	23.3	20.2	25.8	35.5
All manufacturing	17.3	21.6	21.6	20.5	20.4
Return on invested capital[a]					
Apparel	14.9	14	11.7	12.6	18.2
All manufacturing	8.3	10.7	11.1	10.6	10.7
Long-term debt, as percentage of net worth					
Apparel	59.9	51.1	55.7	84.4	77.1
All manufacturing	62.4	57.9	55.2	53.0	50.3

[a]Net fixed assets plus working capital
SOURCE: U.S. Bureau of the Census, *Quarterly Financial Report for Manufacturing,* cited in U.S. International Trade Commission, *Industry and Trade Summary (Apparel),* Publication 3169 (Washington, D.C.: USITC, March 1999).

The stock prices of apparel retail corporations and clothing manufacturers rose rapidly.[6] According to one analyst, public apparel companies were being pushed to see 10 percent earnings growth per year but were generating only 3 to 4 percent. These pressures drove not only retailers but also apparel producers to consolidate.[7]

Only three years later, this highly volatile industry saw profits decline. On January 5, 2001, a *New York Times* headline on Christmas sales for 2000 read, "A Glum Season for Retailers."[8] The article quoted George Strachan, an analyst with Goldman Sachs, as saying, "The consumer spending binge of 1998 and 1999 has finally decelerated." Even Wal-Mart, the "juggernaut of the industry," grew only 0.3 percent. Yet the article reported rising stock prices for the retail industry: "The Lehman Brothers index of 43 major retailers was up 6.3 percent on the day, a result of gains at Kohl's Target, Federated and May, among others. With interest rates expected to fall further after the Federal Reserve's move on Wednesday, investors appear to believe that retailers have seen the worst and that consumer spending will rebound by late spring or early summer." Stock market prices held steady because downturns in the industry were expected to drive new consolidation. Those retailers who withstood the loss of sales that year were expected to merge with or acquire those who had fared poorly or failed.[9]

Despite the optimism at the beginning of the year, after the events of September 11, 2001, consumer spending continued to fall, further intensifying the economic recession that had begun earlier in the year. By November 2001, sales at department stores like Bloomingdale's and Macy's were "running 20 percent below forecast."[10] Discount stores appeared better able to weather the economic storm.[11] According to one observer, consumer confidence "has been badly shaken and sales of both upscale and discount retailers have trailed forecasts in the last two weeks."[12]

According to Carl Steidtman, an economist with Deloitte Touche, retail spending is expected to decline further.[13] Retailers have narrowed their supplier base, building stronger relationships with particular clothing manufacturers and importers.[14] While this has weeded out many apparel producers, it has also led to new advantages for successful fashion producers in the new global trade regime. In the long run, the economic downturn may provide a new opportunity for both successful retailers and their strategic partners in the apparel industry to consolidate further, just as they did a decade ago.

JOB LOSS

If shareholders, executives, and managers are reaping the benefits of a more consolidated and globalized apparel industry, women production workers have suffered most of the losses as the industry has shifted its production to the developing world.[15] Apparel workers have felt the effects of these trends much more acutely than workers in other manufacturing industries. In 1973 "there were more than 2.4 million textile and apparel workers employed in the United States; by 1996, that figure had dropped to 1.5 million. This 39-percent decline contrasts with the 8-percent decline among all manufacturing workers, and the 56-percent rise in employment among all workers over the same period. In addition, job losses appear to be intensifying in the textile and apparel industries, and are projected to continue in the coming decade."[16]

Until quite recently textile employment declined too, but not as severely as apparel employment. The loss of textile jobs was due, in large part, to the growing productivity generated by advanced technologies.[17] Between 1992 and 1996, about 50,000 U.S. textile jobs were lost. However, between 1993 and 1996, 143,000 U.S. apparel jobs were lost—almost three times as many.[18] Employment in textiles and apparel has been projected to decline from 1994 to 2005 by about 300,000 jobs, with most of the job losses in the apparel industry.[19]

Calculations of employment gains and losses, of course, rest to a large extent on assumptions about what represents a job lost, a job saved, and a job gained, and perhaps more important, on how much losing a job "matters" to different workers. Gary Clyde Hufbauer, Diane Berliner, and Kimberly Ann Elliott calculated that the "protectionist" Multifibre Arrangement had *saved* 460,000 jobs in the apparel industry—but at a consumer cost of $39,000 per job.[20] Has saving jobs really hurt American consumers? If so, the 460,000 jobs saved by the MFA can still be seen as a benefit to these almost half-million workers and their families. The money they were able to spend and the taxes they paid added to the gross national product.

For neoliberal Sidney Weintraub, however, the loss of manufacturing jobs is simply irrelevant in the context of full employment. Weintraub commented in his congressional testimony in support of NAFTA,

> Please consider what full employment means. This means that we cannot create any significant number of new jobs without stimulating higher inflation. It means that we are not losing jobs as a result of trade because the country is creating as many jobs as there are takers without stimulating inflation. This gives the lie to those who assert that NAFTA has resulted in hundreds of thousands of job losses. NAFTA could not have done this[,] because the country is at full employment. I want to repeat this simple truth over and over again so that each time some critic of open trade talks about job losses, a direct challenge to his or her credibility is forthcoming.[21]

For economists, eliminating one job and creating another presumably has the same economic value to the overall economy. This is especially true when the job created pays more than the job lost. According to C. Fred

Bergsten of the Institute for International Economics, Americans do not understand the way freer trade promotes Americans' economic welfare. He argues that exports promote high-wage jobs that more than compensate for the loss of low-wage textile and apparel jobs. He writes, "Export jobs pay about 15% to 20% more than nonexport jobs." A *Time* article quotes Bergsten as saying, "Whatever Pat Buchanan saves for Roger Milliken, a major textile employer in South Carolina, he loses for Boeing," which is heavily dependent on aircraft exports. Bergsten adds, "And Boeing jobs pay so much more than textile jobs."[22] This only suggests that the benefits of trade liberalization are distributed differentially in the population.[23] Americans who live in Seattle may be more likely to support the free trade agenda than textile workers and their families who live in eastern states, where apparel firms are closing their doors only to reopen them in Mexico, the Caribbean, Central America, or China.[24]

WAGE LOSS

While large numbers of women workers in America's apparel factories are losing their jobs, those still employed in the industry are seeing a severe deterioration in their wages and working conditions. Production workers in the apparel industry have suffered deeper wage losses than workers in any other U.S. manufacturing industry. Autoworkers, most of whom are men, have also suffered high levels of job displacement since the 1960s. However, in 2000 the smaller labor force that continued to make auto parts and assemble vehicles in U.S. factories was still largely male, despite some employment gains in this industry by women. Auto workers are members of a strong industrial union—which is one reason they have enjoyed during the past forty years a wage higher than that paid in other industries. In 1960 autoworkers earned 134 percent of the average annual manufacturing wage; by 2000 this figure was 149 percent.

Even the low-wage textile workers who remain have fared better than apparel workers in terms of earnings during the past forty years. In 1960, textile workers earned only 77 percent of the average manufacturing wage, and apparel workers only 76 percent. By 2000 textile workers were earning 80 percent of the average manufacturing wage. However, between 1960 and 2000 the wages of apparel workers plummeted from 76 percent to 66 percent of the average manufacturing wage. Starting out at the low end of the wage distribution, apparel workers lost more in wages than did manufacturing workers in any other industry (see figure 2).[25]

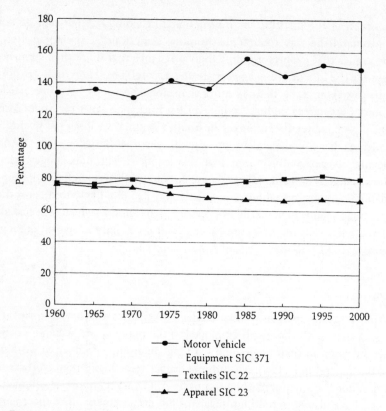

Figure 2.   Average hourly wages of textile workers, apparel workers, and autoworkers as a percentage of average hourly wages of all production workers. *Source:* Bureau of Labor Statistics, National Employment Hours and Earnings, Series ID: EEU00500006, Bureau of Labor Statistics, April 21, 2001.

THE REEMERGENCE OF SWEATSHOPS IN THE UNITED STATES

Official calculations of job displacement and wage losses are based on federally collected data and underestimate the overall job losses that have occurred in the apparel industry since 1960. Sweatshops in the United States are not simply firms that offer undesirable jobs for long hours and poor pay. They are firms paying wages that violate federally mandated minimum wage standards as well as other employment standards set forth in the Fair Labor Standards Act. Sweatshops may employ women without sufficient education for better jobs, or women immigrants, both legal and illegal, who lack language skills. Frequently, official employment and wage data fail to reflect these firms.

Employers in unofficial contracting shops may pay workers in cash "under the table," and may falsify these payments on their official records or fail to report them. Even when such employers do keep records, few report the subminimum wages they may actually pay. Without knowing which firms are violating the law, it is impossible to know how many sweatshops there are, how many workers they employ, and how much they underpay their employees, but a variety of estimates have been made. A recent study of New York's apparel contractors found that 80 percent of the New York firms surveyed complied with the minimum wage laws; however, only 3 percent complied with all wage and hour regulations.[26] UNITE estimates that 75 percent of New York firms are sweatshops. Robert S. J. Ross estimates that fully half of all direct producers employ their workers in sweatshop conditions.[27] Yet even if the number of sweatshops is overestimated— if there were only 20 percent more illegal jobs in U.S. apparel production than officially counted—and the workers in these jobs earned less than minimum wages, the real average wages of apparel workers in the United States would still be substantially less than the officially calculated average wage.

IMMIGRANTS AND SWEATSHOPS

Some have argued that sweatshops reappeared in the 1980s in response to the large-scale immigration that created an "abundance of low wage labor" domestically. Yet this is not sufficient to produce sweatshops, abroad or at home.[28] Although there was much poverty and low-wage labor in the Caribbean countries and Central America fifty years ago, there were few sweatshops. Nor did sweatshops begin to reemerge in significant numbers in the United States—in or outside New York—simply in response to the availability of poor immigrant women.

Despite a large influx of Puerto Rican women into the New York City apparel industry in the 1960s, and despite considerable evidence of discrimination against them, there is little evidence of sweatshop conditions in the city's garment industry during that period. It was only in the early 1980s, with the influx of low-wage, female labor—at a point when immigrant labor was accompanied by higher volumes of low-wage imports than ever before—that sweatshops begin to reappear.[29]

THE CONSEQUENCES OF JOB DISPLACEMENT

The debate about free trade and job displacement has been with us since the nineteenth century. According to Ethan Kapstein, "In seeking to reconcile the conflict between the increased wealth that free trade would bring the country as a whole, and the reduced welfare it would cause rural laborers and landowners, John Stuart Mill posited the 'compensation principle.' "[30] Presumably, "if compensation is paid to those whose incomes fall under free trade, no one would be worse off and everyone could potentially be better off. In this case, free trade would prove best not just for national wealth, but for national welfare as well."[31]

A vast body of research has been collected over the past two decades, nearly all of which demonstrates that workers displaced from manufacturing jobs are downwardly mobile. Many are never reemployed. If and when they do find new jobs, on average their earnings are less than before displacement. Earnings losses over a lifetime are dramatic.

On a human and psychological level, it is now well-recognized that the loss of one's job is a traumatic life event. The resulting stress can lead to psychological and physical illness, drug and alcohol abuse, family violence, and even decreased longevity.[32] These effects may lead to a greater demand for medical care and social services. Yet workers may lose their health insurance when they lose their jobs.

The Trade Adjustment Assistance program for displaced workers was the main federal program used to compensate displaced workers between the Kennedy and Reagan administrations. In 1982 this program was transformed by Reagan into the Job Training Partnership Act (JTPA). Neither effort provided full compensation to permanently displaced workers or compensated all the workers displaced from their jobs as a result of increased imports.[33] Although trade liberalization was dramatically expanded in the late 1980s and 1990s, federal funding through the JTPA for compensation and services to displaced workers was significantly reduced, leaving most of the affected workers and their families to fend for themselves.[34]

Although there is an abundance of research on male workers displaced from their jobs, only a small proportion of studies look at gender differences among displaced workers. Two important studies, however, do compare male and female job losers. One of these is a study of Canadian men and women displaced from manufacturing jobs, a sample controlled for a variety of company policies associated with layoffs—for example, notification, and severance pay and other types of assistance.[35] The study also controlled for union status, education, family status, predisplacement wages, and length of job tenure. It shows that women consistently are paid a smaller proportion of their previous earnings than men when reemployed. The longer the men have worked before they are displaced, the larger are their earnings losses when they are reemployed. The same pattern holds for women, but since they are more likely to find new jobs in gendered work, the women's earnings losses are more than twice as great as those experienced by their male counterparts.

Apparel workers—for example, the women currently being displaced from apparel jobs in the American South—are not typically unionized; they earn significantly less than other manufacturing workers. After two layoffs, in February and June of 1998, in which 2,000 workers lost their jobs, Fruit of the Loom, which subsequently went bankrupt, closed its largest manufacturing plant in the Southeast. A study of reemployment outcomes among these workers showed that "almost 90 percent were female, nearly three-quarters were white and the average age was 40. Sixty-five percent were married or living with someone, the average family size was three, and over half had children presently in the home. Employees had worked at this plant an average of ten years at the time of closing. . . . A majority—about 65 percent—had a high school education or a General Equivalency Diploma."[36] Presumably these women should have been able to get low-wage jobs in the growing sales and service sector. Since apparel workers earn so much less than most manufacturing workers, when reemployed in a sales or service job the women should have been earning as much as they were paid at Fruit of the Loom. On average, the workers made $9.95 per hour before they lost their jobs. The average wage of those reemployed was $7.25 an hour, a loss of 27 percent.

Of these displaced workers, over 40 percent reported they had difficulty paying their bills, and more than half said they had received financial help from their families. Many lost their medical coverage. Even though Fruit of the Loom offered an unusually substantial compensation program to its laid-off workers, over 80 percent were found to be more anxious than normal and nearly half were measured as clinically depressed.

THE RACE TO THE BOTTOM

Job losses, wage reductions, and sweatshops are a result of what Brad Christerson and Richard P. Appelbaum describe as a "race to the bottom."[37] Appelbaum writes, "As the market puts pressure on retailers' profits, the retailers respond by reducing the price they pay to manufacturers (or holding the cost at price point, which in an inflationary environment amounts to the same thing). The manufacturers in turn hold the line on their contractors, reducing the margin they are willing to pay. That leaves the contractor with a simple strategy: reduce costs."[38] As more developing countries are drawn into export-led development, they compete among themselves for foreign investment, outbidding each other to offer concessions to investors designed to reduce the cost of production.[39] As more apparel producers move their assembly operations to low-wage regions, the competitive pressures for domestic manufacturers to move offshore also intensifies, even when they are producing profitably in the United States or for other reasons prefer to produce domestically. In the early 1990s, the apparel maker Guess? produced 97 percent of its clothing in the United States. Then the company was fined by the Department of Labor for violating U.S. labor laws dealing with minimum wages, overtime, and efforts by workers to form a union. After paying the fines, Maurice Marciano, the chief executive officer of Guess?, moved his operations to Mexico, leaving only 35 percent of the company's production in Los Angeles.[40] According to John Sweeney, president of the AFL-CIO, "Mr. Marciano's message is clear: if the U.S. government takes steps to enforce U.S. labor laws that protect working people from exploitation, he and his company will flee, leaving thousands of workers jobless."[41]

As the ability to produce in Mexico became more feasible, competitors like the Gap, Tommy Hilfiger, and others began to produce jeans to target the youth market. J. C. Penney and Sears began to target the lower niche markets, while Donna Karan, Ralph Lauren, and Versace started selling upmarket jeans. By 1997 both price and fashion competition had left Levi Strauss with only 25 percent of the jeans market.[42] As discussed in chapter 9, at that point the firm ended its domestic production and, like its competitors, moved to Mexico.[43] The company closed eleven factories in four states, laying off 3,400 workers.[44] In March of 1999 Levi Strauss announced more layoffs, this time 5,900 more, another 30 percent of its North American workforce. Maintaining its historical commitment to good labor-management relations, Levi Strauss offered a generous severance package to its displaced workers.[45]

THE BENEFIT TO CONSUMERS

Despite the growing job losses, wage losses, and number of sweatshops, supporters of the neoliberal paradigm continue to argue that trade liberalization has reduced the cost of clothing for consumers. Tariffs and quotas that protected apparel jobs were too costly for the economy, they say, and imposed a "tax" on Americans by subsidizing apparel jobs and making clothing cost more. As mentioned, Hufbauer, Berliner, and Elliott argued that the protectionist Multifibre Arrangement had *saved* 460,000 jobs in the apparel industry—at a consumer cost of $39,000 per job.[46]

However, any analysis of the consequences of trade policy and trade invariably rests on the assumptions the analysts use. Steven Suranovic describes the underlying logic of the neoclassical economic rationale for trade liberalization, a view most economists and trade-policy makers would find hard to reject. He writes, "Although for any particular consumer the savings may seem negligible, when summed up over millions of consumers it can represent a sizable amount of additional purchasing power. This increase in purchasing power will raise demand and prices for other products in the economy." He continues, "Exactly which markets will be affected will depend on how those with extra money decide to spend it. In addition, foreign cotton-shirt exporters and others like them will now have larger dollar incomes that will either stimulate demand for our export goods or increase savings in the U.S. financial sector. If the latter occurs, more funds will become available for loans, which, once made, will stimulate demand and raise prices of investment goods (or other consumption goods) in the domestic economy."[47]

In the neoliberal view, then, the value of free trade is its potential to generate and increase national wealth. With lower clothing prices, consumers can spend their money on other goods and services. They can save or invest the money they do not spend on clothing, fueling consumer demand for other products. Such consequences are a potential source of new capital formation and further economic growth, which will make everyone "better off" (wealthier) in the future.

What matters is that economic transactions maximize the accumulation of capital. The job losses and wage declines in certain industries are important only insofar as they contribute to an increase or decrease in the quantity of capital available in the economy. Higher corporate profit, higher stock prices, greater industry concentration, growing exports, foreign investment, and low-wage imports represent greater economic efficiency because they generate more capital in the economy and therefore benefit Americans in general.

One must ask, then, to what extent Americans benefit from lower clothing prices. The evidence suggests that American families today are indeed paying less for clothing than they were twenty-five years ago. Moreover, American consumers can buy more items of clothing at a lower cost per item.[48] In 1995 the average American household spent only about 6 percent of its income on clothing, as compared to about 10 percent in 1970. By September 2001, that figure had dropped to about 4.5 percent.[49] Presumably, the savings has allowed America's families to both enhance the quality of their wardrobes and increase their consumption of other goods and services. Or perhaps instead, the average American family is using its savings on clothing to pay for health care, since the average costs of health care have increased during this period—from 10 percent of family income to 20 percent.[50]

Even if Americans are saving money on clothing, we still need to know how much ending the MFA and eliminating the "tax" on imports has contributed to reduction of clothing costs for Americans. Neoclassical economists like Jeffrey Schott, Gary Hufbauer, and, particularly, William R. Cline have developed highly sophisticated mathematical models to demonstrate in precise dollar values how much trade protection (that is, the tariffs and quotas imposed by the MFA) has cost the U.S. economy and, as a result, artificially subsidized the jobs of domestic apparel workers.[51] In 1987 and again in 1990, Cline argued that reducing tariff and quotas and eliminating other "nontariff barriers" would reduce inefficiencies. He argued for eliminating the Multifibre Arrangement. In 1995, less than a decade later, this was accomplished.

In the late 1980s and early 1990s, other studies done by professional economists found different levels of savings that would accrue to consumers if market barriers were dismantled and trade protection ended.[52] In five of these studies, estimates of savings to consumers ranged from $3.7 billion to $19.3 billion;[53] that is, these were the costs of failing to reduce tariffs further (see table 4). In 1991 U.S. negotiators came to the meetings of the Uruguay Round of the GATT negotiations in Geneva armed with studies showing the billions of dollars that America's consumers would save if the Multifibre Arrangement were eliminated and the "hidden tax" on apparel phased out. James Bovard cited Cline's figures in his popular book, claiming that continued tariffs and quotas were "bleeding the American public."[54]

We can now calculate the cost of the "tax" that Americans were paying for clothing before the MFA was eliminated. Table 4, based on U.S. Census data, shows that in 1990 the median income of the American family was $35,894.[55] A family spending 6 percent of its total income on clothing spent an average of $2,153.64. If we then calculate the savings to the hypothetical median family, at the varying amounts of savings calculated by the five researchers for the different years in which the studies were done, we find that this family would save anywhere from $37.34 to $206.76 per year on clothing, or between 0.1 percent and 0.6 percent of yearly income.

Table 4. Estimates of Median Household Savings as a Result
of Eliminating Tariffs and Quotas

Source	Median Household Income ($)	Number of Households (thousands)	National Tariff Costs ($US billions)	APPAREL SAVINGS PER HOUSEHOLD	
				($)	(as percentage of household income)
Dardis (1988)	35,982	93,830	13.1	139.72	0.4
Metzger (1989)	36,598	93,370	19.3	206.76	0.6
Cline (1990)	35,894	94,312	17.6	186.61	0.5
Trela and Whalley (1990)	35,894	94,312	12.3	130.42	0.4
Scott and Lee (1994); Lee (1991)	34,027	99,087	3.7	37.34	0.1

Median family income and number of U.S. households calculated from: U.S. Bureau of the Census, *Selected Measures of Household Income, 1969–1996: All Households*, Table A5 (as revised February 3, 1999).

If the "tax" imposed on families by trade protection is not bleeding middle-class American families, nevertheless, the demands for trade liberalization have been based on the argument that tariffs and quotas would hurt the less affluent and the poor. Yet new research suggests this is not the case. Jessie X. Fan, Jinkook Lee, and Sherman Hanna have recently found that, while trade protection is, as other researchers argue, a tax on consumers, protection tends to act as a progressive rather than a regressive tax—except when higher tariffs raise the consumer price of articles by 45 percent or more.[56] These authors write, "For price differences under 45 percent, consumer welfare loss from higher apparel prices due to trade restrictions is greater as a percent of total expenditures for wealthy households than for poor households." Low-income families may benefit from buying at retailers like Wal-Mart, but the bargain prices they get are not the result of savings on tariffs, most of which goes, as Scott and Lee argue, to retailers and importers.

Among the studies reported here, Scott and Lee estimate the lowest cost of protection—only $3.7 billion rather than the $17.6 billion that Cline calculates. They make different assumptions in their model, assumptions that help explain why corporate textiles and apparel retailers and suppliers are so concerned with trade liberalization.[57] In the late 1980s the highly concentrated textile, apparel, and retail complex had achieved substantial oligopsonistic power, particularly in women's fashion. As a result the retail industry had unique access to large volumes of low-wage imports that cost them only 58 percent of comparable domestically made merchandise. Today, even the American Apparel Manufacturers' Association can only agree that there has been "a triumph of oligopolies in retail": a smaller number of players in apparel retail and apparel production—each with a greater market share.[58]

This is consistent with the findings of Christerson and Appelbaum, who argue that large producers like Liz Claiborne and the Gap can promise contractors a steady supply of work.[59] As a result they have more bargaining power with offshore assembly producers, who guarantee them a high standard of quality and on-time delivery. Large producers also have the resources to develop personal relationships with government officials who can ease the difficulties associated with customs, transportation, and quotas.

The work of Scott and Lee is also consistent with that of Abernathy and colleagues, who argue that successful retailers use advanced technology and lean retailing. The ability of these corporations to reduce operating costs in their supply chains, market strategically, put greater demands on their suppliers, and increase the volume of low-wage apparel imports may have allowed them, as Scott and Lee argue, to double their share of the U.S. retail market between 1972 and 1987, while smaller firms, less able to source abroad and less competitive, were more likely to fail. Scott and Lee reach the following conclusion: "The biggest transfer of income that would result from trade liberalization . . . would go to domestic apparel retailers and importers, who stand to gain up to $8.7 billion if the MFA is eliminated." And indeed, the MFA has been ended. Consistent with Scott and Lee's predictions, and despite fluctuations in annual sales, Wall Street continues to be confident that the industry will remain healthy.

The steadily increasing stream of low-wage imports due to the reduction of trade barriers allows transnational retail and import corporations to capture market share from domestic producers and is responsible for deflation in the cost of domestically made wholesale apparel. From 1995 to

1998, producer costs for domestically made apparel fell for the first time.[60] By 1998, U.S. apparel productivity was stagnant, while productivity in textile production grew.[61]

Even if low-income families do not benefit from lower clothing prices as a result of reduced tariffs and quotas, when retailers source in places like China, Bangladesh, or Haiti, they help contribute to job displacement and lower wages in domestic apparel production.[62] But perhaps even more significant is the impact this restructuring has had on women in the domestic economy. Few Americans have yet to see the link between the growth of apparel sweatshops and domestic retailing, which has generated a new group of low-wage women workers in the United States. Indeed, one out of five employed women in the nation works in the retail industry. Seventy-nine percent of these women earn $7.91 an hour or less. Working full-time and year-round at these wages, a woman can earn $16,450 a year. Thirty-nine percent of all working women (female wage and salary workers), most of whom are of prime working age, earn $7.91 an hour or less.[63]

THE DILEMMAS OF GLOBALIZATION

Americans today have doubts about the value of free trade. A 1996 poll of American attitudes toward trade policy, reported in *Time* magazine, found that "58% of those surveyed thought free-trade agreements were 'mostly good' for U.S. corporations, but 51% thought the effects for workers were 'mostly bad.' "[64] A survey of public opinion polls found that, while Americans basically supported free trade and were pleased with its effects on the availability and prices of goods, they were worried about the consequences of new trade pacts for jobs, wages, and economic security.[65] Their top priority was protecting the jobs of American workers. The Marymount University Center for Ethical Concerns, in Virginia, conducted surveys of consumer attitudes in 1995, 1996, and 1999. They found that the percentage of respondents saying that retailers and manufacturers should be held responsible for sweatshop abuses increased from 10 percent in 1995 to 19 percent in 1999. In 1999 the group found that "86% of those surveyed would pay an extra dollar on a $20 garment, if it were guaranteed that the garment was made in a legitimate shop."[66] Moreover, a majority of Americans agreed that factories should enforce health and safety standards, allow workers the freedom to organize, and pay their workers a minimum wage.[67]

THE DEBATE ABOUT SWEATSHOPS:
GOOD JOBS OR BAD JOBS

In the early 1980s, feminist researchers began to discover the existence of a large and growing number of women employed in low-wage manufacturing jobs—primarily in electronics and apparel assembly—in the developing world.[68] Today, the dramatic growth in the number of these women, along with continuing reports of low pay and labor abuse, has led to an ongoing debate about the consequences of this enterprise. Are the recent forms of development creating the win-win situation that neoclassical economists and free trade supporters claim? Do the jobs women now hold provide them with better opportunities to earn needed income, at better wages than would otherwise be available to them? Will this export-led growth produce the industrialization and affluence economists predict? Or is the globalization of the apparel industry merely a new way to enrich retailers and clothing manufacturers at the expense of women?

This controversy has been joined by a group of professional economists, many from elite universities and some who regularly participate in policy discussions at the highest levels. On July 29, 2000, six of these individuals—led by Jagdish Bhagwati, a professor of economics at Columbia University, and calling themselves the Academic Consortium on International Trade (ACIT)—signed a letter favoring trade liberalization, which they sent to ninety university presidents. By March 1, 2001, they had been joined by over three hundred other economists, academics, lawyers, and policy makers. Many of the signers were advisers to governments and policy makers. The letter they signed expressed concern that universities were inappropriately supporting student antisweatshop activists represented by the Workers' Rights Consortium and the Fair Labor Association, and it challenged the usefulness of student efforts to press for codes of conduct and a living wage for apparel workers.[69] Bhagwati himself has written elsewhere: "Unions such as UNITE, which represents workers in the apparel industry, are misleading a few gullible undergraduates who then chant on campuses against the 'exploitation' of workers in developing countries. Are they demanding that the wage premium enjoyed by a lucky few who work for multinationals be increased still further?"[70]

This letter is an important document in this debate because it illuminates the way the neoliberal paradigm has helped shape policy perspectives. The letter highlights the argument of neoliberal economists, an argument that ignores, as it legitimates, the abuse that many women workers employed in apparel assembly suffer as a result of the objectives of export-led development.

The letter itself begins by discrediting student antisweatshop activists, implying they lack understanding of the economic processes that contribute to economic growth. Or as the letter puts it, what is required for effective policy making is "careful research, discussion, and debate in a manner appropriate to informed decision making."[71] The letter goes on to argue that apparel workers are paid fairly, that transnationals "commonly pay their workers more on average in comparison to the prevailing market wage for similar workers employed elsewhere in the economy. In cases where subcontracting is involved, workers are generally paid no less than the prevailing market wage." Expressing concern for the welfare of people in developing countries, the authors say that what students are advocating will only make things worse for apparel workers because "shifts in employment . . . will worsen the collective welfare of the very poor workers in poor countries who are supposed to be helped." The authors conclude their letter by pointing to the views of economists and policy makers from developing countries, which are, in fact, not always consistent with the approach of antisweatshop activists. The ACIT letter states, "Little attention has been paid to whether the views of the Anti-Sweatshop campaign are representative of the views of the governments, non-government organizations (NGOs), and workers in the poor countries that are directly involved in the manufacture and in the export of apparel and related goods."

In October 2001 a dissenting group of economists, Scholars Against Sweatshop Labor (SASL), based at the Political Economy Research Institute at the University of Massachusetts, responded to this letter. Endorsed by 434 social scientists, the majority of whom are economists, the SASL response challenges some of the views of the ACIT letter and of Bhagwati himself. It refutes the claim that student antisweatshop activists are ignorant of the real needs of economic growth and its benefits. The SASL letter points to the fact that there is now a large volume of journalistic reports of abuses in apparel factories, and a large corpus of scholarly articles that deal with the impact of trade liberalization in textiles and apparel on workers—both in the United States and in developing countries. The students are well-informed and aware of both the neoliberal approaches to this issue and the research from alternative perspectives.

Moreover, there is no reason for the ACIT members to believe that the students, the faculty who advise them, or the university presidents who support them have not made a careful and reasoned examination of all the issues involved before deciding to support the antisweatshop movement. Faculty advisors have become highly knowledgeable about the issues. Through teach-ins, new courses, and informal meetings, students continue to learn more about the current debate on international trade and globalization that has been taking place in the United States. As the Scholars Against Sweatshop Labor also point out, "The anti-sweatshop movement has prompted a new body of research and discussion that is deepening our understanding of the specific issues at hand. Universities have commissioned much of this new research. . . . No doubt more such work would be beneficial. For now, the anti-sweatshop movement deserves credit for pushing researchers to focus on these issues."

The SASL letter argues that student antisweatshop groups do not act alone. Some coordinate their activities with groups like Global Exchange, the National Labor Committee for Worker and Human Rights, the Campaign for Labor Rights, UNITE, and other comparable groups, many of which disseminate a large amount of information about conflicts and labor struggles at apparel production sites throughout the world. Students seek out information and sometimes work directly with local grassroots organizations in developing countries—nongovernment organizations and indigenous women's and labor activist groups—engaged with workers and their communities.

The ACIT and SASL letters both address the issue of apparel wages. The ACIT letter writers believe that production workers are reasonably paid, even well-paid, given the poverty in many developing countries. The SASL letter points out, "This is true, almost by definition. But the prevailing market wage is frequently extremely low for garment workers in less developed countries": the abuses are real. The SASL letter goes on to cite the most recent International Labour Organization (ILO) report, published in 2000, which notes that this organization found not only that wages are low but also that "serious workplace abuses and violations of workers' rights are occurring in the garment industry throughout the world." SASL argues that a consideration of only the "prevailing market wage in various countries tells us very little about the working and living conditions of the workers who receive these wages." In the same report the ILO has documented abuses against workers in apparel factories, and it has called for a new human resource agenda for export-processing zones, and standards for "decent work" initiatives.[72]

The SASL letter goes on to say, "There is no reason to assume that a country or region that sets reasonable standards must experience job losses. Additional policy measures will also be crucial for enhancing any region's overall employment opportunities and competitiveness." The measures that the members of SASL suggest are debt relief and job expansion programs. They continue by pointing out that consumers in the wealthier countries—the destination of most apparel exports—are willing to pay "somewhat higher retail prices to ensure that garments are produced under non-sweatshop conditions."

Yet the SASL letter does not recognize that the U.S. textile, apparel, and retail complex has become embedded in corporate financial obligations that may now require a race to the bottom. While resources from high corporate profits could be used to finance better wages for workers in apparel production through higher consumer prices, financial and competitive imperatives constrain the global industry from doing this. Without a change in the "Darwinian" market structures on which this industrial complex is now based, it is difficult to see how transnationals might change their low-wage strategy.

The appeal in the ACIT letter for more research is welcome. Certainly, more research needs to be done on these issues. But it is not clear that more research is needed merely to point out the insufficiencies of the current forms of global trade and economic development. What would be particularly valuable today is more interdisciplinary and collaborative research between economists and other social scientists. Such research might benefit from the modification of current economic models in ways that allow for an understanding of how culture, history, and social life affect economic patterns. Only by seeing how social and cultural forces influence trade and economic growth can we truly understand the effects of trade and investment on the different groups involved. Researchers could then explore how to better reconcile the need of corporations to accumulate capital with the economic welfare of the men and women these corporations employ.

Ultimately, universities may prove to be the best, rather than the worst, place for antisweatshop activism. It is important to note that, although some professors support the students' activism, there are in the economics departments of every college and university campus many economists who accept the neoliberal approach. What better place to have a real debate and discussion?

GENDER AND THE GLOBALIZATION OF THE APPAREL TRADE

Most discussions of apparel workers have assumed that they are without gender or that all workers are men. Indeed, in writing about these issues some of the most experienced and insightful economic analysts have tended to ignore the role that gender plays in the labor market and the liberalized trade regime.[73] The implicit assumption is that wages and working conditions for apparel workers are determined by market forces. But we must recognize that the situation of apparel workers can be fully comprehended only within a gendered context. Although there are, of course, some circumstances in which men take these jobs, women make up the vast majority of apparel workers—and this has been the case since clothing production was first industrialized. Indeed, as better technology has de-skilled the production process in this industry, more and more women have been employed in apparel production. These jobs are not gender neutral but have been designed specifically to employ women, often women who are young and unmarried. To understand the problems faced by today's women workers in the global apparel industry, we must consider the gendered labor market and women's wages in the context of women's family circumstances and the changing structure of family economies.

THE LOWELL MODEL

Implicit in the arguments of neoliberal economists is the notion that industrialization will proceed in today's developing countries as it proceeded in the West. This model often serves as a grid through which these economists perceive parallels between the experiences of women in today's export-led apparel industry and those of the women textile workers in Lowell, Massachusetts, at the debut of the nineteenth century. Clearly there are some similarities between the two, but there are also significant differences. Women employed in industrial production in the export-processing zones of developing countries may be gaining freedom from traditional forms of patriarchal authority, but, at the same time, the "new international division of labor" has made women increasingly vulnerable to changes in family structure and to new forms of paid and domestic work.

In the 1830s, American-born "farm girls" were recruited to work in the new textile mills of Lowell and Lawrence, Massachusetts. These young women lived in the dormitories provided privately for them and worked in conditions that would, in twenty-first-century America, be considered exploitative and socially unacceptable. According to Thomas Dublin, "Women worked some 73 hours each week, averaging 13 hours a day Monday through Friday and 8 hours on Saturday. The typical workday began at dawn—or even earlier in the summer—and lasted until 7:00 or 7:30 p.m. with only 30 minute breaks for breakfast and midday dinner."[74]

Although the work was hard, the textile mills of Lowell and Lawrence did offer wages substantially higher than alternative types of employment for young farm women before they married. These women sent money home, sometimes helping to pay the family mortgage, and saved for dowries their parents could not afford. As competition increased in the industry, work was intensified; the wages and working conditions deteriorated. Lowell mill girls organized protests against their employers. By the late 1850s, American-born farm girls were replaced in the textile mills by immigrants willing to work at lower wages and in worse conditions.[75]

A debate among historians about the quality of conditions in the earliest American textile mills mirrors today's debate about women's wages and working conditions in export-processing industries. Just as the historical literature demonstrates positive and negative elements of the Lowell experience, so does the literature about women employed in export-processing zones. As in the past, women today appear to be pushed into the labor force by the needs of their families and pulled by the lure of good wages. Research findings on women workers in Hong Kong, Taiwan, South Korea, and Singapore between the 1960s and the 1980s are divided about whether women are coerced into work by impoverished families,[76] or whether they have chosen to work in factories for the personal advantages offered by wages that are higher than those in the informal economy.

In the early 1980s export-processing zones in the People's Republic of China paid wages that were two-and-a-half-times higher than those outside the zones. Linda Lim writes, "Though it may be inferior to developed country standards, work in modern export factories also generates more income, with shorter working hours and better working conditions than traditional housework, home-based work and unpaid family labor."[77]

In Singapore, "where women export factory workers are the lowest paid workers in the economy, usually earning less than the men in their families, their total family income puts them in an income bracket where, in 1983, 96.2 percent of the households had a refrigerator, 95.9 percent had a television set, 23.1 percent a video cassette recorder, 12.8 percent a motor car, 17.5 percent a motor cycle, 44.7 percent a washing machine, 3.6 percent an air conditioner, and 3.8 percent a piano/organ." In Malaysia, women workers in the export-processing sector "earn enough to save for themselves and/or contribute a large proportion of their incomes to family expenses, even when they are rural-urban migrants who live on their own and not with their families."[78]

In the past two decades, however, growth and competition within the industry appears to have dramatically depressed wages and working and living conditions for women employed in apparel production in export-processing zones. In El Salvador, women make clothing in factories contracting with Wal-Mart, Kmart, and Leslie Fay. They work in zones surrounded by barbed wire. Searched by armed guards as they enter and leave the factories, they work eleven-hour shifts, six days a week; they sometimes work twenty-hour shifts. Women refusing to work overtime are suspended, fined, and, for repeated "offenses" like this, fired. Women must take and pay for pregnancy tests and are fired when they test positive. In the factories, women suffer verbal abuse, sexual harassment, and in some cases, assaults by supervisors. There is no ventilation and no potable water in these factories. Workers may visit the bathroom only once per shift, and the bathrooms are generally dirty.

These women earn, for example, 15 cents for each pair of Kathie Lee pants they sew, a sum that equals 9/10 (.9) percent of the retail price of the garment, which sells for $16.96 at Wal-Mart. Though money is deducted from their pay for health insurance, workers are routinely denied access to the health care clinic. After paying bus fare to and from work, and $57.07 per month in rent for two small rooms, the workers are left with just $1.08 per day. As a result, women cannot afford milk for their children, who are raised on coffee and lemonade.[79]

When workers try to organize, they are summarily fired and blacklisted; some have experienced death threats. Similar conditions prevail in other contracting facilities that make Kathie Lee products in Guatemala and Mexico. In Tijuana's *maquiladoras*, it is "standard procedure to assign difficult and dangerous tasks to pregnant women so they will quit before the companies are obligated to pay officially required maternity benefits." One woman organizer in Honduran *maquiladoras* described the situation of women workers in the following way: "After three or four years of mindless work, . . . the women return to the countryside, tired, worn out and many times sick, possessing the same few options they had when they left."[80]

Reports from other export-processing zones describe similar conditions. Apparel factories in Mexico; in Haiti; in Central American countries like El Salvador, Nicaragua, Guatemala, and Honduras; and in Asian countries like Myanmar, Vietnam, American Samoa, and China employ women in conditions that are coming to resemble indentured servitude.[81] In China, one of the largest exporters of textiles and apparel to the United States, factory conditions are even worse. In Guangdong Province, where new export-processing zones have been established, young women between the ages of sixteen and twenty-five come thousands of miles from their rural families to work in factories and live in state-provided dormitory facilities. The dormitories are large concrete buildings in which rooms measuring about ten by twenty feet house nine to twelve workers. The National Labor Committee reports,

> The bunk beds had hard wooden surfaces covered with paper-thin straw mats. Some workers had been able to secure thin mattresses, while others slept on folded up blankets. The few possessions the workers owned were hung up inside their tiny bunk space. . . . The workers hung blankets or sheets or strips of torn plastic over the outside part of their bunks in order to provide a little privacy. . . . The walls were cinder block, the floors concrete, and one fluorescent light was affixed to the ceiling.[82]

Workers making clothing, shoes, and handbags for Wal-Mart work twelve to thirteen hours a day, six to seven days a week. An examination of the official pay stubs of workers showed they earned from three to ten cents an hour. Nearly half the workers surveyed (46 percent) actually owed the company money after deductions were taken from their paychecks for dormitory fees, food, job placement fees, temporary residency permits, and various fines. When the company began to require workers to purchase food coupons to eat in the company canteen, their jobs offered them only the potential to starve. After protesting, they were all fired. Under these conditions, it is not surprising that, in 1993, 2,500 workers were burned in dormitory fires in China. Workers dismissed from their jobs are typically shipped back to the countryside with nothing to contribute to a potentially impoverished family economy. And because their families live thousands of miles from the factories, they are unable to generate any community pressure on factory managers to provide more humane working conditions and higher wages.[83] Such treatment of workers in China raises serious questions about the potential of free markets to bring civil liberties to China.

In 2001, the National Labor Committee published a new report about apparel workers in Bangladesh titled "Bangladesh: Ending the Race to the Bottom."[84] According to the report, 1.6 million apparel workers are employed sewing 924 million garments a year for export to the United States. Of these workers, 85 percent are young women between the ages of sixteen and twenty-five. They work twelve to fourteen hours a day, seven days a week, with just one or two days off a month. Sometimes there are mandatory twenty-hour shifts; women sleep in the factory for about four hours and go right back to work the next day. Sewers are paid 13 to 18 cents an hour, below the legal Bangladeshi minimum wage and less than half their survival needs. Another reports states, "Outside their workplace, life is yet another hell. The majority of these girls being migrants are separated from their loved ones and live in boardings [sic] like cattle, where sometimes as many as ten share a single 10.5-foot square room, and where sometimes 30 in the boarding are compelled to use a single toilet. Restricted use of water for washing, bathing and sometimes drinking further aggravates their existence outside the factory."[85] Many of the women living in poor countries and employed in apparel production today work even more hours than the women textile workers Dublin described in his study of Lowell, Massachusetts. The former earn less and live in conditions that are considerably more squalid than those encountered by America's farm girls doing similar work almost two hundred years ago.

Some claim that situations like these are atypical, that they cannot be generalized to more successful and more typical zones with better work environments. If atypical horror stories are giving a bad name to production in export-processing zones, greater transparency in disseminating information about conditions in these zones would alter misconceptions. Unfortunately, reports by the International Labour Organization and other monitoring groups confirm that the experiences mentioned above are not merely isolated incidents.[86] Employment conditions would have to change dramatically to comply with corporate codes of conduct that are now in place, or with the nationally legislated labor standards that are formally on the books in these countries.

Such treatment of women workers raises serious questions about the potential for free trade and free markets to bring economic welfare and individual freedom to workers not only in China but also in poor countries throughout the world. If in the past women's subordination was based on relegation to the private sphere, market work as it is now being experienced in apparel production can hardly be described as more liberating.

WOMEN AND THE NEW INTERNATIONAL DIVISION OF LABOR

To understand the new sweatshops, we must see how the "new international division of labor" in the developing world, as discussed by Folker Frobel and his associates, differs from the division of labor that evolved in Europe and America in the nineteenth and early twentieth centuries.[87] In the West, industrial production was largely dominated by a male labor force employed in capital-intensive industries like coal mining, steel production, and auto manufacturing. As Alice Kessler-Harris points out in her book *In Pursuit of Equality,* in the United States, citizenship was allocated to white men on the basis of their "right to work."[88] Embodied in the notion of citizenship was the attribute of "manliness," which derived from the right to sell one's labor for a wage, a right that would allow a man to support his dependent family. Even if men could not always earn enough to support their families, and if wives and daughters contributed resources, the man was the paterfamilias, the head of the family.[89] In the nineteenth century, male industrial workers in Europe and America fought for a family wage for men, and for protective labor legislation for women in order to keep women out of the higher wage, capital-intensive industrial jobs and relegated (at least normatively) to the private sphere.

In this system, unmarried daughters often were the labor force of choice in the low-wage manufacturing sectors like the textile and apparel industries, since the labor of wives and mothers was needed for domestic work and childcare. Indeed, the value of the unpaid domestic work of wives and mothers was too valuable to the family to be sacrificed for the wages that factory work typically offered women. Yet when families were in need, even married women found ways to combine their domestic responsibilities with factory jobs, especially if the wages were high enough. Women's employment in these marginal jobs, and their responsibility for domestic work, supported and was consistent with expectations that women had a right to be sustained by their fathers and husbands. This gendered division of labor was also consistent with the rights of men to exclusive access to the higher paid industrial jobs.

Today's export-processing economy does not duplicate this model; it does not merely transplant older forms of industrialization to the developing world. Transnational corporations relocate the labor-intensive, lower wage work of assembling lower-value-added goods (no longer only textiles and apparel but now toys, jewelry, and electronics as well) to poor countries, allocating the jobs in these industries to women. Unlike in Western nations, where capital-intensive manufacture was central to economic growth, in many developing countries these low-wage industries have become central to the economic growth that is expected to occur. And unlike in the West, where the higher-paid men's industrial jobs were central to the economic welfare of families, in export-processing economies the low-paid women workers make up about 80 percent—the vast majority—of the workforce.

The value of factory jobs to women—two centuries ago in Lowell, Massachusetts, and since then in the growing industrial economies of the West and many parts of the developing world—has resided in the fact that they allow young women, usually as daughters but often as mothers, to supplement a larger family economy, one supported primarily by a male breadwinner. The cash contributions of daughters and mothers to low-income families have allowed them to survive or to raise their standard of living. Such contributions often give women greater bargaining power within the family. Sometimes daughters save their earnings and use them to set up their own households when they marry. But women's factory work typically has never paid enough—in earlier times and certainly not today—to permit women to support themselves. Nor has it ever been enough to permit a woman to independently support her children.

One study compared households in two industrial communities in Mexico—one a community dominated by export processing and the other a traditional, state-led form of indigenous industrial development based on traditionally male forms of industrial employment. The study's author found two "starkly contrasting" types of household formations, the first dominated by female-headed households and the other by male-breadwinner households. The overall standard of living was significantly lower for households in the export-processing zone than for those in the traditional community.[90]

Two other studies support these generalizations. One in El Salvador found that 80 percent of the workers were women between the ages of eighteen and forty; half were single mothers earning only 28 percent of the officially calculated living wage—that is, the wage sufficient to cover the minimum basic needs of the average family of 4.3 people. Thus, in order for women in this gendered labor force to produce and reproduce their families as the next generation's labor force, each family requires three to four women working at the current wage to support it, or it would require one woman earning a wage three to four times higher than the current wage.[91]

In the second study, Naila Kabeer has shown that Bangladeshi wives who live with their families and work in apparel factories—but factories outside the export-processing areas—find work in apparel factories highly desirable. As married women they are supported by their husbands, but their ability to work outside the home allows them to challenge some of the rigid rules of female seclusion, or purdah, which many women in that country are required to follow.[92]

It is hardly surprising that the sex industry is expanding in many of the poorest developing countries. In nineteenth-century America, urban areas saw the growth of prostitution.[93] Indeed, whenever women must live alone on a "woman's wage," prostitution is likely to occur. When women are far from their families, earning barely enough to support themselves, few can survive for long on such a wage, let alone contribute money to their families.

The studies mentioned here are suggestive. It is essential to do more systematic research to explore the effects of the development of export-processing zones on the lives of the young women who work in the factories. It is clear that the new international division of labor in the intensely competitive apparel industry is creating major changes in the family lives and family structures of these women, and in ways that do not bode well for the future of family life. How can women nurture their children in the context of a lengthy workday and abusive working conditions? How can they feed, clothe, educate, and otherwise provide for the future of their children, who make up the next generation? How will women and men make do as they become too old and too infirm to endure the pressures of such employment?

THE RECESSION AND EVENTS OF SEPTEMBER 11

Much of the optimism that characterized the 1990s was based on the economic growth that occurred in the last half of the decade. In the wake of the economic downturn of 2001 and the events of September 11, the potential for the footloose apparel industry to promote economic development in poor countries, and to sustain the welfare of its women workers, looks increasingly dubious. In June of 2001, Pakistan had requested from the United States additional trade benefits—higher quotas and lower tariffs for its clothing exports.[94] After the events of September 11, both the European Union and the United States agreed to provide Pakistan with tariff and quota concessions to "mitigate losses suffered by exports from this country" as a result of the hostilities.[95] Yet by October the retail press was reporting that major U.S. apparel companies had withdrawn their contracts with Pakistan's apparel producers. According to one report, "Major importers of apparel from Pakistan, which now finds itself a military hotspot, have withdrawn their contracts from Pakistan." These included Russell Athletic, Eagle Outfitters, Tommy Hilfiger, Sara Lee, the Gap, Levi-Strauss, and Eddie Bauer. They ended their contracts "largely on expectations that deliveries may be impossible because of US military action in neighboring Afghanistan. And signs are that these companies have already drawn up contingency plans to shift apparel production to another location if the need arises."[96]

Fear of terrorism has resulted in slowed consumption, which in turn has led to large layoffs of apparel workers in export-processing industries throughout the world. Since September 2001, apparel assembly jobs have been lost in Bangladesh.[97] On December 26, 2001, the day after Christmas, articles appeared in both the *Washington Post* and the *Wall Street Journal* about new layoffs in the apparel industry. In Pakistan 68,500 workers lost their jobs. In Mexico there has been a loss of 200,000 *maquiladora* jobs since October 2001.[98] Ginger Thompson in the *New York Times* cites information from an analyst at the economic consulting firm DRI-WEFA, who said that, even after the recession picks up, it will be cheaper to produce in other countries like the Dominican Republic, Indonesia, and China.

Currency devaluations in the Asian countries, concurrent with the phase-out of MFA quotas, have led to a rapid influx of textile products into U.S. markets from this region.[99] Some of the largest U.S. textile corporations—West Point–Stevens, Galey and Lord, Burlington Industries, Cone Mills, and Russell Corporation—have all reported heavy losses this year.[100] *Home Textiles Today* reported that Guilford Mills lost nearly $17 million in the second quarter of 2001, and that it had failed to meet the terms of its loan agreements.[101]

According to the American Textile Manufacturers' Institute, in 1997 the fiscal crisis drove down Asian currencies by 40 percent. As a result, Asian imports increased by 80 percent. Since 1997, ATMI calculates, a total of 398 U.S. textile mills have closed their doors, laying off more than 60,000 workers, or about 10 percent of the industry's workforce. This has hit small southern communities—where 90 percent of these mills are located—extremely hard.[102]

A LIVING WAGE

Before we can assess whether the wages that transnationals pay their apparel workers are reasonable and acceptable, we must find out how well these wages enable the women who earn them to fulfill their economic needs and the needs of their families. We must consider how men in these families earn a living, and how these men, as fathers and husbands, contribute to the family economy.

Wages are always calculated and formulated by employers in terms of what the market will bear. But employers also determine how much a worker will be paid in terms of the social cost of living. Wages represent the power of workers and the social norms that confer on them either high or low esteem. The question we must ask, then, is, at what level can the export-processing economy allow a woman and her family to live? Given the needs of families and the options of family members to earn income, what wage rate would allow for a reasonable standard of living? Such a calculation cannot be defined in terms that are gender neutral. Embedded in the determination of wages and the creation of jobs are gendered assumptions, which include definitions of adequate wages for men and women. Men as breadwinners have been paid a man's wage and sometimes a family wage—enough to provide for dependent wives and children. Women's wages in the past have been based on the assumption that they are supplemental to a family economy where men are the main breadwinners and earnings are pooled.

Feminists have pointed to a link between women's paid work and their economic independence. But export-processing economies in developing countries are not "liberating" women from dependence on patriarchal families. There is no essential link between paid work and women's autonomy. Instead, the link between the two depends on the value of the wages women earn. Equal opportunity is the opportunity to earn enough to support oneself and one's family. There is no link between paid work and economic independence when women are paid a poverty-level wage.

If the new liberalization in the textile and apparel trade is truly intended to promote the greatest good for the greatest number, there are two viable options for fulfilling this intention, both of which take into account the cost of raising children and the value of reproductive work that women do in families. The first option is for transnational corporations to plan their contract sourcing in ways that ensure the employment of male workers who earn a family wage. This would permit the pattern of sex-segregated employment and gendered wages for different jobs to continue. The combined income of men and women would continue to constitute a family wage in a traditional family economy. However, if women are to be the dominant workforce in apparel factories, the second, and more egalitarian, solution is to pay a wage designed not merely to attract the daughters of the poorest families but also to provide significantly more than the current woman's wage that now prevails in these jobs—to pay a wage that would allow women to support themselves and their families. America's families are now willing to bear some of the extra cost of this option.

THE FUTURE OF THE GLOBAL APPAREL INDUSTRY

It is now more than half a century since the end of World War II, when the major powers created a new global trade agenda for the free world.

Since then, the world has seen the demise of communism and the growth of a hegemonic America that is pressing to expand the markets for its transnational corporations, in part through a program of trade liberalization. The growing integration of the world economy may be seen as having fulfilled the original promise of the GATT accords: to end the aggressive and militaristic politics that led to conflicts among the United States, Japan, and Europe—conflicts that were responsible for World War II. The flow of capital and goods across national borders has brought peace—at least among the industrialized countries. But it has not ended armed conflict in the world, and it has yet to create abundance for most of the world's people, the vast majority of whom live in developing nations. Nor is it clear that the availability of lower cost clothing has significantly improved the quality of life for apparel workers at home or abroad or for American families in general.

Rethinking and reordering the market structures of this industry does not mean that we must build fences along our economic borders or preclude the expansion of international trade or investment. But we must begin to work more cooperatively with developing countries to formulate rules that structure markets to produce more equitable forms of exchange in any new industrial growth—both domestically and globally.

John F. Kennedy can hardly be called a protectionist. Yet in negotiating the Short-Term and the Long-Term Agreements in 1961 and 1962, he did recognize that the growing imports of low-wage textile and apparel products on a massive scale would undermine domestic production, and that these labor-intensive and trade-sensitive industries required a trade policy different from those necessary for other, more capital-intensive industries. In 1974 the Multifibre Arrangement provided a way to control the quantity of low-wage textile and apparel imports to the United States and other industrialized countries. While the MFA never protected U.S. apparel producers from imports, it did slow the rate at which imports increased as a proportion of American manufacturers' market share.

The Multifibre Arrangement's quota system may have outlived its usefulness in the face of the growing need of developing countries to participate in the world economy and to strengthen their positions in the global trading system. However, the Agreement on Textiles and Clothing—the new regulatory framework for trade and investment in textiles and apparel—has made America's apparel industry even more footloose. The pressure to open new markets in lower and lower wage regions of the world has led to a Darwinian struggle, which is producing a race to the bottom.

In an industry that so overwhelmingly employs women workers, this is a serious problem, one perhaps generated in part by a theoretical paradigm that recognizes cultural and social factors as distortions in economic models. Such a paradigm may also function—as did earlier views of women's unique nature (for example, their suitability to apparel production because of their patience and "nimble fingers")—as a way to legitimate women's segregation and low wages in this industry. The failure of industry leaders and policy makers to address the gendered work and the gendered wage in this enterprise contributes to these distortions. It is essential to make it clear that abuse is not economic opportunity.

Americans want a fair and equitable economic system, both globally and nationally, and the people of developing countries want increasing access to the goods and services now available primarily to those in the West. Few would question the value of producing more clothing, more cheaply, so that more of the world's people can be adequately and fashionably dressed. Business corporations have a right to profit from such an enterprise. If this goal can be accomplished in lower wage areas of the world, it is reasonable to move production outside our national borders to lower wage areas of the world and to compensate workers who lose their jobs as a result. But America's women apparel workers have not been adequately compensated for the loss of their jobs. Not surprisingly, then, Americans are wary of the ways in which trade affects job security and earnings for them and the workers who may replace them in developing countries. We need new ways of thinking about the rules of international trade and investment in order to create a global economy that offers economic equity to more of the poorest people of the world.

Making Sweatshops has been an effort to examine the causes of job loss, declining wages, and the reemergence of apparel sweatshops in the United States and developing countries. Defining and refining solutions to these problems must wait on the work of others—on intellectuals, policy makers, and activists. I hope this book will be part of a larger effort to ensure that a significant part of the new and emerging global labor force, women apparel workers, will be able to earn a living wage.

Notes

CHAPTER 1

1. "141 Men and Girls Die in Waist Factory Fire: Trapped High Up in Washington Place Building: Street Strewn with Bodies; Piles of Dead Inside," *New York Times*, March 26, 1911.

2. A. H. Raskin, "Dress Union Out in 7 State Strike," *New York Times*, March 6, 1958.

3. Barry Bluestone and Bennett Harrison, *The Deindustrialization of America* (New York: Basic Books, 1983).

4. Annette Fuentes and Barbara Ehrenreich, "Women on the Global Assembly Line," *Ms.* (June 1981); June Nash and Maria-Patricia Fernandez-Kelly, *Women, Men, and the New International Division of Labor* (Baltimore: Johns Hopkins University Press, 1983).

5. Kenneth B. Noble, "Workers in Sweatshop Raid Start Leaving Detention Site," *New York Times*, August 12, 1995, sec. 1, p. 6.

6. James Sterngold, "Raids Link Organized Crime to Sweatshops," *New York Times*, August 25, 1995.

7. Maria Echaveste and Karen Nussbaum, "Viewpoints: 96 Cents an Hour: The Sweatshop is Reborn," *New York Times*, August 6, 1994. Maria Echaveste is the former administrator of the Wage and Hour Division of the Labor Department. Karen Nussbaum was formerly the director of the department's Women's Bureau.

8. International Labour Organization, "Global Employment in Textile, Clothing, and Footwear Industries Holding Stable as Industries Relocate: Asia's Job Share Is Growing Fastest: Clandestine Sweatshops Pose Risks to Industry/Workforce" (International Labour Organization, Geneva, October 16, 2000, photocopy), press release.

9. U.S. House, Committee on Education and Labor, *The Reemergence of Sweatshops and the Enforcement of Wage and Hour Standards: Hearings before the Subcommittee on Labor Standards of the Committee on Education*

and Labor, 97th Cong., 1st sess., 1982, statement of Senator Franz S. Leichter; Elizabeth Petras, "The Shirt on Your Back: Immigrant Workers and the Reorganization of the Garment Industry," *Social Justice: A Journal of Crime, Conflict, and World Order* 19 (spring 1992): 76–114; Susan Headden, "Made in the USA: Sweatshop Labor in the U.S. Clothing Industry," *U.S. News and World Report* 115, no. 20 (November 22, 1993): 48; Patricia R. Pessar, "Sweatshop Workers and Domestic Ideologies: Dominican Women in New York's Apparel Industry," *International Journal of Urban and Regional Research* 18, no. 1 (March 1994): 127.

10. Alan Finder, "Hard Labor—a Special Report: Despite Tough Laws, Sweatshops Flourish," *New York Times,* February 6, 1995, sec. A, Metropolitan Desk, p. 1.

11. U.S. General Accounting Office, *Sweatshops in the US: Opinions on Their Extent and Possible Enforcement Options,* GAO/HRD-88–130BR (Washington, D.C.: GPO, 1988); U.S. General Accounting Office, *Sweatshops in New York City: A Local Example of a Nationwide Problem,* GAO/HRD-89–101BR (Washington D.C.: GPO, 1989); U.S. General Accounting Office, *Garment Industry: Efforts to Address the Prevalence and Conditions of Sweatshops,* GAO/HEHS-95–29 (Washington, D.C.: GPO, 1994); U.S. Department of Labor, Bureau of International Labor Affairs, *Public Hearings on International Child Labor,* June 28, 1996, opening remarks by Robert B. Reich and Joaquin F. Otero; International Labour Organization, "Globalization Changes the Face of Textile, Clothing, and Footwear Industries" (International Labour Organization, Geneva, October 28, 1996, photocopy), press release.

12. Mark Mittelhauser, "Employment Trends in Textiles and Apparel, 1973–2005," *Monthly Labor Review* 120, no. 8 (August 1997): 24.

13. David Kucera and William Milberg, "Gender Segregation and Gender Bias in Manufacturing Trade Expansion: Revisiting the 'Wood Asymmetry,'" (paper prepared for the International Working Group on Engendering Macro and International Economics, 1998). Kucera and Milberg include Australia, Canada, Denmark, France, Germany, Italy, Japan, the Netherlands, the United Kingdom, and the United States.

14. Lauren A. Murray, "Unravelling Employment Trends in Textiles and Apparel," *Monthly Labor Review* 118, no. 8 (August 1995): 62; also see Mittelhauser, "Employment Trends in Textiles and Apparel," 24. Mittelhauser estimates that "almost one million US textile and apparel jobs were lost from 1973 to 1996."

15. Ellen Israel Rosen, *Bitter Choices: Blue Collar Women In and Out of Work* (Chicago: University of Chicago Press, 1987).

16. U.S. General Accounting Office, *Sweatshops in the US;* U.S. General Accounting Office, *Garment Industry: Efforts to Address the Prevalence and Conditions of Sweatshops;* William Branigin, "Reaping Abuse for What They Sew: Sweatshops Once Again Commonplace in US Garment Industry," *Washington Post,* February 16, 1997; Hector Figueroa, "In the Name of Fashion:

Exploitation in the Garment Industry (Report on Transnational Investment),"
NACLA Report on the Americas 29, no. 4 (January-February 1996): 34; Laura
Jo Foo, "The Vulnerable and Exploitable Immigrant Workforce and the Need
for Strengthening Worker Protective Legislation," *Yale Law Journal* 103, no.
8 (June 1994): 2179–12. For a comprehensive listing of activist groups, see
Laura Ho, Catherine Powell, and Leti Volpp, "(Dis)Assembling Rights of
Women Workers Along the Global Assembly Line: Human Rights and the
Garment Industry," *Harvard Civil Rights–Civil Liberties Law Review* 31
(1996): 383–414.

17. While apparel is often referred to as the textiles industry, textiles and
apparel are two separate industries. Textile production involves spinning yarn
from natural or man-made fibers and weaving or knitting fabrics for clothing,
home furnishings, or industrial uses. Apparel production involves marking and
cutting patterns and sewing clothing from textiles. In some countries these
two industries are vertically integrated and organized under a single management; in the United States they have evolved separately and are vertically
integrated and organized under a single management. Yet, however they are
organized, each requires a different type of technology and a different type of
production process.

18. "The Basement Wasn't among Fittest Retailers" *Boston Globe*, Tues-
day, August 24, 1999. A number of clothing retailers have recently declared
bankruptcy or gone into Chapter 11 (bankruptcy protection). Among them
were Filene's Basement, Fedco, Loehmann's, Bradlees, Caldor, and Ames.

19. Stuart Chirls, "Analyst Sees More Change Ahead for Domestic Industry," *Women's Wear Daily* 174, no. 116 (December 16, 1997): 11.

20. Hong Kong, Taiwan, and South Korea have been known variously as
the Big Three, the Asian Dragons, and the Newly Industrializing Countries.

CHAPTER 2

1. Robert Kuttner, *The End of Laissez-Faire: National Purpose and the
Global Economy after the Cold War* (New York: Alfred A. Knopf, 1991). This
contention has been challenged by Alfred Eckes Jr., *Opening America's Market: US Foreign Trade Policy since 1776* (Chapel Hill: University of North
Carolina Press, 1995).

2. Tracy Murray, *Trade Policies for Developing Countries* (New York: Mac-
millan, 1977), 9.

3. Vinod K. Aggarwal, with Stephan Haggard, "The Politics of Protection
in the U.S. Textile and Apparel Industries," in *American Industry in International Competition: Government Policies and Corporate Strategies*, ed. John
Zysman and Laura Tyson (Ithaca: Cornell University Press, 1983), 249–312.
Also see the introduction to Kuttner, *The End of Laissez-Faire*.

4. Secretary of State James Byrne, quoted by Gabriel Kolko, *The Limits of
Power: The World and United States Foreign Policy, 1945–1954* (New York:

Harper and Row, 1972); David B. Yoffie, *Power and Protectionism: Strategies of the Newly Industrializing Countries* (New York: Columbia University Press, 1983), 17.

5. David P. Calleo and Benjamin M. Rowland, *America and the World Political Economy: Atlantic Dreams and National Realities* (Bloomington: Indiana University Press, 1973); Geoffrey R. D. Underhill, *Industrial Crisis and the Open Economy: Politics, Global Trade, and the Textile Industry in the Advanced Economies* (New York: St. Martin's Press, 1998), 8–9. Also see Sylvia Ostry, *The Post–Cold War Trading System: Who's on First* (Chicago: University of Chicago Press, 1997).

6. Bennett Harrison and Barry Bluestone, *The Great U-Turn: Corporate Restructuring and the Polarizing of America* (New York: Basic Books, 1988). Also see MIT Commission on Industrial Productivity, Working Group on the Textile Industry, *The Working Papers of the MIT Commission on Industrial Productivity*, vol. 2: *The US Textile Industry: Challenges and Opportunities* (Cambridge: MIT Press, 1989).

7. Folker Froebel, Jurgen Heinrichs, and Otto Kreye, *The New International Division of Labor* (Cambridge: Cambridge University Press, 1979).

8. I. M. Destler, *American Trade Politics*, 3d ed. (Washington, D.C.: Institute for International Economics and the Twentieth Century Fund, April 1995). There is an extensive historiography on U.S. trade policy that supports free trade. See also Raymond A. Bauer, Ithiel de Sola Pool, and Lewis Anthony Dexter, *American Business and Public Policy* (New York: Atherton Press, 1964); Aggarwal and Haggard, "The Politics of Protection in the U.S. Textile and Apparel Industries"; Robert A. Pastor, *Congress and the Politics of U.S. Foreign Economic Policy, 1929–1976* (Berkeley and Los Angeles: University of California Press, 1980); H. Richard Friman, *Patchwork Protectionism: Textile Trade Policy in the United States, Japan, and West Germany* (Ithaca: Cornell University Press, 1990); Thomas W. Zeiler, *American Trade and Power in the 1960s* (New York: Columbia University Press, 1992); Stephen Sylvia, "Jobs, Trade, and Unions: The Politics of Employment and Protectionism in West German and American Unions" (Ph.D. diss., Yale University, 1990).

9. Peter Passell, "Economic Scene: Loading Trade Agenda with Divisive Issues Could Backfire," *New York Times*, October 14, 1997.

10. Stephen Gill, "Knowledge, Politics, and Neo-Liberal Political Economy," in *Political Economy and the Changing Global Order*, ed. Richard Stubbs and Geoffrey R. D. Underhill (Toronto: McClellan and Stewart, 1994), 79.

11. Adam Smith, *The Wealth of Nations* (1786; reprint, Cambridge: Prometheus Books, 1996); David Ricardo, *Principles of Political Economy and Taxation* (1817; reprint, Cambridge: Prometheus Books, 1991).

12. Kuttner, *The End of Laissez-Faire*, 118–19; Underhill, *Industrial Crisis and the Open Economy*, 14; Robert Heilbroner and William Milberg, *The Crisis of Vision in Modern Economic Thought* (Cambridge: Cambridge University Press, 1995), 36.

13. Heilbroner and Milberg, *The Crisis of Vision in Modern Economic Thought.*

14. Geoffrey R. D. Underhill, "Conceptualizing the Changing Global Order," in *Political Economy and the Changing Global Order,* ed. Richard Stubbs and Geoffrey R. D. Underhill (Toronto: McClellan and Stewart, 1994), 41, n. 32.

15. Heilbroner and Milberg, *The Crisis of Vision in Modern Economic Thought.*

16. William Lazonick, *Business Organization and the Myth of the Market Economy* (Cambridge: Cambridge University Press, 1991), 3; Underhill, "Conceptualizing the Changing Global Order"; Heilbroner and Milberg, *The Crisis of Vision in Modern Economic Thought.*

17. Underhill, "Conceptualizing the Changing Global Order," 28.

18. Heilbroner and Milberg, *The Crisis of Vision in Modern Economic Thought,* 105.

19. Underhill, "Conceptualizing the Changing Global Order," 18.

20. Paul R. Krugman and Maurice Obstfeld, *International Economics: Theory and Policy,* 5th ed. (Reading, Mass.: Addison-Wesley, 2000), 13.

21. See Bernard Elbaum, "Cumulative or Comparative Advantage? British Competitiveness in the Early Twentieth Century," *World Development* 18 (September 1990): 1255–72.

22. Gary Clyde Hufbauer and Jeffrey Schott, *NAFTA: An Assessment,* rev. ed. (Washington, D.C.: Institute for International Economics, 1993); Jeffrey Schott, assisted by Joanna W. Buurman, *The Uruguay Round* (Washington D.C.: Institute for International Economics, 1994); Gary Clyde Hufbauer and Kimberly Ann Elliott, *Measuring the Costs of Protection in the United States* (Washington D.C.: Institute for International Economics, 1994); William R. Cline, *The Future of World Trade in Textiles and Apparel,* rev. ed. (Washington D.C.: Institute for International Economics, 1990).

23. In 1994 the MFA was eliminated and replaced by the Agreement on Textiles and Clothing. All tariffs and quotas on textile and apparel imports will be phased out by 2005.

24. Kim Moody, *An Injury to All: The Decline of American Unionism* (London: Verso Press, 1988).

25. Legally, much of the capital accumulated from such an exchange must be earmarked for repaying Mexico's large debt. Therefore, very little can be used for new capital investment to support indigenous industrialization.

26. Alice Kessler-Harris, *A Woman's Wage* (Lexington: University of Kentucky Press, 1990).

27. Elizabeth Wayland Barber, *Women's Work—the First 20,000 Years: Women, Cloth, and Society in Early Times* (New York: W. W. Norton and Company, 1994).

28. Thomas Dublin, *Women at Work: The Transformation of Work and Community in Lowell, Massachusetts, 1826–60* (New York: Columbia University Press 1979).

29. The "putting-out system," which today incorporates the practice of homework, is an intermediate stage between forms of home and industrial production. Homework persists today in some segments of the industry, but factory production is the norm.

30. Carole Truman and J. Keating, "Technology, Markets, and the Design of Women's Jobs—the Case of the Clothing Industry," *New Technology, Work, and Employment* 3 (spring 1988): 1.

31. Veronica Beechey, "Rethinking the Definition of Work: Gender and Work," in *Feminization of the Labour Process: Paradoxes and Promises,* ed. Jane Jenson, Elizabeth Hage, and C. Reddy (New York: Oxford University Press, 1988); Cynthia Cockburn, *The Machinery of Dominance* (London: Routledge and Kegan Paul, 1988); Angela Coyle, "Sex and Skill in the Organization of the Clothing Industry," in *Work, Women, and the Labour Process,* ed. Jackie West (London: Routledge and Kegan Paul, 1983); A. Game and Rosemary Pringle, *Gender at Work* (Sydney: George Allen and Unwin, 1983); P. Armstrong, "If It's Only Women It Doesn't Matter So Much," in *Work, Women, and the Labour Process,* ed. Jackie West (London: Routledge and Kegan Paul, 1983).

32. See Beechey, "Rethinking the Definition of Work."

33. Sally Hacker, *Pleasure, Power, and Technology: Some Tales of Gender, Engineering, and the Cooperative Workplace* (Boston: Unwin and Hyman, 1989); J. McIlwee and J. G. Robinson, *Women in Engineering: Gender, Power, and Workplace Culture* (New York: State University of New York Press, 1992); W. Faulkner and E. Arnold, *Smothered by Invention: Some Tales of Gender* (London: Pluto Press, 1985).

34. International Labour Organization, "Export Processing Zones Growing Steadily: Providing a Major Source of Job Creation" (International Labour Organization, Geneva, September 28, 1998, photocopy), press release.

35. Leslie Kaufman, "For Clothing Makers, It's Cut or Be Cut," *New York Times,* January 6, 2002.

36. John Galtung, *Peace by Peaceful Means: Peace and Conflict, Development and Civilization* (London: Sage Press, 1996), 4.

CHAPTER 3

1. Chiang Hsieh, "Post War Developments in the Japanese Textile Industry," *International Labour Review* (Geneva) 62, no. 5 (November 1950): 364–88.

2. Ippei Yamazawa, *Economic Development and International Trade: The Japanese Model* (Honolulu: East-West Center, Resource Systems Institute, 1990), 69–70.

3. Deputy Undersecretary of State Murphy, "A Review of United States Foreign Policy," *Department of State Bulletin* (September 26, 1955): 490–93.

Excerpts from an address to the International College of Surgeons at Philadelphia, on September 14, 1955.

4. Hsieh, "Post War Developments in the Japanese Textile Industry," 366.

5. Jerome B. Cohen, *Japan's Economy in War and Reconstruction* (Minneapolis: University of Minnesota Press, 1949), 479. See also Hsieh, "Post War Developments in the Japanese Textile Industry," 369.

6. Stanley Nehmer and Marguerite C. Crimmins, "Significance of Textiles in the Japanese Economy," *Department of State Bulletin* 18, no. 460 (April 25, 1948): 527–33.

7. See ibid., 529.

8. Fred Taylor, *The Textile Mission to Japan: Report to the War Department and the Department of State*, Far Eastern Series 13, Publication 2619 (Washington, D.C., January–March 1946).

9. Nehmer and Crimmins, "Significance of Textiles in the Japanese Economy," 527.

10. J. B. Cohen, *Japan's Economy in War and Reconstruction*, 480; John R. Stewart, *Japan's Textile Industry* (New York: International Secretariat, Institute for Pacific Relations, 1949), 2.

11. Richard J. Barnet and Ronald E. Muller, *Global Reach* (New York: Simon and Schuster, 1974), 67; also see J. B. Cohen, *Japan's Economy in War and Reconstruction*, 392; Warren S. Hunsberger, *Japan and the United States in World Trade* (New York: Harper and Row, 1964), 289.

12. Hsieh, "Post War Developments in the Japanese Textile Industry," 369.

13. Stewart, *Japan's Textile Industry*, 5.

14. Burton I. Kaufman, "Eisenhower's Foreign Economic Policy with Respect to East Asia," in *The Great Powers in East Asia, 1953–1960*, ed. Warren I. Cohen and Akira Iriye (New York: Columbia University Press, 1990), 114–15.

15. Yamamoto Mitsuru, "The Cold War and U.S.-Japan Economic Cooperation," in *The Origins of the Cold War in Asia*, ed. Yonosuke Nagai and Akira Iriye (New York: Columbia University Press; Tokyo: University of Tokyo Press, 1977), 415–16.

16. William H. Draper, Jr., "The Eightieth Congress and the Origins of Japan's 'Reverse Course,'" in *Aftermath of War: Americans and the Remaking of Japan, 1949–1952*, ed. Howard B. Schonberger (Kent, Ohio: Kent State University Press, 1989), 183.

17. Stewart, *Japan's Textile Industry*, 11.

18. Ibid., 10.

19. J. B. Cohen, *Japan's Economy in War and Reconstruction*, 487.

20. Sylvia Ostry, *The Post–Cold War Trading System: Who's on First* (Chicago: University of Chicago Press 1997).

21. Robert Kuttner, *The End of Laissez-Faire: National Purpose and the Global Economy after the Cold War* (New York: Alfred A. Knopf, 1991), 25.

22. Ibid., 49.

23. William Borden, *The Pacific Alliance: United States Foreign Economic Policy and Japanese Trade Recovery, 1947–1955* (Madison: University of Wisconsin Press, 1984). See also George Kennan, *American Diplomacy, 1900–1950* (Chicago: University of Chicago Press, 1951).

24. Richard Barnet, *The Alliance: America, Europe, Japan, and the Makers of the Postwar World* (New York: Simon and Schuster, 1983), 67.

25. Cited in Robert A. Pollard, *Economic Security and the Origins of the Cold War, 1945–1960* (New York: Columbia University Press, 1985), 184–85.

26. Barnet, *The Alliance*, 64, 66, 93–94.

27. David P. Calleo and Benjamin M. Rowland, *America and the World Political Economy: Atlantic Dreams and National Realities* (Bloomington: Indiana University Press, 1973), 198.

28. Barnet, *The Alliance*, 64, 66, 93–94; Howard B. Schonberger, ed., *Aftermath of War: Americans and the Remaking of Japan, 1949–1952* (Kent, Ohio: Kent State University Press, 1989), 175.

29. Pollard, *Economic Security and the Origins of the Cold War*, 120–30; Richard M. Freeland, *The Truman Doctrine and the Origins of McCarthyism: Foreign Policy, Domestic Politics, and Internal Security, 1946–48* (New York: Alfred A. Knopf, 1972), 54–55; Calleo and Rowland, *America and the World Political Economy*, 197–201.

30. Kaufman, "Eisenhower's Foreign Economic Policy with Respect to East Asia," 106; Schonberger, *Aftermath of War*, 182.

31. Theodore Cohen, *Remaking Japan: The American Occupation as the New Deal*, ed. Herbert Passin (New York: Free Press, 1987).

32. T. Cohen, *Remaking Japan*, 1987, 411.

33. Draper, "The Eightieth Congress and the Origins of Japan's 'Reverse Course,'" 184; Stewart, *Japan's Industrial Recovery*, 11.

34. J. B. Cohen, *Japan's Economy in War and Reconstruction*; Nehmer and Crimmins, "Significance of Textiles in the Japanese Economy."

35. Schonberger, *Aftermath of War*, 174.

36. Ibid., 184.

37. Ibid., 183.

38. See Stewart, *Japan's Textile Industry*, 2.

39. Ibid., 13.

40. Murphy, "A Review of United States Foreign Policy," 492; U.S. House, Committee on Ways and Means, *Trade Agreements Extension Act of 1953: A Bill to Extend the Authority of the President to Enter into Trade Agreements under Section 350 of the Tariff Act of 1930*, 83rd Cong., 1st sess., April 27–30; May 1–19, 1953, 20.

41. Yamamoto Mitsuru, "The Cold War and U.S.-Japan Economic Cooperation," 415–16.

42. Kaufman, "Eisenhower's Foreign Economic Policy with Respect to East Asia," 114.

43. Hunsberger, *Japan and the United States in World Trade*, 316.

44. Borden, *The Pacific Alliance*.

45. Freeland, *The Truman Doctrine and the Origins of McCarthyism*, 47; Kaufman, "Eisenhower's Foreign Economic Policy with Respect to East Asia," 105; Barnet and Muller, *Global Reach*, 92–93; Calleo and Rowland, *America and the World Political Economy*, 197.

46. Kaufman, "Eisenhower's Foreign Economic Policy with Respect to East Asia," 107.

47. On Eisenhower's initiatives, see Kaufman, "Eisenhower's Foreign Economic Policy with Respect to East Asia," 113.

48. U.S. Senate, Committee on Interstate Commerce, *A Study of the Textile Industry of the U.S.*, 85th Cong., 2d sess., S. Res. 287, December 2, 1958, Washington D.C., 1770–74.

49. U.S. Senate, Committee on Commerce, *Problems of the Domestic Textile Industry: Hearings on a Study of the Textile Industry of the United States Pursuant to S. Res. 287*, 85th Cong., 2d sess., July 8–10, 1958, 60, 182–84, 235. Japanese textile machinery, at that point, sold for 30 to 50 percent of what the American product cost. It may have been a bargain, but as U.S. textile industry advocates saw it, it supplanted government subsidies to U.S. industries.

50. Samuel P. Hayes, ed., *The Beginnings of Aid to Southeast Asia: The Griffin Mission of 1950* (Lexington, Mass.: D. C. Heath and Company, 1971). The Griffin mission to Southeast Asia lent credence to the need for foreign aid. The United States spent about $60 million in an effort to prevent communist aggression.

51. Hunsberger, *Japan and the United States in World Trade*.

52. "Eximbank Authorizes Credit for Purchase of U.S. Cotton by Japan," *Department of State Bulletin* (August 9, 1954): 211.

53. See Nicholas Lemann, *The Promised Land: The Great Black Migration and How It Changed America* (New York: Alfred A. Knopf, 1991).

54. *Activities under the Agricultural Trade Development and Assistance Act*, Message from the President to the Congress, 84th Cong., 1st sess., *Department of State Bulletin* (January 10, 1955): 200–206.

55. "U.S. and Japan Sign Agreement for Technical Cooperation," *Department of State Bulletin* (April 25, 1955): 701.

56. *Activities under the Agricultural Trade Development and Assistance Act*, Message from the President to the Congress, 84th Congress, 1st session, transmitted on January 10, 1955, 202.

57. U.S. Senate, Committee on Interstate Commerce, *A Study of the Textile Industry of the U.S.*, 1770–74.

58. Ibid.

59. I. M. Destler, *American Trade Politics*, 3d ed. (Washington, D.C.: Institute for International Economics and the Twentieth Century Fund, April 1995), 25.

60. Stewart, *Japan's Textile Industry*, 15.

61. Kaufman, "Eisenhower's Foreign Economic Policy with Respect to East Asia," 117.

62. On the tariff reductions made in each of these years, see Hunsberger, *Japan and the United States in World Trade*, 293.

63. U.S. Senate, Committee on Foreign Relations, *Imports of Cotton Textiles from Japan: Hearings on H.R. 11356*, 84th Cong., 2d sess., June 16, 1956.

64. Yamazawa, *Economic Development and International Trade*, 8.

65. Hunsberger, *Japan and the United States in World Trade*, 292.

66. U.S. Senate, *Imports of Cotton Textiles from Japan*; also see U.S. Senate, Committee on Finance, *Trade Agreements Extension Act of 1951: An Act to Extend the Authority of the President under Section 350 of the Tariff Act of 1930, as Amended and for Other Purposes, Part 1: Hearings on H.R. 1211*, 81st Cong., 1st sess., February 22, 26–28; March 1–3, 6–8, 12–13, 1951, testimony of Senator Henry Cabot Lodge (D-Mass.). Even though Japan did not become a member of the GATT until 1955, it was accorded the same privileges as GATT members when shipping products, including textiles, to the United States, according to E. G. Martin, general counsel to the U.S. Tariff Commission. Martin testified, "I don't believe we have any obligation to extend trade agreement rates to Japan. But we do it as a matter of practice."

67. Calleo and Rowland, *America and the World Political Economy*, 38–40; On postwar British textile protectionism, see Caroline Miles, "Protection of the British Textile Industry," in *Public Assistance to Industry: Protection and Subsidies in Britain and Germany*, ed. W. M. Corden and Gerhard Fels (Boulder, Colo.: Westview Press, 1976), 184–214.

68. Burton I. Kaufman, *Trade and Aid: Eisenhower's Foreign Economic Policy, 1953–1961* (Baltimore: Johns Hopkins University Press, 1982), 40; Kaufman, "Eisenhower's Foreign Economic Policy with Respect to East Asia," 116.

69. Destler, *American Trade Politics*, 54; Kaufman, *Trade and Aid*, 39–41; J. B. Cohen, *Japan's Economy in War and Reconstruction*, 496; Kaufman, "Eisenhower's Foreign Economic Policy with Respect to East Asia," 116.

70. Hunsberger, *Japan and the United States in World Trade*, 244–45.

71. The Association of Southeast Asian Nations was founded in 1967. Members now include Malaysia, Thailand, Singapore, the Philippines, Brunei, Vietnam, Cambodia, and Indonesia.

72. See Richard Appelbaum and Jeffrey Henderson, eds., *States and Development in the Asian Pacific Rim* (Newbury Park, Calif.: Sage Publications, 1992).

73. Y. Dolly Hwang, *The Rise of a New World Economic Power: Postwar Taiwan* (New York: Greenwood Press, 1991), 11.

74. Ramon H. Myers, "The Economic Development of the Republic of Korea, 1965–1981," in *Models of Development: A Comparative Study of Economic Growth in South Korea and Taiwan*, ed. Lawrence J. Lau (San Francisco: Institute for Contemporary Studies Press, 1986), 66–67.

75. United Nations Command, Office of the Economic Coordinator for Korea, *Korea: Stabilization and Program Progress, Fiscal Year 1958*, June 30, 1958.

76. Alice Amsden, *Asia's Next Giant: South Korea and Late Industrialization* (New York: Oxford University Press, 1989), 39.

77. Ibid., 39–40.

78. Neil Jacoby, *U.S. Aid to Taiwan* (New York: Frederick A. Praeger, 1966), 36–37.

79. Ibid., 36.

80. Ibid., 30–32.

81. Ibid., 11.

82. Ibid.

83. Ibid., 21.

84. Louis Turner, introduction to *The Newly Industrializing Countries: Trade and Adjustment,* ed. Louis Turner and Neil McMullen (London: George Allen and Unwin, 1982), 22.

85. Donald B. Keesing, *World Trade and Output of Manufacturers: Structural Trends and Developing Countries' Exports,* Staff Working Paper no. 316 (Washington, D.C.: World Bank, 1979); and Keesing, *Trade Policy for Developing Countries,* Staff Working Paper no. 353 (Washington, D.C., World Bank, 1979).

86. Myers, "The Economic Development of the Republic of Korea," 68.

87. On the rapid economic growth of the region, see James Riedel, "Economic Development in East Asia: Doing What Comes Naturally?" in *Achieving Industrialization in East Asia,* ed. Helen Hughes (Cambridge: Cambridge University Press 1988), 1–38. U.S. funding helped to rebuild the cotton textile industry in many of these countries. Riedel writes, "The purpose of USAID [U.S. Agency for International Development] to Taiwan and the Republic of Korea was mainly to help absorb the burden of their confrontation with neighbouring Communist states. It did, nonetheless, allow investment, mainly in infrastructure, that would not otherwise have been possible given their extraordinary defense obligations." U.S. funding helped to rebuild the cotton textile industry in many of these countries (24–25). See Yamazawa, *Economic Development and International Trade,* 81–86; Kunio Yoshihara, *Japanese Investment in Southeast Asia* (Honolulu: University of Hawaii Press, 1978), 97.

88. Louis Turner, introduction, 18.

89. Louis Turner and Neil McMullen, eds., *The Newly Industrializing Countries: Trade and Adjustment* (London: George Allen and Unwin, 1982), 18.

90. U.S. House, Joint Economic Committee, *Foreign Economic Policy,* 87th Cong., 1st sess., December 4–14, 1961, 122, testimony of Warren Hunsberger; Vinod K. Aggarwal, *Liberal Protectionism: The Politics of Organized Textile Trade* (Berkeley and Los Angeles: University of California Press, 1985), 11–12; Jon Woronoff, *Asia's Miracle Economies,* 2d ed. (New York: M. E. Sharpe, 1992).

91. Yamazawa, *Economic Development and International Trade,* 81.

92. On the Lancashire Agreement and restriction of textile imports, see Caroline Miles, "Protection and Adjustment Problems of the UK Textile In-

264 / Notes to pages 47–51

dustry," in *Public Assistance to Industry: Protection and Subsidies in Britain and Germany*, ed. W. M. Corden and Gerhard Fels (Boulder, Colo.: Westview Press, 1976), 187–88; Aggarwal, *Liberal Protectionism*, 12.

93. Hwang, *The Rise of a New World Economic Power*, 49–50.

94. Myers, "The Economic Development of the Republic of Korea," 73; Seung Noon Lee and No Keun Song, "The Korean Garment Industry: From Authoritarian Patriarchism to Industrial Paternalism," in *Global Production: The Apparel Industry in the Pacific Rim*, ed. Edna Bonacich et al. (Philadelphia: Temple University Press, 1994), 147–48.

95. U.S. Senate, Committee on Commerce, *Problems of the Domestic Textile Industry*, 87th Cong., 1st sess., February 6–7, 1961, 4–5, statement of Congressman Robert Hemphill (R-S.C.).

96. U.S. House, Committee on Education and Labor, *Impact of Imports and Exports on Employment (Textiles)*, 87th Cong., 1st sess., July 19–21, 1961, 212–27.

97. U.S. Senate, *Problems of the US Textile Industry*, 77, statement of W. J. Erwin, president of Dan River Mills, Danville, Va., chairman, Foreign Trade Committee, American Cotton Manufacturers' Institute.

98. U.S. House, Joint Economic Committee, *Foreign Economic Policy*, testimony of Warren Hunsberger.

99. U.S. Senate, *Problems of the US Textile Industry*, 100, statement of James P. Hunder, president of the American Textile Machinery Association.

100. Ibid., 276, statement of William Pollock, general president, Textile Workers Union of America, AFL-CIO; statement of Solomon Barkin, director of research, Textile Workers Union of America, AFL-CIO, accompanied by John W. Edelman, Washington representative, Textile Workers Union of America, AFL-CIO.

101. Nehmer and Crimmins, "Significance of Textiles in the Japanese Economy," 531.

102. Edna Bonacich, Lucie Cheng, Norma Chinchilla, Nora Hamilton, and Paul Ong, eds., *Global Production: The Apparel Industry in the Pacific Rim* (Philadelphia: Temple University Press, 1994), chap. 5.

103. Ibid.

104. Yoshihara, *Japanese Investment in Southeast Asia*, 98.

105. Ibid. Between 1960 and 1972 the price of cotton remained relatively constant, while man-made textile prices dropped by 40 percent (98).

106. Yamazawa, *Economic Development and International Trade*, 8, table 1.3.

107. Yoshihara, *Japanese Investment in Southeast Asia*, 94.

108. Even Kennedy's Short-Term and Long-Term Arrangements (1962 and 1963), which restrained imports from East Asia, imposed quotas on cotton textiles but not on textiles or apparel composed of man-made fibers.

109. See, for example, Annette Fuentes and Barbara Ehrenreich, "Women on the Global Assembly Line," *Ms.* (June 1981); June Nash and Maria-Patricia

Fernandez-Kelly, *Women, Men, and the New International Division of Labor* (Baltimore: Johns Hopkins University Press, 1983).

110. Stewart, *Japan's Textile Industry,* 9.

111. Hsieh, "Post War Developments in the Japanese Textile Industry," 384.

112. Kaji Etsuko, "The Invisible Proletariat: Working Women in Japan," *AOMI* (1973).

113. Hsieh, "Post War Developments in the Japanese Textile Industry," 384–85.

114. Stewart, *Japan's Textile Industry,* 6; Hsieh, "Post War Developments in the Japanese Textile Industry," 380; Hunsberger, *Japan and the United States in World Trade,* 284. Japan's women textile workers, like their male counterparts, were legally entitled to receive employee benefits (health insurance, life insurance, pensions, and unemployment insurance). But these benefits were generally limited to employees in the larger textile firms. About one-third of textile workers, however, were employed by firms with ten or fewer workers.

115. Hunsberger, *Japan and the United States in World Trade,* 279.

116. U.S. Senate, Committee on Commerce, *Problems of the Domestic Textile Industry,* February 6–7, 1961, 4–5, statement of Congressman Robert Hemphill (R-S.C.).

117. Amsden, *Asia's Next Giant,* 9; also see Alice H. Amsden, "Taiwan in International Perspective," in *Taiwan's Enterprises in Global Perspective,* ed. N. T. Wang (New York: M. E. Sharpe, 1992), 25–52, 29.

118. Hunsberger, *Japan and the United States in World Trade,* 279.

119. Gordon Walker, "Made in Japan," *Christian Science Monitor,* December 20, 1955, cited in Leon Stein, ed., *Out of the Sweatshop: The Struggle for Industrial Democracy* (New York: Quadrangle Books and New York Times Book Company, 1977), 321–22.

120. Walker, "Made in Japan." This is consistent with Forbes's account stating that women textile workers were paid $30 a month in 1961.

121. Hsieh, "Post War Developments in the Japanese Textile Industry," 386.

122. Shiou-Chao Wu, "The Structural Transformation of the Textile Industry in Taiwan and Its Impact on Current Women Workers" (Ph.D. diss., Heller School, Brandeis University, 2000).

CHAPTER 4

1. On the U.S. textile and apparel trade in the first quarter-century after the war, see Raymond A. Bauer, Ithiel de Sola Pool, and Lewis Anthony Dexter, *American Business and Public Policy* (New York: Atherton Press, 1964); I. M. Destler, *American Trade Politics,* 3d ed. (Washington, D.C.: Institute for International Economics and the Twentieth Century Fund, April 1995); Vinod

K. Aggarwal with Stephan Haggard, "The Politics of Protection in the U.S. Textile and Apparel Industries," in *American Industry in International Competition: Government Policies and Corporate Strategies,* ed. John Zysman and Laura Tyson (Ithaca: Cornell University Press, 1983), 249–312; Robert A. Pastor, *Congress and the Politics of U.S. Foreign Economic Policy, 1929–1976* (Berkeley and Los Angeles: University of California Press, 1980); H. Richard Friman, *Patchwork Protectionism: Textile Trade Policy in the United States, Japan, and West Germany* (Ithaca: Cornell University Press, 1990); Thomas W. Zeiler, *American Trade and Power in the 1960s* (New York: Columbia University Press, 1992); Stephen Sylvia, "Jobs, Trade, and Unions: The Politics of Employment and Protectionism in West German and American Unions" (Ph.D. diss., Yale University, 1990).

2. Whether or not the industries who chose protection made a strategic error is now, of course, with the defeat of protectionism, moot.

3. Robert Kuttner, *The End of Laissez-Faire: National Purpose and the Global Economy after the Cold War* (New York: Alfred A. Knopf, 1991), 25.

4. The Reciprocal Trade Agreements Act of 1934 is often called the Reciprocal Trade Act, or the RTA. While being renewed every three years, it was at times renamed the Trade Agreements Act and sometimes the Trade Agreements Extension Act.

5. Destler, *American Trade Politics,* 12.

6. U.S. Senate, Committee on Finance, *Trade Agreements Extension Act of 1951: An Act to Extend the Authority of the President to Enter into Trade Agreements under Section 350 of the Tariff Act of 1930, as Amended and for the Purposes, Part 1,* 82d Cong., 1st sess. February 17–23, 1951.

7. Ibid., 7.

8. Ibid.

9. Ibid., statement of Walter J. Mason.

10. Ibid., 410, statement of O. R. Strackbein, executive secretary of America's Wage Earners Protective Conference.

11. Strackbein was to make additional appearances to testify at congressional hearings on trade as a spokesman for labor and industries opposed to further tariff reductions.

12. Kuttner, *The End of Laissez-Faire,* 49.

13. U.S. Senate, Committee on Finance, *Trade Agreements Extension Act of 1951,* February 22, 26–28; March 1–3, 6–8, 12, 13, 1951, pp. 232–34.

14. Bauer, Pool, and Dexter, *American Business and Public Policy,* 40–44.

15. John Foster Dulles, "Security in the Pacific," *Department of State Bulletin* (June 28, 1954): 971–74. Address to the Los Angeles World Affairs Committee at Los Angeles.

16. Deputy Undersecretary of State Murphy, "America, Japan, and the Future of the Pacific," *Department of State Bulletin* (March 22, 1954): 430. Address to the World Affairs Council of Northern California and the American Legion of San Francisco.

17. Everett Drumright, "Problems in the Far East," *Department of State*

Bulletin (October 18, 1954): 573. Presentation to the board of directors of the National Chamber of Commerce, Washington, D.C.

18. Yamamoto Mitsuru, "The Cold War and U.S.-Japan Economic Cooperation," in *The Origins of the Cold War in Asia*, ed. Yonosuke Nagai and Akira Iriye (New York: Columbia University Press; Tokyo: University of Tokyo Press, 1977), 293.

19. Aggarwal and Haggard, "The Politics of Protection in the U.S. Textile and Apparel Industries," 272; see also Bauer, Pool, and Dexter, *American Business and Public Policy*, 54.

20. U.S. House, Committee on Ways and Means, *Trade Agreements Extension Act of 1953: A Bill to Extend the Authority of the President to Enter into Trade Agreements under Section 350 of the Tariff Act of 1930*, 83rd Cong., 1st sess., April 27–30; May 1–19, 1953, p. 1811. This bill was also called the Simpson bill.

21. Bauer, Pool, and Dexter, *American Business and Public Policy*, 40.

22. U.S. House, Committee on Ways and Means, *Trade Agreements Extension Act of 1953*, 681–82.

23. Cited in Bauer, Pool, and Dexter, *American Business and Public Policy*, emphasis in original. See also *Congressional Record*, June 11, 1954.

24. Destler, *American Trade Politics*, 14.

25. Dan Reed's changed vote is not evidence that representatives believed that trade protection was, as Destler puts it, "bad policy." Destler himself argues in his discussion of textiles that congressmen and senators voted for protection when concerted action had some chance for success. See Destler, *American Trade Politics*, 69.

26. Warren S. Hunsberger, *Japan and the United States in World Trade* (New York: Harper and Row, 1964), 289.

27. U.S. Senate, Committee on Interstate Commerce, *A Study of the Textile Industry of the U.S.*, 85th Cong., 2d sess., S. Res. 287, December 2, 1958, Washington D.C., 1716.

28. Stanley Metzger, "Injury and Market Disruption from Imports," in *United States International Economic Policy in an Interdependent World* (Washington D.C.: Commission on International Trade and Investment Policy, 1971), 1:167–91. This volume is also called the Williams Report.

29. U.S. House, Committee on Ways and Means, *Trade Agreements Extension Act of 1953*, 13.

30. Cited in ibid. Also see Metzger, "Injury and Market Disruption from Imports," 167–91: "An agreement in cotton cloth for two years duration was concluded in January 1937 and further renewed for two years on December 18, 1938. The agreements limited Japanese exports to 155 million square yards in 1937 and 100 million square yards for each year thereafter. The signatories were the American Cotton Textile Mission and the representatives of the Japanese cotton textile industry."

31. U.S. Senate, Committee on Finance, *Trade Agreements Extension Act of 1951*, February 22, 26–28; March 1–3, 6–8, 12, 13, 1951, 3.

32. Ibid., 5–7.

33. Ibid., 9–13.

34. Burton I. Kaufman, *Trade and Aid: Eisenhower's Foreign Economic Policy, 1953–1961*(Baltimore: Johns Hopkins University Press, 1982), 42.

35. U.S. Senate, Committee on Interstate Commerce, *A Study of the Textile Industry of the U.S.*, 85th Cong., 2d sess., S. Res. 287, November 12, 13, and 14, 1958, New York City, 1229–30. Statement of Edwin Wilkinson, executive vice president of the National Association of Wool Manufacturers.

36. U.S. Senate, Committee on Finance, *Trade Agreements Extension Act of 1951*, June 20–21, 23–26, 1951, 184.

37. Ibid.

38. U.S. Senate, Committee on Interstate Commerce, *A Study of the Textile Industry of the U.S.*, December 2, 1958, 1748.

39. Ibid., 1726.

40. U.S. Senate, Committee on Commerce, *Problems of the Domestic Textile Industry*, July 8–10, 1958, 22, testimony of Halbert M. Jones, president of the American Cotton Manufacturers' Institute. It was not until 1961, at the debut of the Kennedy administration, that American industrial interests had the opportunity to even attend the sessions of the GATT negotiations.

41. U.S. Senate, Committee on Finance, *Trade Agreements Extension Act of 1951*, February 22, 26–28; March 1–3, 6–8, 12, 13, 1951, 235. The Textile Workers Union of America (TWUA-CIO) passed a resolution supporting the implementation of international labor standards at their convention in the spring of 1950.

42. Despite their official commitment to freer trade, the Europeans had found ways to resist fully opening their markets to imports from Japan and the Newly Industrializing Countries.

43. David B. Yoffie, *Power and Protectionism: Strategies of the Newly Industrializing Countries* (New York: Columbia University Press, 1983), 92.

44. Destler, *American Trade Politics*.

45. Zeiler, *American Trade and Power in the 1960s*, 1–5.

46. Barry E. Truchil, *Capital-Labor Relations in the U.S. Textile Industry* (New York: Praeger, 1988), 111–12.

47. Yoffie, *Power and Protectionism*, 92.

48. Alfred Eckes Jr., *Opening America's Market: US Foreign Trade Policy since 1776* (Chapel Hill: University of North Carolina Press, 1995), 191–92.

49. Cited in ibid., 200.

50. Destler, *American Trade Politics*.

CHAPTER 5

1. Barry E. Truchil, *Capital-Labor Relations in the U.S. Textile Industry* (Greenwood Press, 1988); Seymour E. Harris, *New England's Textiles and the New England Economy: Report by the New England Governors' Textile Com-*

mittee to the Conference of New England Governors (n.p., March 1957), II-40.

2. Harris, *New England's Textiles and the New England Economy*, II-40.

3. U.S. House, Committee on the Judiciary, *The Merger Movement in the Textile Industry: A Staff Report to Subcommittee No. 5 (Anti-Trust Subcommittee)*, 84th Cong., 1st sess., 1955, testimony of Emanuel Cellar, 15–18.

4. Ibid., 2–35.

5. Harris, *New England's Textiles and the New England Economy*, I-9.

6. Truchil, *Capital-Labor Relations in the U.S. Textile Industry*, 65–66; Harris, *New England's Textiles and the New England Economy*. Also see U.S. Senate, Committee on Commerce, *Problems of the Domestic Textile Industry*, July 8–10, 1958, testimony of William Pollock, general president, Textile Workers Union of America, AFL-CIO.

7. Harris, *New England's Textiles and the New England Economy*.

8. Vinod K. Aggarwal, *Liberal Protectionism: The Politics of Organized Textile Trade* (Berkeley and Los Angeles: University of California Press, 1985), 50.

9. Yutaka Matsamura, *Japan's Economic Growth, 1945–1960* (Tokyo: Tokyo News Service, 1961), 378.

10. U.S. House, Committee on the Judiciary, *The Merger Movement in the Textile Industry*, testimony of Emanuel Cellar, 15–18.

11. "Textile Workers Threaten Strike," *New York Times*, April 7, 1955.

12. "Textile Industry Told to Help Industry," *New York Times*, April 10, 1955.

13. "Textile Union Asks Rise: Seeks Ten Percent More from Biggest Producer in New England," *New York Times*, March 15, 1956.

14. Joseph A. Loftus, "Union Organizing Spreads in South: United Labor Is Finally Set to Push Its Campaign in Tobacco and Textiles," *New York Times*, July 11, 1956.

15. Jack Bass and Walter DeVries, *The Transformation of Southern Politics* (New York: Basic Books, 1976), 257. It was not until 1980 that the U.S. Supreme Court upheld the National Labor Relations Board finding and ordered that the workers displaced be compensated.

16. Cited in A. H. Raskin, "Union Sees Crisis in Textile Field: Million Workers Said to Be Condemned by Industry's Declining Standards," *New York Times*, September 25, 1956.

17. Harris, *New England's Textiles and the New England Economy*, II-61. U.S. House, Committee on the Judiciary, *The Merger Movement in the Textile Industry*, testimony of Emanuel Cellar, 5.

18. "Japan's Textiles Stir New Protest," *New York Times*, July 21, 1956.

19. U.S. Senate, Committee on Commerce, *Problems of the Domestic Textile Industry*, 88th Cong., 1st sess., May 22–23, 1963, 71, testimony of Seabury Stanton, chairman of the executive committee of the Northern Textile Association and president of Berkshire Hathaway, New Bedford, Mass.

20. Glenn Fowler, "Imports Shroud Cotton Outlook: Japanese Textiles Are Said to Pose a Life or Death Question for Industry," *New York Times,* April 6, 1956.

21. Thomas Dublin, *Women at Work: The Transformation of Work and Community in Lowell, Massachusetts, 1826–60* (New York: Columbia University Press 1979).

22. U.S. House, Committee on Education and Labor, *Impact of Imports and Exports on Employment (Textiles),* 87th Cong., 1st sess., July 19–21, 1961, 214–15.

23. Ester Boserup, *Women's Role in Economic Development* (London: Allen and Unwin, 1970).

24. Alice Amsden, *Asia's Next Giant* (New York: Oxford University Press, 1989), 9.

25. U.S. Senate, Committee on Commerce, *Problems of the Domestic Textile Industry,* May 22–23, 1963.

26. Harris, *New England's Textiles and the New England Economy,* II-1; also see Glenn Fowler, "Imports Shroud Cotton Outlook: Japanese Textiles Are Said to Pose a Life or Death Question for Industry," *New York Times,* April 6, 1956.

27. U.S. Senate, Committee on Foreign Relations, *Imports of Cotton Textiles from Japan: Hearings on H.R. 11356,* 84th Cong., 2d sess., June 16, 1956, 13–14, testimony of Theodore Francis Green.

28. U.S. Senate, Committee on Commerce, *Problems of the Domestic Textile Industry,* July 8–10, 1958, 21–22, testimony of Halbert M. Jones.

29. Warren S. Hunsberger, *Japan and the United States in World Trade* (New York: Harper and Row, 1964), 166.

30. Harris, *New England's Textiles and the New England Economy.*

31. Raymond A. Bauer, Ithiel de Sola Pool, and Lewis Anthony Dexter, *American Business and Public Policy* (New York: Atherton Press, 1964).

32. William Hays Simpson, *Some Aspects of America's Textile Industry, with Special Reference to Cotton* (Columbia: University of South Carolina Press, 1966).

33. See Richard Hofstadter, *The Age of Reform: From Bryan to FDR* (New York: Vintage, 1955).

34. Ralph Katz, "Textile Pay Rises in South Spread: Unspecified Increases Given by Two Companies in Sequel to Ten Cent Stevens' Grant," *New York Times,* October 3, 1956.

35. Richard L. Rowan and Robert E. Barr, *Employee Relation Trends and Practices in the Textile Industry* (Philadelphia: Industrial Research Unit, Wharton School, University of Pennsylvania, 1987), 9. The industry is concentrated in the Southeast.

36. Barbara Koeppel, "Something Could Be Finer," *The Progressive* (June 1976): 20–23.

37. Truchil, *Capital-Labor Relations in the U.S. Textile Industry,* 105.

38. Ibid.; Philip J. Wood, *Southern Capitalism: The Political Economy of*

North Carolina, 1880–1980 (Durham, N.C.: Duke University Press, 1986); Koeppel, "Something Could Be Finer," 20–23; Jeffrey S. Arpan, Jose de la Torre, and Brian Toyne, *The US Apparel Industry: International Challenge, Domestic Response* (Atlanta: Georgia State University, 1982); Rowan and Barr, *Employee Relation Trends and Practices in the Textile Industry*, 1987.

39. Stephen J. Hudak and Paul T. Bohnslav, *The Textile Industry: A Study of Capital Investment, Technology, and Other Factors Affecting Prescribed Capital Recovery Allowances of Textile Machinery*, a report prepared at the request of the U.S. Office of Industrial Economics, Office of the Assistant Secretary for Tax Policy, Department of the Treasury, February 2, 1976. The study disclosed the availability of significant technological advances, many of which the industry has been slow to adopt. This reluctance was primarily due to the limited availability of capital. These producers had access to internally generated funds, which, because of the low profitability of the industry, were in short supply.

40. Vinod K. Aggarwal with Stephan Haggard, "The Politics of Protection in the U.S. Textile and Apparel Industries," in *American Industry in International Competition: Government Policies and Corporate Strategies*, ed. John Zysman and Laura Tyson (Ithaca: Cornell University Press, 1983), 249–312; Geoffrey R. D. Underhill, *Industrial Crisis and the Open Economy: Politics, Global Trade, and the Textile Industry in the Advanced Economies* (New York: St. Martin's Press, 1998).

41. Aggarwal and Haggard, "The Politics of Protection in the U.S. Textile and Apparel Industries," 252.

42. Thomas W. Zeiler, *American Trade and Power in the 1960s* (New York: Columbia University Press, 1992), 77.

43. Aggarwal and Haggard, "The Politics of Protection in the U.S. Textile and Apparel Industries"; Zeiler, *American Trade and Power in the 1960s*, 76.

44. Hudak and Bohnslav, *The Textile Industry*, vii.

45. Brian Toyne, *The Global Textile Industry* (London: Allen and Unwin, 1984), 44.

46. Harold A. Bratt, "Assisting the Economic Recovery of Import-Injured Firms," *Law and Policy in International Business* 6, no. 4 (1974): 1–37; Samuel D. Rosenblatt, "Trade Adjustment Assistance Programs: Crossroads or Dead End?" *Law and Policy in International Business* 9, no. 4 (1977): 1065–1100.

47. See *Business Week* (December 23, 1961): 28; Truchil, *Capital-Labor Relations in the U.S. Textile Industry*, 111.

48. Denney Freeston Jr. and Jeffrey S. Arpan, *The Competitive Status of the U.S. Fibers, Textiles, and Apparel Complex: A Study of the Influences of Technology in Determining International Industrial Competitive Advantage*, prepared by the Fibers, Textiles, and Apparel Industry Panel; Committee on Technology and Trade Issues of the Office of the Foreign Secretary; National Academy of Engineering; and the Commission on Engineering and Technical Systems, National Research Council (Washington, D.C.: National Academy Press, 1983).

49. Wood, *Southern Capitalism*, 61.
50. Truchil, *Capital-Labor Relations in the U.S. Textile Industry*, 111–12.
51. Freeston and Arpan, *The Competitive Status of the U.S. Fibers, Textiles, and Apparel Complex*, 59.
52. Peter Katzenstein, *Policy and Politics in West Germany: The Growth of a Semi-Sovereign State* (Philadelphia: Temple University Press, 1987). Aggarwal and Haggard, "The Politics of Protection in the U.S. Textile and Apparel Industries"; Jose de la Torre, "Clothing-Industry Adjustment in Developed Countries" (London: Trade Policy Research Centre, 1984); Michael J. Piore and Charles F. Sabel, *The Second Industrial Divide: Possibilities for Prosperity* (New York: Basic Books, 1984). Also see Zeiler, *American Trade and Power in the 1960s*.
53. On the burst of capital spending in the industry, see Truchil, *Capital-Labor Relations in the U.S. Textile Industry*, 36–38; on the increased production in this period, see I. M. Destler, Harohiro Fukui, and Hideo Sato, *The Textile Wrangle: Conflict in Japanese-American Relations, 1969–1971* (Ithaca: Cornell University Press, 1979), 35.
54. Hudak and Bohnslav, *The Textile Industry*, vii.
55. Freeston and Arpan, *The Competitive Status of the U.S. Fibers, Textiles, and Apparel Complex*, 42.
56. Truchil, *Capital-Labor Relations in the U.S. Textile Industry*, 111–12; Roger Milliken argued for a shorter depreciation period for capital expenditures for textiles. U.S. House, Committee on Ways and Means, *Trade Reform: Tax Treatment of Capital Recovery*, 93rd Cong., 1st sess., March 5–6, 1973, testimony of Roger Milliken, president of Deering Milliken Corporation, Spartanburg, South Carolina, on behalf of the ATMI.
57. Rowan and Barr, *Employee Relation Trends and Practices in the Textile Industry*: "A comparison of this productivity index between the textile industry and all manufacturing shows that the relative gain in productivity for textiles is higher, 75.9 versus 64.8 percent for the period 1967 to 1985. Considering that automation in textiles is in its infancy, productivity will certainly continue to improve and outpace [that of] other industries."
58. Wood, *Southern Capitalism*, 173.
59. Hudak and Bohnslav, *The Textile Industry*.
60. *Fortune* vol. 85, nos. 5 and 6 (May and June); vol. 91, nos. 5 and 6 (May and June). These figures do not include Deering Milliken Corporation, because it is privately held. This corporation is a major textile manufacturer and is one of the recognized leaders in implementing new textile technologies. Cited in Hudak and Bohnslav, *The Textile Industry*, 11.
61. Freeston and Arpan, *The Competitive Status of the U.S. Fibers, Textiles, and Apparel Complex*, 32, 39; Arpan, de la Torre, and Toyne, *The US Apparel Industry*, 47.
62. Arpan, de la Torre, and Toyne, *The US Apparel Industry*, 82–83.
63. Ibid., 43–47.
64. Ibid., 48.

65. Ibid.

66. Quote is from ibid., 47. See also U.S. Senate, Committee on Commerce, *Problems of the Domestic Textile Industry,* May 22–23, 1963, 72, testimony of Seabury Stanton.

67. Zeiler, *American Trade and Power in the 1960s,* 240.

68. Alfred Eckes Jr., *Opening America's Market: US Foreign Trade Policy since 1776* (Chapel Hill: University of North Carolina Press, 1995), 201–2.

69. Members of the House Committee on Ways and Means and the Senate Finance Committee were particularly important as advocates of protection.

70. Destler, Haruhiro Fukui, and Hideo Sato, *The Textile Wrangle.*

CHAPTER 6

1. Later the Amalgamated Clothing Workers of America merged with the Textile Workers Union and became the Amalgamated Clothing and Textile Workers' Union.

2. A. H. Raskin, "A Union with Power," *New York Times,* March 13, 1958.

3. Ann Hoffman, Union of Needletrades and Industrial Textile Employees, conversation with the author, July 17, 1996.

4. "Garment Union Wins FTC Suit," *New York Times,* January 9, 1957.

5. Gus Tyler, *Look for the Union Label* (New York: M. E. Sharpe, 1995), 263–64.

6. Richard E. Mooney, "Labor Cautioned on Import Battle: President Warns of Danger of Reprisals If Unions Bar Handling Foreign Goods," *New York Times,* March 9, 1961.

7. A. H. Raskin, "Low Pay Called Pattern in City: Study Finds Apparel Wages Squeezed by Competition," *New York Times,* June 26, 1961.

8. A. H. Raskin, "Dress Union Out in 7 State Strike," *New York Times,* March 6, 1958.

9. Roy Helfgott, research director of the New York Cloak Joint Board of the ILGWU, cited by Milton Bracher, "Garment Center in City Area Seen Losing 15,000 Jobs," *New York Times,* November 9, 1959.

10. A large part of the advantage of moving from New York to New Jersey in the 1920s, or from the Northeast to the South and West in the 1960s, was union avoidance. The system of collective bargaining in the United States, based on individual plant organizing and elections, has made it extremely difficult to achieve high rates of union density in the apparel industry.

11. Raskin, "Low Pay Called Pattern in City."

12. Raskin, "Dress Union Out in 7 State Strike." Also see A. H. Raskin, "Struck Industry Dresses a Nation," *New York Times,* March 11, 1958; A. H. Raskin, "Pact Is Reached in Dress Strike," *New York Times,* March 12, 1958; A. H. Raskin, "Dress Workers to Start Return to Shops Today," *New York Times,* March 13, 1958.

13. Raskin, "A Union with Power."

14. Stephen Sylvia, "Jobs, Trade, and Unions: The Politics of Employment

and Protectionism in West German and American Unions" (Ph.D. diss., Yale University, 1990).

15. Joan M. Jensen, "Inside and Outside the Unions: 1920–1980," in *A Needle, A Bobbin, A Strike: Women Needleworkers in America*, ed. Joan M. Jensen and Sue Davidson (Philadelphia: Temple University Press, 1984), 183–94.

16. A. H. Raskin, "Dressmaker to Pay Union $250,000 in South," *New York Times*, November 14, 1954.

17. "Union Builds a Plant in Civil War on Jobs," *New York Times*, July 27, 1954.

18. "Justices Reject a Curb on Labor," *New York Times*, July 9, 1954; "City Ousts Union Group," *New York Times*, March 13, 1955.

19. "Union Builds a Plant in Civil War on Jobs."

20. Gus Tyler, *Look for the Union Label*, 265.

21. Warren S. Hunsberger, *Japan and the United States in World Trade* (New York: Harper and Row, 1964), 304.

22. Calculated from U.S. House, Committee on Education and Labor, *Impact of Imports and Exports on Employment (Textiles)*.

23. Edna Bonacich, Lucie Cheng, Norma Chinchilla, Nora Hamilton, and Paul Ong, eds., *Global Production: The Apparel Industry in the Pacific Rim* (Philadelphia: Temple University Press, 1994), chap. 5.

24. Denney Freeston Jr. and Jeffrey S. Arpan, *The Competitive Status of the U.S. Fibers, Textiles, and Apparel Complex: A Study of the Influences of Technology in Determining International Industrial Competitive Advantage*, prepared by the Fibers, Textiles, and Apparel Industry Panel; Committee on Technology and Trade Issues of the Office of the Foreign Secretary; National Academy of Engineering; and the Commission on Engineering and Technical Systems, National Research Council (Washington, D.C.: National Academy Press, 1983).

25. U.S. House, Committee on Education and Labor, *Impact of Imports and Exports on Employment (Textiles)*, 212–27.

26. Leo Ullman, letter to the editor, *New York Times*, September 14, 1959.

27. Sylvia, "Jobs, Trade, and Unions," 171.

28. U.S. Senate, Committee on Commerce, *Problems of the Domestic Textile Industry*, February 6–7, 1961.

29. Ibid., 400, statement of Lawrence Phillips of Phillips–Van Heusen.

30. Jose de la Torre et al., "Corporate Adjustments and Import Competition in the U.S. Apparel Industry," *Journal of International Business Studies* 8 (spring-summer 1977): 6.

31. "11 Textile Groups Fight Tariff Cuts," *New York Times*, December 7, 1954. Out of thirteen industry associations mentioned in this article, five were apparel, rather than textile, producers: the National Association of Shirt, Pajama, and Sportswear Manufacturers; Underwear Institute; National Association of Blouse Manufacturers; International Association of Garment Manufacturers; and Southern Garment Manufacturers' Association of Nashville.

32. "U.S. Blouse Group Seeks Tariff Rise," *New York Times*, November 3, 1956.

33. A. H. Raskin, "Union Would Cut Clothing Imports: Amalgamated Scores 'Sweatshop' Competition of Hong Kong and Japan," *New York Times*, July 8, 1959.

34. U.S. Senate, Committee on Commerce, *Problems of the Domestic Textile Industry*, February 6–7, 1961, statement of Jacob S. Potofsky, general president of Amalgamated Clothing Workers of America, AFL-CIO.

35. Raskin, "Union Would Cut Clothing Imports."

36. U.S. Senate, Committee on Commerce, *Problems of the Domestic Textile Industry*, February 6–7, 1961, 545–46, testimony of Jacob S. Potofsky, general president of Amalgamated Clothing Workers of America, AFL-CIO.

37. A. H. Raskin, "Union Threatens to Boycott Japan: Clothing Workers Warn of Action as Talks on Quota Apparently Collapse," *New York Times*, December 29, 1960.

38. Mooney, "Labor Cautioned on Import Battle."

39. "Trade Council Fights Threat of Boycott on Japanese Cloth," *New York Times*, January 11, 1961.

40. David B. Yoffie, *Power and Protectionism: Strategies of the Newly Industrializing Countries* (New York: Columbia University Press, 1983), 4, 6.

41. See William R. Cline, *The Future of World Trade in Textiles and Apparel*, rev. ed. (Washington D.C.: Institute for International Economics, 1990), 4.

42. Robert Kuttner, *The Economic Illusion: False Choices between Prosperity and Social Justice* (Boston: Houghton Mifflin, 1984), 121–22.

43. Ying-Pik Choi, Hwa Soo Chung, and Nicholas Marian, *The Multi-Fibre Arrangement in Theory and Practice* (London: Frances Pinter Publishers, 1985), 17.

44. Cline, *The Future of World Trade in Textiles and Apparel*, 4.

45. In the Pastore Committee hearings of 1961, Lawrence Phillips, vice president of Phillips–Van Heusen, the well-known shirtmaker and spokesman for the Textile/Apparel Coalition for Trade, testified, "The only way it seems to me that this problem can be controlled is to establish a world wide quota based upon our domestic production of the particular items, and upon examination to find out what portion of this production we can absorb by way of imports." U.S. Senate, Committee on Commerce, *Problems of the Domestic Textile Industry*, February 6–7, 1961, 400.

46. Jaleel Ahmad, "The North American Clothing Industry," in *Trade, Protectionism, and Industrial Adjustment: Three North American Case Studies* (Ottawa: North-South Institute, 1989), 116. The Long-Term Arrangement was renewed in 1967 and 1970. By 1973 there were over eighty signatory countries.

47. I. M. Destler, Haruhiro Fukui, and Hideo Sato, *The Textile Wrangle: Conflict in Japanese American Relations, 1969–71* (London: Cornell University Press, 1979), 68; I. M. Destler, Hideo Sato, Priscilla Clapp, and Haruhiro

Fukui, *Managing an Alliance: The Politics of US-Japanese Relations* (Washington, D.C.: Brookings Institution, 1976), 35.

48. Richard Rothstein, *Keeping Jobs in Fashion: Alternatives to the Euthanasia of the US Apparel Industry* (Washington D.C.: Economic Policy Institute, 1989), 108.

49. Yoffie, *Power and Protectionism*, 48.

50. Cline, *The Future of World Trade in Textiles and Apparel*, 13, 41.

51. Rothstein, *Keeping Jobs in Fashion*, 108.

52. Jeffrey S. Arpan, Jose de la Torre, and Brian Toyne, *The US Apparel Industry: International Challenge, Domestic Response* (Atlanta: Georgia State University, 1982), 57.

53. I. M. Destler, *American Trade Politics*, 3d ed. (Washington, D.C.: Institute for International Economics and the Twentieth Century Fund, April 1995), 41–42

54. U.S. Congress, Office of Technology Assessment, *Trade Adjustment Assistance: New Ideas for an Old Program—Special Report*, OTA-ITE-346 (Washington, D.C.: GPO, June 1987), 28.

55. Ibid., 26–27.

56. See Ellen Israel Rosen, *Bitter Choices: Blue Collar Women In and Out of Work* (Chicago: University of Chicago Press, 1987).

57. Ibid.

58. Ahmad, "The North American Clothing Industry," 108; Organization for Economic Cooperation and Development, *Textile and Clothing Industries: Structural Problems and Policies in OECD Countries* (Paris: OECD, 1983).

59. Lauren A. Murray, "Unravelling Trends in Textiles and Apparel," *Monthly Labor Review* 118, no. 8 (August 1995): 62

60. Ahmad, "The North American Clothing Industry," 108; Organization for Economic Cooperation and Development, *Textile and Clothing Industries.*

61. Later on, as we will see, Latin America would become a new and more salient region for American apparel outsourcing.

62. Vinod K. Aggarwal with Stephan Haggard, "The Politics of Protection in the U.S. Textile and Apparel Industries," in *American Industry in International Competition: Government Policies and Corporate Strategies*, ed. John Zysman and Laura Tyson (Ithaca: Cornell University Press, 1983), 250–51.

63. U.S. Bureau of the Census, *1987 Census of Manufacturers: Concentration Ratios in Manufacturing*, MC87-S-6 (Washington, D.C., February 1992), table 5.

64. U.S. House, Committee on Education and Labor, *Impact of Imports and Exports on Employment (Textiles)*, 227, testimony of R. Dave Hall, president of the American Cotton Manufacturers' Institute, citing Secretary of State George W. Ball.

65. U.S. Senate, Committee on Finance, *A Bill to Amend the Trade Act of 1974: Hearing on S. 2920*, 95th Cong., 2d sess., August 15, 1978, 4.

CHAPTER 7

1. On the international division of labor, see Folker Froebel, Jurgen Heinrichs, and Otto Kreye, *The New International Division of Labor* (London: Cambridge University Press, 1980); on the deindustrialization of America, see Michael Dertouzos et al., *Made in America: Regaining the Productive Edge* (Cambridge: MIT Press, 1989). Also see MIT Commission on Industrial Productivity, Working Group on the Textile Industry, *The Working Papers of the MIT Commission on Industrial Productivity* (Cambridge: MIT Press, 1989).

2. U.S. House, Committee on Ways and Means, *The U.S. Trade Deficit*, 98th Cong., 2d sess., March 28–29, April 5, 10, 12, and 25, 1984. In this hearing Sam Gibbons pointed out that "the U.S. trade deficit has grown from $13 billion in 1976 to $69 billion in 1983. That is, of course, the merchandise trade deficit."

3. United Nations Conference on Trade and Development, Division on Transnational Corporations and Investment, *World Investment Directory*, vol. 4: *Latin America and the Caribbean, 1994* (Geneva: United Nations, 1994); United Nations Conference on Trade and Development, Division on Transnational Corporations and Investment, "World Investment Report, 1993: Transnational Corporations and Integrated International Production; an Executive Summary," prepared by David Gold, *Transnational Corporations* 2, no. 2 (August 1993): 99–123.

4. Elizabeth Martinez and Arnoldo Garcia, "What Is 'Neo-Liberalism'?: A Brief Definition for Activists," *Corporate Watch*, http://corpwatch.org/trac/issues/global/background/2000/neolib.html.

5. There are a number of ways of calculating the import penetration rate. This calculation is based on the value of domestic production plus imports, minus exports.

6. On Capitol Hill's concerns, see U.S. House, Committee on Ways and Means, *Current Conditions in the Textile and Apparel Industries*, 99th Cong., 1st sess., Washington, D.C., April 3, 1985; Helen, Georgia, April 5, 1985; Washington, D.C., July 15, 1985, 11, testimony of Walter C. Lenahan, Deputy Assistant Secretary for Textiles and Apparel, U.S. Department of Commerce.

7. Calculated from U.S. International Trade Commission, *US Imports of Textiles and Apparel under the Multifibre Arrangement*, Publication 2075 (Washington, D.C.: USITC, March 1988).

8. See Joseph Pelzman, "China's Economy Looks toward the Year 2000," in *Economic Openness in Modernizing China, Selected Papers*, Joint Economic Committee of the Congress of the United States, 99th Cong., vol. 2, Washington, D.C., May 21, 1986, Committee Print, 385, 405.

9. U.S. Congress, Office of Technology Assessment, *The US Textile and Apparel Industry: A Revolution in Progress* (Washington, D.C.: GPO, April 1987), 177–78.

10. Richard Wightman, "Retailers Hit Countervailing Duty Requests," *Daily News Record* 14 (August 3, 1984): 2.

11. "The Caribbean Clothing Industry: US and Far East Connections," Special Report No. 147, *Textile Outlook International* (London) (October 1988): 41.

12. "Over 20 Retailers, Trade Associations, Mobilize to Fight Import Quotas," *Discount Store News* 23 (July 9, 1984): 2; Jeffrey Arlen, "Some Big Stores Plan Ads to Fight Textile Bill," *Daily News Record* 15 (May 24, 1985): 4. According to Arlen, "RITAC has been opposing the administration's new system of automatic calls to negotiation and the new country of origin regulations, developing an industry consensus on preliminary negotiations to renew the MFA, and most recently opposing the Textile and Apparel Trade Enforcement Act of 1985."

13. "Customs Takes Notice of Fake Chinese Textile, Apparel Visas," *Daily News Record* 15 (March 27, 1985): 11; Mark Hosenball, "Imports from Communists Rise," *Women's Wear Daily* 155, no. 30 (February 12, 1988): 12.

14. Fariborz Ghadar, William H. Davidson, Charles S. Feigenoff, *U.S. Industrial Competitiveness: The Case of the Textile and Apparel Industries* (Lexington, Mass.: Lexington Books, 1987), 5.

15. "The Caribbean Clothing Industry," 46.

16. This suggests that the permeability of the MFA may owe more to how the U.S. government has chosen to implement this international agreement than to the requirements of the treaty, which are internationally binding.

17. U.S. House, Committee on Ways and Means, *Current Conditions in the Textile and Apparel Industries*, 22, testimony of Walter Lenahan.

18. Ibid.

19. Ibid., 11–12.

20. U.S. House, Committee on Ways and Means, *Current Conditions in the Textile and Apparel Industries*, July 15, 1985.

21. Ibid., April 3, 1985.

22. Stephen L. Lande, "Textiles," in *US Perspectives in US-Mexican Integration: The Road to Free Trade*, ed. Sidney Weintraub, with Luis F. Rubio and Alan D. Jones (Boulder, Colo.: Westview Press, 1991), 222; "Manufacturers, Unions Fight Apparel Imports; Prices, Supplies Would Be Affected," *Discount Store News* 24 (May 27, 1985): 2.

23. Thomas R. Howell and William A. Noellert, *The EEC and the Multifibre Arrangement: A Study Prepared for the Fiber, Fabric, and Apparel Coalition for Trade (FFACT)* (n.p.: FFACT, 1986); "The Caribbean Clothing Industry," 63.

24. In the face of import competition, some segments of the U.S. textile industry began to focus on developing new products, making textiles for household and industrial uses in lieu of apparel.

25. Cecil V. Crabb Jr. and Pat M. Holt, *Invitation to Struggle: Congress, the President, and Foreign Policy* (Washington, D.C.: CQ Press, 1992), 211.

26. "The Caribbean Clothing Industry," 44.

CHAPTER 8

1. I will refer to the countries that participated in the Caribbean Basin Economic Recovery Act of 1983 and its Special Access Program for Textiles and Apparel in 1986 as the CBI countries. Although the act referred to the Caribbean, some participating countries were in Central America. Over the years the number of participating countries has changed.

2. On the larger struggle between East and West, see Robert A. Pastor, "The U.S. and the Caribbean: The Power of the Whirlpool," *Annals of the American Association of Political and Social Science* 553 (May 1994): 25–28. On the maintenance of a secure environment for trade and investment in the region, see Leslie Sklair, "The CBI: An Overview," in *Imperial Power and Regional Trade: The Caribbean Basin Initiative,* ed. Abigail B. Bakan, David Cox, and Collin Leys (Waterloo, Ont.: Wilfrid Laurier University Press, 1993), 1–9; Nina M. Serafino, "Central America: Continuing U.S. Concerns," in *The Caribbean Basin: Economic and Security Issues,* study papers submitted to the Joint Economic Committee, 102d Cong., 2d sess., January 1993, S. Print 102–110, 179; *Caribbean-Central America Economic Revitalization Act of 1982,* 97th Cong., 2d sess., July 26, 1982, Report 97–665, pt. 1, p. 5.

3. Among them are theories of the new international division of labor, the commodity chain theory, the state-centered theories of Evans and others, the dependency theory, the dependent development theory, and so on.

4. Emilio Pantojas Garcia, "Restoring Hegemony: The Complementarity among the Security, Economic, and Political Components of US Policy in the Caribbean Basin during the 1980s," in *Conflict, Peace, and Development in the Caribbean,* ed. Jorge Rodriguez Beruff, J. Peter Figueroa, and J. Edward Greene (New York: St. Martin's Press, 1991), 30.

5. Quoted in Pastor, "The U.S. and the Caribbean," 28.

6. Jonathan E. Sanford, "U.S. Foreign Assistance to Central America: Policy and Programs, FY 1980 to 1993," in *The Caribbean Basin: Economic and Security Issues,* study papers submitted to the Joint Economic Committee, 102d Cong., 2d sess., January 1993, S. Print 102–110, 271.

7. Garcia, "Restoring Hegemony," 27.

8. *Caribbean-Central America Economic Revitalization Act of 1982,* 5.

9. William Corbett Jr., "A Wasted Opportunity: Shortcomings of the Caribbean Basin Initiative Approach to Development in the West Indies and Central America," *Law and Policy in International Business* 23, no. 4 (summer 1992): 951–85.

10. U.S. Senate, Committee on Foreign Relations, *National Bipartisan Report on Central America,* 98th Cong., 2d sess., February 7–8, 1984, testimony of Henry Kissinger.

11. The figure for U.S. aid comes from U.S. General Accounting Office, *Foreign Assistance: US Support for Caribbean Basin Assembly Industries,* GAO/NSIAD-94-31 (Washington, D.C.: GPO, December 1993), 20. Sanford, "US Foreign Assistance to Central America," 271.

12. U.S. General Accounting Office, *Foreign Assistance: Aid's Private Sector Assistance Program at a Crossroads*, GAO/NSIAD-93-55 (Washington, D.C.: GPO, January 1993), 2.

13. Sanford, "U.S. Foreign Assistance to Central America."

14. U.S. House, Committee on Ways and Means, *Caribbean Basin Economic Recovery Act*, 98th Cong., 1st sess., 1983, H. Rept. 98–266, 2.

15. Mark P. Sullivan, "Overview," in *The Caribbean Basin: Economic and Security Issues*, study papers submitted to the Joint Economic Committee, 102d Cong., 2d sess., January 1993, S. Print 102–110, vii–xxvii; Carmen Diana Deere et al., *In the Shadows of the Sun: Caribbean Development Alternatives and US Policy* (Boulder, Colo.: Westview Press, 1990); Garcia, "Restoring Hegemony," 27; also see U.S. Senate, Committee on Finance, *Hearing on S. Rept. 504 and H. Rept. 3299*, 101st Cong., 2d sess., testimony of U.S. Trade Representative Carla Hills.

16. Jean Marie Burgaud, "The New Caribbean Deal: The Next Five Years," Report No. 240, *Textile Outlook International* (London) (March 1986): 9.

17. U.S. House, Committee on Ways and Means, *Caribbean Basin Economic Recovery Act*, 97th Cong., 2d sess., December 10, 1982, H. Rept. 97–958, 3–4.

18. Carmen Diana Deere et al., *In the Shadows of the Sun*, 156–57.

19. The Del Monte Company had done this in Costa Rica by investing in a pineapple plantation, which enabled it to bring the fruit from Costa Rica rather than Hawaii.

20. U.S. General Accounting Office, *Caribbean Basin Initiative: Impact on Selected Countries, July 1988*, report to the chairman, Subcommittee on Western Hemisphere and Peace Corps Affairs, Committee on Foreign Relations, U.S. Senate, July 1988, 8. In December 1984, the president had directed "all Administration officials to give programs relating to the Caribbean Basin their personal attention and the institutional support needed for success."

21. U.S. House, Committee on Ways and Means, *Review of the Impact and Effectiveness of the Caribbean Basin Initiative*, 99th Cong., 2d sess., February 25 and 27, 1986, 162, statement of Thomas O. Kay, administrator of the Foreign Agricultural Service, U.S. Department of Agriculture.

22. Ibid., 69, 72, statement of Bruce Smart, undersecretary of commerce, International Trade Administration, Department of Commerce, Basin Business Information Center.

23. Ibid., 69–72.

24. U.S. House, Committee on Ways and Means, *Report on the Committee Delegation Mission to the Caribbean Basin and Recommendations to Improve the Effectiveness of the Caribbean Basin Initiative*, 100th Cong., 1st sess., May 6, 1987, Committee Print WMPC 100–9; *Caribbean-Central America Economic Revitalization Act of 1982*, 7.

25. Serafino, "Central America," 179.

26. U.S. House, Committee on Ways and Means, *Review of the Impact and Effectiveness of the Caribbean Basin Initiative*, 418–19, statement of Craig

VanGrasstek. VanGrasstek documents that 47.87 percent of the value of all CBI imports was ineligible by statute. Another 33.42 percent was not dutiable, while 5.67 percent was duty-free as a result of privileges under the Generalized System of Preferences. Finally, 6.59 percent remained ineligible for benefits. Thus only 6.45 percent of CBI exports that year were newly provided with duty-free entry.

27. U.S. House, Committee on Ways and Means, *Hearing before the Subcommittee on Oversight*, 101st Cong., 2d sess., April 3, 1990, Serial 101–97.

28. Eva Paus, "A Critical Look at Nontraditional Export Demand: The Caribbean Basin Initiative," in *Struggle against Dependence: Export Growth in Central America and the Caribbean*, ed. Eva Paus (Boulder, Colo.: Westview Press, 1988), 202–3.

29. U.S. House, Committee on Ways and Means, *Report on the Committee Delegation Mission to the Caribbean Basin and Recommendations to Improve the Effectiveness of the Caribbean Basin Initiative*. In November 1985, the Customs Service ruled in favor of ethanol imports from the Tropicana company. See Burgaud, "The New Caribbean Deal," 22.

30. U.S. Senate, Committee on Finance, *Caribbean Basin Initiative Hearing*, 101st Cong., 2d sess., 1989.

31. U.S. House, Committee on Ways and Means, *Review of the Impact and Effectiveness of the Caribbean Basin Initiative*, 415, 420.

32. U.S. General Accounting Office, *Caribbean Basin Initiative: Need for More Reliable Data on Business Activity Resulting from the Initiative*, NSIAD-86–201BR (Washington, D.C.: GPO, August 1986). This report indicated that the Department of Commerce study which had claimed that a large number of investments had been made by U.S. companies in the Caribbean countries and Central America as a result of the CBI was unsubstantiated and incorrect.

33. See Sullivan, "Overview."

34. Business International Corporation, *Improving International Competitiveness through Sourcing in Latin America* (New York: Business International Corporation, 1989), 126–27.

35. Ibid., 127.

36. Stephen L. Lande, "Textiles," in *US Perspective in US Mexican Integration: The Road to Free Trade*, ed. Sidney Weintraub, with Luis F. Rubio and Alan D. Jones (Boulder, Colo.: Westview Press, 1991), 223. From 1977 to 1987 the mill sector increased productivity by an average of 3.9 percent annually, mostly as a result of investments in weaving mills. Productivity in overall manufacturing increased at an average annual rate of 3.1 percent. Imports of textile mill products accounted for less than 10 percent of U.S. consumption of such products, compared with apparel imports, which accounted for almost one-third of U.S. consumption. Capital expenditures in the textile mill industry from 1984 to 1986 were 14.8 percent higher than from 1981 to 1983. The investment rate climbed even more dramatically in 1987, rising 17.4 percent over that of the previous year.

37. U.S. International Trade Commission, *Imports under Items 806.30 and 807.00 of the Tariff Schedules of the United States, 1982–1985*, Report No. 1920 (Washington, D.C., December 1986), p. 1–1.

38. Ibid., pp. 1–4, 1–5, 1–9.

39. U.S. House, Committee on Ways and Means, *The Trade Reform Act of 1973: Hearings on H.R. 6767*, 93rd Cong., 1st sess., May 10–11, 1973. Aside from Lazare Teper, the panel consisted of Sol Stetin, general president of the TWUA; and Howard Samuel, vice president of the ACWA.

40. Joseph Grunwald and Kenneth Flamm, *The Global Factory: Foreign Assembly in International Trade*, ed. Joseph Grunwald and Kenneth Flamm (Washington, D.C.: Brookings Institution, 1985), 14–17.

41. "Lovable's Costa Rican Operation Thrives," *Bobbin Magazine* (April 1985): 66–70; Edna Bonacich, "The Swimwear Sector of the Los Angeles Garment Industry" (unpublished manuscript, 1991).

42. U.S. International Trade Commission, *Imports under Items 806.30 and 807.00 of the Tariff Schedules of the United States, 1982–1985*, pp. 4–6 to 4–8.

43. "The Caribbean Clothing Industry: US and Far East Connections, Special Report, No. 147," *Economist Intelligence Unit* (October 1988): 21.

44. See U.S. Tariff Commission, *Economic Factors Affecting the Use of Item 807.00 and 806.30 on the Tariff Schedules of the United States*, Tariff Commission Publication No. 339 (Washington, D.C.: GPO, 1970), 9.

45. Barry E. Truchil, *Capital-Labor Relations in the U.S. Textile Industry* (Greenwood Press, 1988), 114.

46. Thomas G. Travis, "807 Decision 'Unexpected,'" *Bobbin Magazine* (July 1985): 157–58; U.S. House, Committee on Ways and Means, *Current Conditions in the Textile and Apparel Industries*, 99th Cong., 1st sess., July 15, 1985, 243, statement of Ronald Kohn, president of the American Caribbean Trade Association.

47. Calculated from U.S. Agency for International Development, *Latin America and the Caribbean: Selected Economic and Social Data* (Washington D.C., 1991). Eight countries—Costa Rica, El Salvador, Guatemala, Honduras, Panama, the Dominican Republic, Haiti, and Jamaica—produced the vast majority of these exports.

48. Stuart B. Chirls, "Charge US Does Little to Encourage 807 Plant," *Daily News Record* 15 (July 2, 1985): 2.

49. Lloyd Schwartz, "Manufacturers, Importers Again Slug It Out in Capitol," *Daily News Record* (September 27, 1984): 8.

50. Anna Cifelli, "Friends of Free Trade," *Fortune* 110 (August 20, 1984): 153; Richard Wightman, "Retail Group Being Formed to Fight for Freer US Trade," *Women's Wear Daily* 147 (June 21, 1984): 7.

51. Richard I. Hersch, "Discounters Must Keep Fighting Harmful Reform," *Discount Store News* 24 (January 21, 1985): 6.

52. Travis, "807 Decision 'Unexpected,'" 157–58; "Blue Bell Is Alive and Operating in Honduras," *Bobbin Magazine* (November 1985): 131–37. Mem-

bers of RITAC included Kmart, Zayre Corporation, May Department Stores, Associated Dry Goods, Federated Department Stores, R. H. Macy, Tandy, Associated Merchandising Corporation, Balliet's, Batus Retail Group, Dayton Hudson Corporation, Edison Bros. Stores, Proffitts, Selber Bros., Spiegel, and Zale Corporation. Associations in RITAC included the Association of General Merchandise Chains, National Mass Retailing Institute, American Retail Federation, National Retail Merchants Association, American Retail Federation, and Volume Footwear Retailers of America. See Cifelli, "Friends of Free Trade"; Mark Hosenball, "Caribbean-Based Firms Ask Trade Concessions on Apparel," *Daily News Record* 14 (September 21, 1984): 16.

53. Richard Wightman, "Stores Aim Big Guns at Trade Bars," *Women's Wear Daily* 14 (June 28, 1984): 1; Wightman, "Retail Group Being Formed to Fight for Freer US Trade," 7; Lisa Lockwood, "Importers, Stores Sue over Rules," *Women's Wear Daily* 148 (August 30, 1984): 1.

54. Cifelli, "Friends of Free Trade."

55. Wightman, "Retail Group Being Formed to Fight for Freer US Trade," 7.

56. Jeffrey Arlen, "Retailers to Seek Allies in Free Trade Battle," *Daily News Record* 15 (January 17, 1985): 1. Arlen writes, "On its own RITAC will spend $1 million in 1985 to further its efforts to eliminate existing apparel quotas as dictated by the Multifibre Arrangement."

57. Scott Wylie, "CBI Related Developments," *Business America* 8 (January 7, 1985): 6. The Lome Convention was signed December 8, 1984, extending duty-free access to the EEC for five years. The aid, trade, and investment benefits of Lome III apply to sixty-four African, Caribbean, and Pacific (ACP) countries, including eleven CBI beneficiaries. The program provides $6.4 billion in EEC economic aid worldwide over the five-year period, and allows one-way duty-free access for virtually all ACP exports meeting the newly simplified rules of origin. Thus, using both CBI and Lome Convention benefits, U.S. firms with Caribbean manufacturing sites can gain duty-free access to EEC and U.S. markets.

58. Cifelli, "Friends of Free Trade."

59. Lande, "Textiles," 222; "Manufacturers, Unions Fight Apparel Imports: Prices, Supplies Would Be Affected," *Discount Store News* 24 (May 27, 1985): 2.

60. "US Textile Executives Invited to Eye Jamaica for '807,'" *Daily News Record* 14 (July 23, 1984): 3.

61. "Holderman Gives 807 Program the 'Old College Try,'" *Daily News Record* 14 (December 10, 1984): 10.

62. Garcia, "Restoring Hegemony," 33–34.

63. William E. James and Masaru Umemoto, "NAFTA Trade with East Asia," *ASEAN Economic Bulletin* 17, no. 3 (December 2000): 293; Kala Krishna and Anne O. Krueger, "Implementing Free Trade Areas: Rules of Origin and Hidden Protection," in *New Directions in Trade Theory*, ed. Alan

Deardorf, James Levinsohn, and Robert Stern (Ann Arbor: University of Michigan Press, 1995); Anne O. Krueger, "Free Trade Agreements versus Customs Unions," *Journal of Development Economics* 54 (1997): 169–87.

64. Kenneth M. Chanko, "Quota Rollbacks Best Import Tonic," *Daily News Record* 14 (December 13, 1984): 1.

65. "The Caribbean Clothing Industry: U.S. and Far East Connections," 46.

66. Calculated from U.S. International Trade Commission, "Production Sharing: US Imports under Harmonized Tariff Schedule Subheadings 9802.0060 and 9802.0080, 1986–1989," in *Summary Report*, USITC Publication 2349 L (Washington, D.C.: GPO, January 1991), 29, table 22.

67. U.S. Department of Commerce, International Trade Administration, *1991 Caribbean Basin Investment Survey* (Washington, D.C., February 1991); *The Caribbean Basin: Economic and Security Issues*, study papers submitted to the Joint Economic Committee, 102d Cong., 2d sess., January 1993, S. Print 102–110; "The Caribbean Clothing Industry: U.S. and Far East Connections."

68. Travis, "807 Decision 'Unexpected,' " 158.

69. "The Caribbean Clothing Industry: U.S. and Far East Connections," 9.

70. "807: Our Domestic Industry's White Knight," *Bobbin Magazine* (January 1986): 22.

71. U.S. House, Committee on Ways and Means, *Caribbean Basin Free Trade Agreement Act*, 103rd Cong., 1st sess., June 24, 1993, 113, statement of Andrew F. Postal, president of Judy Bond, New York, on behalf of Caribbean/ Latin American Action.

72. Calculated from "The Caribbean Clothing Industry: U.S. and Far East Connections."

73. Ibid.

74. "Asian Tigers Leap into Central America," *Business Latin America: A Weekly Report to Managers of Latin American Operations* (December 16, 1991): 401–2. Also see Charles Kernaghan and Barbara Briggs, *Paying to Lose Our Jobs* (New York: National Labor Committee in Support of Worker and Human Rights in Central America, 1992). This report documents the U.S. apparel firms having investments in Honduras and Guatemala.

75. U.S. General Accounting Office, *Foreign Assistance*, 44.

76. U.S. House, Committee on Ways and Means, *Current Conditions in the Textile and Apparel Industries*, statement of Ronald Kohn, president of the American Caribbean Trade Association.

77. U.S. Agency for International Development, *Latin America and the Caribbean*.

78. Calculated from U.S. International Trade Commission, *Annual Statistical Report on US Imports of Textiles and Apparel*, Investigation No. 332–343, Publication 3102 (Washington, D.C., April 1998), 15.

79. Joel Millman, "It's Working," *Forbes* 145, no. 4 (February 19, 1990): 10.

80. Business International Corporation, *Improving International Compet-*

itiveness through Sourcing in Latin America, 17; Khosrow Fatemi, ed., *The Maquiladora Industry: Economic Solution or Problem?* (New York: Praeger 1990), 12.

81. U.S. House, Committee on Ways and Means, *Caribbean Basin Economic Recovery Act,* H. Rept. No. 97–958, December 10, 1982, 37, cited in Devanand J. Ramnarine, "The Philosophy and Development Prospects of the CBI," in *Imperial Power and Regional Trade: The Caribbean Basin Initiative,* ed. Abigail B. Bakan, David Cox, and Collin Leys (Waterloo, Ont.: Wilfrid Laurier University Press, 1993).

82. Business International Corporation, *Improving International Competitiveness through Sourcing in Latin America,* 8, 12.

83. Ibid., 13.

84. Ibid., 7–10.

85. Kernaghan and Briggs, *Paying to Lose Our Jobs,* 17–18.

86. U.S. General Accounting Office, *Foreign Assistance,* 24.

87. According to one source, CINDE maintained an office in Stamford, Connecticut, "in order to be close to apparel manufacturers in New Jersey and New York." Linda Corman, "Local Companies Consider the Caribbean," *Boston Business Journal* (August 8, 1988). The Spanish acronyms FIDE, CINDE, FUSADES, and IPC refer to the Foundation for Investment and Development in Honduras, Costa Rican Investment and Development Agency, Foundation for Economic and Social Development in El Salvador, and Investment Promotion Council of the Dominical Republic, respectively.

88. U.S. General Accounting Office, *Foreign Assistance,* 27.

89. See Kernaghan and Briggs, *Paying to Lose Our Jobs;* "We're Creating Jobs in the Third World: AID's Role," *New York Times,* August 1, 1995; Helen Zia, "Made in the USA," *Ms.* 6, no. 4 (January-February 1996): 66; Frederick C. Deyo, ed., *The Political Economy of the New Asian Industrialization* (Ithaca: Cornell University Press, 1987).

90. U.S. General Accounting Office, *Foreign Assistance,* 27.

91. The report pointed out that *maquiladoras* had developed without any financial assistance because low-wage labor and proximity to U.S. markets were the major incentives for apparel assembly. However, this GAO report does not provide sufficient evidence to reach a conclusion about the role played by U.S. foreign aid in the growth of CBI apparel assembly.

CHAPTER 9

1. U.S. Senate, Committee on Foreign Relations, *Trade vs. Aid: NAFTA Five Years Later,* 106th Cong., 1st sess., April 13, 1999, testimony of Charles W. McMillion, MBG Information Services, Washington, D.C.

2. U.S. General Accounting Office, *U.S.-Mexico Trade: The Maquiladora Industry and U.S. Employment,* GAO/GGD-93–129 (Washington, D.C.: GPO, July 1993), 1.

3. Twenty-Eighth Mexico–United States Interparliamentary Conference,

"United States–Mexico Economic Relations: An Overview," Congressional Research Service Report for Congress, February 1988, 244–52.

4. Khosrow Fatemi, introduction to *The Maquiladora Industry: Economic Solution or Problem?* ed. Khosrow Fatemi (New York: Praeger, 1990), 9; Twenty-Eighth Mexico–United States Interparliamentary Conference, "United States–Mexico Economic Relations," 244–52.

5. Joseph Grunwald and Kenneth Flamm, *The Global Factory: Foreign Assembly in International Trade,* ed. Joseph Grunwald and Kenneth Flamm (Washington, D.C.: Brookings Institution, 1985), 149–50.

6. U.S. International Trade Commission, *Imports under Items 806.30 and 807.00 of the Tariff Schedules of the United States, 1982–1985,* Report No. 1920, December 1986, 1–8. Also see Grunwald and Flamm, *The Global Factory,* 149.

7. Fatemi, introduction to *The Maquiladora Industry,* 9.

8. According to Grunwald and Flamm, "In dollars, maquiladora wages increased until 1981, interrupted only by a temporary decline as result of the 1976 devaluation of the peso. Thus, dollar wages increased more than 50% between 1973 and 1975—while Mexican purchasing power of assembly wages increased 13%—and about 80% between 1977 and 1981." See Grunwald and Flamm, *The Global Factory,* 149–50.

9. Joan B. Anderson, "Maquiladoras in the Apparel Industry," in *The Maquiladora Industry: Economic Solution or Problem?* ed. Khosrow Fatemi (New York: Praeger, 1990), 103–6.

10. Barbara A. Crispin, "Employment and Manpower Development in Mexico," in *The Maquiladora Industry: Economic Solution or Problem?* ed. Khosrow Fatemi et al. (New York: Praeger, 1990); Marc N. Scheinman, "Report on the Present Status of Maquiladoras," in *The Maquiladora Industry: Economic Solution or Problem?* ed. Khosrow Fatemi (New York: Praeger, 1990), 22; U.S. General Accounting Office, *International Trade: Commerce Department Conference on Mexico's Maquiladora Program: Briefing Report to the Chairman, Subcommittee on Commerce, Consumer Protection, and Competitiveness, Committee on Energy and Commerce House of Representatives* (Washington, D.C., April 1987).

11. David Gold, "World Investment Report 1993: Transnational Corporations and Integrated International Production: An Executive Summary," *Transnational Corporations* 2, no. 2 (August 1993): 99–123.

12. Ibid.

13. Jean Marie Burgaud, "The New Caribbean Deal: The Next Five Years," *Textile Outlook International,* Economist Intelligence Unit, Report No. 240, March 1986, 15.

14. U.S. General Accounting Office, *North American Free Trade Agreement: U.S. Mexican Trade and Investment Data* (Washington, D.C., September 25, 1992), 8–9.

15. U.S. Agency for International Development, *Latin America and the*

Caribbean: Selected Economic and Social Data (Washington D.C., 1991), 65–77.

16. Ibid.

17. Jaleel Ahmad, "The North American Clothing Industry," in *Trade, Protectionism, and Industrial Adjustment: Three North American Case Studies* (Ottawa: North-South Institute, 1989), 74.

18. Eduardo Lachica, "US and Mexico Reach Trade Pact Covering Textiles," *Wall Street Journal,* January 6, 1988.

19. William A. Reed and Miguel Montero, "Will NAFTA-Mexico Be a Plus or Minus for You?" *Textile World* 143, no. 2 (February 1993): 33.

20. The 807 trade regime was renamed USTS 9802 in 1987.

21. Calculated from U.S. International Trade Commission, *Annual Statistical Report on US Imports of Textiles and Apparel, 1997,* 15.

22. U.S. House, Committee on Ways and Means, *Caribbean Basin Free Trade Agreements Act, Written Statement of the Florida International Affairs Commission, Addressing H.R. 1403,* 103d Cong., 2d sess., June 24, 1993, 104.

23. Glen Segal and Thomas M. Rosenthal, "Putting Textile and Apparel Trade in One Basket: Hialeah—South Florida's Workhorse," *Bobbin Magazine* (January 1990): 12–16; Alan G. Milstein, "Miami Postured for Apparel Boom," *Bobbin Magazine* 32, no. 7 (March 1991): 64–71; "Lectra Opens 807 Facility in Miami," *Daily News Record* 20, no. 71 (April 11, 1990): 8.

24. Andrew Lowry, "Caribbean Basin: US Firms in Good Position to Share in Future Growth," *Business America* 3, no. 8 (April 23, 1990): 27.

25. Elizabeth Chute, "Bush Seeks Action on CBI Expansion," *Daily News Record* 19, no. 233 (November 29, 1989): 6.

26. Lowry, "Caribbean Basin."

27. United Nations Conference on Trade and Development, Division on Transnational Corporations and Investment, *World Investment Directory,* vol. 4: *Latin America and the Caribbean, 1994.*

28. Ibid.

29. David Hale, "The Trade Revolution," *Wall Street Journal,* November 3, 1993, sec. A, p. 22.

30. Richard Rothstein, *Keeping Jobs in Fashion: Alternatives to the Euthanasia of the US Apparel Industry* (Washington D.C.: Economic Policy Institute, 1989).

31. U.S. House, Committee on Ways and Means, Subcommittee on Trade, *President's Comprehensive Review of the North American Free Trade Agreement,* 105th Cong., 1st sess., September 11, 1997, testimony of Sidney Weintraub, William E. Simon Chair in Political Economy, Center for Strategic and International Studies.

32. Ibid., testimony of Larry A. Liebenow, president and chief executive of Quaker Fabric Corporation, Fall River, Massachusetts, and chairman, Western Hemisphere Task Force, U.S. Chamber of Commerce.

33. Mike Youssef, "International Trade and Development: Mexico Still to

288 / *Notes to pages 161–164*

Face a Large Foreign Debt and Costly Debt Screening," *International Economic Review* (December 1996–January 1997): 10.

34. Ibid.

35. Stephen L. Lande, "Textiles," in *US Perspective in US Mexican Integration: The Road to Free Trade*, ed. Sidney Weintraub, with Luis F. Rubio and Alan D. Jones (Boulder, Colo.: Westview Press, 1991), 27–28. Also see U.S. International Trade Commission, *The Likely Impact on the United States of a Free Trade Agreement with Mexico*, Publication 2353 (Washington, D.C.: USITC, February 1991), viii; Refik Erzan and Alexander Yeats, *Free Trade Agreements with the United States: What's in It for Latin America?* World Bank Policy Research Working Paper No. WPS827 (Washington D.C.: World Bank, January 1992).

36. Charles W. McMillion, *Assessing NAFTA: What Is So Different about US-Mexico Trade Six Years after NAFTA?*, rev. ed. (Washington, D.C.: MBG Associates, 1997; September 1999), 2. McMillion cites the *International Financial Statistics Yearbook: 1998* (Washington, D.C.: International Monetary Fund, 1998), 626–27.

37. U.S. House, Committee on Government Operations, *North American Free Trade Agreement: Are There Jobs for American Workers?* 103rd Cong., 1st sess., May 27, 1993, statement of Thea Lee, Economic Policy Institute.

38. Ibid., statement of Jeffrey Schott, Institute for International Economics.

39. U.S. Senate, Committee on Foreign Relations, *Trade vs. Aid: NAFTA Five Years Later*, testimony of Deputy U.S. Trade Representative Richard W. Fisher.

40. Ibid., testimony of Charles W. McMillion.

41. U.S. Department of Labor, Bureau of Labor Statistics, *International Comparisons of Hourly Compensation Costs for Production Workers in Manufacturing, 1975–1998* (Washington, D.C., September 1998), table 1.

42. U.S. Senate, Committee on Foreign Relations, *Trade vs. Aid*, testimony of Charles W. McMillion.

43. "Is the Mexican Model Worth the Pain?" *Wall Street Journal*, March 8, 1999, p. 1.

44. American Textile Manufacturers' Institute, "Study Shows Increases in US Textile Industry Shipments and Employment with Yarn-Forward Caribbean Basin Initiative Trade Legislation—Doubles US Shipment and Employment from Alternative Proposal" (Washington, D.C.: American Textile Manufacturers' Institute, September 20, 1999, photocopy), press release. This document includes a statement by Doug Ellis, president of American Textile Manufacturers' Institute, regarding the Senate filibuster on the Caribbean Basin Initiative Trade Bill that took place October 28, 1999.

45. Reed and Montero, "Will NAFTA-Mexico Be Plus or Minus for You?"

46. Rachael Kamel and Anya Hoffman, eds., *The Maquiladora Reader: Cross Border Organizing since NAFTA* (Philadelphia: American Friends Service Committee, 1999).

47. U.S. International Trade Commission, *Production Sharing: Use of US*

Components and Materials in Foreign Assembly Operations, 1992–1995, Publication 3032 (Washington, D.C.: USITC, April 1997).

48. Joyce Barrett, "US Apparel Makers Plan Big Push for CBI Parity," *Women's Wear Daily* 174, no. 12 (July 17, 1997): 14; Joyce Barrett, "US Makers Split on CBI Parity," *Women's Wear Daily* 174, no. 31 (August 17, 1997): 12.

49. U.S. International Trade Commission, *Production Sharing,* 1–9.

50. Larry Luxner, "CBI Grows but Mexico Dominates," *Bobbin Magazine* (November 1995).

51. U.S. House, Committee on Ways and Means, *The Caribbean Basin Trade Security Act,* 104th Cong., 1st sess., February 10, 1995, 110, testimony of Howard A. Vine, representative of the Central American–Caribbean Textile and Apparel Council.

52. Mimi Whitefield, "What Mexico Has, Caribbean Wants," *Miami Herald,* April 7, 1997.

53. Ibid.

54. Larry Rohter, "Backlash from NAFTA Batters Economies of Caribbean," *New York Times,* January 30, 1997; Mimi Whitefield, "NAFTA: Cost Factors Blamed in Closings of Jamaican Apparel Factories," *Tribune Business News,* April 13, 1997; Mimi Whitefield, "Tearing the Fabric of an Industry," *Miami Herald,* April 7, 1997.

55. U.S. International Trade Commission, "Customs Value of Apparel Imports for All Countries, U.S. Imports for Consumption, Annual Data" (http://dataweb.usitc.gor/REPORT.asp), January 10, 2001; "99 Percent Perspiration: Honduras," *Economist* 343, no. 8022 (June 21, 1997): 36. Apparel exports have increased most rapidly from some of the CBI countries that, in the early 1980s, were regions of political instability and left-wing insurgency, e.g., the Dominican Republic, Honduras, Guatemala, El Salvador, Haiti, and Nicaragua.

56. Dani Rodrik, *Democracies Pay Higher Wages,* National Bureau of Economic Research Working Paper 6364, revised October 1998. Cited by Jay Mazur in his congressional testimony; see U.S. House, Committee on Ways and Means, *The Caribbean and Central American Relief and Economic Stabilization Act: Hearing on HR 984,* 106th Cong., 1st sess., March 23, 1999, testimony of Jay Mazur, president of UNITE.

57. Comision Economic para America latin y el Caribe, Maquila y transformacion productive en Mexico y centroamerica, LC/Mex/r.6.30, 28 de octubre de 1997. Translated by UNITE from the original Spanish.

58. U.S. House, Committee on Government Operations, *North American Free Trade Agreement: Rules of Origin and Enforcement Issues, Fourth Report,* 103d Cong., 1st sess., November 22, 1993, 11–15.

59. Peter Buxbaum, "When Your Shipment Doesn't Arrive Intact," *Transportation and Distribution* 36, no. 8 (August 1995): 43.

60. Charles R. Harris, "Global Benchmarks Measure Tomorrow's Apparel Firms," *Apparel Industry Magazine* 55, no. 10 (October 1994): 56–62.

61. Geoffrey Bannister and Patrick Low, "Textiles and Apparel in NAFTA:

A Case of Constrained Liberalization," World Bank Policy Research Working Paper WPS994 (Washington D.C.: World Bank, October 1992), 11–12.

62. Shirley H. Jones and Graham Anderton, "Shaping Strategic Alliances in Mexico," *Bobbin Magazine* (January 1995). Also see Susan S. Black et al., "Outlook Bright, but Not without Hurdles for Americas, CBI," *Bobbin Magazine* (May 1997); Suzette Hill, "Burlington Adds Retail-Ready with Garment Services," *Apparel Industry Magazine* (January 2000).

63. Lisa C. Rabon, "Make Room for New Mindsets," *Bobbin Magazine* (September 1996): 114–20.

64. Barbara Foxenberger, "Major Technology Show Debuts in Mexico City This Month," *Apparel Industry Magazine* 55 (March 1994): 56–58.

65. Black et al., "Outlook Bright, but Not without Hurdles for Americas, CBI."

66. "Joint Ventures Industrializing Latin America," *Apparel Industry Magazine* (April 1998).

67. Jones and Anderton, "Shaping Strategic Alliances in Mexico."

68. David Brookstein, "US Textiles Has Global Opportunities," *Textile World* 147, no. 2 (February 1997): 79–81.

69. Hector Figueroa, "In the Name of Fashion: Exploitation in the Garment Industry" (Report on Transnational Investment), *NACLA Report on the Americas* 29, no. 4 (January-February 1996): 34–40. It is hardly surprising, then, that so much of the casual clothing purchasable in retail outlets is made of denim.

70. Christopher Palmeri and Jose Aguayo, "Goodbye Hong Kong, Hello Jalisco," *Forbes* 159, no. 3 (February 10, 1997): 76.

71. Jane Bussey, "Changes in the Material World: NAFTA Paving Way for Mexican Apparel Industry," *Miami Herald*, April 7, 1997.

72. Figueroa, "In the Name of Fashion," 3; Raye Rudie, "Textile Report: Mills Making Apparel," *Bobbin Magazine* (September 1997): 134–52.

73. Rudie, "Textile Report," 134–52.

74. National Labor Committee in Support of Worker and Human Rights in Central America, "Who's Who: Top US Apparel Companies Contracting Production in China," January 25, 2000 (http://www.nlcnet.org/China/whos who.htm).

75. Judi Kessler, "Tarrant, GSI on Successful Expansion in Mexico" *Bobbin Magazine* (November 1999).

76. Jules Abend, "Sourcing: US Mills Move South," *Bobbin Magazine* (November 1999).

77. "New Ventures, New Markets," *Apparel Industry Magazine* (June 1999).

78. Abend, "Sourcing."

79. Ibid.; Suzette Hill, "Burlington Adds Retail-Ready with Garment Services," *Apparel Industry Magazine* (January 2000).

80. Abend, "Sourcing."

81. Ibid.

82. "Zaga Rally in Mexico to Fight Asian Imports," *Apparel Industry Magazine* (May 1999).

83. "How Levi's Trashed a Great American Brand: While Bob Haas Pioneered Benevolent Management, His Company Came Apart at the Seams," *Fortune* 139, no. 7 (April 12, 1999): 82; Stacy Perman, "Levi's Gets the Blues: The Once Cool Brand Is Out of Step with Young Buyers," *Time* 150, no. 21 (November 17, 1997): 66.

84. Jeff Moad, "Coming Unzipped: Levi Strauss' Business Process Reengineering Plan's Demise," *PC Week* 14, no. 48 (November 17, 1997): 141.

85. "How Levi's Trashed a Great American Brand," 54.

86. "Patching Up Levi's: Levi Strauss & Company Tries to Catch Market Share," *US News and World Report* 126, no. 9 (March 8, 1999): 54.

87. Moad, "Coming Unzipped," 141; Perman, "Levi's Gets the Blues," 66.

88. Maintaining its historical commitment to good labor management relations, Levi Strauss offered a generous severance package to its displaced workers. "Levi's Offers Package for Laid Off Workers," *Business Insurance* (March 15, 1999): 47.

89. "UNITE Reacts to Strauss Plant Closings," United Press International (New York), February 22, 1999, p. 1008053u2004.

90. Holly Welling, "Differentiation: Drano for the Denim Glut?" *Apparel Industry Magazine* (January 2000).

91. "Mexico's Fast Trip to the Top," *Women's Wear Daily* 170, no. 109 (December 12, 1995): 7.

92. Calculated from U.S. International Trade Commission, U.S. Department of Commerce, DATAWEB, February 13, 2000.

93. Gary Gereffi, Martha Martinez, and Jennifer Blair, "Torreon: The New Blue Jeans Capital of the World" (paper presented to the Annual Meeting of the American Sociological Association, Washington, D.C., August 2000).

94. Elizabeth Chute, "Mexico Key in Trade Talks," *Women's Wear Daily* 168, no. 58 (September 25, 1990): 12.

95. Andres Serbin, "Towards an Association of Caribbean States: Raising Some Awkward Questions," *Journal of Interamerican Studies and World Affairs* 36, no. 4 (winter 1994): 61.

96. Larry Luxner, "Regional Integration Effects Produce Winners, Losers," *Bobbin Magazine* (November 1996): 49–54.

97. Thomas G. Travis, "NAFTA in a Nutshell for Textile and Apparel Producers," *Apparel Industry Magazine* (October 1998).

98. James A. Morrissey, "Textile Trade Grows between US, Latin America," *Textile World* 146 (April 1996): 26.

99. Jim Ostroff, "New Players to Join NAFTA?: A Look at the Impact of Various Trade Pacts throughout the Western Hemisphere," *Women's Wear Daily* 174, no. 35 (August 19, 1997): 11.

100. U.S. International Trade Commission, U.S. Department of Commerce,

DATAWEB, February 13, 2000. These countries include Colombia, Peru, Brazil, Bolivia, Ecuador, Uruguay, Venezuela, Argentina, Paraguay, Bermuda, Anguilla, and the Cayman Islands.

101. Ibid.

102. Welling, "Differentiation."

103. "Sourcing Moves West, Thanks to NAFTA," *Women's Wear Daily* 169, no. 34 (February 21, 1995): 39.

104. U.S. Senate, Committee on Foreign Relations, *Trade vs. Aid*, testimony of U.S. Deputy Trade Representative Richard W. Fisher.

105. Jules Abend, "CMA Grapples with Sourcing Issues," *Bobbin Magazine* (July 1997): 8–10.

106. Amy Glasmeier, James M. Campbell, and June M. Henton, "Tequila Sunset? NAFTA and the US Apparel Industry," *Challenge* (November-December 1993): 37–45.

107. See Edna Bonacich and Richard Appelbaum, *Behind the Label: Inequality in the Los Angeles Apparel Industry* (Berkeley and Los Angeles: University of California Press, 2000).

CHAPTER 10

1. Frederick H. Abernathy, John T. Dunlop, Janice H. Hammond, and David Weil, *A Stitch in Time: Lean Retailing and the Transformation of Manufacturing—Lessons from the Apparel and Textile Industries* (New York: Oxford University Press, 1999). This book is among the most scholarly and empirically sound treatments of this position.

2. Barry Bluestone et al., *The Retail Revolution: Market Transformation, Investment, and Labor in the Modern Department Store* (Boston: Auburn House, 1981), 11.

3. See Jack Kaikati, "Don't Discount Off-Price Retailers," *Harvard Business Review* (May-June 1985); Samuel Feinberg, *The Off-Price Explosion* (New York: Fairchild Publications, 1984); Bluestone et al., *The Retail Revolution.*

4. Bluestone et al., *The Retail Revolution.*

5. Sergio A. Pais, "An Analysis of the Retailing Industry: Future Trends and Perspectives" (Master's thesis, Sloan School of Management, MIT, June 1986), 37.

6. Bennett Harrison and Barry Bluestone, *The Great U-Turn: Corporate Restructuring and the Polarizing of America* (New York: Basic Books, 1988).

7. Lucie Cheng and Gary Gereffi, "US Retailers and Asian Garment Production," in *Global Production: The Apparel Industry in the Pacific Rim*, ed. Edna Bonacich et al. (Philadelphia: Temple University Press, 1994).

8. Leonard Berry, "The New Consumer," in *Competitive Structure and Retail Markets*, ed. E. Hirschman and R. Stampfl (Chicago: American Marketing Association, 1980), 1–11; Pais, "An Analysis of the Retailing Industry," 68.

9. Pais, "An Analysis of the Retailing Industry," 19.

10. Ibid., 38–39.

11. Jeannette Jarnow and Kitty C. Dickerson, *Inside the Fashion Business* (Englewood Cliffs, N.J.: Prentice Hall, 1997), 72.

12. David Moin, "Store Nets Will Slide for '84," *Women's Wear Daily* 149 (February 22, 1985): 8.

13. Meyer Lasker, Irwin Cohen, and Laurence N. Garter, "The Retail Industry: In Search of Real Profits in the 80s," *Retail Control* (February 1981).

14. Holly Klokis, "Retail Layoffs: Where Will Everyone Go?" *Chain Store Age Executive* 63, no. 4 (April 1987): 104, 106.

15. Steven E. Haugen, "The Employment Expansion in Retail Trade, 1973–1985," *Monthly Labor Review* (August 1986).

16. Natalya Iwach, "Shifting Relations between Retailing and Manufacturing in the U.S. Apparel Industry" (Master's thesis, Sloan School of Management, MIT, 1991).

17. Robert M. Frazier, "Quick Response in Soft Lines," *Discount Merchandiser* 26, no. 1 (January 1986): 40–46.

18. Michael Dertouzos et al., *Made in America: Regaining the Productive Edge* (Cambridge: MIT Press, 1989); Bertrand Frank, "Merchandising Management: Turnaround Revisited," *Bobbin Magazine* (January 1988): 98–102.

19. Jarnow and Dickerson, *Inside the Fashion Business*, 172–73.

20. Ibid.

21. James Lardner, "Annals of Business: The Sweater Trade," *New Yorker* (January 11 and 18, 1991).

22. Cheng and Gereffi, "US Retailers and Asian Garment Production," 64–66.

23. Not surprisingly, these corporations were staunch supporters of the Special Access Program of the Caribbean Basin Initiative of 1986.

24. Gary Gereffi and Mei-Lin Pan, "The Globalization of Taiwan's Garment Industry," in *Global Production: The Apparel Industry in the Pacific Rim*, ed. Edna Bonacich et al. (Philadelphia: Temple University Press, 1994), 134.

25. Pais, "An Analysis of the Retailing Industry," 23.

26. Mark Henricks, "Private Labeling: Who Said the Stores Would Get Tired of Manufacturing?" *Apparel Industry Magazine* (March 1998).

27. Cheng and Gereffi, "US Retailers and Asian Garment Production," 66.

28. Carol Warfield, Mary Barry, and Dorothy Cavender, "Apparel Retailing in the USA—Part I," *Textile Outlook International* (London) (March 1995); Susan Sherreik, "Attention, Shoppers: Brand Name Stores," *New York Times*, August 14, 1994, sec. 9, p. 1.

29. Pete Born, "Retailers Cautioned on Private Label Expansion," *Women's Wear Daily* 149 (January 16, 1985): 6.

30. Cheng and Gereffi, "US Retailers and Asian Garment Production," 68.

31. Gereffi and Pan, "The Globalization of Taiwan's Garment Industry," 135.

32. Cheng and Gereffi, "US Retailers and Asian Garment Production," 68.

33. "Retailers Promote Private Label to Counter Off-Price Threat," *Ad Forum* (November 1983). According to Bluestone and colleagues (*The Retail Revolution*, 1983), the figure in 1984 was between 5 and 6 percent of "all national brand apparel sales in the same clothing categories," a figure predicted to rise to between 9 and 10 percent by 1990.

34. U.S. Senate, Committee on the Judiciary, *Hearings on S. 408*, 94th Cong., 1st sess., May 12, 1975, 70–75, testimony of Kurt Barnard; U.S. House, Committee on the Judiciary, *Hearings on H.R. 2384*, 94th Cong., 1st sess., March 25 and April 10, 1975.

35. Daniel W. J. Raff and W. J. Salmon, "Allied, Federated, and Campeau: Causes, Outcomes, and Implications" (manuscript, Harvard, 1991), 5–6.

36. Bluestone et al., *The Retail Revolution*.

37. Pais, "An Analysis of the Retailing Industry," 19.

38. Raff and Salmon, "Allied, Federated, and Campeau"; Natalya Iwach, "Shifting Relations between Retailing and Manufacturing in the U.S. Apparel Industry" (Master's thesis, Sloan School of Management, MIT, 1991), 33.

39. See Gary Vineberg and Nancy R. Shapiro, "Off-Price Market Share Seen Hitting 1–20% by '90," *Footwear News* 39 (November 7, 1983): 1.

40. Samuel Feinberg, "Atkins Has Big Start in Off-Price Merchandise Subsidiary," *Women's Wear Daily* 147 (January 27, 1984): 13.

41. Vineberg and Shapiro, "Off-Price Market Share Seen Hitting 1–20% by '90," 1.

42. Irene Daria, "Batus Singing the Praises of Imported Goods for US," *Women's Wear Daily* 148 (September 19, 1984): 63. Also see "Stores Have Problems of Their Own," *Daily News Record* 15 (June 6, 1985): 2; Feinberg, *The Off-Price Explosion*, ix.

43. Gereffi and Pan, "The Globalization of Taiwan's Garment Industry," 140; and Harvard Apparel Seminar, Harvard Business School, 1990–94.

44. Ferd O. Lawson Jr. and Peter Zimmerman, "Frederick Atkins Exec Tells Meeting That Price Lures Business Offshore," *Women's Wear Daily* 149 (June 6, 1985): 17.

45. Ron Cohen, "Off-Price Retailing Growing Up Quickly," *Women's Wear Daily* 146 (November 2, 1983): 42.

46. Donna Heiderstadt, "Markdown Madness Takes Toll on '84 Net," *Footwear News* 41 (February 11, 1985): 57; also see Ron Cohen, "Frederick Atkins Reports Fast Growth of Private Labels; Sees Doubled Volume by 88," *Women's Wear Daily* 146 (September 16, 1983): 11.

47. Daria, "Batus Singing the Praises of Imported Goods for US," 63.

48. Jeremy Main, "Merchants' Woe: Too Many Stores," *Fortune* 111 (May 13, 1985): 62; Feinberg, *The Off-Price Explosion*.

49. Lasker, Cohen, and Garter, "The Retail Industry." Also see Ernest H. Risch, "Operating Profit in the Conventional Department Store: A Statistical Prognosis," *Retail Control* (January 1986).

50. "Managing the Productivity Loop," *Women's Wear Daily* 172, no. 59 (September 25, 1996): 18.

51. Ibid.

52. Cited in Pais, "An Analysis of the Retailing Industry," 52; also see "State of the Industry, *Chain Store Age Executive* (June 1984).

53. Daniel J. Sweeney, "Retailing—an Industry under Siege," *Retail Control* (December 1991).

54. "Managing the Productivity Loop," 1996.

55. Sidney Rutberg, "NRF to Hear Chapter, Verse on Chapter 11," *Daily News Record* 21, no. 6 (January 10, 1991): 15; also see Alan G. Milstein, "The Check Is in the Mail," *Bobbin Magazine* (December 1991): 18–19.

56. Sidney Rutberg, "Where the LBO Money Comes From," *Women's Wear Daily* 151 (February 11, 1986): 17.

57. "Retail LBOs: Good or Evil, the Pace Quickens," *Chain Store Age Executive with Shopping Center Age* 61 (December 1985): 11.

58. Rutberg, "Where the LBO Money Comes From," 17.

59. Sidney Rutberg, "Tough to Pick Targets for LBOs: Retail Analyst," *Daily News Record* 16 (January 15, 1986): 8.

60. Rutberg, "Where the LBO Money Comes From," 17.

61. Louis S. Richman, "Retailers Get Lean," *Fortune* 128, no. 14 (November 29, 1993): 24.

62. Anna Cifelli, "Friends of Free Trade," *Fortune* 110 (August 20, 1984): 153.

63. Karen Paxton, "New Customs Regulation to Hurt Many, Aid Few," *Discount Store News* 23 (September 17, 1984): 6.

64. Ibid.

65. In 1998, the president of the ATMI, Patrick Danahy, supported this position; see "Fifteen Minutes with Danahy, President of ATMI," *Apparel Industry Magazine* (June 1998).

66. James A. Morrissey, "China Looms over World Textile Trade," *Textile World* (August 1996): 146.

67. "Over 20 Retailers, Trade Associations, Mobilize to Fight Import Quotas," *Discount Store News* 23 (July 9, 1984): 2.

68. Jeffrey Arlen, "Retailers to Seek Allies in Free Trade Battle," *Daily News Record* 15 (January 17, 1985): 1.

69. Richard Wightman, "Retail Group Being Formed to Fight for Freer US Trade," *Women's Wear Daily* 147 (June 21, 1984): 7.

70. "Over 20 Retailers, Trade Associations, Mobilize to Fight Import Quotas," 2.

71. "Chain Spokesmen Testify vs. Tighter Garb Quotas," *Discount Store News* 24 (April 29, 1985): 2.

72. Paul Charles Ehrlich, "RITAC Says Restrictive Bilaterals in Asia Threaten MFA Renewal," *Daily News Record* 16 (June 25, 1986): 8; Richard Wightman, "Stores Aim Big Guns at Trade Bars," *Women's Wear Daily* 14

(June 28, 1984), 1; Richard Wightman, "RITAC May Put Roadblocks on Path to MFA Talks," *Women's Wear Daily* 151 (March 26, 1986): 8.

73. Richard Wightman, "AMC Exec Packs US Retail Position for Far East Trip," *Daily News Record* 16 (April 16, 1986): 7.

74. Ibid.

75. Jim Ostroff, "Stores Hit Draft of GATT Trade Plan," *Daily News Record* 20, no. 229 (November 20, 1990): 4.

76. Julie Ritzer Ross, "Changes Afoot in Textiles/Apparel Sourcing Patterns," *Global Trade* 112, no. 3 (March 1992): 26.

77. Joyce Barrett, "Retailers Will Fight for China's MFN," *Women's Wear Daily* 163, no. 44 (March 4, 1992): 19.

78. Joyce Barrett, "Retailers Start New Campaign for Free Trade," *Women's Wear Daily* 163, no. 36 (February 21, 1992): 1.

79. "The Federation Strikes Back!" *Chain Store Age Executive* 72, no. 11 (November 1996): 54–62.

80. Joyce Barrett, "NRF Launches Letter-Writing NAFTA Drive," *Women's Wear Daily* (June 28, 1993).

81. Jeff Black, "AMC Explores New Apparel Sourcing Areas," *Daily News Record* (February 28, 1992).

82. David Moin, "Atkins Sets Munich Conference to Find East Europe Sources," *Women's Wear Daily* 160, no. 65 (October 3, 1990): 28.

83. Black, "AMC Explores New Apparel Sourcing Areas."

84. Vicki M. Yount, "Seeking Options in Asia," *Women's Wear Daily* 175, no. 26 (February 10, 1998): 20.

85. See U.S. Department of Labor, "Dynamic Change in the Garment Industry: How Firms and Workers Can Survive and Thrive," Fashion Industry Forum (Washington, D.C., July 9, 1996).

86. *Standard and Poor's Industry Survey*, Retailing: General, September 24, 1997.

87. "The Globalization of Sweatshops," *Sweatshop Watch* 6, no. 2 (summer 2000).

88. Fairchild News Service, "Retail Financing: Alternate Sources" (Fairchild News Service, Minneapolis, 1996, photocopy), press release.

89. *Standard and Poor's Industry Surveys*, Retailing: General, September 24, 1997.

90. William C. Woodard, "The Game's the Same but the Rules Can Be Different," Coopers and Lybrand report on Global Powers of Retailing, *Chain Store Age* (December 1996); Warfield, Barry, and Cavender, "Apparel Retailing in the USA—Part I."

91. *Standard and Poor's Industry Survey*, Retailing: General, July 24, 1997.

92. Rachel Beck, "Markdowns Lure Shoppers to Stores in January," *Associated Press*, February 5, 1998.

93. Carol Warfield, Mary Barry, and Dorothy Cavender, "Apparel Retailing in the USA—Part II," *Textile Outlook International* (London) (July 1995).

94. Warfield, Barry, and Cavender, "Apparel Retailing in the USA—Part I."

95. Michael Niemira, "The Supply of, and Demand for, Apparel Goods," *Chain Store Age* (September 1997); also see *Apparel Strategist* (May 1998): 7.

96. Kathleen DesMarteau, "US Apparel Contractors: Can They Beat the Odds?" *Bobbin Magazine* (February 1997).

97. Carl Proper, "Keeping New York in Fashion" (manuscript, University of Massachusetts, January 2, 2000). Paper written by a UNITE member for a program on union leadership and administration.

98. See ibid.

99. Abernathy et al., *A Stitch in Time.*

100. Ibid., 53.

101. Ibid., 57.

102. Trevor A. Finnie, "Outlook for the US Apparel Industry," *Textile Outlook International* (London) (September 1997). Finnie also reports such partnership arrangements.

103. Abernathy et al., *A Stitch in Time,* 236–37.

104. Deborah Catalano Ruriani, "Logistics Challenge 2000," *Apparel Industry Magazine* (September 1999).

105. Edna Bonacich and Richard Appelbaum, *Behind the Label: Inequality in the Los Angeles Apparel Industry* (Berkeley and Los Angeles: University of California Press, 2000), 90.

106. "Thinking Globally, Selling Locally," *Futurist* (Washington, D.C.) (July-August 1993); the quote is from Madhav Kacker, "Coming to Terms with Global Retailing," *International Marketing Review* (London) 3, no. 1 (spring 1986): 7–21.

107. Joseph Ellis, "Global Retailing '97," *Chain Store Age* (December 1997); Mark Carr, "The New Era of Global Retailing," *Journal of Business Strategy* (May-June 1996).

108. Jay L. Johnson, "The Globetrotters: Retail's Multinationals," *Discount Merchandiser* 35, no. 9 (September 1995).

109. Coopers and Lybrand, "Global Powers of Retailing," *Chain Store Age* (December 1995).

110. "Consulting Firms Examine Global Markets," *Discount Store News* 33, no. 3 (February 7, 1994).

111. Woodard, "In Global Retailing—the Game's the Same but the Rules Can Be Different."

112. Elaine Underwood, "Storebrands," *Brandweek* (January 9, 1995); J. Henton, M. Barry, and C. Warfield, "Setting the Pace for Global Retailing," *Textile Outlook International* (London) (July 1997); "Retailing's Great Global Gold Rush," *Chain Store Age Executive* (December 1997).

113. Coopers and Lybrand, "Global Powers of Retailing."

114. "Retailing's Great Global Gold Rush."

115. Dan O'Connor, "Global Retailing and Sourcing," *Discount Merchandiser* 36, no. 5 (May 1996).

116. Jay L. Johnson, "Going Global: An Evolving Saga," *Discount Merchandiser* (September 1994): 46–58.

CHAPTER 11

1. Linda Shelton and Robert Wallace, "World Textile and Apparel Trade: A New Era," in *Industry, Trade, and Technology Review* (Washington, D.C.: U.S. International Trade Commission, October 1996), 1.

2. U.S. International Trade Commission, *Assessment of the Economic Effects on the United States of China's Accession to the World Trade Organization*, Investigation 332–403, Publication 3229 (Washington, D.C.: USITC, September 1999), chap. 8, p. 15.

3. U.S. House, Committee on Ways and Means, *Caribbean Basin Free Trade Agreement Act*, 103rd Cong., 1st sess., June 24, 1993, 113, statement of Andrew F. Postal.

4. "Clinton Faces Limited Support on Wider NAFTA," *Daily News Record* 22, no. 234 (December 9, 1994): 2.

5. "USAIC Addresses Real-World 807," *Daily News Record* 20, no. 243 (December 13, 1990): 2; Joyce E. Santora, *Bobbin Magazine* 30, no. 9 (May 1989): 94–100.

6. "Caribbean High Tech Dreams," *Business Week*, no. 3694 (August 14, 2000): 38.

7. South Center, *Lopsided Rules of North-South Engagement: The African Growth and Opportunity Act* (Geneva: South Center, February 1999).

8. Stephen E. Lamar, "The Apparel Industry and African Economic Development," *Law and Policy in International Business* 30, no. 4 (summer 1999): 1999.

9. Robert Weisman, "Waiting to Export: Africa Embraces Export-Processing Zones," *Multinational Monitor* 17, nos. 7–8 (July-August 1996): 12.

10. U.S. International Trade Commission, *Likely Impact of Providing Quota-Free and Duty-Free Entry to Textiles and Apparel from Sub-Saharan Africa*, Publication 3056 (Washington, D.C.: USITC, September 1997), D-13.

11. Brenda Jacobs, "HR 1432 Could Propel Sub-Saharan Sourcing," *Bobbin Magazine* (July 1997): 88–89.

12. U.S. House, Committee on Ways and Means, *U.S. Trade Relations with Sub-Saharan Africa*, 106th Cong., 1st sess., February 3, 1999, testimony of Carlos Moore, vice president of the American Textile Manufacturers' Institute.

13. Simone Field et al., "The Second-Hand Clothes Trade in the Gambia," *Geography* 81, no. 4 (1996); Karen Tranberg Hansen, "Second Hand Clothing

Encounters in Zambia: Global Discourses, Western Commodities, and Local Histories," *Africa* 69, no. 3 (summer 1999).

14. Lamar, "The Apparel Industry and African Economic Development."

15. Joanna Ramey, "ATMI Loosens Position on Africa/CBI Textiles," *Women's Wear Daily* (April 5, 2000).

16. South Center, *Lopsided Rules of North-South Engagement*.

17. Jacobs, "HR 1432 Could Propel Sub-Saharan Sourcing," 88–89.

18. Kathleen DesMarteau, "TDA Implementation: The Clock Is Ticking," *Bobbin Magazine* (November 2000); Jordan K. Speer, "CBI Splashdown," *Bobbin Magazine* (November 2000).

19. Holly Welling, "Caribbean Boon: Lurching after NAFTA," *Apparel Industry Magazine* (July 31, 2000).

20. Speer, "CBI Splashdown."

21. See Pelzman, "China's Economy Looks toward the Year 2000," 385, 405. Between 1953 and 1978, the annual increase of textile and apparel production was 7 percent. Between 1979 and 1985, the annual increase in production was 14 percent. James Glasse, "Textiles and Clothing in China: Competitive Threat or Investment Opportunity?" Report No. 268, *Textile Outlook International* (London) (January 1995): 29; "China: An Export Strategy to Pay for Modernization," *Business Week* (January 15, 1979).

22. Richard Wightman, "Retailers Hit Countervailing Duty Requests," *Daily News Record* 14 (August 3, 1984): 2.

23. "How China Will Alter the Far Eastern Market," *Business Week* (March 5, 1979): 46; "China: An Export Strategy to Pay for Modernization," 48.

24. Glasse, "Textiles and Clothing in China," 29; "China: An Export Strategy to Pay for Modernization."

25. See Pelzman, "China's Economy Looks toward the Year 2000."

26. "How China Will Alter the Far Eastern Market," 46; "China: An Export Strategy to Pay for Modernization," 48. Also see Pelzman, "China's Economy Looks toward the Year 2000."

27. Paul Charles Ehrlich, "China to Put $440 Million into Upgrading Apparel Units," *Daily News Record* 17, no. 239 (December 10, 1987): 10.

28. "China Needles US," *Far Eastern Economic Review* (January 24, 1991): 34–35.

29. U.S. International Trade Commission, *Assessment of the Economic Effects on the United States of China's Accession to the World Trade Organization*, chap. 8, p. 5.

30. Susumu Awanohara, Jonathan Burton, and Mark Clifford, "Frayed Relations: China's Textile Trade Expected to Draw US Ire," *Far Eastern Economic Review* 156, no. 5 (February 4, 1993): 46–47.

31. Office of the U.S. Trade Representative, Executive Office of the President (Washington, D.C., February 2, 1997), press release; U.S. International Trade Commission, *Assessment of the Economic Effects on the United States of China's Access to the World Trade Organization*, 12.

32. The president of the ATMI at that time, Patrick Danahy, supported this position; see "Fifteen Minutes with Danahy, President of ATMI," *Apparel Industry Magazine* (June 1998).

33. U.S. House, Committee on Ways and Means, *US-China Trade Relations and the Possible Accession of China to the World Trade Organization,* 106th Cong., sess. 1, June 22, 1999, statement of the American Textile Manufacturers' Institute.

34. American Textile Manufacturers' Institute, "China's Entry into World Trade Organization Would Cost 154,000 US Jobs and Billions of Dollars in Lost US Textile and Apparel Sales—ATMI Provides US International Trade Commission with Study Findings" (ATMI, September 31, 1999, photocopy), press release.

35. U.S. International Trade Commission, *Assessment of the Economic Effects on the United States of China's Accession to the World Trade Organization,* 3.

36. Ibid.

37. Jesse Rothstein and Robert Scott, *The Cost of Trade with China: Women and Low Wage Workers Hit Hardest by Job Increases in All Fifty States,* Issue Brief No. 122 (Washington, D.C.: Economic Policy Institute, October 28, 1997).

38. There is no disaggregation with respect to CBI nations, which are categorized here as part of "all other" importing nations.

39. National Labor Committee, "Who's Who: Top US Apparel Companies Contracting Production in China" (http://www.nlcnet.org/China/whos/who.htm), December 5, 1999; "Made in China: The Role of U.S. Companies in Denying Human and Worker Rights," December 12, 2001 (http://www.nlcnet.org/).

40. Kym Anderson, "The WTO Agenda for the New Millennium," *Economic Record* 75, no. 228 (March 1999): 77.

41. Trevor A. Finnie, "Outlook for the US Textile Industry," *Textile Outlook International* (London) (September 1995): 101; U.S. International Trade Commission, *US Implementation Draws Criticism* (Washington, D.C.: USITC November 26, 1996).

42. "Clash over Textiles at WTO Summit," United Press International (Geneva), November 30, 1999.

43. T. J. Zheng, "One Year After," *Time* (July 1998); "Learning to Capitalize on Asia's Crisis," *Financial Times* (July 28, 1998); "Concessions Made in Face of 'Most Difficult Year So Far': SHKP Cuts Retail Rents but Not for Prime Sites," *South China Morning Post,* July 29, 1998.

44. American Textile Manufacturers' Institute, "US Textile Industry Hit Hard by Flood of Low Cost Asian Imports: Industry President Calls on US Government to Take Action" (ATMI, February 23, 1999, photocopy), press release.

45. American Textile Manufacturers' Institute, "US Textile Industry Mid Year Trade and Economic Report; Imports Reach Record Level: Exports to

NAFTA and CBI Partners Strong" (ATMI, August 23, 1999, photocopy), press release.

46. American Textile Manufacturer's Institute, *Promises Unkept: A Report on Market Access for US Textile and Apparel Products Five Years into the WTO* (Washington, D.C.: American Textile Manufacturer's Institute, March 17, 2000).

47. Richard Tomlinson, "The China That Clinton Won't See," *Fortune* (July 6, 1998); U.S. International Trade Commission, *Assessment of the Economic Effects on the United States of China's Accession to the World Trade Organization*, 11.

48. Helene Cooper and Kathy Chen, "US and China Announce Tariff Targets as Both Nations Step Up Trade Rhetoric: Sanctions Will Take Effect June 17 Unless Accord Is Reached on Pirating," *Wall Street Journal*, May 16, 1996, sec. A, p. 3.

49. "Selling Dallas to Mexico," *Women's Wear Daily* 164, no. 18 (July 27, 1992): 8; "NAFTA Looms over AAMA Meeting," *Women's Wear Daily* 163, no. 89 (May 6, 1992): 23.

50. Jennifer Steinhauer, "Prices Starting to Drop from Asian Crisis," *New York Times*, May 1, 1998.

51. Josephine Bow, "Parley Stresses Ties with Asia," *Daily News Record* 23, no. 233 (December 9, 1993).

52. Kathleen DesMarteau, "Contexpo Preview: The Meeting of the Americas," *Bobbin Magazine* (February 1996): 74–77.

53. Raye Rudie, "Textile Report: Mills Making Apparel," *Bobbin Magazine* (September 1997): 134–52.

54. Finnie, "Outlook for the U.S. Textile Industry," 101.

55. William E. Dawson, "American Textiles and Apparel: Export Promotion Equals Export Success," *Business America* 115, no. 6 (June 1994): 20.

56. See Trevor A. Finnie, "Outlook for the US Textile Industry," *Textiles Outlook International* (London) (May 1997): 127.

57. Data compiled from the US International Trade Commission, various years (http://dataweb.usitc.gov/scripts/REPORT.asp).

58. Frederick H.Abernathy, John T. Dunlop, Janice H. Hammond, and David Weil, *A Stitch in Time: Lean Retailing and the Transformation of Manufacturing—Lessons from the Apparel and Textile Industries* (New York: Oxford University Press, 1999), 223–24; Patricia Alisau, "Mexico 2000: Managing Growth Intelligently," *Apparel Industry Magazine* (September 1999).

59. Judi Kessler, "NAFTA, Economic Development, and Regional Reconfiguration: The Southern California–Mexico Apparel Commodity Chain" (paper presented to the Annual Meetings of the American Sociological Association, Washington, D.C., August 2000).

60. Christopher Palmeri and Jose Aguayo, "Goodbye Guangdong, Hello Jalisco," *Forbes* 159, no. 3 (February 10, 1997): 76.

61. Scott Malone, "Parity Puzzle: Mills Aim to Finesse CBI," *Women's Wear Daily* (June 20, 2000).

62. Jules Abend, "AAMA Outlook Gives Global Guidance" *Bobbin Magazine* (February 1996): 36–42.

63. Trevor A. Finnie, "Profile of Kellwood Company," *Textile Outlook International* (London) (January 1995): 76–94.

64. Jules Abend, "Hungary Comes to Call," *Bobbin Magazine* (March 1996): 12–16; Jules Abend, "Exporters Tout Western Europe," *Bobbin Magazine* (September 1996): 36–40.

65. American Textile Manufacturers' Institute, "Crisis in U.S. Textiles: The Impact of the Asian Currency Devaluations and the U.S. Government Actions" (http://www.atmi.org/TheTextileCrisis/index.asp/December 30, 2001).

CHAPTER 12

1. U.S. International Trade Commission, "Import Growth in Textile and Apparel Sector Accelerates in 1997," press release; *Annual Statistical Report on US Imports of Textile and Apparel: 1997*, Publication 3102 (Washington, D.C.: USITC, April 28, 1998).

2. U.S. Bureau of the Census, *Quarterly Financial Report for Manufacturing, Mining, and Trade Corporations, Fourth Quarter 1997* (Washington, D.C., 1998), and various back issues, cited in U. S. International Trade Commission, *Industry and Trade Summary*, Publication 3169 (Washington, D.C.: USITC, March 1999), 7.

3. U.S. International Trade Commission, "Import Growth in Textile and Apparel Sector Accelerates in 1997."

4. Diane E. Picard, "Most Apparel CEO's Saw Their Incomes Swell during 1996," *Women's Wear Daily* 173, no. 105 (June 2, 1997): 2.

5. Sidney Rutberg, "Lenders Eager to Throw Money at Qualified Apparel Companies: Loan Rates Go Below Prime as Bankers Fight to Serve Shrinking Customer Base," *Daily News Record* 27, no. 148 (December 12, 1997): 10.

6. Jennifer L. Brady, "Growth of Big Brands Heightens the Appeal of Apparel for Wall Street," *Women's Wear Daily* 173, no. 17 (January 27, 1997): 1; also see "Market Rise Smiles on Industry Stocks," *Women's Wear Daily* 173, no. 86 (May 2, 1997): 2.

7. Brent Shearer, "Like Hemlines, Assets Are Shifting in the Apparel-Making Industry," *Mergers and Acquisitions* 35, no. 7 (July 2000): 20.

8. Leslie Kaufman, "A Glum Season for Retailers," *New York Times, Business Day*, January 5, 2001.

9. Shearer, "Like Hemlines, Assets Are Shifting in the Apparel-Making Industry," 20.

10. Just-Style.com, "Editor's Weekly Highlights," issue 87, September 26, 2001 (http://www.Just-Style.com).

11. Just-Style.com, "Editor's Weekly Highlights," issue 96, November 28, 2001 (http://www.Just-Style.com).

12. Just-Style.com, "Editor's Weekly Highlights," issue 87, September 26, 2001 (http://www.Just-Style.com).

13. Deloitte Touche, "There's Still a Silver Lining for Some Retailers Despite Gloomy 2001 Holiday Sales Outlook," PRNewswire (New York), October 15, 2001.

14. David Moin, "Sears Gets Tough with Its Softer Side," *Women's Wear Daily* (January 24, 2001); Just-Style.com, "Editor's Weekly Highlights," issue 70, May 30, 2001 (http://www.Just-Style.com).

15. Mark Mittelhauser, "Employment Trends in Textiles and Apparel, 1973–2005," *Monthly Labor Review* 120, no. 8 (August 1997): 24.

16. Ibid.

17. The textile industry has increased its capital intensity. Its consolidation, then, is not the result of low-wage imports, which in part may have been responsible in the 1950s. In that sense, textile production is more like other traditional manufacturing industries.

18. Historical employment figures are from the Current Employment Statistics survey of the U.S. Bureau of Labor Statistics. This survey is establishment-based and collected in cooperation with state agencies from a sample of more than 390,000 reporting units employing over 47 million nonfarm wage and salary workers. Projections are from the Office of Employment Projections, Bureau of Labor Statistics. For more information on these programs, including methodology and background, see U.S. Bureau of Labor Statistics, *Handbook of Methods,* Bulletin no. 2490 (Washington, D.C.: Bureau of Labor Statistics, 1997), cited in Mittelhauser, "Employment Trends in Textiles and Apparel, 1973–2005," 24.

19. James C. Franklin, "Industry Output and Employment Projections to 2005," *Monthly Labor Review* (November 1995): 45–59; George T. Silvestri, "Occupational Employment to 2005," *Monthly Labor Review* (November 1995): 60–84.

20. Gary Clyde Hufbauer, Diane Berliner, and Kimberly Ann Elliott, *Trade Protection in the United States: 31 Case Studies* (Washington, D.C.: Institute for International Economics, 1986), 148.

21. U.S. House, Committee on Ways and Means, *President's Comprehensive Review of the NAFTA,* 105th Cong., 1st sess., September 11, 1997, testimony of Sidney Weintraub.

22. George J. Church, "Where He Rings True: Free Trade Isn't Always Fair," *Time* 147, no. 10 (March 4, 1996): 28.

23. Robert E. Scott, Thea Lee, and John Schmitt, "Trading Away Good Jobs: An Examination of Employment and Wages in the US, 1979–1994," (Washington, D.C.: Economic Policy Institute, 1997).

24. "Bobbin and Weaving: Mills Fight to Survive," *Business North Carolina* 17, no. 2 (February 1997): 107; Richard Lawson, "Losses in Apparel Industry Trim Manufacturing," *Memphis Business Journal* 19, no. 24 (October 20, 1997): 22; also see David Fisch, "Strong Arming Workers," *U.S. News and World Report* 120, no. 11 (March 18, 1996): 63.

25. U.S. Bureau of Labor Statistics, *National Employment Hours and Earnings,* Series ID: EEU00500006 (Washington, D.C.: April 21, 2001).

26. Mark Levitan, *Opportunity at Work: The New York City Garment Industry* (New York: Community Service Society of New York, 1998).

27. Robert S. J. Ross, professor of sociology, conversation with the author, Clark University, March 2000.

28. As noted earlier, a "sweatshop," as understood here, is not merely a firm which offers poorly paid jobs, and/or an authoritarian system of industrial relations. The wages they pay are below the federally mandated minimum, and/or the conditions of employment they provide are substandard in terms of the criteria set by the U.S. Fair Labor Standards Act (FLSA). Employers who provide such jobs violate the federal law. The FLSA has been on the books in this country since 1938. The growing prevalence of sweatshops in the United States means the law is not being enforced.

29. Robert S. J. Ross, Ellen I. Rosen, and Karen McCormack, "The Global Context of the New Sweatshops" (paper given at the annual meeting of the Society for the Study of Social Problems, New York, 1996).

30. Ethan Kapstein, "Trade Liberalization and the Politics of Trade Adjustment Assistance," *International Labour Review* 137, no. 4 (winter 1998): 501.

31. Douglas Irwin, *Against the Tide* (Princeton: Princeton University Press, 1996), 183, cited in Kapstein, "Trade Liberalization and the Politics of Trade Adjustment Assistance."

32. V. L. Hamilton, William S. Hoffman, Clifford L. Broman, and David Arum, "Unemployment, Distress, and Coping: A Panel Study of Autoworkers," *Journal of Personality and Social Psychology* 6, no. 2 (August 1993): 234–47; J. B. Turner, "Economic Context and the Health Effects of Unemployment," *Journal of Health and Social Behavior* 36, no. 3 (September 1995): 213–29; David Dooley, Ralph Catalano, and Georgina Wilson, "Depression and Unemployment: Panel Finding from the Epidemiological Catchment Area Study," *American Journal of Community Psychology* 24, no. 6 (December 1994): 745–65.

33. Kapstein, "Trade Liberalization and the Politics of Trade Adjustment Assistance."

34. Scott, Lee, and Schmitt, "Trading Away Good Jobs"; Robert E. Scott and Jesse Rothstein, "NAFTA and the State: Job Destruction Is Widespread" (Washington, D.C.: Economic Policy Institute 1997).

35. Thomas F. Crossley, Stephen R. G. Jones, and Peter Kuhn, "Gender Differences in Displacement Cost: Evidence and Implications," *Journal of Human Resources* 29, no. 2 (spring 1994): 461.

36. Cynthia Rocha and Felicia McCant, "Closing Time: Workers' Last Call," *Forum for Applied Research and Public Policy* 14, no. 1 (spring 1999): 65.

37. Brad Christerson and Richard P. Appelbaum, "Global and Local Subcontracting: Space, Ethnicity, and the Organization of Apparel Production," *World Development* 23, no. 8 (August 1995): 1363.

38. Richard B. Appelbaum and Gary Gereffi, "Power and Profits in the Apparel Commodity Chain," in *Global Production: The Apparel Industry in*

the Pacific Rim, ed. Edna Bonacich et al. (Philadelphia: Temple University Press, 1994).

39. Jason Abott, "Export Processing Zones and the Developing World," *Contemporary Review* 270, no. 1576 (May 1997): 232.

40. William H. Holstein, "Guess Who's Moving to Mexico?" *U.S. News and World Report* 122, no. 3 (January 27, 1997): 65.

41. U.S. House, Committee on Ways and Means, *President's Comprehensive Review of the NAFTA,* testimony of John Sweeney, president of the AFL-CIO. This appears to be a typical pattern for manufacturing companies. See Kat Bronfenbrenner, "Final Report: The Effects of Plant Closing or Threat of Plant Closing on the Right of Workers to Organize" (manuscript, Cornell University, Program on Labor Education Research, September 1996).

42. "How Levi's Trashed a Great American Brand: While Bob Haas pioneered benevolent management, his company came apart at the seams," *Fortune* 139, no. 7 (April 12, 1999): 82.

43. "Patching Up Levi's: Levi Strauss & Company Tries to Catch Market Share," *US News and World Report* 126, no. 9 (March 8, 1999): 54.

44. Jeff Moad, "Coming Unzipped: Levi Strauss' Business Process Reengineering Plan's Demise," *PC Week* 14, no. 48 (November 17): 141; Stacy Perman, "Levi's Gets the Blues: The Once Cool Brand Is Out of Step with Young Buyers," *Time* 150, no. 21 (November 17, 1997): 66.

45. "Levi's Offers Package to Laid Off Workers," *Business Insurance* (March 15, 1999): 47.

46. Hufbauer, Berliner, and Elliott, *Trade Protection in the United States,* 148.

47. Steven Suranovic, "Why Economists Should Study Fairness," *Challenge* 40, no. 5 (September–October 1997): 109.

48. Frederick H. Abernathy, John T. Dunlop, Janice H. Hammond, and David Weil, *A Stitch in Time: Lean Retailing and the Transformation of Manufacturing—Lessons from the Apparel and Textile Industries* (New York: Oxford University Press, 1999), 47.

49. U.S. Department of Commerce, "Apparel's Falling Share of Wallet, June 1991 to June 2001," cited in *Apparel Strategist* (September 2001): 1.

50. Cost of clothing purchases is from *Visions of the New Millennium: Evolving to Consumer Response,* cited in Jeannette Jarnow and Kitty C. Dickerson, *Inside the Fashion Business* (Upper Saddle River, N.J., and Columbus, Ohio: Merrill, Prentice Hall, 1997), 72.

51. Gary Clyde Hufbauer and Jeffrey Schott, *NAFTA: An Assessment,* rev. ed. (Washington, D.C.: Institute for International Economics, 1993); Jeffrey Schott, assisted by Joanna W. Buurman, *The Uruguay Round* (Washington D.C.: Institute for International Economics, 1994); Gary C. Hufbauer and Kimberly Ann Elliott, *Measuring the Cost of Textile Protection in the US* (Washington, D.C.: Institute of International Economics, 1994); William R. Cline, *The Future of World Trade in Textiles and Apparel,* rev. ed. (Washington D.C.: Institute for International Economics, 1990).

52. Julian M. Alston, Kenneth A. Foster, and Richard D. Greene, "Estimating Elasticities with the Linear Approximate Almost Ideal Demand System: Some Monte Carlo Results," *Review of Economics and Statistics* 76 (May 2, 1994): 351–56; C. Fred Bergsten, "The Cost of Import Restriction to American Consumers," *American Importers Association* (1972); Cline, *The Future of World Trade in Textiles and Apparel;* Jessie X. Fan, Jinkook Lee, and Sherman Hanna, "Household Expenditures on Apparel: A Complete Demand System Approach," in *Consumer Interest Annual: Proceedings of the American Council on Consumer Interests,* ed. Irene Leech (Columbia, Mo.: American Council on Consumer Interests), 42, 173–80; Hufbauer and Elliott, *Measuring the Costs of Protection in the United States;* Michael R. Metzger, "A Recalculation of Cline's Estimates of the Gains to Trade Liberalization in the Textile and Apparel Industries," Working Paper no. 174 (Washington, D.C.: Federal Trade Commission, U.S. Bureau of Economics, 1989); Rachel Dardis, "International Trade: The Consumer's Stake," in *Research in the Consumer Interest,* ed. E. Scott Maynes (Columbia, Mo.: American Council on Consumer Interests, 1988), 329–60; Julie A. Nelson, "Individual Consumption within the Household: A Study of Expenditures on Clothing," *Journal of Consumer Affairs* 23, no. 1 (summer 1989): 21–44.

53. Cline, *The Future of World Trade in Textiles and Apparel;* Metzger, "A Recalculation of Cline's Estimates of the Gains to Trade Liberalization in the Textile and Apparel Industries"; Dardis, "International Trade," 329–60; Irene Trela and John Whalley, "Global Effects of Developed Country Trade Restrictions on Textiles and Apparel," *Economic Journal* 100, no. 403 (December 1990): 1190–205; Robert E. Scott and Thea Lee, "The Costs of Trade Protection Reconsidered: US Steel, Textiles, and Apparel," in *US Trade Policy and Global Growth,* ed. R. A. Blecker (Washington, D.C.: Economic Policy Institute, 1994), 108–35.

54. James Bovard, "Viewpoints: Drop Textile Tariffs, for GATT's Sake," *New York Times,* November 7, 1993, Financial Desk, p. 11. Also see James Bovard, *The Fair Trade Fraud: How Congress Pillages the Consumer and Decimates American Competitiveness* (New York: St. Martin's Press, 1991).

55. U.S. Bureau of the Census, "Money Income in the United States," in *Current Population Reports* (Washington, D.C., 1996).

56. Jessie X. Fan, Jinkook Lee, and Sherman Hanna, "Are Apparel Trade Restrictions Regressive?" *Journal of Consumer Affairs* 32, no. 12 (winter 1998): 252.

57. Robert E. Scott and Thea M. Lee, *Reconsidering the Benefits and Costs of Trade Protection: The Case of Textiles and Apparel,* Working Paper no. 105 (Washington, D.C.: Economic Policy Institute, April 1991).

58. Carl Steidtmann, "Global Economics and the Apparel Industry: Sharpening Your Consumer-centric Edge," *Apparel Industry Magazine* (March 2000).

59. Christerson and Appelbaum, "Global and Local Subcontracting," 1363–74.

60. Michael Niemira, "The Supply of, and Demand for, Apparel Goods," *Chain Store Age* (September 1997); also see *Apparel Strategist* (May 1998): 7.

61. "Industry News," *Apparel Industry Magazine* (January 1999). In the United States, according to this report, textile industry "productivity rose, with the industry producing 37 square yards per hour, versus fewer than 35 yards per hour last year." At the same time, "textile imports totaled $12.8 billion, up 7 percent over 1997, versus textile exports of $9.1 billion, up 1% over 1997, for a total trade deficit of $3.7 billion, up 25% over last year."

62. "Wal-Mart and WTO Tagged for Globalizing Poverty," U.S. Newswire, November 29, 1999, p. 100832n0024; National Labor Committee, "Wal-Mart's Shirts of Misery," December 5, 1999 (http://www.nlcnet.org).

63. Marlene Kim, "Women Paid Low Wages: Where They Are and Where They Work," *Monthly Labor Review* (September 2000).

64. Church, "Where He Rings True: Free Trade Isn't Always Fair," 28.

65. See Ian Robinson, "Reconstructing Globalization: Ways out of the Current Impasse" (paper presented to the annual meeting of the American Sociological Association, Washington, D.C., August 2000). Also see Economic Policy Institute, "The Pulse on Trade," November 16, 1999 (http://www.epinet.org).

66. Marymount University, Center for Ethical Concerns, "The Consumer and Sweatshops," 1999 (http://www.marymount.edu/news.garmentstudy/).

67. Maryland University, Program on International Policy Attitudes, "American Globalization: A Study of U.S. Public Attitudes," March 28, 2000 (http://www.pipa.org).

68. See, for example, June Nash and Maria-Patricia Fernandez-Kelly, *Women, Men, and the New International Division of Labor* (Johns Hopkins University Press, 1983); Lydia Kung, *Factory Women in Taiwan* (Ann Arbor: University of Michigan Press, 1983); Barbara Ehrenreich and Annette Fuentes, "Life on the Global Assembly Line," *Ms.* (January 1981): 53–59; Susan Tiano, "Maquila Women: A New Category of Workers?" in *Women Workers and Global Restructuring*, ed. Kathryn Ward (Ithaca, N.Y.: ILR Press, 1990), 193–225.

69. The five others who signed the letter were Robert E. Baldwin, University of Wisconsin; Alan V. Deardorff, University of Michigan; Arvid Panagariya, University of Maryland; T. N. Srinivasan, Yale University; and Robert M. Stern, University of Michigan.

70. Jagdish Bhagwati, "Comment and Analysis: Nike Wrongfoots the Student Critics," *Financial Times* (London), May 2, 2000.

71. Quotes are from the letter written by the Academic Consortium on International Trade.

72. International Labour Organization, *Labour Practices in the Footwear, Leather, Textiles, and Clothing Industries: Report for the Discussion at the Tripartite Meeting on Labour Practices in the Footwear, Leather, Textiles, and Clothing Industry* (Geneva: ILO, 2000).

73. Louis Uichitelle, "International Business: Globalization Marches On as U.S. Eases Up on the Reins," *New York Times*, December 17, 2001.

74. Thomas Dublin, *Women at Work: The Transformation of Work and Community in Lowell, Massachusetts, 1826–60* (New York: Columbia University Press 1979), 80.

75. Ibid.; Tamara K. Hareven, *Family Time and Industrial Time: The Relationship between the Family and Work in a New England Industry* (Cambridge: Cambridge University Press, 1982).

76. Ehrenreich and Fuentes, "Life on the Global Assembly Line"; Maria Mies, *Patriarchy and Accumulation on a World Scale* (London: Zed Books, 1986); Nash and Fernandez-Kelly, *Women, Men, and the International Division of Labor*; Tiano, "Maquila Women," 193–225.

77. Linda Lim, "Women's Work in Export Factories: The Politics of a Cause," in *Persistent Inequalities: Women and World Development*, ed. Irene Tinker (New York: Oxford University Press, 1990).

78. Ibid.

79. Melissa Connor et al., *The Case for Corporate Responsibility: Paying a Living Wage to Maquila Workers in El Salvador* (New York: National Labor Committee, 1999); also published on the NLC Web site (http://www.nlcnet.org/resources/e_salv.htm). This study was done for the National Labor Committee, Program in Economic and Political Development, School of International and Public Affairs, Columbia University.

80. Susan Tiano, *Patriarchy on the Line: Labor, Gender, and Ideology in the Mexican Maquiladoras* (Philadelphia: Temple University Press, 1994).

81. International Labour Organization, "Labour Issues in the Textile and Clothing Sector: A Sri Lankan Perspective" (paper presented to the International Labour Organization, Sectoral Activities Program, November 2000).

82. National Labor Committee, "Visiting the Company Dorm," December 2000 (http://www.nlcnet.org).

83. National Labor Committee, "Wal-Mart's Shirts of Misery," December 2000 (http://www.nlcnet.org).

84. National Labor Committee, "Bangladesh: Ending the Race to the Bottom," December 2001 (http://www.nlcnet.org).

85. National Labor Committee, "Wal-Mart's Shirts of Misery."

86. International Labour Organization, *Labour Practices in the Footwear, Leather, Textiles, and Clothing Industries*.

87. Folker Froebel, Jurgen Heinrichs, and Otto Kreye. *The New International Division of Labor* (London: Cambridge University Press, 1980).

88. Alice Kessler-Harris, *In Pursuit of Equity: Women, Men, and the Quest for Economic Citizenship in Twentieth Century America* (New York: Oxford University Press, 2001).

89. Alice Kessler-Harris, *A Woman's Wage* (Lexington: University of Kentucky Press, 1990); Kessler-Harris, *In Pursuit of Equity*.

90. Altha Cravey, *Women and Work in Mexico's Maquiladoras* (Lanham, Md.: Rowman and Littlefield, 1998).

91. Connor et al., *The Case for Corporate Responsibility*.

92. Naila Kabeer, *The Power to Choose: Bangladeshi Women and Labour Market Decisions in London and Dhaka* (London: Verso, 2000), 82–84.

93. Christine Stansell, *City of Women* (Urbana: University of Illinois Press, 1987).

94. Financial Times Information, Global News Wire, Business Recorder, June 3, 2001.

95. Financial Times Information, Global News Wire, Business Recorder, October 2, 2001; Reuters, "EU and US Offer Pakistan Trade and Aid Concessions: Country's Frontline Status in the War on Terrorism Is Tearing It Apart," *Vancouver Sun*, October 17, 2001, final ed.

96. Leslie Kaufman, "Companies Cut Textile Orders from Pakistan," *New York Times*, October 31, 2001; Just-Style.com, "Editor's Weekly Highlights," issue 89, October 10, 2001 (http://www.Just-Style.com); Paul Blustein, "A Pakistani Setback," *Washington Post*, December 26, 2001.

97. Financial Times Information, Global News Wire, Business Recorder, "Bangladesh Facing Decline in Garment Production," September 12, 2001.

98. Blustein, "A Pakistani Setback"; Ginger Thompson, "Fallout of U.S. Recession Drifts South into Mexico," *New York Times*, December 26, 2001.

99. Just-Style.com, "Editor's Weekly Highlights," issue 82, August 22, 2001 (http://www.Just-Style.com).

100. Just-Style.com, "Editor's Weekly Highlights," issue 79, August 1, 2001 (http://www.Just-Style.com).

101. Don Hogsett, "Guilford Sales Down Close to $17M in 2Q," *Home Textiles Today* (May 14, 2001): 24.

102. American Textile Manufacturers' Institute, *Crisis in U.S. Textiles: The Impact of the Asian Currency Devaluations and the U.S. Government Actions* (Washington D.C.: ATMI, August 2001).

Index

Page numbers in *italic type* refer to figures and tables.

neoliberal economic paradigm as context of, 23–25; restructuring in, 7, 116–18; shift away from New York City, 98–99, 273n10; shift to East Asia in, 103–6; shift to low-wage countries in, 22–23; shift to South in, 99–103; sourcing of, 117–18, 197–200, 217–19, 276n61; textile industry distinguished from, 103, 255n17; trade liberalization's impact on, 20–23; unique qualities of, 4. *See also* apparel manufacturers, U.S.; apparel production; apparel workers; export-processing zones (EPZs); trade protection

Apparel Industry Committee against Imports, 107

Apparel Industry Magazine, 199

apparel manufacturers, U.S.: cultural background of, 96; differences among, 145–48; dilemmas faced by, 105–6; export-led development supported by, 141–42; expositions for, 169; of fashion vs. standard/basic clothing, 164–67; free trade supported by, 103; global competition and, 214–17; offshore options sought by, 129–30, 137–43, 211–12; protectionism of, 106–7, 127, 275n45; retailers' conflicts with, 203–4; retail restructuring and, 180–82; union's cooperation with, 97–98; union's difficulties with, 99–103; vertical integration of, 164, 167–72, 183. *See also* "just-in-time" delivery (a.k.a. quick response); profits

apparel production: of fashion vs. standard/basic clothing, 164–67; "full package" type of, 153; as gendered, 23–24; global competition in, 214–15; low wage for, 22–23, 49–50, 103–6; in *maquiladoras*, 153–56; offshore location of, 117–18, 128, 136–43, 216–17, 276n61; in outside vs. inside shops, 97; political influences on, 148; women's low-wage labor as critical to, 51–54, 116–17.

See also apparel workers; export-processing zones (EPZs); productivity and production systems; sweatshops

apparel republics, concept of, 136–43

apparel retailing and retailers: Asian trade and, 213–14; bankruptcies in, 189, 190, 195–96, 229, 234, 255n18; concentration and integration of, 164, 167–72, 183, 194–97; Darwinian struggle of, 8–9; declining sales of, 222–23; economics of fashion and, 182–84; global trade and, 191–94, 200–201, 214–17; historical context of, 177–78; overview of, 11; producers' conflicts with, 203–4; profitability paradox for, 188–89, 195–96; restructuring in, 180; SAP opposed by, 145; sourcing abroad and, 197–200, 217–19. *See also* apparel imports; clothing; department stores; discount stores; "just-in-time" delivery (a.k.a. quick response)

apparel workers: CBI opposed by, 164–65; displacement of, 113, 115–16, 118, 228–29, 235; gender of, 239–40; jobs lost by, 4, 9, 99, 150–52, 174–76, 223–25; poverty of, 80–82, 96–97, 241–43; in sweatshop debate, 236–38; unionization efforts and, 99–103; wages lost by, 225, 226

Appelbaum, Richard, 199, 229–30, 234

Appomattox (Va.): ILGWU plant in, 101

Arlen, Jeffrey, 278n12, 283n56

Armco, 135

Arpan, Jeffrey S., 92, 94

ASEAN (Association of Southeast Asian Nations), 43, 112–13, 262n71

Asher, Jerome, 105–6

Asia: competition with, 199–200, 205, 207–12; currency devaluations in, 248; financial crisis in, 174, 212–14, 218, 248; textile industry's role in,

Asia *(continued)*
43; trade not aid for, 33–34, 38, 72.
See also East Asia; Southeast Asia;
specific countries
Asian miracles, 46, 143. *See also*
South Korea; Taiwan (earlier, For-
mosa)
Associated Dry Goods, 192, 282–
83n52
Associated Merchandising Corpora-
tion, 178, 184, 192, 214, 282–83n52
Association of Caribbean States (trade
agreement), 173
Association of General Merchandise
Chains, 192, 282–83n52
Association of Southeast Asian
Nations (ASEAN), 43, 112–13,
262n71
ATC. *See* Agreement on Textiles and
Clothing (ATC)
Atkins, Frederick, 184, 186–87, 194
ATMI. *See* American Textile Manu-
facturers' Institute (ATMI)

Baldwin, Robert E., 307n69
Ball, George, 61, 118
Bangladesh: apparel exports of, 216;
apparel jobs lost in, 248; export-
processing zones of, 243–44; new
international division of labor in,
246; trade agreements of, 212
Bankers' Trust, 190
banking industry, investments by, 189–
90
Barbados: apparel exports of, 138; as
CBI participant, 135
Barnard, Kurt, 185
Barnet, Richard, 32
Batus Retail Group, 184, 282–83n52
Bauer, Raymond A., 64, 86–87
Beale, W. T. M., 66, 70–71
Beechey, Veronica, 24
Benetton (company), 200
Bergsten, C. Fred, 224–25
Berliner, Diane, 224, 231
Bethlehem Steel Corporation, 135
Bhagwati, Jagdish, 236, 237

Big Three. *See* Hong Kong; South
Korea; Taiwan (earlier, Formosa)
Bloomingdale's (company), 178, 180,
212, 223
Blue Bell–Wrangler, 139
Bluenthal, Michael, 142
Bluestone, Barry, 2, 16
Bobbin Contextpo, 169
Bobbin Magazine, 145, 146, 169, 174,
196
Bolivia, trade agreements of, 173
Bonacich, Edna, 199
Borden, William, 36
Border Industrialization Program, 154
Boserup, Ester, 83
Boston Associates, 77
Boston Globe, 8
Boston Store, 180
Bosworth, Barry, 142
Bovard, James, 232
boycotts and protests, 79, 106, 109.
See also strikes
Bradlees (company), 255n18
Brady Plan, for Mexico, 160–61
Bretton Woods negotiations, 31, 56–
57
Brooks Brothers (company), 183–84
brown lung disease, 89
Brunei: as ASEAN member, 262n71
Buchanan, Pat, 86, 225
Bullis, Harry, 61
Bullock's North (company), 180
Burdines (company), 180
Burlington Industries: joint ventures
of, 215; labor organizing efforts at,
81, 87; Mexican investment by, 169–
71; sales of, 93, 248
Burroughs Manufacturing Company,
61
Bush, George H. W.: bill vetoed by,
127–28; protectionism defeated un-
der, 76; trade liberalization under,
7, 17, 158–59, 193–94
Business International Corporation,
149–50
Business Promotion Council (under
CBI), 134

41–42; increased imports due to, 59; Japan's status in, 42, 262n66; Mexico's joining of, 160; politics of, 56–57; tariff negotiations under, 66–68; Uruguay Round of, 17, 128, 192–93, 194, 202, 212, 232; violations of, 123, 209

General Electric Credit Company, 190

Generalized System of Preferences, 136, 206, 280–81n26

General Mills (company), 61

Geneva negotiations, 31, 56

Gereffi, Gary, 182–83, 184

Germany, labor laws in (FRG), 102

Gibbons, Sam, 125–26, 277n2

Gifford, Kathie Lee, 2. *See also* Kathie Lee (company)

Gilder, George, 120–21

Gillette (company), 61

Glasmeier, Amy, 174, 176

global economy: Asian financial crisis in, 174, 212–14, 218, 248; emergence of, 14–15; Reagan's approach to, 120–21; sterling bloc and U.S. dollars in, 35–36; tripartite nature of, 16–17

Global Exchange, 238

globalization: cost reduction in, 9; dilemmas of, 235; economic recession in context of, 247–48; free trade in context of, 214–17; gender and, 239–40; historical context of, 13; retailing in context of, 191–94, 200–201; sweatshops in context of, 6; trade liberalization's role in, 7

global textile, apparel, and retail complex: capabilities necessary in, 207; competition in, 153, 177–78; consumers and, 230–35; emergence of, 118; future of, 249–51; gender in, 239–40; job losses due to, 223–25, 228–29; lean retailing in context of, 197–200, 234; Limited (company) as example of, 187; overview of, 220–21; race to bottom and, 229–30; Reagan's approach to, 121–23; sourcing's role in, 217–19; wage

losses due to, 225, 226; winners in, 221–23

Gold Circle (company), 180

Goldman Sachs, 222–23

Great Britain. *See* United Kingdom

Greater East-Asian Co-Prosperity Sphere, 37

Great Society programs, 120

Grenada: as CBI participant, 135; U.S. role in, 133

Griffin mission (1950), 261n50

Grunwald, Joseph, 154–55, 286n8

Grupo Alfa of Mexico, 170

Grupo Industrial Zaga, 171

G-3 Agreement (trade agreement), 173

Guaranteed Access Levels (GALs), 143–46

Guatemala: apparel exports of, 167, 182, 282n47; export-processing zones of, 242; investment in, 147, 284n74

Guess? (company), 230

Guilford Mills, 169–70, 171, 248

Haggar (company), 139

Haggard, Stephen, 89

Haiti: apparel exports of, 138, 167, 282n47; export-processing zones of, 242

Hammond, Janice H., 197–98, 199

Hanna, Sherman, 233

Harris, Seymour, 78–79, 86

Harrison, Bennett, 2, 16

Hawley-Smoot Tariff Act, 14, 58

Hayes, Chuck, 174

Hays, Thomas A., 194

Hecht's (company), 2

Heckscher-Ohlin-Samuelson theory, 18

Hemphill, Robert, 48, 52

Henton, June M., 174, 176

Hillman, Sidney, 98

holding companies, 178, 179–80

Home Textiles Today, 248

homework, 258n29

sex industry, expansion of, 246–47
sex segregation. See gender
Shea, John J., 193–94
Sherman Act, 186
Shillito's (company), 180
Short-Term Arrangement: description
of, 73–75; goals of, 110–12, 250;
historical context of, 202; limits of,
264n108
silk fibers and fabrics, 28, 29, 210
Simpson, Richard, 61
Singapore: apparel exports of, 182; as
ASEAN member, 262n71; offshore
buying offices in, 184; reasons for
women working in, 241; textile and
apparel industry development in,
47–48; U.S. support for, 43
Smith, Adam, 18, 21, 105, 147
Smoot-Hawley (Hawley-Smoot Tariff
Act), 14, 58
social contract. See industrial relations; New Deal social contract
South Africa: apparel exports of, 205–
6
South America. See Central America;
Latin America; specific countries
South Carolina: conference in, 143;
protests and boycotts in, 79; textile
industry in, 88
Southeast Asia: Griffin mission to,
261n50; poverty in, 36; raw materials exports of, 30; sweatshops in, 3.
See also specific countries
Southern African Clothing and Textile Workers Union, 205
South Korea: apparel and textile exports of, 106, 113, 121–23, 182,
211, 216; market-opening initiatives in, 21; North's invasion of, 38–
39; offshore buying offices in, 184;
reasons for women working in, 241;
sourcing by, 146–47; textile and apparel industry development in, 47;
U.S. support for, 43–46; wages in,
52, 83, 213
South Sea Textile Manufacturing Co.,
Ltd., 48, 82–83

Soviet Union: China's alliance with,
38; containment of, 31–32; fear of,
62–63, 72; Reagan's approach to,
120, 129, 131
Spang, Joseph, Jr., 61
Special Access Program (SAP) for
Textiles and Apparel: description
of, 143–44; discourse on, 145–46,
293n23; influence on, 141; as infrastructure for export-processing
zones, 148–52; maquiladoras under, 155; NAFTA compared to, 166;
permanency of, 158; production
sharing fostered by, 147–48; Special
Regime compared to, 157, 198;
USAID as adjunct to, 151
Special Regime (Mexico-U.S.), 157–
58, 198
specification contracting, concept of,
182–83
Spiegel (company), 194, 212, 282–
83n52
Springs Industries, 93
Sri Lanka: apparel exports of, 216; as
ITCB member, 212; U.S.-owned fa-
cilities in, 217
Srinivasan, T. N., 307n69
Stanton, Seabury, 81
Stassen, Harold, 64
Steidtman, Carl, 223
Stein, Herbert, 142
Stitt, Nelson A., 109
Strachan, George, 222–23
Strackbein, O. R., 59–60, 266n11
Strategic Defense Initiative ("Star
Wars" or SDI), 120
strikes, 61, 99. See also protests and
boycotts
Super 807. See U.S. Tariff Schedule
(USTS) 807
Supreme Commander of Allied Powers
(SCAP): intergovernmental trans-
fers and, 49–50; Japanese textile in-
dustry reconstruction and, 27–31,
35; Kennan's ideas vs., 32–33; U.S.
market opening and, 40; women's
low-wage labor and, 51–52

Warnaco Group, 194
Washington Post, 248
Weil, David, 197–98, 199
Weintraub, Sidney, 224
Western Hemisphere Free Trade Association, 158–59
West Point–Pepperell (company), 93
West Point–Stevens (company), 248
Wexler, Jack, 187
Wexner, Leslie, 193–94
Wilkinson, Edwin, 69
Wolfensohn, James, 212
women: as labor organizers, 97–98; as losers in globalization, 221; roles of, 23–24. *See also* women workers
Women's Wear Daily, 187, 192, 206, 216, 221
women workers: displacement of, 113, 115–16, 228–29, 235; in export-processing zones, 241–44; fashion changes and, 112, 182–83; globalization's impact on, 223–25; as neglected factor, 9, 251; in new international division of labor, 240, 244–47; preference for, 23–25; reason for working, 241–42; status of Japanese, 51–54; in U.S. vs. East Asia, 82–84. *See also* sweatshops

wool textiles, 60–61, 69
Workers' Rights Consortium, 236
World Bank: CBI and, 135; criticism of, 22; as influence, 19; infrastructure built by, 149; neoliberalism of, 5, 8; trade accords fostered by, 158–59
World Trade Agreement (WTA): GATT superseded by, 77; global sourcing and, 218; ITCB members on, 212; overview of, 11; requirements of, 202–3; timing of, 21–22. *See also* Agreement on Textiles and Clothing (ATC)
World Trade Organization (WTO): ATC's requirements for, 202; China's membership in, 206, 209, 210, 211, 218; criticism of, 213; formation of, 17, 119, 128, 212; neoliberalism of, 5; politics and norms of, 19

"yarn forward" rule, 165, 204
Yoffie, David B., 112

Zale Corporation, 282–83n52
Zayre Corporation, 192, 282–83n52
Zeiler, Thomas W., 89–90

Indexer: Margie Towery
Compositor: Binghamton Valley Composition
Text: 10/13 Aldus
Display: Aldus
Printer and Binder: Maple-Vail Manufacturing Group